AS
ECONOMICS

SJ GRANT

PEARSON

Longman

Pearson Education Limited
Edinburgh Gate
Harlow
Essex
CM20 2JE
England

First published 2003
Fifth impression 2006

ISBN-10: 0-582-50185-7
ISBN-13: 978-0-582-50185-0

Designed by Linda Males MSCD

Printed in China
PPLC/05

The publishers' policy is to use paper manufactured from sustainable forests.

We are grateful to all copyright holders whose material appears in this work.

ACKNOWLEDGEMENTS

We are grateful to the following for permission to reproduce copyright material:

The Copyright Clearance Center Inc for an extract from 'Time to reboot: PC makers say farewell to 15 year boom'
by Clark and Buckman; HMSO for tables 15.8, 15.9 and 16.1 from *Monthly Digest of Statistics* April 2002 and an
extract from *Social Trends 31* Office for National Statistics 2001; The Labour Party for an extract from *The Labour
Party Manifesto 2001*; and Oxford University Press Inc and for an extract from *Human Development Report 2001* by
United Nations Development Programme, © 2001.

Contents

Introduction

What is economics?

Economics is concerned with the key issues facing us today, including globalisation, pollution and poverty. It is essentially about choice: why different sorts of people and groups of people, such as governments, have to make choices; the choices they make; and the consequences of those choices. The work of economists transforms people's lives.

Studying economics can be compared with studying medicine. Medical students learn about the human body, what can go wrong and how to remedy it. Economics students learn how an efficient economy and markets in the economy should work, how market failure can occur and how governments can seek to improve economic performance.

Microeconomics and macroeconomics

Microeconomics is the study of markets for individual items, such as the market for CDs. It involves examining the decisions and behaviour of customers, manufacturers and retailers.

In contrast, macroeconomics is concerned with the study of the whole economy. The topics it covers include unemployment, changes in a country's price level, a country's international trade position and changes in the number of goods and services a country is producing.

Social science

Economics is a social science, which means it is concerned with the study of human behaviour. Economists develop theories about how people, the firms they run and the economy they live in behave. In physics or chemistry, theories can be tested under controlled conditions in laboratories. This is not possible in social science. Economists assess how accurate and useful their theories are by studying what is happening in the economy.

The role of economists

The number of people working as economists grew significantly in the second half of the twentieth century and is continuing to grow in the twenty-first century. There are economists working in the media, in universities, for companies, for banks, for the government and for international organisations. Their vital role is to analyse and interpret economic information, to give advice on how the institutions they work for should respond to and influence economic events and to make forecasts about future economic trends.

The advantages of studying AS economics

Economics is a highly regarded subject and qualification. Studying economics will develop your ability to think logically, assess arguments and communicate in a clear way. Now is a good time to study economics as there is a worldwide shortage of economists.

AS Specifications

Table 1: AS level specification					
AQA	**Sections**	**Edexcel**	**Sections**	**OCR**	**Sections**
Module 1: Markets and market failure	1, 2, 3 & 4	Module 1: Markets: how they work	1, 2 & 5	Module 1: The market system	1, 2 & 5
Module 2: The national economy	6, 7 & 8	Module 2: Markets: how they fail	3, 4 & 5	Module 2: Market failure and government intervention	3, 4 & 5
Module 3: Markets at work	5	Module 3: Managing the economy	6, 7 & 8	Module 3: The national and international economy	6, 7 & 8

All specifications seek to develop candidates' knowledge and understanding of economic concepts and theories, their ability to apply these and their ability to analyse, explain and evaluate economic issues and arguments.

Table 1 shows how the modules of the three mains specifications are covered in this book.

Key skills

A good economist needs to communicate clearly, manipulate and interpret statistics, use information technology and work with others.

Communication

The quality of written communication is assessed in AS examinations. It is therefore important to write as clearly as possible. Be careful with spelling, grammar and punctuation. When writing longer answers, use a separate paragraph for each important point you make.

Manipulating and interpreting statistics

In AS and A level economics, the emphasis is on calculating percentages, percentage changes and averages, and interpreting statistics. However, the mathematical knowledge required is no more than GCSE level. Even if you have not gained a C grade or above in maths GCSE, the practice you will get while working through this book will enable you to reach the required standard.

The main numerical tools used by economists are as follows.

Percentage. A percentage is a proportion of a total. To calculate the percentage of females in the class, for example, divide the number of females by the total number of people in the class and multiply by 100. If there are 8 females in a class of 20, the percentage of females is:

$$\frac{8}{20} \times 100 = 40\%$$

Percentage change. This is also known as the rate of change. To calculate the percentage change, first work out the actual change by subtracting the original figure from the current figure. Then divide the change by the original figure and multiply by 100. For example, if an economics class starts with 15 students and then increases to 20, the percentage change in the class size is:

$$20 - 15 = 5$$

$$\frac{5}{15} \times 100 = 33.33\%$$

Average. There are three main ways of calculating an average: the mean, the median and the mode. The most commonly used average, and the one you may have to calculate, is the mean or arithmetic mean. This is found by totalling the individual figures and dividing by the number of figures used. For example, in a test marked out of 20, one candidate may have gained 15 marks, another 10 marks, another 20 marks and another 3 marks. The average mark achieved would be:

$$15 + 10 + 20 + 3 = 48$$

$$\frac{48}{4} = 12$$

You are unlikely to be asked to calculate an average using the median or the mode, but you may have to comment on averages found by these methods.

The median is the middle value of a series of figures when the figures are placed in ascending order. For example, weekly incomes of five workers may be £300, £320, £380, £460 and £500. In this case the median would be £380.

The mode is the most frequently occurring figure. For example, if 15 out of a possible 18 pieces of homework are handed in during the first week, 18 in the second week, 2 in the third week, 15 in the fourth week and 15 in the fifth week, the mode would be 15.

Index numbers. You will not have to calculate index numbers, but you may see them in activities and data response questions. Index numbers enable changes to be compared easily, especially where large numbers are involved. To convert actual numbers into a series of index numbers, first select a base year. This is given a value of 100. Then calculate the subsequent index numbers by dividing the actual figures by the base year figure and multiplying by 100. For example, the output of a country for a five-year period might be as shown in Table 2.

Table 2: Output 2000–05	
Year	Output (£ billion)
2000	820
2001	861
2002	984
2003	1,066
2004	1,230
2005	1,435

The output in 2000 would be given a value of 100. Then the index number for 2001 would be calculated by:

$$\frac{861}{820} \times 100 = 105$$

The index number for 2002 would be:

$$\frac{984}{820} \times 100 = 120$$

The figures for 2003, 2004 and 2005 would be calculated in the same way, giving the index series shown in Table 3.

Table 3: Output 2000–05	
Year	Output (2000 = 100)
2000	100
2001	105
2002	120
2003	130
2004	150
2005	175

In Table 3 it can be seen clearly that output increased by 5% from 2000 to 2001, 20% from 2000 to 2002, 30% from 2000 to 2003, 50% from 2000 to 2004 and 75% from 2000 to 2005.

Activity 1

a 36 students in a sixth form of 200 choose to study AS economics. Calculate the percentage of students selecting AS economics.

b An economics teacher's wage is raised from £500 a week to £600 a week. Calculate the teacher's percentage increase in income.

c Six economics students work part-time in a local supermarket. Their weekly wages are £20, £14, £52, £26 and £18. Calculate the students' average wage rate, using the arithmetic mean.

Information technology

You will benefit from using IT throughout your course. Appropriate websites can keep you up to date with economic developments, help you research for homework assignments, give you guidance on examination techniques and enable you to build economic models. You can also use a word-processor for assignments and investigations.

Improving your learning and performance

Studying economics obviously improves your understanding of economics and your economic skills. It also develops your ability to investigate a complex subject, to think logically, to write clearly, to analyse data, to evaluate arguments and to meet targets.

Problem-solving

Much of economics is about problem-solving. For example, you will analyse and discuss how firms may increase their profits, how pollution could be tackled and how unemployment could be reduced. In the activities and data response questions, you will explore problems, select methods of tackling them and compare the effectiveness of the methods chosen.

Assessment objectives

Examination questions test four levels of skills. In ascending order, these are knowledge and understanding, application, analysis and evaluation.

Knowledge and understanding is concerned with a sound awareness of economic terms, concepts, theories and problems. Examination questions that require you to demonstrate your knowledge and understanding usually start with words such as 'define', 'give', 'identify' or 'state'. For example, you may be asked to define inflation.

Application is a higher order skill. This requires you to use your knowledge to answer a particular question. For example, from a set of economic data on different countries, you may be asked which country was experiencing the most serious economic problems. You might also be asked which policies might be used to tackle a particular economic problem.

Analysis is an even higher skill. This involves examining economic problems and issues. The key directive (or trigger) words here are 'explain', 'examine' and 'analyse'. You may be asked, for instance, to explain what effect a rise in government spending may have on unemployment.

Evaluation is the highest order skill. This requires you to assess economic arguments and to make informed judgements based on sound analysis. The key directive words for this skill include 'discuss', 'assess', 'consider', 'comment on' and, of course, 'evaluate'. For example, you may be asked to discuss the costs and benefits of economic growth or to assess the arguments for and against an increase in income tax.

Each examination board awards 30 per cent of marks for knowledge, 30 per cent for application, 20 per cent for analysis and 20 per cent for evaluation.

Use of diagrams

Economists use diagrams such as pie charts, bar charts and graphs to present data and economic relationships. The most commonly used diagrams are graphs. Figure 1 shows a time series graph.

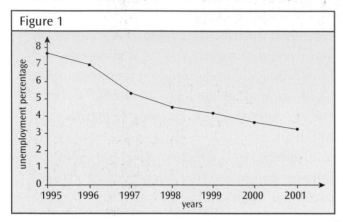

In Figure 1 the unemployment rate is measured on what is known as the vertical axis and time is measured on the horizontal axis. The diagram shows clearly that the unemployment rate fell between 1995 to 2001.

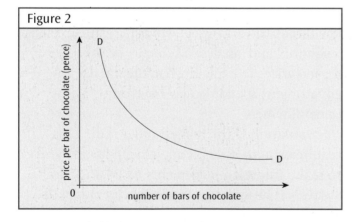

Figure 2 shows the relationship between demand for a chocolate bar and the price of the bar.

The demand curve shows that as price rises, fewer bars are demanded.

You will interpret and draw diagrams. It is important that your diagrams are clear. Do not make them too small. For most diagrams, one-third of a page is an appropriate size. Label appropriately the axes and any curves you include.

1 The economic problem

1 Positive and normative statements

In the previous section you started to explore the nature of economics. In this unit you will discover the distinction between **positive** and **normative statements** in economics and how **value judgements** influence economic decision making.

Positive and normative statements

Positive statements deal with facts. 'Hong Kong is now part of China', 'the National Health Service employs more than 1 million workers' and 'Jane Smith achieved a grade A in AS level Economics' are all positive statements. If a disagreement arises over a positive statement, it can be settled by looking at the facts and seeing whether or not they support the statement. Positive statements are either true or false.

In contrast, **normative statements** usually include or imply the words 'ought' or 'should'. They reflect people's opinions and views. They are expressions of what some individuals or groups think ought to be done. 'The UK should join the single currency', 'more aid should be given to developing countries' and 'income should be distributed more equally'. These statements are based on **value judgements** and express views of what is 'good' or 'bad', 'right or wrong'.

The distinction between positive and normative statements

Economists distinguish between positive and normative statements because different techniques are used to study them. For positive statements, a scientific approach is adopted. They can be assessed by examining real world data and events.

Unlike positive statements, normative statements cannot be proved right or wrong by looking at the facts. Disagreements about such statements are settled by persuasion and voting.

In practice, issues facing economists usually have both positive and normative aspects.

For example, economists studying whether the tax on cigarettes should be increased or not have to consider whether the tax is already too high (normative) and whether a higher tax will reduce demand (positive).

Activity 1

Decide whether each statement is a positive or a normative statement.

a More students sit English AS level than sit Maths AS level.

b The average US citizen has a higher income than the average Indian citizen.

c Income tax rates are too high.

d Russell Crowe is the best actor in the world.

e Maurice Green is the fastest 100 metres runner.

f The government should build more athletic stadiums.

Activity 2

Explain briefly how you would assess whether the following positive statements are true or false.

a The country's most recent inflation rate is below 5%.

b Females perform better at AS level than males.

c You may be asked questions about inflation in your AS level examination.

d Switzerland is a member of the European Union.

Value judgements

Value judgements influence economic decision making and policy. A government has to decide on its economic priorities. For example, it may make reducing unemployment its prime objective. Among its other decisions may be whether to spend more on education or health care, whether to increase or reduce government intervention in the economy and whether to raise the retirement age. Such decisions will be informed by positive economics. In the case of raising the retirement age, government economists will calculate the expected future costs of pensions and the expected future size of the labour force. However, once all the information has been collected and analysed, the decision will be influenced by the government's and voters' views on the appropriate age for retirement and whether the level of state pensions should rise, fall or remain unchanged.

Economists can assess whether different results would occur if different value judgements were made. For example, it may be assumed that workers prefer income to leisure. In this case, a rise in the wage rate per hour would be expected to encourage workers to work more hours. If it were thought that workers prefer leisure, however, the outcome would be a reduction in the number of hours worked.

Current issue: immigration

Immigration is a controversial issue which has both positive and normative aspects. People and politicians make normative statements about the issue.

The start of the twenty-first century has seen an increase in immigration into EU countries from Eastern Europe and from countries in Africa and Asia.

This has led some newspapers and some politicians to claim that the EU is being 'flooded' by 'illegal immigrants' (people moving into countries without permission) and 'bogus asylum seekers' (people claiming they are suffering persecution but who are really migrating in search of improved living conditions). Some people are saying that the EU is already 'full up' with people and that immigration is threatening their jobs, culture, access to services including hospital treatment, benefits and housing, and sense of identity. They are calling for tighter immigration laws and for all asylum seekers to be locked up in detention centres until their claims can be processed.

EU governments, however, are relaxing immigration laws and are actively seeking to employ doctors, nurses, IT specialists, farm workers and other groups from countries such as the Philippines, Russia and India. This is because the population of EU countries is falling. As Europeans have fewer children but live longer, there is also a reduction in the proportion of workers to pensioners. The shortage of workers is particularly serious in some high-skill jobs, such as information technology and medicine, and in some low-skill jobs, such as farm work, cleaning and public transport, which EU workers are becoming increasingly reluctant to do. *The Economist* newspaper has estimated that the EU

Activity 3

The government places taxes on alcohol consumption, driving and smoking but not on books, papers and magazines. Some argue that books and magazines with a high content of violence and/or pornography should be taxed.

a What value judgement may governments have made in deciding not to tax books, papers and magazines?

b What value judgement is being made by people who argue that books and magazines with a high content of violence and/or pornography should be taxed?

c Discuss one difficulty a government would encounter in implementing a tax on books and magazines with a high content of violence and/or pornography.

would have to attract 13.5 million immigrants a year to keep the ratio of workers to pensioners constant.

Many of the issues raised about the effects of immigration, however, are based on positive statements which can be analysed, for example population sizes, skill shortages, housing vacancies and net contributions of immigrants and indigenous people to state finance. In practice, most people debating immigration do not consider the available evidence.

Summary

In this unit you have learned that:

- **Positive statements** are statements of facts which can be proved right or wrong.

- **Normative statements** are statements of opinion based on value judgements.

- Economists distinguish between positive and normative statements as different techniques are used to assess them.

- **Value judgements** influence economic decision making and government policy.

Multiple choice questions

1 Which of the following statements involves a value judgement?
A   Unemployment fell in 2001.
B   The government must increase its spending on education.
C   Men earn more per hour worked than women.
D   A cut in income tax should increase household spending.

2 Which of the following is a normative economic statement?
A   Free nursery education should be provided for all children aged between 2 and 5.
B   Increased government expenditure on secondary education will raise the examination performance of pupils.
C   Extra funding for state education could be obtained by reducing spending on health care.
D   The UK government devotes a higher percentage of its expenditure to education than the government of France.

3 What is economics the study of?
A   the management of personal services
B   government expenditure and taxation
C   the operation of the domestic economy
D   the allocation of scarce resources to satisfy unlimited wants

4 What do positive economic statements contain?
A   facts
B   opinions
C   optimistic views
D   value judgements

5 'Doctors should be paid more than footballers.' This is an example of a normative statement because it is:
A   wrong
B   objective
C   testable
D   based on an opinion

6 Which of the following is a positive statement?
A   The price of beer is too high.
B   A rise in the price of beer will result in less beer being demanded.
C   The consumption of alcohol in public parks and shopping centres should be banned.
D   The penalties for drunk and disorderly behaviour are too lenient.

Data response question: education standards

Education remains Labour's top priority. Excellence for the many, not just the few is our driving passion. Our goal is to develop education to harness the individual talents of every pupil.

Since 1997 rising standards have been achieved through major new investment and significant reforms; 17,000 schools have had vital repairs or refurbishment; 20,000 schools are now connected to the internet; there are nearly half a million fewer primary pupils in classes of more than 30; over 150,000 teachers are set to receive a £2,000 pay rise above the usual annual increase.

Transforming secondary education is the critical challenge of the next decade.

Standards have risen in the past four years particularly among pupils in less advantaged areas. Strong school leadership and better teaching have turned around 700 failing schools. But the challenge ahead is immense. Too many pupils fall back and become disillusioned in the first two years of secondary school. Just half of 16 year olds

currently gain good school-leaving qualifications, and levels of drop-out remain too high.

(Extracts from Labour's manifesto 2001, Ambitions for Britain, *HH Associates, p. 18.)*

a Explain why 'transforming secondary education is the critical challenge of the next decade' is a normative statement. [3]

b Identify a positive statement from the extract and explain why it is positive. [5]

c i In a positive statement, give one additional way in which standards may have risen in the past few years. [3]

ii Explain why your statement is positive. [3]

d Identify an alternative to education as a top priority for government. [2]

e Discuss a benefit of an improvement in secondary education. [4]

2 Choice, scarcity and opportunity cost

In this unit you will examine the key economic concepts of **scarcity**, **choice** and **opportunity cost**. You will investigate what is often called the **economic problem**, why choices have to be made and the implications of those choices.

Choices

Every day we make choices:

Yesterday I bought a DVD as a present for my sister. I had thought about buying her a book but decided she would prefer the DVD. I was also invited out by one friend to a party and by another to a concert. I chose to go to the party.

We decide how to spend our time and our money. People as buyers, workers, producers and members of organisations and governments make choices all the time. Managers in industry have to choose what to produce, the administrators and doctors of a hospital who to treat, the police which crimes to tackle and government ministers whether to build a new school or a new road.

Constraints

Why do we have to make choices? It is because we have limited income, time and **resources**. The employee in Activity 1 had a limited

Activity 1

An employee of a local wildlife park is sent to a pet shop specialising in exotic birds. She is given £2,000 to spend. Using the price list below, give three different ways she could use the money.

◆ Price list ◆

Blue and Gold Macaw	£750 each
Green Wing Macaws	£1,300 pair
Redsided Eclectus	£1,000 pair
African Greys	£500 pair
Cuban Amazon	£700 each
Leadbeaters Cockatoo	£2,000 each
Maroon Conures	£100 pair

Activity 2

Identify two factors which limit the AS levels a school or college can offer.

Activity 3

In 2000 the number of teacher vacancies in schools increased by more than 70%. A survey by the Department for Education and Employment showed that unfilled posts in schools jumped from 2,870 at the beginning of 2000 to 4,980 in January 2001.

a In what ways does the example of unfilled posts illustrate the concept of scarcity?

b In what sense is education scarce in the developing countries of Mali and Bangladesh?

c In what sense may luxury cars be regarded as scarce in the UK?

budget, just as the vast majority of people who cannot afford to buy all that they would like. We are also constrained by time.

There are only 24 hours in a day. If I teach an Economics class between 2pm and 3.30pm on a Wednesday afternoon, I cannot spend the same time writing.

Crucially, there is always a limited number of workers, machines, equipment, factories, offices and farms available so only a certain number of **goods** can be produced or **services** provided. If a hospital has to treat more patients for pneumonia and broken bones during a prolonged cold spell, it may not have enough beds and medical staff to carry out some routine operations. If a school builds a science laboratory on a field it owns it cannot use it as a playing field, and if a retailer uses its floor space to sell clothes it cannot sell food there.

Scarcity

Economists refer to resources as being **scarce**. This emphasises that there are not enough resources to meet all of people's wants. In every country people would like to have more goods and services than its resources can produce, for example more consumer items such as mobile phones and DVD players and better health care. Our wants are unlimited but our resources are scarce. The fact that our wants exceed resources is known as the **economic problem**.

Over time, as workers improve their skills and technology develops, countries are able to produce more, but as wants also increase so scarcity continues. Indeed, wants often grow more rapidly than the quality and quantity of resources. For example, in the UK more resources are continuing to be devoted to health care but demand still exceeds the supply of health care. This is because advances in technology (making more complex operations possible), the development of new drugs, people living longer and rising expectations of the quality of life are increasing demand for health care faster than more doctors and nurses can be trained and more hospital beds can be created.

Opportunity cost

When we make choices we consider alternatives. The next best alternative achieved within the same amount of time, with the same amount of income or resources, is called the

opportunity cost. This is often referred to as the true or real cost of a decision as it emphasises what has been sacrificed.

Recently I bought a new digital television. First, I considered spending the money on a variety of items including new carpets, a foreign holiday and opening a savings account. Finally the decision came down to buying the television or going on the foreign holiday. So the opportunity cost of my buying the television was the foreign holiday.

Activity 4

Identify the opportunity cost of:

a you studying AS level Economics

b buying an economics textbook

c spending an hour reading your Economics homework

d working for a local supermarket on a Saturday

Economic goods

Most **products** are what economists call **economic** or **scarce** goods. This means that resources are used to produce them. As resources are limited so are the numbers of economic goods that can be produced. The need to use resources in production also means that economic goods have an opportunity cost. For example, workers, machines, equipment and offices used to produce insurance services could be used instead to produce banking services.

Activity 5

Identify three resources used in the production of an Economics course.

Free goods

Only a few products do not require scarce resources to produce them and so have no opportunity cost. These are known as **free goods**. This term must be used carefully. Some products are provided for people without charge.

For example, the state provides free education for children, and the National Health Service (NHS) does not require patients to pay for treatments. Retailers use promotional tactics such as bogofs (buy one, get one free) to provide goods without charge. However, none of these products are what economists call free goods. This is because resources are required to produce them so they have an opportunity cost. Teachers, books, IT facilities and buildings are needed to provide state education but these resources could be used for other purposes, for example teachers could work as accountants and the school buildings could be used as offices.

An example of a free good is sunlight. We benefit from sunlight without having to use resources to obtain the sunlight. Sea and air can usually be regarded as free goods, but there are circumstances when even these are not free goods. For example, most of us can take advantage of air without having to use resources, but resources have to be used to provide air in underground buildings and submarines.

Activity 6

One of the problems is that we expect Internet resources to be free. Curious, this. Do we expect anything else good to be free? The BBC, the British Library and the Public Record Office provide wonderful access to tremendous original sources and add value by suggesting classroom uses of this priceless material. What does this prove? To begin with, they are the exceptions that prove the rule. Secondly, they are not entirely free. Taxes that could have gone into other education resources went into those websites. (BBC History Magazine, Ben Walsh, 2001)

a Explain why the BBC education websites are not free goods.

b Identify a possible opportunity cost of producing 'free' education websites.

Current issue: foot-and-mouth outbreak

In early April 2001 the Cotswold Wildlife Park near Burford reopened. It had been closed to visitors for more than five weeks because of the outbreak of foot-and-mouth disease.

The park, which attracted 350,000 visitors in 2000, was founded in 1970 by John Heyworth.

Like nearly all other major zoological attractions in the UK, we closed voluntarily to protect our potentially susceptible animals and to express solidarity with the local farming community.

Although ideally all zoos, wildlife and safari parks would remain closed until the country is free of foot-and-mouth disease, to do so would lead to insolvency. We have nearly 80 full-time staff and outgoings of £120,000 a year in food and vets' bills. The park costs £28,000 a week to run, with or without visitors. We have lost £120,000 in the past month. To lose even a relatively unimportant month is a blow, but if we did not open in time for Easter, we would have lost nearly £300,000.

In March 2001 there was even talk that the park would have to close permanently, with the animals being sold to other zoological parks and the land being sold for housing or agricultural use.

This example can illustrate choice, scarcity and opportunity cost in various ways.

- **Choice** The park's owner had to decide whether to open the zoo or keep it closed during the foot-and-mouth outbreak. He also had to decide whether to keep the park going in the long run.
- **Scarcity** Land, workers and animals are scarce resources with alternative uses.
- **Opportunity cost** Closing the park meant that it had to forgo £120,000 of revenue. However, deciding to reopen the park meant putting the animals at risk of catching foot-and-mouth disease. Keeping the park open in the long term means the land and workers cannot be used for other purposes.

A wider perspective can also be taken of how the outbreak of foot-and-mouth should have been tackled and the role of wildlife parks.

Summary

In this unit you have learned that:

- We have to make **choices** because there are not enough resources to produce everything we want.

- Wants are unlimited but resources are **scarce**.

- Making choices involves going without something else. **Opportunity cost** is the best alternative forgone and so represents the true cost of the choice selected.

- The vast majority of products are **economic goods**. They need resources to make them and so their production involves an opportunity cost.

- A few items are **free goods**. These require no resources to make them and so their production does not involve an opportunity cost.

Multiple choice questions

1 Which of the following is a free good?

A dental treatment for children

B state education

C a promotional gift given away by a company

D wind which drives a windmill

2 A factory worker decides to leave her job in order to take a full time university degree course in Economics. What is the opportunity cost of this decision?

A current earnings

B future earnings

C books which have to be purchased for the course

D tuition fees

3 What is opportunity cost?

A extra resources needed to increase the variety of products on offer

B the best alternative forgone

C the time taken to make a decision

D a reduction in the range of choices available

4 Which of the following explains why people have to make choices?

A wants exceed resources

B resources grow more rapidly than wants

C wants are scarce whereas resources are unlimited

D most products are free goods

5 An economic good is one which:

A is produced cheaply

B has a lower price than rival products

C has an opportunity cost

D makes a profit

6 Five years ago a man bought a car for £9,000. It develops an electrical fault that would cost £400 to repair. A new model would now cost £12,000 but the man would only receive £4,000 should he sell his own car on the second-hand market. What is the present opportunity cost of him owning the car?

A £400

B £4,000

C £8,000

D £9,000

Data response question: health care spending

In 2000 the government published a National Health Service (NHS) plan in which it promised to increase government spending on health care by a third by 2004. The money would be spent on recruiting extra staff, providing more beds and extending NHS care. It was announced that among the additional spending would be £570m to pay for new screening programmes and more cancer drugs. The NHS breast-screening programme for women aged 50–64 would be extended to women aged 65–70, involving 400,000 more patients a year. However, not all forms of health care were to benefit and prostrate screening was still not introduced.

Ian Bogle, chairman of the British Medical Association, doubted that the extra resources would ever be enough to meet the expanding demand for health care. He pointed out that waiting lists for inpatient treatment at NHS hospitals were still increasing. In April 2001 he said:

'We have to accept the prospect of treatments being excluded from the NHS if we want to maintain a universal service, one which is available to everyone and essentially free at the point of use.'

a Explain one possible opportunity cost of increasing government spending on health care. [3]

b Discuss an opportunity cost of not screening for prostrate cancer for:
i men with prostrate cancer [3]
ii the NHS. [5]

c Explain how NHS treatment illustrates the concept of scarcity. [5]

d Discuss whether NHS treatment is a free or an economic good. [4]

3 Economic resources

In the previous unit you saw that resources are in limited supply and have an opportunity cost. In this unit you will examine these resources in more depth.

Economists refer to resources as economic resources, factors of production or inputs. There are four categories of resources – **labour**, **enterprise**, **capital** and **land**.

Labour

Labour consists of all human effort, both physical and mental, used in the production of goods and services. So the hours of work undertaken by a car worker and a journalist contribute to the country's labour force.

The labour force can be categorised in various ways. One is into sectors in which workers are employed.

- The primary sector includes the **industries** involved in extracting raw materials and food, such as agriculture, coal mining, fishing and forestry.
- The secondary sector covers manufacturing industries and the building and construction industry, including publishing, chemicals, toys, jewellery and housing.
- The tertiary sector is concerned with industries providing services, such as banking, education, retailing and transport.

Most workers in the UK are employed in the tertiary sector. Employment in this sector is expanding while fewer people are being employed in the manufacturing and primary sectors. In 2001, 82% of workers were employed in the tertiary sector, 15% in the manufacturing sector and 3% in the primary sector.

Some economists separate out a section from the tertiary and call it the quaternary sector. This consists of services concerned with the collection, processing and transmission of information (such as microtechnology), research and development (such as higher education) and administration and financial management (such as accountancy).

The mobility of labour

At any time some industries are expanding and some are contracting, which makes it important for workers to be able to change jobs easily and to move from one area to another. Various factors hinder the **occupational** and **geographical mobility** of labour. For instance, some workers may find it difficult to change jobs because they lack the skills, training or qualifications needed. Some may also experience difficulties moving from one location to another because of differences in house prices and rents in different areas, family ties and lack of awareness of opportunities elsewhere.

The quantity and quality of labour

At any time there is only so much labour in the country – the supply is finite. However, over time both the quantity and quality of labour can change. Immigration, a higher retirement age and an increased willingness and ability of single parents to work will increase the supply of labour. The main reason for a rise in the quality of the labour force is an improvement in **human capital**. If workers receive more or better education and training they will be capable of producing more goods and services.

It is well known that the UK economy has experienced structural change in the post-war period, with a decline in the manufacturing sector and an increase in service industries.

Jobs in the service industries have increased by 36 per cent, from 15.6 million in 1978 to 21.2 million in 2000, while those in manufacturing have fallen by 39 per cent from 7.0 million to 4.2 million over the same period. Virtually all the increase in women's labour market participation has been through taking up jobs in the service sector. The total number of jobs done by men is now 15.1 million, compared with 13.0 million by women. (Extracts from Social Trends 31, *Office for National Statistics, 2001)*

a The extract mentions the service and manufacturing sector. Which sector is not mentioned?

b Give two examples of jobs in:
  i the service sector
  ii the manufacturing sector

c Explain two ways in which the labour force can decrease.

Enterprise and the entrepreneur

Some economists view **enterprise** as a distinct economic resource, and an **entrepreneur** as someone who takes risks and organises the other economic resources. The first function involves bearing the risks involved in a business not being a success. Some risks, including fire, theft and flood, can be insured against but others, including costs of production rising, tastes changing and the emergence of new competitors, cannot. Entrepreneurs such as Stelios Haji-Ioannou (easyJet and internet cafes), Charles Dunstone (mobile phones) and Sir Alan Sugar (computers) may make a large profit but they risk losing their money.

Organising labour, capital and land involves deciding what to produce, how resources are used and where to locate the firm. A **firm** is an institution that hires factors of production and organises those factors to produce and sell goods and services.

The mobility of the entrepreneur

The entrepreneur is considered to be the most mobile of economic resources. People who have the skills to recognise new opportunities, to develop new businesses and new products, and to organise resources are usually able to transfer those skills to a range of different business ventures. They are also often willing to move from one area to another and indeed from one country to another.

The quantity and quality of entrepreneurs

Successful entrepreneurs have initiative, the ability to take decisions and a willingness to take risks. Some concern has been expressed about the lack of entrepreneurial spirit in the UK.

In firms, particularly large ones, the role of the entrepreneur is often divided. The organisation of the economic resources may be undertaken by directors and managers while the shareholders bear the risks of business failure.

James Dyson appeared as the 37th richest person in the UK in *The Times Rich List 2001* with assets of £700 million. He made his fortune from the dual-cyclone bagless vacuum cleaner, which he invented and launched in 1993. By 2001 he was selling approximately 100,000 cleaners a month. He continues to develop new products, including a new type of washing machine and a more advanced, eight-cyclone vacuum cleaner.

a Explain why James Dyson is considered to be an entrepreneur.

b Identify two risks entrepreneurs bear.

Capital

When economists discuss capital they are usually referring to physical capital, which consists of man-made goods that are used to produce other goods and services. Examples include factories, offices, warehouses, railways, power stations, machinery, lorries, equipment and processed raw materials. The category of **capital goods** also includes social capital, which consists mainly of goods and services produced not for sale but for the benefit of the community, such as hospitals, schools and roads.

Capital goods, which can also be called producer goods, are distinct from **consumer goods**. Capital goods are not wanted for their own sake but for what they will produce. They do not provide immediate satisfaction. In contrast, consumer goods do give immediate satisfaction and are wanted for their own sake. Whether a good is considered to be a capital or a consumer good depends on its use. For example, a computer is a capital good if it is used in an insurance company to process claims, but a consumer good if it is used in a home to play computer games.

It is important to distinguish between capital and **financial capital**. Economists define capital as producer goods, whereas financial capital covers financial assets, such as shares, savings accounts and government bonds.

The mobility of capital

The mobility of capital goods varies. Most machines, equipment and processed raw materials are geographically mobile, but goods such as factories, offices and railways are not. Similarly, some capital goods can be used for various purposes and so are occupationally mobile. For example, an office could be used by an accounting firm or an advertising agency and a photocopying machine by a school or a telecommunications firm. Other capital goods, including blast furnaces, coal mines and sausage machines, are specialised and are occupationally immobile.

The quantity and quality of capital goods

An increase in the quantity of capital goods may involve a short-term opportunity cost in the form of consumer goods. If all, or nearly all, economic resources are currently being used, making more capital goods will require some resources to be switched away from making consumer goods. This will, however, only be a short-term sacrifice as in the long term more capital goods will enable the economy to produce even more consumer goods.

The quality of capital goods is improved by advances in technology. Inventions create new capital goods and together with technical modifications increase the quantity and quality of consumer goods that capital goods can make.

Activity 3

Eddie and William Stobbart run the largest private haulage company in the UK. It is currently growing at 27% a year, and the company is buying more lorries to fit out in its distinctive green and red colours.

a Explain why the company's lorries are capital goods.

b Classify the following into capital and consumer goods:
 i a suite of furniture bought by a couple moving into a new home
 ii a car bought by a company for use by one of its sales people
 iii a television used by a television critic
 iv a bookcase bought by a library
 v shampoo used in a hairdressers' salon
 vi a CD player bought by woman as a present for her partner

c Give two examples of capital goods, other than lorries, that might be owned by the Stobbart company.

Land

In economics, **land** means all natural resources that can be used to produce goods and services. This covers not only land as we conventionally think of it but also the sea and air and things that occur naturally on the land, below the land, under the sea and in the air, including forests, gold, fishing grounds, oil, wind and rain.

These gifts of nature can be divided into **renewable** and **non-renewable resources**. Renewable resources are replaced automatically by nature and so can be used on a continual basis, for example rivers, air, tidal power and wind power. In contrast, non-renewable resources are not automatically replaced. They are depletable and so will run out with use. They include the fossil fuels of coal, oil and natural gas and minerals such as gold and silver.

Some resources can change from renewable to non-renewable if they are overexploited. For example, overfishing may reduce fish stocks to unsustainable levels.

The mobility of land

The earth's surface, oceans and fossil fuel deposits show clearly that land itself is geographically immobile. It is not possible to move land from the north of Scotland to London, where there is a shortage of space for offices, homes and places of entertainment. Even in the case of wildlife and rivers, the resources are immobile in their natural form. Animals can be moved into zoos and safari parks, but then they have to be maintained and housed by people. Similarly, rivers can be diverted but they then become man-made rather than gifts of nature.

In contrast to its complete lack of geographically mobility, land is probably the most occupationally mobile of economic resources. In most cases its use can be changed easily and quickly. For example, an area of land could be used for farming, housing, recreation or industry. Only in a few cases is land restricted in its occupational mobility. An area used to bury nuclear waste may not have an alternative use, and it takes time for landfill sites to change their use.

The quantity and quality of land

Although the supply of land for a particular use can be increased, the total supply of land changes little over time. Soil erosion and land reclamation alter the quantity of land slowly and by only small amounts. The quantity of water in the world is affected by evaporation and climate change, but it does not alter much.

The quality of natural resources is affected by various factors including fertilisers, purification measures and infrastructure.

Activity 4

For centuries rice was grown in Madagascar under flooded conditions. Now more Madagascan farmers are keeping the soil automatically wet only when the plant is producing grain. The rest of the time the fields are dry during the day and irrigated in the evening. The farmers are finding their yields are greater because the plants receive more oxygen from the atmosphere and get more benefit from the warmth of the sun.

a What forms of land are being discussed here?

b In what sense is land itself immobile?

Current issue: ageing populations

In Europe, the USA and Japan the population is ageing as well as shrinking. This is reducing the ratio of workers to pensioners and leading to skill shortages. In Japan, the ratio of working people to retired people will have shrunk from 4:1 in 2000 to 2:1 by 2030. In Italy more than 35% of the population will be 65 or over by 2050.

Governments and firms are reacting to these changes in various ways. Immigration controls are being relaxed and governments are considering raising the retirement age. Firms are reducing the opportunities for their workers to take early retirement, and are seeking to retain more of their current staff and to encourage more mothers and disabled people to work for them. Some firms are spending more on training and capital goods in order to achieve a higher output per worker.

This example shows that many countries are experiencing significant changes in their labour forces, which creates a challenge for governments and entrepreneurs. Making it easier for migrants to enter the country and raising the retirement age will increase the number of workers available. Entrepreneurs and their firms are seeking to maintain or increase their labour forces by, for example, offering some workers the opportunity to work more flexible hours, to work from home and to become more involved in the firm's decision making. Some firms are offering crèche facilities to attract more mothers, and some are adapting their buildings and equipment to make it easier for disabled people to enter their labour force.

The example shows that firms are aware of the importance of improving human capital. It also shows that resources are combined to produce goods and services, and that when labour is combined with better quality capital goods, output will rise.

Summary

In this unit you have learned that:

- **Economic resources** can also be referred to as factors of production and inputs.

- The four factors of production are **labour**, **enterprise**, **capital** and **land**.

- Most workers in the UK are employed in the tertiary sector.

- Workers will find it difficult to move from one job to another if they lack skills, training and qualifications.

- **Geographical mobility** of labour is limited by people's social ties, lack of awareness of vacancies and differences in the price and availability of housing in different locations.

- The quantity of labour in a country would be increased by a rise in the retirement age and immigration.

- The quality of labour is improved by training and education.

- The key functions of the **entrepreneur** are to bear risks and to organise the other economic resources.

- The entrepreneur is the most mobile factor of production.

- **Capital goods** are man-made resources used to produce other goods and services.

- The mobility of capital varies.

- To increase the quantity of capital goods may involve a short-term opportunity cost in terms of consumer goods.

- The quality of capital goods is improved by advances in technology.

- **Land** covers all natural resources.

- Land itself is geographically immobile but **occupationally mobile**.

Multiple choice questions

1 Factors of production include:

A man-made resources

B man-made and human resources

C human and natural resources

D man-made, human and natural resources

2 Which of the following is a capital good?

A a share

B a government bond

C a child's toy

D a luxury liner

3 Which of the following is an entrepreneur?

A a police officer

B a sales assistant

C a self-employed window cleaner

D a government tax officer

4 In what way does land itself differ from the other three factors of production?

A it is man-made

B it is unlimited in supply

C it is geographically immobile

D it is occupationally immobile

5 Which of the following is an example of human capital?

A a saving account

B universities and schools

C experience people have gained while working

D new-born children

6 Which of the following risks does an entrepreneur bear?

A a flood destroying stock

B a fire burning down a warehouse

C a competitor introducing a superior rival product

D a hurricane tearing off the roof of the firm's head office

Data response question: Snappy Snaps

In 1983 Don Kennedy, who gave up his accountancy and law studies, and Tim MacAndrews, who resigned from his accountancy job, set up Snappy Snaps. This proved a successful move as the business revolutionised photocopying. The company expanded from one to three shops in its first year, and grew rapidly in the late 1980s and early 1990s by taking over Anglia SuperColour and Express Photo Labs. By 2001 Snappy Snaps had 90 shops throughout the UK and planned to open shops abroad.

But the business was facing increasing competition. During the 1980s and 1990s more photo-processing specialists entered the market, and more supermarkets, petrol stations and newsagents started to offer the service. The late 1990s brought another threat in the form of digital cameras, which do not require film.

Snappy Snaps has responded to the increased competition by extending its range of services to include not only traditional developing but also the transfer of images on to CD and image scanning.

a What was the opportunity cost to Tim MacAndrews of starting up Snappy Snaps? [2]

b i What risk faced by entrepreneurs is discussed in the passage? [3]

ii Explain two other risks that entrepreneurs have to bear. [6]

c Discuss how Snappy Snaps has continued to be successful. [5]

d Explain two factors that motivate entrepreneurs. [4]

4 Production possibility curves

Economic resources are used to produce goods and services, and choices are made in terms of how they are used. In this unit you will explore how **production possibility curves** can be used to examine the issues of scarcity, opportunity cost, production decisions and **productive efficiency**.

Production possibility curves

A **production possibility curve** (see Figure 1) shows the maximum output of a combination of two types of products that an economy, area, firm or individual can produce with its current resources and technology. This curve can also be called a production possibility boundary, a production possibility frontier or an opportunity cost curve.

On this curve has been plotted all the combinations of capital and consumer goods the country is capable of producing. For example, it could make no consumer goods and 50 million capital goods, or 40 million consumer goods and 40 million capital goods, or 60 million consumer goods and 28 million capital goods, or no capital goods and 80 million consumer goods.

Production possibility curves and scarcity

A production possibility curve shows that there is a limit to what a country can produce. Scarcity of economic resources limits output to points on or below the production possibility curve. Figure 2 shows that although an economy may want to produce 60 million consumer goods and 60 million capital goods, it cannot do so because it does not have enough resources. Thus points A, B, C, D and any other point to the right of a production possibility curve are unattainable output points with the existing quantity and quality of resources.

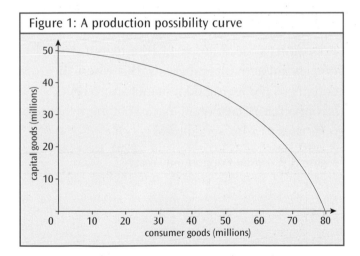

Figure 1: A production possibility curve

Activity 1

Using Figure 1 and a ruler state:

a the maximum number of capital goods which can be made if the economy makes 20 million consumer goods

b the maximum number of consumer goods which can be made if the economy makes 10 million capital goods

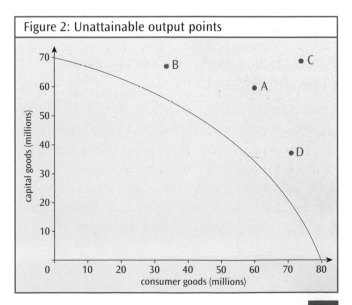

Figure 2: Unattainable output points

Activity 2

Using Figure 3 and a ruler, state which of the following combinations of agricultural and manufactured goods are attainable and which are unattainable.

a 60m agricultural goods and 30m manufactured goods

b 50m agricultural goods and 38m manufactured goods

c 40m agricultural goods and 45m manufactured goods

d 30m agricultural goods and 65m manufactured goods

e 10m agricultural goods and 65m manufactured goods

f 0m agricultural goods and 72m manufactured goods

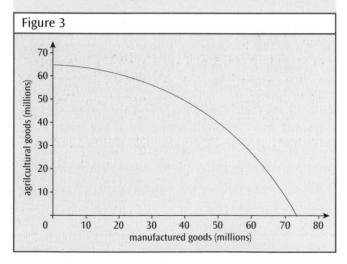

Figure 3

Production possibility curves and opportunity cost

Production possibility curves show the opportunity cost of increasing the production of one type of product in terms of another type. In Figure 4 the economy starts by producing 30m agricultural goods and 68m manufactured goods. If it decides to increase its output of agricultural goods to 40m, it has to reduce its output of manufactured goods to 60m. It has given up 8m manufactured goods.

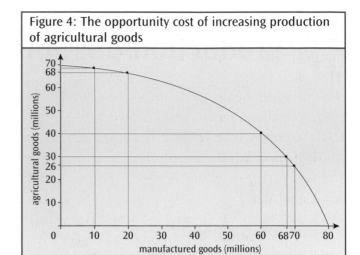

Figure 4: The opportunity cost of increasing production of agricultural goods

Most production possibility curves curve outwards. This shows that as more of one product is produced, the opportunity cost of extra units of it increases. This is because some resources are better suited to making one type of product, such as manufactured goods, and are likely to be used first. So when a large quantity of one product is being produced, to produce more will require the use of increasing quantities of the less well-suited resources. In Figure 4, when the economy is producing 10m manufactured goods, the opportunity cost of an extra 10m manufactured goods is 2m agricultural goods. But when the economy is producing 60m manufactured goods, the opportunity cost of an extra 10m manufactured goods rises to 14m agricultural goods.

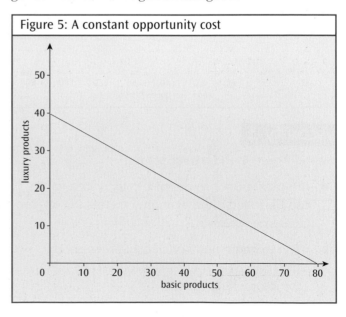

Figure 5: A constant opportunity cost

In the few cases, where economic resources are equally good at producing both types of products, the opportunity cost will be constant. This is illustrated by a downward sloping, straight line production possibility curve as shown in Figure 5. Whatever quantity of luxury products is made, the opportunity cost of an extra 1m luxury goods stays at 2m basic products.

Activity 3

Figure 6 shows a production possibility curve for an economy capable of producing both capital and consumer goods. Estimate the opportunity cost of a 5m increase in the output of consumer goods when the output of consumer goods is:

a 20m

b 60m

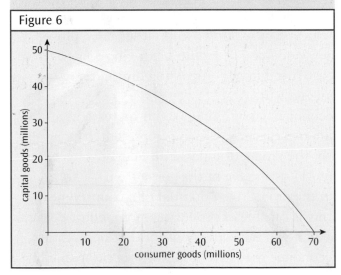

Figure 6

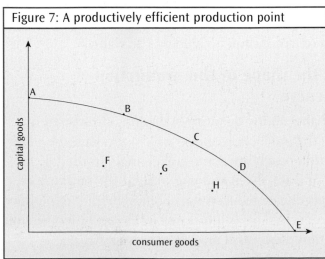

Figure 7: A productively efficient production point

Production possibility curves and efficiency

When an economy is producing on its production possibility curve it is working to its full capacity and making full use of its economic resources. Such a production point is described as **productively efficient**.

Points A, B, C, D and E in Figure 7 are all productively efficient output points. The economy could not produce any more with its existing resources. In contrast, points F, G and H are productively inefficient points. The economy is not making full use of its resources. It could increase output by employing some or all of the unemployed resources. In this case there is no opportunity cost involved in increasing output. For example, when the economy moves from point G to point C, the output of both capital and consumer products rises.

Activity 4

Using Figure 8, identify which points are productively efficient, which are productively inefficient and which are currently unattainable.

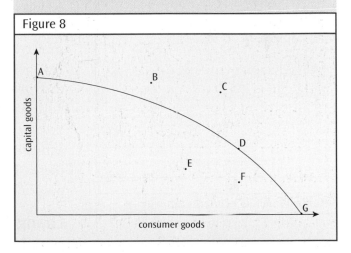

Figure 8

Shifts in production possibility curves

A change in the position of a production possibility curve illustrates a change in productive capacity. A shift to the right shows an increase in a country's ability to produce more goods and services. A shift to the left shows a decrease in its productive capacity.

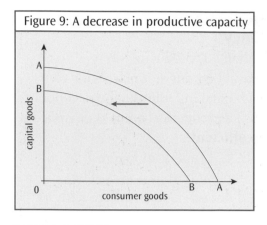

Figure 9: A decrease in productive capacity

Activity 5

Decide whether the following would cause a country's production possibility curve to shift to the right or left:

a an increase in investment

b a rise in the retirement age

c major floods

d net immigration

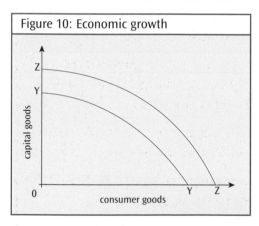

Figure 10: Economic growth

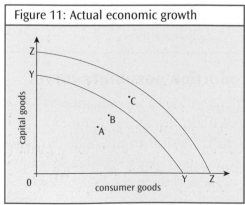

Figure 11: Actual economic growth

Over time most countries' productive capacity increases. This is because the quality and quantity of resources usually increases. Workers become better educated and trained and the quantity of capital goods rises.

In a few cases the productive potential of countries declines. Wars and natural disasters are likely to reduce a country's ability to produce. Capital goods may be destroyed, some workers may lose their lives, the health of others may be harmed and education and training will be disrupted. Figure 9 shows a decrease in productive capacity from AA to BB owing to a decrease in the quantity and quality of resources.

Economic growth

Economists refer to a rise in a country's productive potential as **economic growth**. Figure 10 illustrates the production possibility curve shifting out to the right from YY to ZZ.

Some economists distinguish between what they call actual and potential economic growth. Actual economic growth is an increase in the output of goods and services. This can be achieved by making use of either unemployed resources or new resources. In Figure 11 the movements from point A to point B and from point A to point C represent actual economic growth.

Potential economic growth refers to an increase in a country's productive capacity, which is represented by an outward shift in the production possibility curve. This is shown in Figure 11 as a move of the curve from YY to ZZ. An increase in the productive potential of a country means that its economy is capable of producing more, but it does not necessarily mean it will take advantage of that opportunity. So potential economic growth is not always accompanied by actual economic growth. However, for an economy to keep increasing its output, it is important for its production possibility curve to continue to shift to the right.

Changes in the shape of the production possibility curve

If there is a change in the quantity or quality of resources that are specific to the production of one type of product, the slope of the production possibility curve will change. In the UK in 2001 the cull of cows, sheep and pigs to fight the outbreak of foot-and-mouth disease reduced the country's ability to produce agricultural products. This is illustrated in Figure 12 by the shift of the production possibility curve from AA to AB.

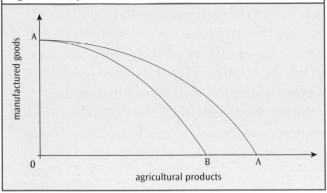

Figure 12: A reduction in the ability to produce agricultural products

Activity 6

Egypt is undertaking vast land reclamation schemes. Currently its 66 million people are crowded into less than 5% of its land. The rest of the country is virtually uninhabited desert. The government hopes that by 2017 it will have increased the inhabited area of the country by 25%, adding 3.4 million acres of agriculturally viable land and land suitable for manufacturing industry.

a Explain, using a production possibility curve, what the Egyptian government hopes will happen by 2017.

b Identify another two causes of a movement in a production possibility curve.

Activity 7

A country can produce wheat and cotton. There is an improvement in the quality of training that cotton workers receive. Using a production possibility curve, illustrate the effect of such a change.

Current issue: Singapore's labour force

Singapore has a shortage of talented young workers. Its labour force is not growing fast enough and the average age of workers has increased from 32.8 to 37.4. There are many vacancies for professional, technical and managerial workers. The government is seeking to tackle the situation in various ways. For example, it is promoting dating agencies and

Summary

In this unit you have learned that:

■ A **production possibility curve** shows the maximum output of a combination of two types of products that can be produced with current resources and technology.

■ Production possibility curves illustrate the concepts of opportunity cost, scarcity, choice and efficiency.

■ Any point on or inside a production possibility curve is attainable.

■ Any point outside a production possibility curve is unattainable.

■ Most production possibility curves are curved outwards as the opportunity cost of producing one more unit of a product increases as more of it is produced.

■ A straight line production possibility curve indicates a constant opportunity cost.

■ Any point on a production possibility curve is a **productively efficient** point.

■ A point inside a production possibility curve is an inefficient point and results from some resources being unemployed.

■ Changes in the quantity or quality of resources shift a production possibility curve.

■ Actual **economic growth** is an increase in the output of goods and services and is represented by a shift to the right of the production point.

■ Potential economic growth is an increase in the productive potential of the economy and is represented by a shift to the right of the production possibility curve.

■ If there is a change in the quantity or quality of resources that are specific to the production of one type of product, the slope of the production possibility curve will alter.

encouraging Singaporean women to have more children. It is also trying to develop lifelong training and to encourage firms to recruit more foreign specialists.

Slow growth in the labour force will restrict the outward movement of the production possibility curve. If the government succeeds in encouraging more immigrants to enter the country's labour force and developing lifelong training, the country's production possibility curve will shift to the right. First, because there will be more resources (workers), and second, because the quality of resources (workers) will have improved. Increasing the birth rate may, in the short run, reduce the supply of labour as parents take time off work to bring up their children. However, when the children are old enough to work, the labour force will increase.

Multiple choice questions

1 What does a production possibility curve show?
A the quantity of capital and labour available
B the combinations of two products which give people equal satisfaction
C the relationship between the resources devoted to the production of two types of products
D the maximum possible output of one type of product for any output of a second type, given existing technology and resources

2 What does production point X on Figure 13 illustrate?
A unemployed resources
B full utilisation of resources
C a productively efficient output
D an impossible position at which to produce with existing resources and technology

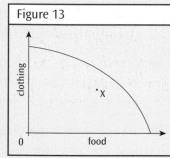
Figure 13

3 Which of the following would cause the production possibility curve to move from YY to ZZ?
A greater use of existing resources
B an increase in the number of capital goods
C greater concentration on the production of basic necessities
D a more efficient allocation of resources

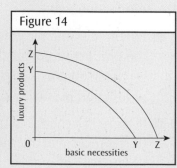
Figure 14

4 What does a downward sloping, straight line production possibility curve indicate?
A people value both products equally
B efficiency declines as output increases
C the opportunity cost of one type of product in terms of the other is constant
D the opportunity cost of one type of product in terms of the other increases by constant amounts

5 Figure 15 shows the production possibility of an economy. What is the opportunity cost of producing 80m consumer goods?
A 30m capital goods
B 40m capital goods
C 70m capital goods
D 110m consumer goods

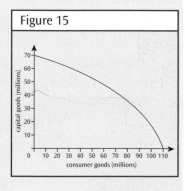
Figure 15

6 Which of the following could have caused the move of the production possibility curve from AA to AB?
A improved technology in the car industry
B an increase in the number of cotton firms
C an increase in the country's labour force
D a switch of resources from the production of clothes to the production of cars

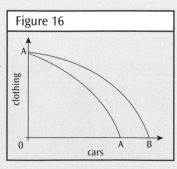
Figure 16

Data response question: Ireland's economic growth

In the 1990s the Irish economy grew rapidly. The country's output grew, on average, by 8% from 1991 to 1999. Unemployment in 1993 was 16% but by 1999 it had fallen to 4%.

Economic growth was driven by increases in the quality and quantity of the labour force and capital goods. The government had increased its spending on universities and had succeeded in raising the number of computer science graduates from 500 in 1996 to 2,400 in 2001. The labour supply had grown through more women seeking employment and through immigration. The government's training agency actively sought to attract workers from overseas and immigration rules were eased. Investment increased with domestic and foreign entrepreneurs spending more on capital goods.

a Explain, using a production possibility curve, the effect on output of a fall in unemployment. [5]

b Which two resources are not mentioned in the passage? [2]

c Explain, using a production possibility curve, the effect of an increase in the quality and quantity of the labour force. [5]

d Discuss one factor which could lead to an improvement in the quality of capital. [3]

e Explain and illustrate on a production possibility diagram the effect on a country of some of its workers emigrating to Ireland. [5]

5 Specialisation and division of labour

In Unit 4 you learned that countries have to make a choice about what to produce and that switching resources involves an opportunity cost. In this unit you will examine the meaning, benefits and risks of **specialisation** and compare the difference between **domestic** and **international trade**.

Specialisation

Specialisation means the concentration by workers, firms, areas or countries on a particular product or a few products, or a particular task or a narrow range of products.

Specialisation and trade

Trade and **money** enable people, firms, areas and countries to specialise.

I sell my skills as a teacher and am paid a wage. With the money I earn I buy a range of products, including food, housing and clothing. If I could not sell what I produce for money and then use that to buy what other people produce, I would have to

Activity 1

Figure 1 shows the production possibility curve for country X. It is currently producing at point A.

a Identify which product the country is concentrating on.

b Would there be any opportunity cost involved in increasing the output of weapons from point A to point B?

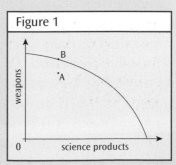

Figure 1

make everything I use. For example, I would have to grow my own food, build and maintain my own home and make my own clothes.

Firms buy **raw materials**, services and capital goods and sell their products to other areas within their own countries and to other countries. This exchange of products, helped by money, enables people, firms, areas and countries to concentrate on what they are best at producing. Economists refer to **domestic trade** and **international trade**. Domestic trade, also called internal trade, is the exchange of products within a country. International trade, also called external trade, is the exchange of goods and services across international boundaries. Products sold by one country to other countries are known as **exports** and products bought from abroad are called **imports**.

Activity 2

Decide whether the following are examples of domestic or international trade:

a a Dutch citizen buying a German car

b a citizen in Singapore buying a computer produced in China from parts made in Singapore

c a Nigerian insurance company selling a policy to a Nigerian maize exporter

d a farm in Kent, southern England, selling hops to a brewery in Scotland

Domestic and international trade

Trading with other countries is complex and may cost more than domestic trade. Firms may have to deal with cultural differences, different promotional techniques and different legal and technical requirements. Production costs can be higher because currencies may have to be changed, transport distances may be longer and communications may be more expensive.

However, improving communication links, faster and more efficient transport and the increasing similarity of tastes throughout the world mean that the differences between international trade and internal trade are diminishing.

Activity 3

American dot.com companies, including Amazon (seller of books, music and videos), are seeking to expand further into Europe. They see it as a largely untapped market. 'The rate of growth for Amazon in Europe is dramatic, much more dramatic than it has been historically in the US', Jeff Bezos told an industry conference in Stockholm. Amazon launched its French site in 2000 and is aiming to achieve a local presence in every country.

a Why are American dot.com companies seeking to expand further into Europe?

b Explain two additional costs a US bookseller may experience in selling books to Europe.

Benefits of specialisation

Specialising enables countries, areas, firms and individuals to concentrate on what they are best at producing. The UK has a reputation for producing medicines, scientific instruments, financial and business services and civil aviation.

In the UK, the Isle of Wight, with its good climate and beaches, has many people employed in tourism. The City of London, with its international reputation, long tradition and excellent communication links, has many people employed in financial services such as banking and insurance.

General Motors, a US company, specialises in car production and has car plants throughout the world, and De Beers, a South African company, concentrates on diamond production.

By concentrating on areas of strength, the quality and quantity of output produced should be high. With their suitable climate and fertile soil, Caribbean countries produce excellent sugar. A high proportion of agricultural land in Bangladesh, China, Indonesia and Madagascar is devoted to growing rice. Higher output increases the number of goods and services people can enjoy and so raises their material standard of living.

Activity 4

In Madagascar rice yields per hectare increased dramatically between 1990 and 2000 without the use of chemical fertilisers, pesticides or expensive seed varieties. This was the result of a new technique called the System of Rice Intensification (SRI), which involves planting seedlings earlier than usual, planting them individually, and not keeping them continually submerged in water. SRI was developed by Henri De Laudani, an agricultural specialist, who drew on the experience of the country's farmers.

a   Identify two benefits of being able to increase rice yields without the 'use of chemical fertilisers'.

b   Why are countries which have specialised in a product for some time likely to develop new techniques?

Risks of specialisation

Specialisation can increase output but it also carries risks. Concentrating on a narrow range of products may prove to be unwise if demand for the products falls, the costs of producing the products increase or difficulties arise in producing the products. Fewer people may want the products if tastes change or if new competitors start to produce them more cheaply or to a higher standard. Costs of producing the products can increase if, for example, workers' wages or the prices of raw materials rise. As a result, fewer products may be sold. Demand may remain high but there may be problems meeting that demand. In the case of agricultural products, output can be disrupted or destroyed by poor weather conditions and disease. With minerals there is a risk that supplies will run out.

Activity 5

Tobacco is Zimbabwe's largest export, accounting for approximately 30% of its export earnings. In 2001 production was disrupted by war veteran invasions, farmer evictions and the destruction of seed beds on an estimated 250 of the 1,600 commercial tobacco farms.

a   Identify another factor that could disrupt the production of tobacco.

b   Discuss one factor that could reduce demand for tobacco in the future.

Division of labour

For firms to sell their products at home and abroad they have to be **price competitive**. One way of keeping costs low is to have workers specialising. The specialisation of labour on particular tasks is known as **division of labour**. For example, in a sausage factory some workers may specialise in preparing the sausage skins, some in making the ingredients and some in putting the sausages into cellophane.

The main advantage claimed for division of labour is higher **productivity**. This leads to lower costs per unit of output produced. For example, if ten workers, each earning £40 a day and not specialising, produce 20 CD players between them, the labour cost per CD player produced is £20 (£400/20). However, if each worker performs just part of the process, instead of making the whole CD player him or herself, output may rise to 40 CD players. This will reduce the labour cost per CD player to £10 (£400/40).

Output per worker may increase when workers specialise for various reasons. One is that the more a worker performs a task the more skilled he or she may become – 'practice makes perfect'. A teacher who has taught economics for some time has, hopefully, become proficient in explaining the subject and preparing students for examinations. Another reason is that when workers are performing one or a limited range of tasks they can be trained more quickly. As a result, they start contributing to output more quickly and need less updating training once at work.

Division of labour can also cut costs by reducing the amount of equipment each worker requires. For example, if each worker produced a complete computer they would each need a full set of tools. But if each one specialised in a particular task, he or she would need only a few tools.

Concentrating on a particular task also saves time as workers do not have to move from one job to another.

In addition, breaking down production into separate tasks may make it possible to devise machinery to carry out each individual operation. This may also cut costs.

Not all firms can take advantage of the division of labour. For it to take place, production has to be on a certain scale. For example, a small bakery producing only 120 loaves a day and employing two workers will have little scope for the workers to specialise. In a large bakery producing 14,000 loaves a day and employing 100 workers there will be much more opportunity for them to concentrate on particular tasks.

The risks of division of labour

Despite the advantages claimed for division of labour, there is a risk that workers specialising may result in higher costs for firms and disadvantages for the workers themselves.

When workers perform the same task each day there is a danger that they will become bored. If this happens they may reduce their effort or not work as efficiently, make mistakes or even resign. In each case labour costs will rise. In the first case output per worker will fall, in the second some of the output will have to be rejected and in the third there will be extra recruitment and training costs.

Specialisation of its labour force may also reduce a firm's flexibility. If a specialised worker is ill or on a training course, or if demand for a particular task rises quickly, other workers may not be able to perform the function. For example, if the Spanish teacher is off sick, no other teacher in the school may be able to teach the students Spanish that day.

Workers who have been trained to perform just one or a few tasks may experience problems finding alternative work if demand for the task falls or it is mechanised. Specialisation, however, may help workers find new jobs more quickly. Firms that employ people to carry out a limited number of functions know that the training period is short, so they may be willing to take on people who have no experience.

Activity 6

A town has two doctors' surgeries, North and South. North surgery has eight doctors who do not specialise. South surgery employs one doctor who sees patients aged under 16, two who concentrate on treating patients aged over 60, one specialising in alternative medicine, one who concentrates on patients with cancer, one who treats patients with heart disease, one who sees all other female patients and one who sees all other male patients.

a Explain one benefit a patient may receive from visiting the South surgery.

b Explain one benefit a patient may receive from visiting the North surgery.

Activity 7

Northampton, a town in England, used to be well known for shoemaking. Since the late 1950s, however, the industry has suffered because of cheaper imports from abroad. Many Northampton shoemakers have gone out of business and shoemaking in Northampton is now in decline. However, other types of industries, such as Barclaycard, have moved to Northampton and unemployment remains below the national average.

a What are the risks of a person specialising as a cobbler (shoemaker) in Northampton?

b What does the passage suggest about the ability of workers in Northampton to transfer their skills?

Moves away from division of labour

To avoid the problems of worker boredom, low-quality output, high **labour turnover** and lack of flexibility, some companies, including car manufacturer Volvo, have moved away from division of labour. They train their workers in a variety of tasks to see which ones they are best at performing and so they can cover for absent colleagues. Carrying out a number of tasks can increase workers' motivation, enable them to appreciate the role of other workers and increase the range of jobs they can apply for in the future.

Activity 8

In 1992 London Zoo decided to cut the number of staff it employed to save costs. The managers also decided that staff would receive training in more than one section. For example, staff working in the aviaries received training in looking after the big cats.

a What benefits may London Zoo receive from having its staff trained in a number of areas?

b Why may some staff have been unhappy with the change in policy?

Current issue: the problems of specialisation

The terrorist attack on September 11th 2001 disrupted production in the USA. The halt in flights and extensive delays at border controls meant that many American companies, including car and technology companies, experienced difficulties in obtaining supplies of components.

Many car and technology companies now base their components factories abroad or buy parts from foreign firms. For example, Ford imports component parts from Europe, Asia and Africa. Its inability to obtain crucial component parts forced the company to close a number of factories on the days after the attack.

These difficulties illustrate one of the problems of specialisation. When firms or their plants rely on parts or services from other firms and plants they become interdependent. Problems at a plant or with transport can cause difficulties throughout the industry and related industries. The purchase of goods and services across international boundaries is increasing rapidly. Capital is also becoming more geographically mobile, and many firms are prepared to base some of their plants abroad to save costs.

Summary

In this unit you have learned that:

■ **Specialisation** is the concentration on a particular or limited number of products or tasks.

■ **Trade** and the use of **money** enable specialisation to take place.

■ **International trade** is trade between countries and **domestic trade** is trade within a country.

■ International trade can involve extra costs but can also bring more benefits than domestic trade.

■ The main benefits of specialisation are increased output and higher living standards.

■ Specialisation carries risks since demand and supply conditions change.

■ **Division of labour** is the specialisation of workers on particular tasks.

■ Output may increase when workers specialise because they can concentrate on the tasks they are best at, can be trained quickly, need less equipment and have to move around less, and machinery can be developed to assist the production process.

■ The quantity and quality of output may be adversely affected by division of labour if it results in workers becoming bored. As workers are trained to perform specific tasks, a firm's flexibility may be reduced. Division of labour may also adversely affect a worker's ability to obtain alternative employment.

■ To increase the motivation and flexibility of their labour force some firms have moved away from division of labour.

Multiple choice questions

1 Specialisation and trade can improve people's standard of living. This is because:

A firms can increase their prices

B people can work longer hours

C the output of goods and services should increase

D governments can impose taxes on imported products

2 Which of the following makes trade easier?

A differences in countries' technical requirements

B high transport costs

C money

D taxes

3 What is the main benefit claimed for division of labour?

A a reduction in the use of machinery

B a decrease in the average cost of production

C an increase in the job satisfaction workers experience

D a rise in the amount of training given to workers

4 A country's farmers specialise in corn production. Which of the following would reduce the benefits of such specialisation?

A an increase in the productivity of the country's agricultural workers

B an increase in world demand for corn

C a reduction in the number of other countries producing corn

D a prolonged period of bad weather in the country which reduces crop yields

5 Which of the following may result from the introduction of division of labour in a firm?

A a reduction in mechanisation

B a reduction in the range of workers' skills

C an increase in the quantity of equipment per worker

D an increase in the number of tasks a worker carries out

6 Why might a firm decide to move away from division of labour?

A to reduce the training given to workers

B to reduce labour turnover

C to reduce labour flexibility

D to increase the specialisation of workers

Data response question: oil production in Kazakhstan

Kazakhstan, a former Soviet republic, gained independence in August 1995. It is expected to become an important energy producer in the next few years. It has major oil fields, notably in Tengiz and Karachaganak. As Kazakhstan is landlocked (it has no sea port), it has to pipe its oil to the Black Sea, the Caspian Sea and the Mediterranean and then on to customers. It uses two Russian pipelines and a third built with the help of foreign finance in 2001. It sells most of its oil to Russia.

In 1999 Kazakhstan's economy suffered because a financial crisis in Russia meant it was unable to buy so much oil and a general slowdown in world economic activity reduced world commodity prices, including oil prices.

Economists are concerned that Kazakhstan is too dependent on one resource and therefore too heavily influenced by what happens in Russia and the price of oil.

They are worried about what would happen if world economic activity declines in the future.

Kazakh officials have said that they are aware of the dangers of overdependence on one commodity and are taking measures to build up other industries.

a What advantage does Kazakhstan have in oil production? [2]

b What risks does Kazakhstan run in piping its oil to its customers? [4]

c Discuss three risks Kazakhstan faces in specialising in oil production. [6]

d Discuss four ways an oil company could reduce its average cost of production by engaging in division of labour. [8]

6 Economies of scale

In this unit you will see that by trading internationally firms can produce large quantities of goods and services. Producing on a large scale can bring many benefits, but if firms grow too large, they may experience problems. You will examine some of these problems.

Economies of scale

The term **economies of scale** refers to the benefits of producing on a large scale. When firms and industries increase the scale of their operation there can be advantages which reduce the average (unit) cost of their output. For example, producing 2,000 units may cost £8,000 (giving an average cost of £4), but producing 6,000 units may cost £18,000 (giving a lower average cost of £3).

Activity 1

A firm's cost schedule is given in Table 1. Calculate the average cost for each level of output and state at which level average cost is minimised.

Table 1	
Output (units)	Total cost ($)
100	600
200	1,100
300	1,500
400	1,800
500	2,500
600	3,300

Internal economies of scale

Internal economies of scale are the benefits, in the form of lower average costs, which a firm can gain from increasing its size. Among these benefits are the following.

- **Technical economies** When a firm increases its output it can use larger machinery, which is often more efficient, producing output at a lower unit cost. A larger output may also allow the firm to take advantage of specialisation of capital goods and to link some production processes together.

- **Marketing economies** Large firms can save money when they buy raw materials and equipment and when they sell their products. When a firm buys large quantities, often referred to as buying in bulk, it usually pays a lower price for each item. Selling can become cheaper. For example, advertising costs can be spread over more units of output. Packaging and transport costs per unit can also be lower. For example, a large lorry does not cost twice as much to run as a lorry half its size.

- **Managerial economies** A large firm can employ specialist staff including accountants, market researchers and human development managers and spread the cost of their wages over a large number of units of output.

- **Research and development (R&D) economies** A large firm is more likely to have an R&D department than a small firm, and the larger the firm, the larger that department will probably be. R&D departments benefit from being large because it is important for researchers to share ideas and brainstorm.

- **Financial economies** As a firm grows it usually becomes easier and cheaper for it to borrow and to sell shares. Banks like to lend to well-known firms with valuable assets. They think such loans are less risky than loans to smaller firms. Large loans are not much more expensive to process than small loans, so the interest charged per pound lent is often lower than on small loans. Individuals and financial institutions are also more willing to buy shares in large, well-known firms than in small, lesser-known firms.

■ **Risk bearing** Large firms can produce a range of products. This reduces their vulnerability to sudden changes in demand or cost conditions. For example, a firm producing baby food, crisps, postcards and perfume would be less badly hit by a fall in the birth rate than a firm concentrating on baby food. The spreading of risks is often referred to as not putting all your eggs in one basket.

Internal diseconomies of scale

Figure 1 shows that as the output of a firm increases to 20,000 units its average cost (AC) falls.

When output rises above 20,000, however, average costs start to rise. The firm is becoming too large and is starting to experience **internal diseconomies of scale**. The possible disadvantages a firm can experience if it grows too large include the following.

■ **Control** It can be difficult for managers to keep track of everything that goes on in a large firm.
■ **Co-ordination** Because of the difficulty of controlling a large firm, several tiers of management and decision making are often used. As a result the firm may be slower to respond to changes in market conditions.
■ **Communication** In a small firm communication between employers and workers is usually straightforward and quick. In a large firm extra costs may be incurred to ensure clear and quick lines of communication between managers and workers.
■ **Industrial relations** There appears to be a strong link between the size of a firm and relationships between workers and employers. Generally, the larger the firm the poorer **industrial relations** are. One reason for this is that it can take longer for problems to be resolved because more people are likely to be involved. In a small firm a worker may be able to meet the manager (who may also be the owner) to talk over an issue. In a large firm a worker may have to discuss the issue first with his or her line manager, who may then have to raise it with the head of department, who may

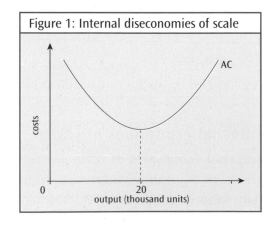

Figure 1: Internal diseconomies of scale

then have to take it to a senior manager before a decision can be made. Another reason is that a large firm will have more staff. The more people there are, the more opportunity there is for people to disagree.

■ **Prices of resources** As a firm grows its demand for resources will increase. Its higher demand is likely to increase its bargaining power with suppliers and so reduce the prices it pays. If the resource is becoming scarce, however, its high demand may drive up the price.

As you will have noticed, many of these disadvantages relate to the problems of management. Managing a large firm is complex and there are many views on the most appropriate management strategies.

Activity 3

In early 2001 Kingfisher, a retail conglomerate, tried to sell its Woolworths and Superdrug operations because it wanted to concentrate on its more successful DIY and electrical stores. It was unable to find a suitable buyer so it decided to reorganise. In June 2001 it announced its intention to run Woolworths and Superdrug as separate companies.

a Explain why it may be easier to manage a smaller, more focused firm.

b Discuss one possible advantage of producing a variety of products.

External economies of scale

A firm can experience lower average costs either by increasing its size or by being in a growing industry. The benefits that firms in a growing industry gain are called **external economies of scale**. These include the following.

■ **Skilled labour force** A firm in a large industry can draw on a pool of trained and skilled labour. This reduces its training costs.
■ **Specialised suppliers of raw materials, equipment and capital goods may develop** For example, a number of firms produce

clothes and food for Marks and Spencer, a UK chain store.
■ **Specialised services** Suppliers of services may find it worthwhile to supply specialised services to the industry, such as banking, insurance and education.
■ **Specialised markets** If the industry is large, specialised selling places and arrangements may be made. An example is Lloyds of London, which serves the insurance industry.
■ **Improved infrastructure** The growth of an industry may give rise to new transport facilities and communications. For example, new road links were built and cables laid to service the growing IT industry in Silicon Valley in California in the USA.
■ **Good reputation** If an area develops a good reputation for the production of a good or service, firms producing there, in effect, receive free advertising.

Many of these external benefits depend on firms in the same industry being based in the same area. These are sometimes referred to as economies of concentration.

Activity 4

Cambridge is becoming the UK's technological centre, attracting IT, telecommunications, biotechnology and e-commerce firms. It has a cluster of more than 1,300 high-tech firms employing more than 38,000 people, including ARM Holdings (microchip design), Celltech Chiroscience (Europe's biggest biotechnology company) and Autonomy Corporation (a producer of software used to organise information). Cambridge University and the Massachusetts Institute of Technology (MIT) are setting up an institute to teach entrepreneurship, technology and productivity.

a Which external economy of scale is referred to in the passage?

b Discuss one other external economy of scale the Cambridge high-tech firms could enjoy.

External diseconomies of scale

Firms' average costs may increase because the industry they are in grows too large. There are several possible **external diseconomies of scale**. When an industry expands, it demands more economic resources, including labour, equipment, raw materials and appropriate sites. Firms compete for these resources, which may drive up their prices and increase their costs.

If the firms are concentrated in one area, the growth of the industry will increase the volume of traffic required to move raw materials, equipment and workers. This may cause congestion. Firms' transport costs will then rise because of the extra time taken transporting raw materials, equipment and products.

The effect of external economies and diseconomies of scale

When firms are able to take advantage of external economies of scale their average costs fall at any level of output. This effect can be illustrated by a downward shift in the average cost curve as shown in Figure 2.

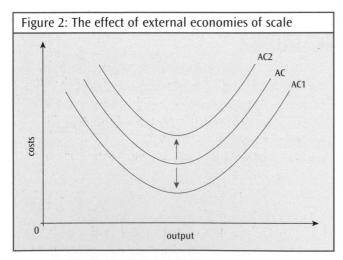

Figure 2: The effect of external economies of scale

The effect of external diseconomies of scale on a firm's average costs is, of course, the opposite. Being part of an industry that has grown too large will push up a firm's average costs. This is shown by the rise in the average cost curve to AC2 in Figure 2.

Current issue: the benefits of mergers

In September 2001 Hewlett-Packard and Compaq, two large US computing companies, announced they were merging. The new company used the name Hewlett-Packard and was based at Hewlett-Packard's headquarters in Palo Alto, California. The chief executive of the new company argued that it would be better placed to challenge IBM and Sun Microsystems in the computer business and would be a strong force in the growing computer services and consulting business. It immediately became the top firm in the PC market, with a 19% market share, overtaking Dell Computer, with 13.4%.

The merged company has operations in 160 countries with more than 158,000 workers. One of its first objectives was to cut costs by $2.5 billion by mid-2004.

The size of firms in computing and other areas, including banking, car production and food retailing, has continued to grow in recent years. One of the main reasons for this is firms seeking to take advantage of economies of scale. If they succeed they can reduce their costs and become more internationally competitive. The internal economies of scale available to a computer firm include technical, marketing, managerial and financial economies. For example, it can use larger, more efficient capital equipment, receive discounts on its advertisements, employ more specialised staff and borrow at lower interest rates. With recent changes in demand and technology, diversification and risk-bearing economies of scale are particularly important to computing firms.

A computing firm, like any other firm, has to be careful that it does not grow too large and experience diseconomies of scale. For example, it may be harder to achieve efficient control and co-ordination of the new Hewlett-Packard than it was in the case of the two smaller firms.

Summary

In this unit you have learned that:

- **Economies of scale** are the benefits, in the form of lower average costs, of producing on a large scale.

- **Internal economies of scale** are the benefits a firm gains from growing in size. These include technical, marketing, managerial, research and development, financial and risk-bearing economies.

- **Diseconomies of scale** are the disadvantages, in the form of higher average costs, experienced when firms grow too large.

- **Internal diseconomies of scale** are the disadvantages a firm experiences when it grows too large. They include problems of control, co-ordination and communication, and possibly having to pay higher prices for resources.

- **External economies of scale** are the benefits firms in an industry can gain from their industry growing in size. They include a skilled labour force, specialised supplies of raw materials, specialised services, specialised markets and infrastructure.

- **External diseconomies of scale** are the disadvantages firms in an industry experience from the industry growing too large. They include higher costs of resources and congestion.

Multiple choice questions

1 Economies of scale occur when:
A average costs fall
B average revenue rises
C output rises by a smaller percentage than the increase in the number of factors of production employed
D output rises by the same percentage as the increase in the number of factors of production employed

2 What are financial economies of scale?
A lower average costs enjoyed by large financial institutions
B lower average costs resulting from a firm increasing the scale of its operation
C a reduction in the average cost of borrowing and issuing shares experienced by firms as they increase in size
D a fall in average costs experienced by larger firms arising from the more efficient handling of revenue

3 Which of the following is most likely to result in a firm being able to benefit from external economies of scale?
A an increase in its output
B a diversification into a wider range of products
C locating in the same area as other firms in the industry
D introduction of new, more capital-intensive methods of production

4 What explains the typical U-shaped long run average cost curve?
A internal economies of scale
B internal and external economies of scale
C internal and external diseconomies of scale
D internal economies of scale and internal diseconomies of scale

5 Which of the following is an example of an external economy of scale?
A a firm's advertising costs not rising in proportion with output
B a firm spreading the cost of improving products over a large level of output
C a firm's managers experiencing problems exercising control and co-ordination
D a firm sending some of its staff to a local FE college which provides specialist training for the industry

6 A firm's average cost curve shifts downwards. What would have caused this movement?
A internal economies of scale
B external economies of scale
C internal diseconomies of scale
D external diseconomies of scale

Data response question: the benefits of clusters

Michael Porter, a professor at Harvard Business School, argues that clusters of firms with the same activity provide significant benefits for customers and the firms themselves. He believes that the concentration of firms in the same area puts constant pressure on them to raise quality. He gives Silicon Valley, Hollywood and Wall Street as examples.

According to his theory, self-seeded clusters in the UK enjoy external economies of scale – benefits that companies would have to pay for were they not part of a cluster. Such benefits include shared suppliers, access to skilled workers and high, stable demand.

Clusters attract scores of customers because they offer a wide variety of quality products in one area. A cluster allows each member to benefit as if it had joined with others without sacrificing its flexibility, he claims.

Clusters also mean that even in an increasingly global market, where a firm decides to be located is still significant. Indeed, Professor Porter argues that location has become more important and that a firm will find it harder to be competitive unless it is in a cluster.

Fans of the cluster theory – that success breeds success – could use Hay in the UK as a neat example. The medieval town of 1,300 inhabitants, about 400 yards within the Welsh border, is now famous the world over for its 67 second-hand bookshops and its annual literary festival.

In 1962 the first second-hand bookshop was opened in Hay. Now its picturesque lanes are chock-a-block with stores specialising in children's books, poetry, antiquarian books, detective fiction and the occult.

Adapted from 'Bookworms make town a bestseller', Jim Pickard, *Financial Times*, 4 September 2000.

a What are the main industries in Silicon Valley, Hollywood and Wall street? [3]

b i Explain what is meant by external economies of scale. [3]

 ii Identify and explain one example of an external economy of scale not mentioned in the passage. [4]

c Describe how customers can benefit from clusters. [4]

d Discuss three benefits a bookshop might receive from setting up in Hay. [6]

7 The role of markets

In Unit 5 you saw that products are traded both domestically and internationally. In this unit you will examine the nature of **markets**, their role and the objectives of participants in markets. You will see that markets operate on various levels, from the small scale to the global (world) scale.

Markets

When we hear the word **market** most of us think of a street market. In economics the word has a wider meaning. It covers any arrangement which allows buyers and sellers to exchange products and to agree on the price and the quantity of products to be exchanged. Buyers and sellers make contact in a variety of ways. Products can be bought and sold in shops, by auction, through newspaper advertisements and on the internet.

The scope of markets

Markets operate on three main levels: local, national and global (or international or world). Each town has its own housing market with estate agents, housing trusts, landlords and landladies trading in accommodation. There are national markets in many products. For example, car insurance, chocolate and magazines are marketed throughout the country. Direct Line sells car insurance to drivers in Cardiff and Leeds, Mars Bars are bought and sold in Inverness and Cornwall and the Radio Times can be found in newsagents from the Channel Islands to the Orkney Islands.

Certain products have been traded on a global scale for some time. For example, dealers have traded in foreign currencies, minerals, coffee, tea and sugar on global markets for centuries. With advances in technology, communications and transport and increasing similarity in tastes, more and more products are being exchanged on global markets. For example, some people in the UK buy books directly from US publishers, some pay for eye operations carried out in Indian hospitals and some choose to work in foreign countries.

The role of markets

Markets play a key role in allocating resources. If a product becomes more popular, people will be prepared to pay more for it. The higher price will encourage entrepreneurs to make more of it. They will seek to employ more land, labour and capital to produce it. In contrast, resources move away from the production of products with falling popularity.

In the UK the increased interest in football is boosting attendance at football matches and encouraging people to spend more on supporting their team. As a result larger, more luxurious football stadiums are being built and more people are employed in producing and selling football merchandise. In contrast, playing and watching snooker is becoming less popular. As a result snooker clubs are being closed and the sport is being given less coverage on television.

A competitive market

A competitive market is one in which there are many buyers and sellers. It is also one in which it is easy to start or stop producing the product.

The large number of buyers and sellers and the ease of entry and exit means that no one buyer and no one seller has much **market power**. If a seller decides to raise the price of her products, buyers will switch to rival sellers. Similarly, if a buyer wants to pay a lower amount for a product, the sellers will sell to other buyers.

In such a market, resources should move quickly and smoothly to reflect changes in buyers' demand. If the product

Activity 1

Sotheby's, a fine-art auctioneer based in Bond Street, London, holds hundreds of auctions each year at its auction houses in the UK, Europe and the USA. It also deals in middle and low-priced antiques on the internet.

a What types of markets are discussed in the passage?

b Identify one other arrangement used for the purchase and sale of antiques.

Activity 2

McDonald's has outlets in many countries. Its branches are so widespread that *The Economist* newspaper is able to base its annual analysis of the purchasing power of different currencies on the price of a McDonald's burger in different countries.

a On what scale is the market for a McDonald's burger?

b What does your answer to (a) suggest about the degree of similarity of tastes throughout the world?

Activity 3

The development of the PC, with its word processing facility, has led to a significant decline in the popularity of typewriters.

a What do you think has happened to:
   i the number of people employed producing PCs
   ii the number of people employed producing typewriters
   iii the number of firms concentrating on producing typewriters
   iv the number of teachers of keyboard skills?

b Identify a product, other than a PC, which has largely replaced another product.

becomes more popular and buyers are able and willing to pay a higher price for it, more will be sold. Suppliers will expand their production and new suppliers, encouraged by the higher price and the prospect of high profits, will start to make the product. If, however, the product becomes less popular, its price will fall. Some suppliers will reduce the quantity they produce and sell, and some will stop making the product.

In practice, many markets are not very competitive. In some, a few suppliers exercise considerable market power. There are also markets where one or a few buyers can dictate the price they pay to suppliers. For example, multinational coffee companies are such large buyers of coffee beans that they can dictate the prices they pay to the coffee producers of Brazil, Ecuador, Indonesia, Vietnam and other **developing countries**.

Participants in markets

Various groups may be involved in a market. We have already mentioned buyers. Firms buy raw materials, capital goods, land and the services of workers. The government buys resources and products in order to provide education, health care and other services. However, the major buyers of products are people who live in households. They buy the products for the satisfaction the products will give them. Economists refer to buyers as **consumers**.

Buyers deal with sellers who are also known as **suppliers**. Members of households sell soft toys and other articles at car boot sales, and sometimes they sell their homes. Some members of households are workers who sell their services as, for example, nurses, electricians and financial advisers. The government also supplies goods and services, some of which are provided free, such as health care and education. Firms are major suppliers. Some firms, including high street retailers, insurance companies and double glazing firms, sell directly to households. Others, such as food-processing firms, plastic moulding firms and staff agencies, sell their goods and services to other firms.

As well as its roles as consumer and supplier, the government intervenes in markets as a regulator. In the labour market it sets health and safety standards and has passed legislation requiring firms to pay their workers at least the minimum wage. In product markets it seeks to promote competition, to reduce pollution and to ensure that the products sold are safe.

Activity 4

The street market in the centre of Cambridge in the UK sells a range of products but specialises in fresh fruit and vegetables. There are several apple sellers. The prices they charge are similar, but each trader usually lowers his or her prices during the last hour of trading and raises them on a Saturday.

a Why can't one apple trader charge a significantly higher price than the other traders?

b Why do you think apple traders usually:

  i lower their prices during the last hour of trading

  ii raise their prices on a Saturday?

Activity 5

The global oil market is extremely volatile. The quantity of oil offered for sale and the price have varied considerably since 1973. For example, in 2000 the price of oil rose from $10 to $32. The high profits that can be earned continue to encourage firms to search for new oil fields on land and at sea.

a Identify three groups of participants in the global oil market.

b Explain how one group would be adversely affected by a rise in oil prices.

c Which group, and why, may be opposed to the search for new oil fields?

Environmental groups influence some markets. Concerns about wildlife and the environment, expressed by groups including the World Wide Fund for Nature, Friends of the Earth and Greenpeace, have led to the introduction of dolphin-friendly fishing nets to catch tuna and an increase in the recycling of paper, bottles and other materials.

Objectives of participants

Consumers want low prices, high quality and ready availability of products. They try to gain as much satisfaction as possible from their purchases as well as the best value for money.

In contrast, most suppliers want high prices in order to make as much profit as possible. Profit is the difference between the revenue firms receive from selling their products and the cost of producing them. The higher the price they can obtain and the lower they can keep their costs, the more profit they will make.

When the government supplies products or pays other firms to supply products, it does not aim to make a profit. Its objectives are to ensure that products are provided in the right quantities and that poor people have access to what are perceived as essential goods and services.

Environmental groups, as the term suggests, seek to protect the environment and conserve wildlife. They aim to reduce pollution, stop the tropical rainforests being cut down and prevent animal and plant species becoming extinct.

Connection between markets

Events in one market can have an impact on other markets. For example, a rise in the price of one product will cause some consumers to switch their spending to substitute products. If strawberries become more expensive, some people will buy other fruit instead.

A change in demand for one product will also affect spending on products that are bought to use with it. Economists call products that are used together **complements**. A fall in demand for strawberries is likely to reduce sales of cream. If more people buy a car, demand for car insurance is likely to rise.

Some products are supplied together. Lead and zinc are found in the same ore. Hides and beef both come from slaughtered cows.

The markets of products and factors of production are also linked. If people buy more cars, demand for car workers and the machines and factories to produce the cars will rise. The decrease in demand for UK steel resulted in 3,000 job losses at Corus steel works in Wales in 2001.

Activity 6

In October 2001 a price war broke out among the UK's supermarkets. Tesco, the biggest supermarket chain, made price cuts on 3,500 lines totalling £100 million. It published its new prices on the internet, comparing them with its rivals' prices. Asda, the UK's third biggest supermarket chain, responded by announcing a plan to introduce price cuts worth £200 million.

Supermarkets that engage in price wars believe in what is called a grocery virtuous circle. This is the view that a cut in prices will lead to an increase in sales volume which will reduce costs. The lower costs then raise profits and allow the firms to cut their prices further.

a What motivated Tesco to cut its prices?

b Explain two ways in which consumers may have benefited from the supermarket price war.

c Explain in what sense, and how, increased 'sales volume' reduces costs.

Current issue: the housing market

In the first half of 2001 the UK housing market experienced a boom. House prices rose significantly, giving windfalls of thousands of pounds to millions of homeowners.

By August 2001 the Council of Mortgage Lenders predicted a severe slowdown in the housing market. They believed this would occur because of falling consumer confidence resulting

Activity 7

The computer games market had sales worth $20 billion in 2001. Among the important games software companies were Nintendo, Microsoft, Sony Computer Entertainment, Ubisoft and Electronic Arts.

The companies spend hundreds of millions of dollars each year during the crucial winter holidays developing computer games, and refinements and additions to games. By 2004 sales are expected to have increased by 20–25%, largely because of the marketing of Microsoft's and Nintendo's new consoles.

a Explain what effect a rise in the sales of computer games may have on the sales of:
  i board games
  ii games consoles

b Give two reasons why a person may choose to buy one computer game rather than another.

from fears about the global economy and the announcement of high-profile job cuts.

The UK housing market is a volatile and important market. House prices can change dramatically and are heavily influenced by changes in consumer confidence.

A rise in activity in the housing market provides benefits for other markets. When more people move home, demand for a range of goods and services rises. People often buy new furniture and carpets. They pay people to decorate their homes and/or spend money on DIY materials. They also pay estate agents, surveyors and removal companies to handle the process of selling and buying homes. This rise in demand creates more jobs and increases in incomes.

Rising property prices increases the value of people's main asset, and this encourages them to spend more. With more activity in the housing market it becomes easier for workers to move from one area to another. This increases the geographical mobility of labour.

Summary

In this unit you have learned that:

■ **Markets** take various forms, but they all enable buyers and sellers to exchange products.

■ Markets operate on local, national and global levels.

■ Markets allocate resources. They move resources from products experiencing a decline towards those experiencing an increase in demand.

■ A competitive market contains many buyers and sellers, has no restrictions on entry and exit and responds quickly to changes in consumer demand.

■ In many markets competition is limited, with sellers and/or buyers exercising considerable **market power**.

■ The participants in markets include **consumers**, **suppliers**, the government and environmental groups.

■ Consumers seek low prices, high quality and ready availability of products. Firms aim for high profits. The government seeks to ensure that products are provided in the right quantities and that poor people have access to essential goods and services. Environmental groups try to protect the environment and conserve wildlife.

■ Markets are interlinked, with a rise in demand for one product tending to reduce demand for substitutes and increase demand for **complements** and for the resources which produce it.

Multiple choice questions

1 What does the existence of scarcity imply?

A all goods are economic goods

B people have to make choices

C it is not possible to increase resources

D production occurs within the production possibility frontier

2 Which of the following combinations of products are in joint supply?

A fish and chips

B lamb and wool

C paper and pens

D DVDs and DVD players

3 What effect will a rise in demand have on a competitive market?

A a rise in price and a fall in supply

B an increase in the number of suppliers

C a reduction in the quantity of resources devoted to producing the product

D a cut in the profits earned by firms in the market

4 Which of the following is a characteristic of a competitive market?

A many buyers and sellers

B firms with considerable market power

C a slow response to changes in consumer demand

D factors which make it difficult for firms to enter or leave the industry

5 Many firms' main objective is to:

A protect the environment

B keep prices as low as possible

C increase the number of their competitors

D earn as high a profit as possible

6 The price of a product rises. What effect will this have on demand for a substitute and a complement to the product?

	substitute	complement
A	rise	rise
B	rise	fall
C	fall	fall

Data response question: terrorist attacks and the airline market

The terrorist attacks in the USA on 11 September 2001 had a major impact on the airline market. Airlines faced falling revenue as passenger numbers dropped and costs, including for insurance and security, rose. Most airlines responded by reducing their operations, which led to cuts in services and jobs. Virgin Atlantic grounded 5 of its 31 aircraft, reduced its transatlantic flights by 20% and made 1,200 workers (13% of its labour force) redundant. British Airways, which experienced a 32% drop in passengers travelling to the USA, cut its capacity by 18% and its labour force by 12,000. The effects were worldwide. For example, American Airlines cut services by 23% and 11,000 jobs, Alitalia cut 2,500 jobs and Aer Lingus cut its operations by 25%.

The reduction in passengers and the cuts in services meant fewer aircraft were needed, so aircraft orders were reduced. This hit the aerospace industry. Boeing laid off more than 30,000 workers.

With fewer people travelling to the UK from the USA and the Far East, British tourism was also adversely affected. Attractions such as the London Eye, the Tower of London and Stratford upon Avon experienced a drop in visitors. A week after the attack audiences at London theatres had fallen by 10%, hotel bookings by 20%, restaurant bookings by 15% and department store sales by 30%.

The attacks on the USA did, however, benefit some firms. Demand for BT's video conferencing and teleconferencing services tripled, and Virgin Trains saw an increase in business travellers using its London to Manchester and London to Glasgow services. Some budget airlines were able to avoid a reduction in passengers by aggressively marketing price reductions.

a Identify three participants in the airline market. [3]

b Explain what effect a decline in its operations may have on an airline's average costs. [5]

c Discuss what is likely to have happened to BA's profits in the weeks after the terrorist attacks. [3]

d What effect did the decline in passengers have on the factors of production employed in the airline industry? [3]

e Discuss the relationship between demand for passenger flights and:

  i demand for foreign holidays [3]

  ii demand for rail travel [3]

8 The importance of money and exchange

Money is crucial to the smooth operation of the economy. This is because, as you saw in Unit 5, it enables specialisation and exchange to take place. In this unit you will explore the significance of exchange, the link between money and exchange, and the functions, characteristics and forms of money.

Markets, money and exchange

Products are exchanged in markets. For example, in the UK newspaper market News Corporation sells *The Times*, *The Sunday Times* and the *Sun*, Trinity Mirror sells the *Mirror* and General Trust sells the *Daily Mail*. Consumers buy these papers in newsagents, supermarkets and train stations and some have them delivered to their homes.

These companies buy paper, word processors, printing presses and other products from other firms. They also buy the services of workers and entrepreneurs. These exchanges enable firms, workers and entrepreneurs to specialise and thereby increase output.

Products are exchanged throughout the world. People in Thailand can buy UK newspapers, Italian shoes and Malaysian rubber, and they can watch TV programmes produced in the USA.

Money makes these exchanges easier and so increases the number of market transactions that take place. Without money, people would have to **barter** products. Barter is the direct exchange of one product for another product.

I may swap, with a friend, a book for two CDs. This exchange may satisfy both of us, but for most exchanges barter poses problems. For example, it may be difficult to make comparisons of the value of different products. I may think that one of my paintings is worth two of your chairs. However, you may think it is worth only one and a half chairs. Even if you convince me that you are right, another problem arises. If you give me two chairs for your painting, how can I give you change? Neither of us would be happy if I sawed one of the chairs in two halves and returned one half to you.

There is also the problem that if I want to save to obtain something in the future, what do I save? It should be some item or items that will be in demand in the future, but what will they be?

The main problem with barter is that it depends on what is known as the double coincidence of wants. I have to find someone who both wants my painting and has chairs to exchange. The alternative is to swap my painting for another product and then swap that product for chairs, but I may have to make a number of exchanges before I get the chairs. All of this takes time and effort, which could be used instead for producing goods and services or leisure.

The use of money overcomes these problems. I can sell my painting for money and then use that money to buy chairs. Money enables me to give and receive change. If I buy an item costing £12 and give a £20 note, I can receive £8 in change. Money enables a value to be placed on goods, services and resources. My painting may be priced at £120. If you value your chairs at £80, I can sell the painting and buy one chair or add an extra £40 and buy two chairs. I can also save money, knowing that people will accept it in the future when I want to buy goods and services.

Activity 1

Over time methods of exchange and items used as money have changed. Products have been exchanged by means of barter and various forms of money. As money has evolved it has made exchange even easier, and this has led to higher output.

a Discuss two disadvantages of barter.

b Explain how easier exchange increases output.

Functions of money

The uses of money in the examples above illustrate three of the four functions of money.

■ To be a **medium of exchange**. This is the most important function. It enables people to sell products and then use the money received to buy other products, thus making the exchange of products easier.

■ To be a **unit of account** or measure of value. Both terms refer to the use of money to put a value on goods and services. For example, a standard Dyson vacuum cleaner was priced at £169 in 2001. Placing a value on products is important because for an exchange to take place people have to agree what one thing is worth in terms of another.

■ To enable people to save. This is because money acts as a **store of value**. It keeps its value over time and because it is generally acceptable it can be spent at a later date.

The fourth function, known as the **standard for deferred payments**, is also influenced by money's ability to retain its value. This concerns money's ability to allow people to lend and to borrow. People who lend now know that the money that is repaid to them in the future can be used to buy products.

Characteristics of money

To act as money an item has to be able to carry out the four functions of money. To do this it has

Activity 2

In 1922 and 1923 Germany experienced hyperinflation. This is a situation where prices rise dramatically. As a result, money rapidly loses its value. This means that the money supply has to be increased rapidly so people to have enough to pay for everyday products. At the start of 1923 German inflation had reached 300% a month. By October it had accelerated to 32,000% a month. The price of an egg rose to 4 billion marks and of a loaf of bread to 400 billion marks. The German government had to use 30 paper mills and 100 private printing firms to produce the high volume of notes required. Workers had to take suitcases and wheelbarrows to collect their pay.

As inflation continued to rise, workers and shopkeepers started to refuse marks. Instead they accepted a variety of items, including cigarettes. On November 23rd the German government had to declare the old Reichsmark invalid. It replaced it with the new Rentenmark. One of these was worth 1,000 billion old marks.

a What function of money does the passage concentrate on?

b Discuss how the function identified is affected by hyperinflation.

c Explain how the function of store of value would be influenced by hyperinflation.

to have certain characteristics. It is essential that it is generally acceptable. If people lose confidence in an item's ability to continue to be acceptable, it will cease to act as money. As we saw above, in 1923 in Germany marks were losing their value so rapidly that people asked to be paid in other items. Shopkeepers also refused to accept marks and the government had to replace the currency.

One of the reasons German marks became unacceptable was because too many notes had been printed and too many coins minted. When the supply of anything increases significantly, its value tends to fall. So to keep its value as money, the supply of an item has to be limited. We do not use stones as money as their supply is abundant. Why should a retailer accept stones as payment for products when she can go out and pick up stones from her garden?

Stones lack some of the other characteristics needed to act as money. They are not homogeneous. This means that they are not all the same. Individuals may not mind which £5 note they are offered, but they may prefer one stone to another. They are also not easily recognisable. It is possible to confuse stones and pebbles, and particularly to confuse stones of 'different values'. To increase the recognisability of coins the image of the ruler's face was placed on them.

Stones do, however, have some of the characteristics of money. They are durable, which means they last for some time. They are also divisible, that is they can be divided into smaller units. Large stones can be used as high denominations, say $50, middle-sized stones as $10, small stones as $1 and very small stones as 1 cent.

Activity 3

In medieval England there were no notes and coins were in short supply. Because of their scarcity coins were used only for large transactions, such as the purchase of land and the payment of taxes. If people wanted small change they had to cut a silver penny into halves or quarters. Even these quarters, which became known as farthings, were too valuable to pay for small items such as bread and eggs.

a What characteristic of money does the passage suggest coins lacked in medieval times?

b How may people have obtained eggs in medieval times?

Forms of money

Although stones have some of the characteristics of money, they do not have all the characteristics needed. Critically, they are not generally acceptable.

Throughout history a variety of items have acted as money. Most people are aware that gold and silver have been used as money, but so have other items such as strips of leather, stamps, shells, cloth and furs. What eventually stopped these less familiar items performing the functions of money was their lack of general acceptability.

Today the main forms of money in most countries are notes, coins and bank accounts. Of these, the most common form is bank accounts. Most payments are made from bank accounts.

Bank accounts have all the characteristics needed to act as money. It is interesting to note, however, that they do not have two of the characteristics that some people incorrectly think are necessary for money to have. They do not have any intrinsic value. This means that they do not have value in themselves. Their value comes only from their role as money. They are not used for any other purpose. This contrasts with, for example, gold, silver, leather and stamps, all of which have alternative uses.

Bank accounts are also not **legal tender**. A payment from a bank account, however it is made (for example, by cheque, direct debit or bank card), can always be refused. Such payments do not, by law, have to be accepted in settlement of a debt.

Activity 4

Paris was learning yesterday how to make do without cash as a week-long national strike by security couriers left banknote dispensers empty of notes. Improvisation was the name of the game as consumers used credit cards for big transactions but other forms of payment – bread and packets of Gauloises – instead of francs. (Extract from 'Welcome to the Gauloises economy', Charlotte Denny and Larry Elliott, Guardian, 18 July 2000)

a Identify two disadvantages of using bread as money.

b What characteristics of money do cigarettes possess?

Current issue: the 'cashless' society

Bankers and economists talk about the UK moving towards being a 'cashless' society. This is because more people are using cheques drawn on bank accounts, direct debit and various credit arrangements to buy more and more products. Most of the adult population now has a bank account and a high proportion use some form of bank card. With advances in technology, the sophistication of these bank cards continues to increase. Many have cash point (ATM = automatic teller machine), cheque guarantee, direct debit and credit card facilities.

Cash is increasingly being restricted to the purchase of small items. In a few cases people use cash to buy products they do not want recorded on a bank or credit card company statement. This may be because they do not want members of their family to know what they have been buying.

The items purchased with a bank card are paid for initially by the card company, which transfers money from its bank account to the creditors, and then by the customers, who transfer money from their bank accounts to the card company.

Bank cards have a number of advantages. People do not have to carry around large amounts of cash, purchases can be made by phone and over the internet, and items purchased are guaranteed for a period of time.

However, bank cards can be stolen and criminals can hack into people's bank account details. It has also been argued that credit facilities, especially if they are easily available, encourage people to spend more than they can afford and so get into debt.

Summary

In this unit you have learned that:

- Exchange permits specialisation and increases output.

- Money avoids the need for **barter** and increases the number of market transactions.

- The main disadvantage of barter is the need for a double coincidence of wants.

- For an item to act as money it must be a **medium of exchange**, **unit of account**, **store of value** and **standard for deferred payments**.

- The most important characteristic an item needs to act as money is general acceptability. Other characteristics include being limited in supply, homogeneous, recognisable, portable, durable and divisible.

- The main forms of money now used in most countries are notes, coins and bank accounts, with bank accounts being overwhelmingly the most important.

Multiple choice questions

1 What is the essential characteristic an item has to possess to be used as money?

A indivisibility

B general acceptability

C intrinsic value

D unlimited in supply

2 Which function of money enables people to buy and sell products?

A a medium of exchange

B a standard for deferred payments

C a store of value

D a unit of account

3 What is the main form of money in developed countries?

A bank accounts

B cheques

C coins

D notes

4 Which function of money enables people to save?

A medium of exchange

B standard for deferred payments

C store of value

D unit of account

5 Barter depends on the double coincidence of wants. Which function of money overcomes this problem?

A medium of exchange

B standard for deferred payments

C store of value

D unit of account

6 For an item to act as money, which of the following characteristics should it have?

A durability

B indivisibility

C immovability

D limited acceptability

Data response question: the launch of the euro

On 1 January 2002 the euro entered circulation in 12 member states of the European Union: Austria, Belgium, Finland, France, Germany, Greece, Ireland, Italy, Luxembourg, the Netherlands, Portugal and Spain. On that day it became legal tender for 300 million people. It was estimated that the metal contained in the coins would have been enough to build 24 Eiffel towers. Notes and coins in the national currencies also had to be collected in.

In preparation for the launch, staff in shops, department stores and banks were trained to recognise the notes and coins and learned the exchange rate. The European Central Bank spent 80 million euros launching the new currency and making people familiar with the new notes and coins. There was also a two-month period when national notes and coins continued to be legal tender alongside the euro.

Euro notes are identical throughout the euro area. There are 5, 10, 20, 50, 100, 200 and 500 euro notes. Coins have a uniform side and a national side.

a What major form of money is not discussed in the passage? [1]

b Identify two possible opportunity costs of the minting of the coins put into circulation on 1 January 2002. [4]

c Explain what is meant by legal tender. [3]

d Discuss three characteristics of money that the European Central Bank was seeking to achieve by issuing notes of seven denominations and spending money on the launch of the euro. [6]

e Explain three of the four main functions of money. [6]

9 Advantages of international trade

In Unit 5 you learned that the main advantage of international trade is increased quantity and quality of output. In this unit you will examine in more depth why output increases, and you will explore the other advantages of international trade.

Absolute advantage

Countries specialise and trade with each other because they have different abilities to produce products. Some countries are good at producing wine, for example, because of the fertility of their land and their climate. Others are good at producing manufactured products because of the skills of their workers, and some benefit from having rich mineral deposits. London, for instance, has an advantage in producing financial services because of the expertise and range of institutions it has built up. It is also in a favourable time zone, which means traders can connect with the USA, Japan and the EU at convenient times.

A country is said to have an **absolute advantage** in producing a product when it can produce it using fewer resources than another country. So if with the same quantity of resources the UK can make 1,000 aspirins and Jamaica only 200, the UK is said to have an absolute advantage in aspirin production. Jamaica may be able to produce 500 bananas compared with the UK's 50 with the same quantity of resources. This would give Jamaica an absolute advantage in banana production.

It used to be thought that most international trade could be explained by absolute advantage. It was believed that a country would trade with other countries that made products it could not produce or produced inefficiently. So, for example, the UK would import natural rubber and tropical fruits.

However, most of the products that countries import they could, and often do, produce themselves. The UK imports products such as cars, computers, beef, paper and jeans, all of which it produces itself. The UK's main trading partners, the USA, Germany, France and the Netherlands, have similar economic tastes and resources. So economists now argue that only a small proportion of international trade can be explained in terms of absolute advantage.

Activity 1

China is opening up its economy by joining the World Trade Organisation, which seeks to promote free international trade. Membership requires it to remove restrictions on imports and foreign investment, and subsidies on exports.

Engaging in more international trade provides China with benefits but also challenges. It is, for example, uncompetitive in agriculture. In terms of hectares of land per worker, the USA has 1.4, the EU has 0.5 and China has only 0.1. The prices of many Chinese farm goods are higher than prices on international markets.

Chinese car production is also a high-cost industry. Cars are produced in factories that are too small and inefficient.

In contrast, China produces textiles, toys and shoes at low average cost. Its **labour-intensive industries** have a ready supply of cheap labour, which appears to be inexhaustible. This will preserve China's competitive edge in these industries for the foreseeable future.

a In what products does China appear to have an absolute advantage?

b In what products does China appear to have an absolute disadvantage?

c Explain why costs are high in the Chinese car industry.

Comparative advantage

Absolute advantage can explain only a small proportion of international trade. Most is based on what economists refer to as **comparative advantage**. Countries can make a range of products, but they often specialise in certain products and trade with other countries.

Countries try to concentrate on producing products in which they have a comparative advantage – the products they can produce at a lower opportunity cost than other countries. Compared with Canada, the USA has an absolute advantage in producing computer software and wheat. With each resource it can produce more of both products. It appears that it does not pay the USA to trade with Canada. This is not true. The two countries benefit from the USA concentrating on computer software, which it is even better at producing, and Canada concentrating on wheat, which it is not bad at producing. This will increase the output of both products, and after trading each country should end up consuming more software and wheat. By concentrating on products in which they have a lower opportunity cost and by engaging in international trade, countries can consume a combination of products outside the production possibility curve.

We can observe the principle of comparative advantage in the decisions individuals and organisations make. A school may employ a person who is the best in the institution at teaching both economics and history. She has an absolute advantage in teaching both subjects. She will have a comparative advantage in economics if she is significantly better at teaching the subject than other staff in the school. Another teacher or teachers may be nearly as good at teaching history. In this case the students' performance will be maximised if the teacher concentrates on teaching economics.

Tom Cruise can both direct and act in films. In most film projects he is associated with, the producers decide that they want him to spend most of his time acting. They think that the opportunity cost of him acting is less than the opportunity cost of him directing.

Activity 2

Jobs in the steel industry are declining in the EU and the USA as the West experiences increasing competition from developing countries. Jobs are also moving from the West to the East in car production, computer production, computer programming, data input and other back-office functions.

The UK's comparative advantage is shifting from secondary to tertiary industries. It now appears to be increasingly in creative and knowledge-based industries, including music, literature, theatre, the development of software and pharmaceuticals, car design and business services.

a What causes comparative advantage to change?

b What advantages will the UK gain by shifting resources from car production to the development of software and pharmaceuticals and car design?

Other advantages of international trade

Engaging in international trade provides benefits for countries, principally higher output and thus higher consumption. It also gives consumers more choices. In UK supermarkets consumers can buy fresh fruit and vegetables from around the world. South African citizens can buy cars produced in the country or imported from the USA, the UK, Germany, France and other countries.

The ability to buy products from many countries gives consumers more variation and allows more tastes to be catered for. For example, suits made in Italy differ from suits made in Hong Kong, French wine has a different taste from wine produced in Australia, and US comedy shows contain more jokes but less irony and satire than UK comedy shows.

International trade increases the number of countries competing for the custom of a country's consumers. This increased competition benefits consumers by keeping prices down and raising quality.

Producers also gain from international trade. They can buy the cheapest and best-quality raw materials and services, and selling to a larger market enables them to take greater advantage of economies of scale. If a Belgian chocolate company sold only to people in Belgium, its sales would be limited to 10.3 million consumers. By selling on the world market, the company has a potential market of 6 billion consumers. Even if it captures only a small proportion of this market, its output would be much greater than if it was catering only for the home market.

Trading internationally also brings firms into contact with foreign firms and consumers. This helps to spread ideas and advances in technology. In the early 1990s China built up its personal computer industry by using information obtained by buying and examining US PCs.

Current issue: changes in comparative advantage

Over time comparative advantage changes. This is because relative costs change as access to technology and minerals, quality of education, training and the fertility of land change.

In recent decades, developing countries have become more competitive in agricultural products and labour-intensive manufactured products. However, developing countries complain that they cannot take full advantage because international trade does not take place on fair terms. They argue that rich countries make it difficult for them to sell their products. For example, they place taxes, known as tariffs, on agricultural products from developing countries averaging over 40%. Other obstacles include artificially high technical regulations and health and safety standards.

Activity 3

Countries such as Australia, New Zealand, the UK and the USA have marketed university education to China. Australia, New Zealand and the UK are now selling secondary education to the country. Chinese students are becoming an important market for the UK. The number of Chinese students applying to study in the UK rose from 3,862 in 1997 to 12,133 in 2001. Rich, ambitious Chinese parents are prepared to pay boarding-school fees as high as Rmb240,000 (about £20,000) a year for top UK schools.

a Why may Chinese parents buy UK education for their children?

b Identify three benefits for the UK of UK schools selling education to Chinese students.

Summary

In this unit you have learned that:

■ International trade occurs because countries have different abilities to produce products.

■ A country has an **absolute advantage** when it can produce a product using fewer resources.

■ Most trade is based on **comparative advantage**. A country has a comparative advantage in a product if it can produce it at a lower opportunity cost than other countries.

■ The main benefit of international trade is higher output. Other benefits include, for consumers, more choice, more variation, lower prices and higher quality. Firms can benefit from access to more sources of raw materials and services, an increased ability to take advantage of economies of scale and contact with new ideas and advanced technology.

Multiple choice questions

1 International trade can reduce a firm's costs by increasing:

A   the size of its market

B   the distances it products have to travel

C   the amount of research it has to undertake into market tastes

D   the range of currencies earned by selling products

2 Which of the following is a benefit of international trade?

A   increased opportunity to diversify production

B   increased specialisation and division of labour

C   reduced exploitation of economies of scale

D   reduced competition for domestic firms

3 A country has a comparative advantage in a product when it:

A   can produce it at a lower opportunity cost than another country

B   can produce a greater quantity than another country

C   imports more of it than it exports

D   has been producing the product for longer than another country

4 Table 1 shows the output of corn and cars per worker which can be made in two countries, X and Y. What can be deduced from this information?

A   Country X has the absolute advantage in producing cars

B   Country X will import corn

C   Country Y has the absolute disadvantage in producing cars

D   Country Y will export cars

Table 1: Output per worker		
	Corn (units)	Cars (number)
Country X	100	10
Country Y	50	30

5 Two countries, X and Y, are considering trading with each other in machinery and fish. Country X has the absolute advantage in both products. Country X has a comparative advantage in machinery and Country Y in fish. What can be concluded from this information?

A   trade would not benefit either country

B   trade would benefit Country X but not Country Y

C   trade would benefit Country Y but not Country X

D   trade would benefit both countries

6 The basis of most international trade is differences in countries':

A   absolute advantage

B   comparative advantage

C   population sizes

D   productive potential

Data response question: South Africa's car industry

In the last six years South Africa has emerged as a notable car producer and a key supplier of motor industry components, including windscreens and exhaust pipes.

Multinational car producers, including BMW, Fiat and Renault, have opened plants in the country. In 2001 South Africa exported 100,000 cars. It earned 5 billion rand from exporting fully built cars and 11 billion rand from exports of components. Its main success is in the production of catalytic converters. The country has massive platinum and palladium deposits and has exploited this advantage to make 10% of the world's production of anti-pollution components. Economists predict that this will rise to 25% by 2004 and that employment in the industry will increase significantly. This is particularly important in a country which, in 2001, had a 40% unemployment rate.

The government has built up the world-class car and components industry by encouraging multinational car companies to set up plants in the country. They have raised the productivity of car workers from 40 cars a day in 1998 to 220 cars a day in 2001 by increasing their spending on capital goods and training. For example, BMW invested 1 billion rand upgrading its Rosslyn plant near Pretoria.

a   Explain why South Africa has a comparative advantage in the car and components industry? [6]

b   Explain why the average cost of producing cars in South Africa may fall as the output of cars increases. [4]

c   Discuss three advantages the people of South Africa may gain from international trade. [6]

d   Explain:

i   where in relation to its production possibility curve South Africa was producing in 2001 [2]

ii   the effect of an increase in capital goods and training in the car and components industry on South Africa's production possibility curve. [2]

10 Economic systems

In this unit you will discover the essential features of the three types of **economic systems** – **market**, **planned** and **mixed** – and analyse the advantages and disadvantages of the market system. You will learn why most economies are mixed economies and examine the economic effects that East European economies are experiencing in making the transition from planned (command) to market economies

Economic systems

All societies face three fundamental economic questions: what goods and services to produce, how to produce them and who should receive them. Germany, for example, devotes proportionately more of its resources to the production of health care than the UK. France uses more **capital-intensive** (a high proportion of capital relative to labour) production methods than India. The distribution of income, and so access to goods and services, is more even in Sweden than in the USA.

The institutions, organisations and methods used to answer these questions are described as the society's economic system.

Activity 1

The government imposes a tax on people's income (income tax), the profits of firms (corporation tax) and firms' employment of labour (national insurance contributions). It also provides cash and non-cash benefits for children and unemployed, disabled, sick and elderly people, subsidies for some train companies and farmers, and education and health care.

Which of the three fundamental questions faced by any economic system are influenced by the forms of government taxation and expenditure mentioned?

Types of systems

There are three main types of economic systems: planned, market and mixed. A **planned economy** is also known as a command, centrally planned or collectivist economy. The government makes the decisions on what to produce, how to produce it and who gets it. The state owns the factors of production and determines output, prices and wages. It usually keeps the prices of basic necessities low and makes sure everyone has a job.

In the former Soviet Union, for example, there was a central planning agency called Gosplan. It drew up five-year plans, which set production targets for firms, and with specialised state planning organisations determined prices and wages of workers.

In contrast, in a **market economy** the government plays little part in economic activity. The interaction of the market forces of demand and supply answer the three fundamental economic questions.

Consumer sovereignty is said to exist as firms, motivated by profit, seek to produce what consumers want. If consumer preferences change, prices will alter, which will encourage resources to move to reflect the change in tastes. For example, if computer games become more popular people will be prepared to pay more for them. This will increase the profits that can be earned from producing computer games so more firms will make them. In contrast, fewer firms will make board games if they become less popular.

There is private ownership of land and capital. For example, in the UK the Duke of Westminster owns parts of Mayfair in London and other valuable property, and shareholders of US company General Motors each own a portion of the firm. Ownership of land and capital gives rise to income and the ability to make production decisions. Workers' pay depends on demand for their services. Workers whose services are in high demand, such as David Beckham, receive the highest incomes. People with the highest incomes are able to buy the most goods and services.

The USA is close to being a market economy and Cuba to being a planned economy. However, in practice no country is a pure market or planned economy. In the USA, the government controls the defence industry and provides benefits for poor people, and in Cuba some agricultural produce is sold on private markets. Most economies are **mixed economies**, which means they contain features of both planned and market economies. They are trying to gain the advantages and avoid the disadvantages of both systems.

Activity 2

In North Korea firms are run by the government, which sets production targets. and fixes wages and prices. The country's foreign trade for a year is equivalent to the amount of goods and services exchanged between Canada and the USA in only 36 hours.

In contrast, in South Korea individuals and groups of individuals own most firms. Most prices and wages are determined by demand and supply and South Korea exported $170bn worth of goods and services in 2001.

a Does the economy of North Korea come closest to a planned or market economy?

b Does the economy of South Korea come closest to a planned or market economy?

Activity 3

The Indian government has been slowly increasing the role of market forces in its economy. It has carried out a **privatisation** programme, selling some state-run industries to the private sector. It has also removed some government labour laws and reduced government subsidies to industries.

In 2000 it allowed private and foreign firms to compete in its insurance market. Before then insurance in the country was provided by just two state-run firms which were overstaffed and underworked.

a Explain one reason why the Indian government may have wished to increase the role of market forces in its economy.

b Explain why insurance premiums may now be lower in India than they were in 2000.

Advantages of free markets

Many countries are moving towards greater reliance on the market system. They are reducing the role of the government in the ownership of factors of production, in regulating industries and in raising taxes, because of the benefits they think this will bring.

One of the principal advantages claimed for market forces is that they promote efficiency. Competition among firms will keep costs and prices low. Consumers will not buy from firms that charge high prices and that do not produce the products they want.

The profit motive provides an incentive for entrepreneurs to produce high-quality products and to innovate. Similarly, the possibility of high wages encourages workers to train, work hard and take on extra responsibility.

Changes in consumer tastes and demand for workers are signalled quickly and automatically through the price mechanism. Consumers and workers have more economic freedom than in a planned economy to pursue their own self-interest. Instead of having to buy from one government-run firm, they may have a choice of producers and can seek low prices and high quality. Producers can choose what to make and can select the prices that they believe consumers will pay and that will cover their costs. Workers can move from job to job in search of the highest pay.

Disadvantages of free markets

Allowing markets to operate without government intervention can potentially bring the advantages of efficiency, consumer sovereignty and speed of response to changes in consumer tastes. However, markets do not always perform well and they may fail to produce an outcome that maximises benefits to society. One reason for this is that in seeking to reduce their costs, firms may create pollution by dumping their waste materials and depleting non-renewable resources. Their self-interest may conflict with the needs of the environment and the long-term needs of the economy. For example, the faecal filth of salmon farming has driven wild salmon from many of the sea lochs and rivers of Scotland.

Another reason is that private-sector firms only have an incentive to produce products that consumers want and are willing to pay for. Goods and services that consumers do not want to pay for directly may not be produced. For example, if defence were sold on the market, some people would not be prepared to buy it. This is because they know that if the armed forces defend anyone, they cannot be excluded. They can act as 'free riders'.

In the absence of government intervention, consumers may not choose to consume the socially desirable levels of all products. This is because of a lack of information on which to base decisions. Some beneficial products, such as seat belts, education and health care, may be underconsumed. Other products, such as cigarettes and alcohol, may be consumed in greater quantities than is beneficial, and undesirable products, notably hard-core pornography and non-prescription drugs, may be traded.

Consumer sovereignty can be reduced by advertising and by producer power. Advertising may persuade people to buy products they would not otherwise have chosen or to spend more than they originally planned. The power of consumers is also reduced in markets where there is little competition between firms. Over time a market may become dominated by one or a few firms which collude together to set prices. In this case the firm or groups of firms can charge prices well above costs as consumers will have no choice.

Some economists describe market economies as economic democracies with consumers expressing their preferences by voting with their purchases. However, they are not true democracies as people do not have equal 'voting power'. This is because people have different income levels and so different purchasing power. Those with the highest purchasing power have the most influence on what is produced. Some products wanted by poor people will not be produced.

Market economies often have a more unequal distribution of income than planned economies. This is because the ownership of factors of production can become concentrated in a few hands and because people have different earning capacities. This situation tends to be self-perpetuating. Those who own property and shares earn incomes which they can reinvest to earn more income. The people with high incomes can spend more on their own and their children's health care, education and training. This further increases their and their children's earnings. In contrast, people with low earning capacity may fall into poverty. The people most likely to be poor include the sick, the disabled, the old and those people whose skills are in low demand. In a market economy, there is no guarantee that everyone will be in employment and people may not make adequate provision for illness, disability and old age.

Activity 4

Four firms dominate the pharmaceuticals industry: Merck, Pfizer, GlaxoSmithKline and Eli Lilly. It is thought that they sometimes act together to keep prices high. They also patent their medicines. This gives them 20 years' exclusive rights to a drug. They argue that such protection is necessary if they are to be able to charge a price high enough to recoup costs and make profits. High profits, they claim, are needed to develop new cures for diseases, including those affecting poor people. However, critics argue the main motive behind patents is to prevent cheap drugs from developing countries coming on to the market.

Explain why private ownership of pharmaceuticals firms may:

a benefit poor people

b harm poor people

Causes of transition

In the 1990s the countries of Eastern Europe started to move from planned to market economies. The role of market forces was also increased in many African and Asian countries.

Consumers in these economies were becoming increasingly dissatisfied with the poor quality of some products and shortages and surpluses of others. These problems arose largely because of poor planning and co-ordination. It proved to be difficult and expensive to gather up-to-date information about consumer preferences and production capabilities.

It was also found to be easier to set targets for and monitor quantity than quality. Indeed, a target mentality arose with producers often sacrificing quality and environmental concerns in order to meet quantity targets. High levels of pollution occurred in all the East European countries. For instance, more than 90% of rivers in Poland were heavily polluted.

Activity 5

In November 1989 the Berlin Wall, dividing West and East Germany, was demolished and the East German authorities removed all border barriers. *The Times* reported how people from the planned economy of East Germany streamed into the market-oriented West Germany to visit the shops.

From Lubeck in the north to Hof in Bavaria, hundreds of thousands of East Germans headed home last night, many burdened with bags of food, clothes and electrical goods bought in an unprecedented shopping spree in the West.

The hordes of visitors snatched everything from lettuce to radios, cleaning out stores in West German cities and towns near the border. The big shock was the price of everything. 'It's much more than I realised', said Jo'm Reschke, on his third trip in three days. ('Visitors besiege Western stores', Michael Binyon and Graham Lees, The Times, 11 November 1989)

From the information given, explain:

a one advantage the citizens of the former East Germany are likely to have gained from the move away from a planned economy

b one disadvantage they may have experienced from the movement

Effects of transition

Several East European countries, particularly Russia, are experiencing difficulties in making the transition. The Russian government had kept prices below those charged by private-sector producers. When it removed price controls in 1992, prices soared.

In the early stages of transition output fell in Russia and other East European countries, including Armenia, Azerbaijan and Turkmenistan. This was because some of the state-run enterprises failed to survive when exposed to market forces. Unemployment soared.

Poverty and homelessness became a problem. Before the transition, state-run enterprises provided education, health care and housing for their employees. Under the planned economy system there was no official unemployment and no social security system, so when the transition started the appropriate welfare systems were not in place. Vulnerable groups suffered and some cases continue to suffer.

There is now more economic freedom, a wider choice of goods and services and the opportunity to earn high profits and high incomes. However, there is also a wider income gap between rich people and poor people and crime has risen.

The performance of transitional economies such as Poland, Hungary and the Czech Republic, which started market reforms earlier, has been stronger. They have built up stronger social security systems, more developed markets for goods, services, labour and capital and stronger trading links with the EU and USA.

Activity 6

Since the collapse of the Soviet Union, Russia's output has fallen by a third. Corruption has risen significantly and more than 40% of economic activity is not declared either because it is illegal or because people want to avoid paying taxes. Average male life expectancy has declined to just 60 years and AIDS is increasing rapidly. While more than a third of the population live in poverty, the country imports more luxury cars and jewellery than most West European countries.

a From the information in the passage, discuss what appears to have happened to the distribution of income in Russia since the economy started to move towards a market economy.

b Discuss whether the passage suggests that the move towards a market economy has achieved success in Russia.

Current issue: planned versus market economies

Many countries in Eastern Europe, Asia and Africa are changing from largely planned to more market-oriented economies.

Some people have welcomed the change, including the entrepreneurs whose firms are succeeding, workers whose skills are in high demand and some consumers who are enjoying a greater range and higher quality of products. Victims of the high crime levels, and unemployed and poor people, are less happy and look back fondly to the days of the planned economy.

The appropriate economic system for a country is influenced by the state of its economy. For example, some countries do not have the right conditions for the successful working of a market economy. They do not have a foundation for a private banking system and stock exchange to build on, appropriate social security schemes are not in place and the infrastructure is poor.

In assessing the merits of a planned or market economy for a particular country, economists use the concepts of efficiency and **equity**. A system is considered preferable if it results in greater efficiency and equity. An economy is efficient if it is producing the maximum possible output with its existing resources and technology and that output reflects consumers' tastes. Equity is fairness. Consideration of equity involves normative judgements. For example, people disagree about what is a fair distribution of income.

Summary

In this unit you have learned that:

■ The three fundamental economic questions that all societies have to consider are what to produce, how to produce it and who receives what is produced.

■ **Economic systems** can be classified as **planned**, **market** and **mixed**.

■ In a planned economy the government owns the factors of production and makes the key economic decisions.

■ In a market economy there is private ownership of land and capital, consumers decide what is produced and resources are allocated through the price mechanism.

■ The advantages of a free market include **consumer sovereignty**, efficiency, choice and quick response to changes in consumers' tastes.

■ The disadvantages of a free market include the risks of pollution, the lack of incentive for firms to produce products consumers are unwilling or unable to pay for, the possibility that consumers may underconsume beneficial products and overconsume harmful products, the chance that producers may gain more power than consumers and the risk of people falling into poverty.

■ There was a movement from planned to market economies in Eastern Europe, Africa and Asia in the 1990s because of dissatisfaction with government planning.

■ Some East European countries have encountered problems in making the transition from planned to market economies. These include unemployment, poverty, lack of an adequate social security system and a rise in income.

Multiple choice questions

1 What are the fundamental questions facing all economic systems?

A how to control inflation and unemployment

B how to reduce pollution and preserve wildlife

C the appropriate levels of taxation and government spending

D what, how and for whom to produce

2 What is a major difference between a planned and a market economy? In a market economy:

A most land and capital goods are privately owned

B the government decides who receives the products produced

C government directives, rather than prices, are the main mechanism for allocating resources

D wages are set by the state

3 What is meant by consumer sovereignty?

A products are sold at low prices

B consumers are able to satisfy all their wants

C the preferences of consumers determine the allocation of resources

D consumers have the power to ensure that firms do not deplete non-renewable resources

4 In principle, an advantage of a market economy is that:

A output is produced at the highest average cost

B output reflects producers' preferences

C poor people have as much influence on what is produced as rich people

D profits act as an incentive to move resources quickly

5 A possible disadvantage of a market economy is that:

A competition will keep costs and prices low

B slow response to changes in consumer tastes

C consumer sovereignty can be reduced in markets where there is little competition among firms

D the even distribution of income discourages people to undertake jobs in high demand

6 Some economies are seeking to move from planned to market economies. They are seeking to achieve:

A a more even distribution of income

B increased government intervention

C a reduction in consumer sovereignty

D greater efficiency

Data response question: East European economies

The performance of East European transitional economies continues to vary. Poland, in central Europe, now has a large market sector. It enjoyed an average increase in its national output of 5.4% per year between 1995 and 2000, and in 2000 income per head was $10,802.

In contrast, Romania, a poor country on the eastern side of the Balkans, has been struggling to make the transition from a planned to a market economy. In 1999 the European Commission named Romania as the worst performer among the East European countries seeking to join the EU. It had experienced an average fall in output of 2.2% a year between 1995 and 2000, and in 2000 income per head was only $1,753.

The Romanian government has privatised some firms including Sidex, the largest steel works and biggest loss-making industrial plant, Banca Commerciale Romana, the biggest bank, and two gas and two electricity distributors. It has not been easy to sell state-run concerns. Investors have complained of red tape, corruption and administrative inconsistency.

There are still many loss-making state enterprises. In 1999 and 2000 the government gave large pay increases to some public-sector workers and made others redundant. The first policy contributed to dramatic price rises, and inflation reached over 40% in 1999. The second policy increased both the number of people in poverty and unemployment.

In 2000, 41% of Romanians were living below the official World Bank poverty line and unemployment reached 11%. Some of the unemployed poor left the cities and returned to subsistence farming.

Romania was once known as the bread basket of Europe, but a poorly managed privatisation process has reduced the productivity of Romanian agriculture. Many of the former state co-operatives were split up and sold off as small, uneconomic holdings. Some of these are now used for subsistence farming and most are unable to take advantage of economies of scale.

a Explain what is meant by a 'transitional' economy. [2]

b Identify two differences between a planned and a market economy. [4]

c Explain two difficulties Romania has experienced in changing its economic system. [4]

d Discuss two benefits Poland may have received as a result of moving towards a market economy. [4]

e Explain:
  i a possible opportunity cost of operating a market economy [2]
  ii a possible economy of scale which large farms could enjoy [2]
  iii a benefit Poland could gain as a result of trading with Romania. [2]

2 How markets work

1 Demand

In Section 1, Unit 10, you learned how the forces of **demand** and supply play a significant role in a market economy. In this unit you will examine the meaning of demand. You will learn how to draw demand curves and explore the key influences on demand.

The meaning of demand

In economics demand is not the same as desire, need or want. This is because the strength of the desire for something will not, in itself, have any influence on the output or the price of the product.

For example, I may really want an expensive sports car, but because I cannot afford it, I cannot place an order.

Only when desire is supported by the ability and willingness to pay the price does it become **effective demand** and have an influence on the market. Demand, in economics, means effective demand. It is the quantity of a product which people are willing and able to buy at any given price over some given period of time.

Activity 1

Mid-October is the crab season in Shanghai. In mid-October 2001 eager customers queued up to two hours for a table at a restaurant serving the crab meat. New restaurants had been opened earlier in 2001 in preparation for the feeding frenzy, but the queues just got longer.

a Did restaurateurs underestimate or overestimate demand for crab meat dinners?

b Explain one possible reason why demand for crab meat may have varied from expectations.

The relationship between price and demand

For the majority of goods and services, demand rises as price falls and demand falls as price rises.

When the price of a product falls people are more able and more willing to buy it. With a cheaper price people's purchasing power increases. For instance, if a product initially is priced at £1 per item, £8 will buy eight items. If the price falls to 80p, ten items can be purchased. A fall in price also increases the price competitiveness of the product relative to rival products. For example, a luxury bar of chocolate may be priced at £1.20. Rival bars may be priced at £1, 90p, 85p and 70p. If the price of the luxury bar falls to £1.05 it will still be more expensive than the other bars. The price difference, however, will have fallen and may tempt people to buy more of the luxury bar.

Activity 2

On 24 October 2001 Morrisons, a supermarket chain, cut the price of petrol by 2p. This took it below 70p for the first time since April 1999. In response to this move, Esso, Shell and BP lowered the cost of a litre of unleaded to 69.9p in areas where they compete directly.

a What effect would you expect the fall in the price of petrol to have on demand for petrol?

b Why do you think Esso, Shell and BP also cut their prices?

Individual and market demand

It is possible to study individual demand. This is the relationship between the quantity demanded of a product by a single individual and the price of that product.

It is also possible to study **market demand**. This is the total demand for the product. It is found by adding the quantities demanded by each individual buyer at each price. For example, one buyer's demand for crisps at the current price may be four packets a week and the total demand of all buyers may be 30,000 packets a week.

Market demand depends on how the market is defined. For example, the total demand for all brands of crisps may be studied, or the total demand for one particular brand or the total demand for snacks (of which crisps are a part). It is also possible to examine the demand for crisps from one particular supermarket, or one particular town might be studied or indeed the world.

Demand schedules and curves

Individual and market demand information can be expressed in the form of **demand schedules** and **demand curves**. A demand schedule is a table giving the quantities demanded at a range of prices (Table 1).

A demand curve can be drawn which plots the information on a graph with price on the vertical axis and quantity demanded at a range of prices. This is shown on Figure 1.

A market demand schedule, and a corresponding market demand curve, can be calculated by adding up the amounts each individual demands at different prices (Table 2).

Table 2: Quantity demanded per week

Price	A	B	C	D	E	F	Market demand
5	50	20	40	25	30	70	235
4	80	50	80	50	62	140	462
3	130	90	130	86	96	230	762
2	190	140	200	140	135	340	1,145
1	300	200	280	200	210	500	1,690

The demand curve shows what happens to the quantity demanded when price changes and there is no change in any of the other factors influencing demand (such as income, taste and fashion). Demand curves slope down from left to right. Figure 2 shows a typical demand curve.

Table 1: A demand schedule

Price (£)	Quantity demanded (per week)
5	50
4	80
3	130
2	190
1	300

Figure 1: A demand curve

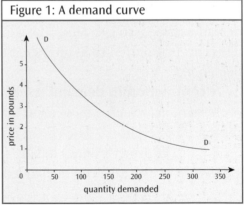

Figure 2

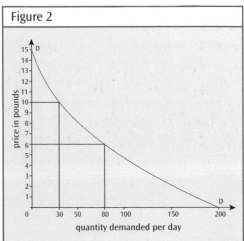

At a price of £10 the quantity demanded would be 30. If price fell to £6 quantity demanded would rise to 80. Alternatively, the demand curve can be used to find the maximum price consumers are willing to pay for a given quantity. Figure 2 shows that the maximum consumers are willing to pay for 80 units is £6.

The demand curve also shows the price at which the product would be priced out of the market. At £15 none of the product would be demanded. If the product were to be provided free, 200 units would be demanded.

The areas of the rectangles under the demand curve represent the total revenue/total expenditure which would occur at different prices, since they are equal to price x quantity. At a price of £6, consumers spend a total of £240 (£6 x 80) and so suppliers receive £240 in revenue.

Movements along a demand curve

A movement along a demand curve can only be caused by a change in the price of the product itself. Such movements can be referred to as extensions and contractions in demand or changes in the quantity demanded.

An **extension in demand** for a product is a rise in demand caused by a fall in its price. Figure 3 shows an extension in demand from Q to Q1 caused by a fall in price from P to P1. This can be referred to as an increase in the quantity demanded.

A **contraction in demand** results from a rise in the price of the product. Such a movement up the demand curve is illustrated in Figure 3. The rise in price from P to P1 causes demand to contract from Q to Q1. This can be referred to as a decrease in the quantity demanded.

Consumer surplus

Consumer surplus is the extra amount that consumers would be prepared to pay for a product above what they actually pay. So it arises when people pay less for a product than they are willing to. Figure 4 shows an individual's demand for wine.

The person would have been prepared to pay £6 for the first bottle, £4 for the second, £3.50 for the third and £2 for the fourth. If the actual price charged is £3.50, the person will buy three bottles. He will receive consumer surplus of £2.50 on the first bottle, £1.50 on the second and no consumer surplus on the third bottle. The total consumer surplus received is £4 (£2.50 + £1.50).

Activity 4

Table 3 is a demand schedule for a product.

a Plot this information on a demand diagram.

b Calculate consumers' expenditure when price is £7.

Table 3	
Price (£)	Quantity demanded
10	20
9	30
8	40
7	50
6	60
5	70

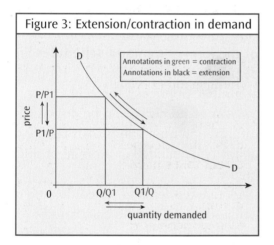

Figure 3: Extension/contraction in demand

Annotations in green = contraction
Annotations in black = extension

Activity 5

In 2001 the price of train travel rose and the price of digital TVs fell.

Explain, using diagrams, what effect the price changes would have had on the demand for:

a train travel

b digital TVs

So a change in the price of a product affects the amount of consumer surplus people receive. A rise in price reduces consumer surplus and a fall in price raises consumer surplus.

Changes in demand

A **change in demand** means that one or more of the factors that determine demand (other than the price of the product) have changed, and therefore the whole demand curve will move. An **increase in demand** means that more is now demanded at each and every price. Figure 5 illustrates an increase in demand with the demand curve shifting to the right.

An increased quantity is now demanded at any given price. For example, at the price P the quantity demanded has increased from Q to Q1 and at the price P1 the quantity demanded has increased from Q2 to Q3.

A **decrease in demand** means that less is demanded at each and every price. Figure 5 shows that at price P, demand falls from Q to Q1 and at price P1, demand decreases from Q2 to Q3. The demand curve has shifted to the left.

Causes of changes in demand

Various factors can cause a change in demand and thus a shift in the demand curve.

■ A change in the level of incomes, specifically real, disposable incomes. **Disposable income** is income after **direct taxes** have been deducted and cash state benefits have been added. **Real disposable income** is actual money nominal income adjusted for inflation. For example, if money incomes rise by 5% but over the same period prices rise by 10%, real incomes will have fallen and so people's ability to buy products will also have fallen.

Demand for most goods and services increases as real, disposable incomes rise. Goods which have this positive relationship between income and demand are called **normal goods**. There are a few goods and services that have an inverse relationship with income, that is, as income rises, demand falls. These are called **inferior goods** and include, for example, cheaper basic foodstuffs (such as supermarkets' own brands), and cheaper clothing and bus travel.

■ A change in the distribution of income. If income becomes more unevenly distributed, demand for luxury products will increase and demand for basic necessities,

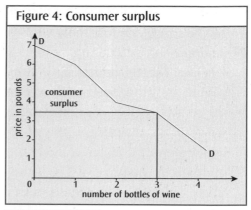

Figure 4: Consumer surplus

Activity 6

A man buys four cakes for £2 each. He would have been willing to pay £5 for the first cake, £4.75 for the second, £4.25 for the third and £3.30 for the fourth.

Calculate the consumer surplus he enjoys.

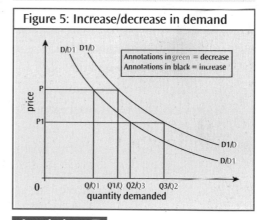

Figure 5: Increase/decrease in demand

Annotations in green = decrease
Annotations in black = increase

Activity 7

As the football season approaches more football shirts are sold. Many clubs bring out new strips and sell the shirts and shorts in the former strip at reduced prices.

a   Does the approach of the new football season cause an extension or an increase in demand for new football shirts?

b   Is a reduction in the price of shirts in the former strip likely to result in an extension or an increase in demand for the shirts?

such as heating and bread, will decrease as poorer people struggle to find money for these products.

■ Changes in the prices of related goods and services. Most products have **substitutes**, so people are influenced in their purchases by the relative prices of competing goods and services. For example, if the price of cod falls, the demand for plaice is likely to decrease. An increase in the price of *The Times* newspaper is likely to lead to a contraction in demand for *The Times* and an increase in demand for the *Daily Telegraph*.

■ Changes in the prices of complementary goods and services. Products are called **complements** when they are jointly demanded – the use of one requires the use of the other. For example, the demand for car insurance is associated directly with the demand for cars. A sharp increase in the price of cars may cause demand for car insurance to fall.

■ Changes in taste and fashion, particularly in the clothing and music industries. Peer group pressure can influence demand for products. For example, in 2000 many primary school children in the UK bought (or had bought for them) Pokemon cards.

■ Advertising influences taste and fashion and has a powerful effect on demand in many markets. Its aim is to move the product's demand curve to the right and at the same time to move the demand curves for competing products to the left.

■ Changes in population size and age distribution. An increase in population size will increase demand for most goods and services. The UK, most of Europe, Japan, the USA and some other countries have ageing populations. They have a high proportion of elderly people in their populations who are living longer than before. This causes an increase in demand for health care, residential care and holidays designed for the elderly.

Other influences can affect demand for particular products. For example, if it becomes easier or cheaper to borrow, demand for homes, furniture, foreign holidays and cars is likely to increase. Changes in weather conditions will alter the demand for a range of products. For example, a period of hot weather is likely to increase demand for suntan lotion, barbecues, ice creams and lager and decrease demand for heating, umbrellas and hot drinks, and a major sports event can increase tourism in a country.

Activity 8

Decide whether the following events would cause a movement along a demand curve (extension or contraction) or a shift in the demand curve (increase or decrease) for Ford cars:

a a fall in the price of petrol

b a fall in the price of Saab cars

c a fall in the price of Ford cars

d a rise in real disposable incomes

e an advertising campaign for Ford cars

f an increase in the punctuality and comfort of rail travel

Current issue: rising real disposable incomes

The trend is for real disposable incomes to rise over time. So, for example, average incomes in India and China were higher in 2001 than they were in 1991 and are expected to be higher still in 2011.

This means that over time there is a tendency for demand for normal goods to rise and demand for inferior goods to fall. So firms which produce inferior goods face the prospect of falling demand. They are then faced with two main choices: they can switch to producing other products or seek to transform inferior goods into normal goods. The latter strategy has been adopted with a number of products.

For example, in Western Europe and the USA rice is now regarded not as a basic, staple food but as a good-quality, healthy food. This has been achicved by offering a greater variety of rice, the increasing popularity of foreign food and advertising. Bicycle producers have sought to keep demand for bicycles high by bringing out models to appeal to a wide range of income groups and by advertising the health benefits of cycling.

Summary

In this unit you have learned that:

- **Demand** in economics means not only the willingness to buy a product but also the ability to buy it.

- For most products, price and demand are inversely related. So a rise in price causes a fall in demand and a fall in price causes a rise in demand.

- Individual demand is the relationship between the quantity demanded of a product by a single individual and the price of that product. **Market demand** is the total demand for a product.

- A **demand schedule** shows the different quantities demanded at a range of prices. Information from a demand schedule can be plotted on to a **demand curve** with price on the vertical axis and quantity demanded on the horizontal axis.

- A movement along a demand curve can be caused only by a change in the price of the product. An **extension in demand** is caused by a fall in the price of the product and a **contraction in demand** is caused by a rise in the price of the product.

- **Consumer surplus** arises when people pay less for a product than they were willing to pay.

- A **change in demand** is caused by a change in any influence on demand other than the price of the product. An **increase in demand** is illustrated by a shift of the demand curve to the right and a **decrease in demand** by a shift of the demand curve to the left.

- Among the factors that can cause a change in demand are changes in **real disposable income**, the distribution of income, prices of related products, taste and fashion, advertising, population size and age distribution.

Multiple choice questions

1 What is the only cause of a movement along a demand curve for a product? A change in:

A consumers' tastes

B consumers' income

C the price of the product

D the size of the population

2 What is the relationship between price and demand in a typical demand schedule?

A direct

B inverse

C proportional

D unrelated

3 Figure 6 shows the demand for a product. Its price falls from P to P1. What is the increase in consumer surplus which results from the fall in price?

A RPS

B P1PST

C OPSQ

D OP1TQ1

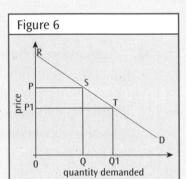

Figure 6

4 Which of the following would result in a contraction in demand for strawberries?

A a rise in the price of strawberries

B a rise in the price of cream

C a fall in the price of raspberries

D a fall in incomes

5 The demand curve for a normal good will shift to the right if:

A the price of the good falls

B there is a decline in incomes

C a rival product becomes more popular

D the price of a substitute product increases

6 What would cause demand for petrol by private motorists to decrease?

A a fall in the price of cars

B a fall in bus and train fares

C a rise in incomes

D a rise in the size of the population

Data response question: a change in demand

Audio cassettes were invented in 1963 by Philips, a Dutch company. Sales of audio cassettes overtook LPs as the most important music format in 1985. They held this dominant position until 1992. Cassettes are, however, still the dominant music format in developing countries in Asia and Latin America.

In 2001 demand for audio cassettes fell dramatically in the UK. The number of single cassettes sold fell by 31.4% and album sales by 60%. In the US market sales of recorded music in the cassette format fell from 55% 1990 to 5% in 2000.

There are thought to be several reasons for this decline, all linked to a rival product, CDs. More and more households have compact disc players, CD prices are falling and it is now standard to install CD players in new cars.

a What is the relationship between audio cassettes and:

  i cassette players [2]

  ii CDs [2]

b Using a diagram, explain what is happening to demand for audio cassettes in the UK and the USA. [8]

c What do you expect to happen to demand for audio cassettes in Asia and Latin America in the future? [4]

d Discuss two influences on demand for audio cassettes not mentioned in the passage. [4]

2 Supply

In this unit you will examine the response to demand – **supply**. You will learn to distinguish between movements along a **supply curve** and shifts in supply curves and will discover the key influences on supply. You will find that the terms and concepts you learned in connection with demand will prove useful in analysing supply.

The meaning of supply

Supply is the willingness and ability to sell a product at any given price over some given period of time. It is not the same as the amount of a product produced or the existing stock. This is because not all products produced or in existence are offered for sale. For example, the supply of housing in a town consists of houses, bungalows, flats and so on that are for sale. It is not the total number of properties in the town or the total number of new properties that have been built.

Activity 1

In his lifetime, a sixteenth-century Italian painted approximately 200 pictures. Since his death they have increased in popularity. In 1987 the high price of £20m paid at auction for his mother with child picture encouraged some museums and private collectors to sell their pictures by this painter. In 1988, 12 of his paintings were auctioned.

Was the supply of the painter's pictures in 1988 12 or 200? Explain your answer.

The relationship between price and supply

In most cases, higher prices create more supply. A higher price usually results in higher profits. This provides the incentive for suppliers to increase their production and the quantity they offer for sale. If the price falls, the willingness and ability of firms to supply the product declines.

This is because a low price will not generate enough revenue for firms to cover their costs and make a profit from the sale of the product.

Activity 2

In 2001 the price of mobile phones fell so some firms reduced their output and cut their staff. Ericsson closed two plants in Nottinghamshire and Lincolnshire with the loss of 1,200 jobs and Motorola closed its Scottish plant and laid off 3,000 workers.

a What happened to the supply of mobile phones in 2001?

b Explain how the supply of mobile phones could rise for a couple of months without their production increasing.

Individual and market supply

It is possible to study supply on an individual or market level. Individual supply is the relationship between the quantity supplied of a product by a single firm or **business unit**, such as a factory, office or shop. **Market supply** is the total supply of the product. It is obtained by adding the quantities supplied by each producer at each price.

Market supply can be studied on several levels. The market supply of cars, for example, can be examined in terms of the supply of cars in a particular town, country or the world. The market supply of a particular model, group of models or all cars can also be studied.

Activity 3

Identify three types of institutions which are part of the education market.

Supply schedules and curves

As higher prices create more supply, supply curves slope up from left to right. Figure 1 shows a **supply curve** based on the **supply schedule** in Table 1.

Activity 4

Table 2 is a supply schedule for a product.

a Plot this information on a supply diagram.

b Calculate producers' revenue if 70 products are sold.

Table 2

Price (£)	Quantity supplied (per week)
10	80
9	70
8	60
7	50
6	40
5	30

Movements along a supply curve

Movements along the supply curve are referred to as extensions and contractions in supply or as changes in the quantity supplied. Such movements can only be caused by a change in the price of the product. Figure 2 shows an **extension in supply**. A rise in price from P to P1 causes an increase in the quantity supplied from Q to Q1.

Figure 2 also shows a **contraction in supply**. A fall in price from P to P1 causes a decrease in the quantity supplied from Q to Q1.

Producer surplus

Producer surplus is the extra amount that producers are paid above what they were willing to accept to supply a product. Figure 3 illustrates producer surplus experienced by a firm selling washing machines.

Activity 5

In 2001 the price of pet food rose and the price of air travel fell. Explain, using diagrams, the effect on the supply of:

a pet food of the rise in the price of pet food

b air travel of the fall in the price of air travel

Table 1: A supply schedule

Price (£)	Quantity supplied (per week)
50	250
40	220
30	180
20	120
10	50

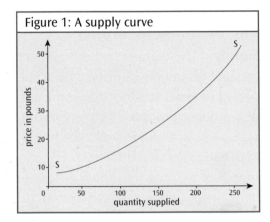
Figure 1: A supply curve

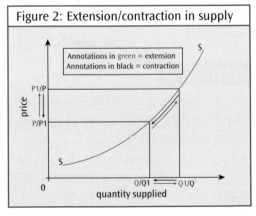
Figure 2: Extension/contraction in supply

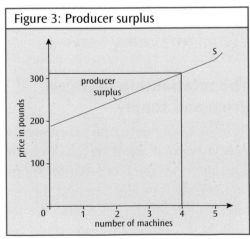
Figure 3: Producer surplus

Activity 6

A firm sells four units of a product for £10 each. It would have been willing to accept £5 for the first unit, £7 for the second, £9 for the third and £10 for the fourth.

Calculate the producer surplus the firm enjoys.

The firm would have been prepared to accept £220 for the first washing machine, £250 for the second, £280 for the third, £310 for the fourth and £340 for the fifth. If consumers pay £310, the firm will sell four machines. It will receive producer surplus of £180 (£90 on the first machine, £60 on the second and £30 on the third).

So a change in the price of a product affects the amount of producer surplus firms receive. A rise in price increases producer surplus and a fall in price reduces producer surplus.

Changes in supply

An **increase in supply** means that more is supplied at each and every price. A **decrease in supply** means that less is supplied at each and every price. Figure 4 illustrates an increase in supply from SS to S1S1. This leads to an increase in the quantity supplied at any given price. For example, at price P suppliers are now prepared to offer Q1, whereas under the original supply conditions, at this price they were only prepared to supply quantity Q. Similarly at price P1, the quantity supplied has increased from Q2 to Q3.

A shift to the left of the supply curve illustrates a decrease in supply. Figure 4 shows a supply curve shifting to the left from SS to S1S1. The effect will be to reduce the quantities supplied at all prices.

Causes of changes in supply

A shift in the supply curve indicates that there has been a change in the conditions governing supply. Various factors influence these conditions.

■ Changes in costs of production. Increases in wages, the prices of raw materials, fuel and power, interest rates, rent and other factor prices will cause supply to decrease.
■ Changes in the productivity of labour. If workers' productivity rises, costs of production will fall so supply will increase.
■ Advances in technology allow more products to be produced with fewer resources, thus causing supply to increase.

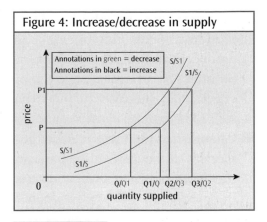

Figure 4: Increase/decrease in supply

Annotations in green = decrease
Annotations in black = increase

Activity 7

During a period of hot weather there is likely to be a bumper crop of tomatoes. As Christmas approaches, tomato growers raise the price they charge.

a Will a period of hot weather cause an extension or an increase in the supply of tomatoes?

b Will a rise in the price of tomatoes, as Christmas approaches, cause an extension or an increase in the supply of tomatoes?

Activity 8

Decide whether the following events would cause a movement along a supply curve (extension or contraction) or a shift in the supply curve (increase or decrease) for Ford cars:

a the use of advanced technology in Ford car plants

b a fall in the cost of car components

c a strike by Ford car workers

d a rise in the productivity of Ford car workers

e a rise in the indirect tax imposed on cars

f a rise in the price of Ford cars

■ **Indirect taxes** and subsidies. The imposition of indirect taxes adds an extra cost for producers and causes a decrease in supply. Subsidies to producers have the opposite effect. They increase the incentive and reward for producers and cause supply to increase.

■ Changes in the prices of other goods and services. If, because of increases in demand, the prices of other goods and services increase, the production of these products will become more profitable and resources will move towards the industries that make them. The production of products with unchanged prices will become less attractive.

In the case of products that are substitutes (in competitive supply), a rise in the price of one product will cause the supply of that product to extend and that of the other product/products to decrease. However, some products are in joint supply. For instance, petrol and paraffin are produced together. So if there is a rise in the price of petrol this will cause the supply of petrol to extend and the supply of paraffin to increase.

■ If new firms enter the market. For instance, the entry of new firms offering low-cost air travel has increased the number of range of flights available.

■ Changes in weather conditions and disease can influence the supply of agricultural products. Bad weather conditions adversely affect the harvest of arable crops. Disease can affect crops and livestock.

■ Unexpected events. For example, flights on Concorde were suspended for more than a year after the Air France Concorde crash in Paris in 2000 in which 113 people died.

Current issue: advances in technology

At the end of the nineteenth century, advances in technology, notably the development of electricity, the internal combustion engine and the radio-wave revolution, altered the way products were produced, reduced transport costs and created new industries. These included the car industry, air transport and television.

Technological change also accelerated at the end of the twentieth century. Since 1995 there has been an acceleration of technical change in computer production, accompanied by the invention of web browsers and widespread internet access. This information technology revolution is raising the productivity of workers, reducing production and communication costs and creating new industries, such as mobile phones and dot.com firms. So for a number of products the supply curve is shifting to the right and new supply curves are being created.

Summary

In this unit you have learned that:

■ **Supply** means the willingness and ability to sell a product.

■ For most products, price and supply are directly related. So a rise in price causes a rise in supply and a fall in price causes a fall in supply.

■ Individual supply is the relationship between the quantity supplied of a product by a single firm or plant. **Market supply** is the total supply of a product.

■ A **supply schedule** gives the different quantities supplied at a range of prices. Information from a supply schedule can be plotted on to a **supply curve** with price on the vertical axis and quantity supplied on the horizontal axis.

■ A movement along a supply curve can be caused only by a change in the price of the product. An **extension in supply** is caused by a rise in the price of the product and a **contraction in supply** is caused by a fall in the price of the product.

■ **Producer surplus** arises when firms receive a higher price for a product than they were willing to receive.

Summary continued

■ A **change in supply** is caused by a change in any influence other than the price of the product. An increase in supply is illustrated by a shift of the supply curve to the right and a decrease in supply by a shift of the supply curve to the left.

■ Among the factors which can cause a change in supply are changes in the costs of production, the productivity of labour, advances in technology, indirect taxes, subsidies, prices of other products, number of firms in the industry and, in the case of agricultural products, weather and disease.

Multiple choice questions

1 A supply curve slopes up from left to right. What effect will a rise in the price of the product have?

A   a shift to the left of the supply curve

B   a shift to the right of the supply curve

C   a decrease in the quantity supplied

D   an increase in the quantity supplied

2 Which area on Figure 5 shows producer surplus?

A   PRS

B   TPS

C   TRS

D   OTSQ

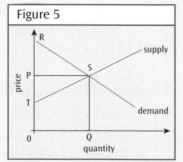

Figure 5

3 Figure 6 shows an industry's supply curve.

Which of the following could explain the shift in the supply curve from S to S1?

A   a reduction in the indirect tax placed on the product

B   an increase in the wage rate paid to the workers making the product

C   a reduction in the number of firms making the product

D   an increase in the cost of raw materials used to make the product

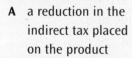
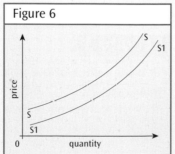

Figure 6

4 Advances in technology reduce the cost of producing a product. How would this be illustrated on a supply diagram?

A   a shift to the left of the supply curve

B   a shift to the right of the supply curve

C   a movement to the right along the supply curve

D   a movement to the left along the supply curve

5 What is the relationship between price and supply in a typical supply schedule?

A   direct

B   inverse

C   proportional

D   unrelated

6 Which of the following would cause the supply of beef to decrease?

A   a fall in the price of lamb

B   a decrease in vegetarianism

C   an outbreak of foot-and-mouth disease

D   an increase in the fertility of beef cattle

Data response question: pork production

Pork production in the UK fell by 10% in 2001. Pork prices fell to 75p a kilo from 120p a kilo in 1999. Pig farmers estimated they needed 90p a kilo to break even. The National Pig Association estimated than one in ten of the 4,000 pig producers in England, Wales and Scotland faced going out of business. Others were cutting back significantly the number of pigs they were keeping and breeding.

Pig farmers also faced other problems, including extra costs imposed by the need for higher health standards following the BSE crisis and the requirement to fit wider stalls for breeding pigs.

Cheaper pork imports increased, in some cases from countries that did not meet the high welfare standards required of UK farmers. To compete with cheaper imports

and to cover their costs, UK pig farmers asked the government to subsidise their industry.

a Explain and illustrate the effect of:
  i a change in the price of UK pork in 2001 on the supply of UK produced pigs. [5]
  ii the extra costs imposed on UK pig farmers on the supply of UK produced pork. [5]

b Discuss why, despite the problems faced by UK pig farmers, the supply of pork in the UK may have risen. [3]

c Explain, and illustrate, the effect of a subsidy to UK pig farmers on the supply of UK produced pork. [5]

d Discuss an influence on the supply of pork not mentioned in the passage. [2]

3 Price elasticity of demand

The response of demand to a price change is measured by **price elasticity of demand**. In this unit you will examine the different degrees of response of demand to a change in price, how to calculate price elasticity of demand, the key influences on price elasticity of demand and the significance of price elasticity of demand for consumers, firms and the government.

Elasticity

Three of the most important influences on the demand for a product are its price, people's incomes and the price of related products. Economists study how changes in these influences affect demand using the concept of **elasticity**. In economics, elasticity is the extent to which one **variable**, for example demand, responds to a change in another variable, for example price.

Activity 1

To what extent (more or less than 10%) do you think demand for the following products would contract if their price rose by 10%:

a milk

b a luxury brand of perfume

b a particular newspaper

Price elasticity of demand

Price elasticity of demand (PED) measures the responsiveness of demand for a product to a change in its price. When demand is very responsive to a change in price it is said to be elastic. A change in price will bring about a greater percentage change in quantity demanded. When demand is relatively unresponsive to a change in price it is inelastic. A change in price will cause the quantity demanded to change by a smaller percentage. So price elasticity of demand is the relationship between the percentage change in price and the percentage change in quantity demanded.

Activity 2

In the summer of 2001 the budget airlines cut their fares. Ryannair cut its fares by 5%. As a result, its passenger numbers increased by 42% to 2.4 million.

Does this information suggest demand for budget air travel is elastic or inelastic?

Calculating price elasticity of demand

Price elasticity of demand is calculated by comparing the percentage change in quantity demanded with the percentage change in price which brought it about. The formula is:

$$PED = \frac{\text{percentage change in quantity demanded}}{\text{percentage change in price}}$$

This can be abbreviated to: $PED = \frac{\%\Delta QD}{\%\Delta P}$

The $\%\Delta QD$ is found by dividing the change in quantity demanded by the original quantity demanded multiplied by 100:

$$\frac{QD \times 100}{\text{original QD}} = \%\Delta QD$$

Similarly, the $\%\Delta P$ is found by dividing the change in price by the original price multiplied by 100:

$$\frac{P}{\text{original P}} \times 100 = \%\Delta P$$

For example, if the price of a product rises from £20 to £24 and demand falls from 400 to 300, the PED will be:

$$\frac{-25\%}{20\%} = -1.25$$

Activity 3

Calculate the PED, up to two decimal places where appropriate, in the following:

a a fall in price from £10 to £6 causes demand to extend from 100 to 150

b a rise in price from 90p to £1.20 results in a contraction in demand from 300 to 200

c the price of a product increases from $8 to $9 which causes demand to contract from 800 to 200

d a cut in price from 48 euros to 36 euros causes demand for a product to rise from 200 to 210

e demand extends from 2,580 to 3,120 when price falls from £12 to £9

f demand contracts from 19,000 to 10,000 when price rises from 65p to 75p

Degrees of price elasticity of demand

In the majority of cases, the relationship between price and demand is inverse. This means that PED is usually negative. To make comparisons between the different degrees of PED, however, economists find it easier to ignore the minus sign.

Demand for most products is elastic or inelastic. **Elastic demand** is when a given percentage change in price causes a greater percentage change in demand. In this case, the numerical value (coefficient) of PED is greater than 1 and less than infinity. Elastic demand is usually illustrated by a shallow downward sloping demand curve as shown in Figure 1.

When a given change in price causes a smaller percentage change in demand, the product has **inelastic demand**. In this case, the numerical value (coefficient) of PED is greater than 0 and less than 1. Inelastic demand is usually illustrated by a steep downward sloping demand curve as shown in Figure 2.

The other degrees of price elasticity of demand are less common but may occur under certain circumstances.

Unit price elasticity of demand occurs when a percentage change in price results in an equal percentage change in demand. The numerical value (coefficient) is 1 as shown in Figure 3.

The area OPAB and OP1CD are equal as consumers' expenditure stays the same.

Perfectly inelastic demand is when a change in price causes no change in the quantity demanded. The numerical value is 0. For instance, a person with a serious illness may be prepared to buy the same quantity of medicine when its price rises and may not find it beneficial to increase the quantity taken when its price falls. Figure 4 shows perfectly inelastic demand over the price range, with a rise in price from P to P1 having no effect on the quantity demanded.

When demand is perfectly elastic a change in price will cause an infinite change in the quantity demanded. The numerical value is infinity. For example, suppose people are selling a group's CDs at one of its concerts. If one person reduced her prices below those of her competitors she may capture all the custom of all the consumers at the concert. Figure 5 illustrates perfectly elastic demand.

Activity 4

Decide in the case of each of your answers to Activity 3 whether demand is elastic, inelastic, unity, perfectly inelastic or perfectly elastic.

Determinants of price elasticity of demand

A number of factors influence the type of price elasticity of demand of a product. The main factor is the availability of close substitutes. Products with close substitutes in the same price range have elastic demand. A rise in their price will cause many consumers to switch to a substitute. For example, if the price of a brand of bleach rises, more consumers are likely to buy an alternative brand.

The extent to which a product has close substitutes, and thus the extent to which demand is elastic or inelastic, is influenced by how the product is defined. Products that are widely defined have few (or no) substitutes and demand is

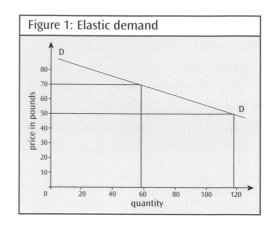

Figure 1: Elastic demand

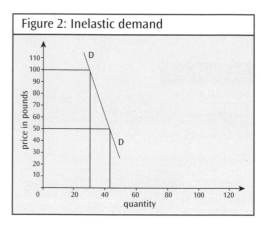

Figure 2: Inelastic demand

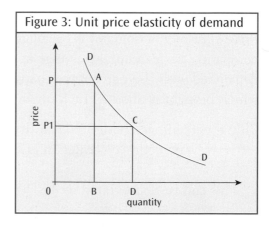

Figure 3: Unit price elasticity of demand

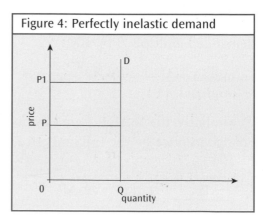

Figure 4: Perfectly inelastic demand

inelastic. For example, there are no substitutes for food. Products that are more narrowly defined have more elastic demand. For example, demand for one brand of cider is elastic, demand for cider in general is less elastic and demand for alcohol is even less elastic.

PED is also influenced by the proportion of income taken up by expenditure on a product. Expenditure on a new garage, for example, takes up a large proportion of income, so a rise in price is likely to have a significant impact. Consumers are likely to seek an alternative and so PED is usually high. Expenditure on a newspaper, however, takes up only a small proportion of income, so even if the price rises it is unlikely to have much impact. Consumers are unlikely to switch to an alternative and so PED will be low.

Luxuries may or may not take up a large part of someone's income but they usually have elastic demand. They are not essential purchases so a rise in the price of, for example, strawberries and jewellery is likely to result in a significant fall in demand. However, demand for necessities, such as soap and toilet paper, is usually inelastic, not only because they are essential but also because they often do not have close substitutes.

Habit-forming products have inelastic demand. If the prices of all brands of cigarettes rise, demand will not fall significantly as smokers find it hard to give up smoking.

Demand is often inelastic for products whose purchase can be postponed. For example, if the price of double glazing rises some households will postpone having their windows and doors replaced.

With most products, demand becomes more elastic over time. This is because it takes time for people to notice price changes and to switch between products. For example, if the price charged for meals in a restaurant rises, people may initially reduce the number of times they eat in the restaurant. When they have had time to sample food in other restaurants, they may stop going to it altogether.

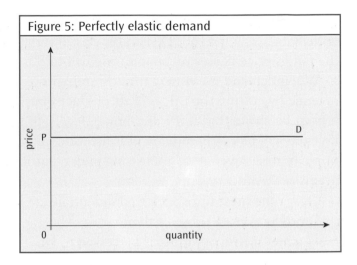

Figure 5: Perfectly elastic demand

Activity 5

Decide whether the following products are likely to have elastic or inelastic demand:

a tooth paste

b champagne

b cut flowers

d bandages

e one brand of pepper

Significance of price elasticity of demand

Most consumers have not heard of price elasticity of demand, but changes in price can have a significant impact on them. As prices rise, consumers become more sensitive to further price rises. Their willingness and ability to buy a product decrease as it becomes more expensive. If its price rises too much, a product can price itself out of the market. In contrast, when prices fall demand becomes more inelastic. When a product has a low price, consumers may still be able and willing to buy it even if its price rises.

Consumers' reactions to price changes in their products can have an important influence on firms' revenue. When demand is elastic, price and revenue move in opposite directions. A rise in price will cause a fall in revenue and a fall in price will result in a rise in revenue. For example, a product may be priced at £10 and demand may be 100. So total revenue is £1,000. A 20% fall in price to £8 may result in a greater percentage rise in demand, 60%, to 160. Demand is elastic and the fall in price causes revenue to rise to £1,280.

When demand is elastic a firm can raise its revenue by cutting the prices of its products, but it must be aware that if it raises prices, its revenue will fall. When demand is inelastic, a firm can raise revenue by increasing prices, but if it lowers them its revenue will fall.

Over time most firms seek to differentiate their products from those of their rivals. The more scarce a firm's product is perceived to be, the more inelastic demand will be. Making demand more inelastic increases a firm's market power. It will be in a stronger position to raise its prices and, if its unit costs remain the same, the profit it earns.

Price elasticity of demand also has implications for the government. It can raise its revenue if it imposes a tax on products with inelastic demand. If it wants to discourage the consumption of certain products, it will be more effective if demand is elastic. PED also affects the government in its role as a producer and consumer. For example, the UK government and its agencies sell postal services and university education to overseas students and buy equipment for hospitals, schools and the armed services.

Current issue: taxing tobacco products

The government originally taxed tobacco and tobacco products to raise revenue. It now also taxes them to discourage their consumption.

However, demand for these products is inelastic. It has been estimated that the price elasticity of demand for cigarettes is -0.77.

If the government forces up the price of cigarettes by raising excise duty, demand falls by a smaller percentage. So although government tax revenue rises, smoking is not significantly discouraged.

When demand is inelastic, a government cannot significantly influence demand by altering price so it uses other measures. To discourage smoking, the government requires cigarette companies to place warnings on cigarette products, spends money on anti-smoking campaigns and has passed legislation preventing cigarettes being sold to people aged under 16.

Activity 6

A UK travel agent specialises in holidays to Spain, Greece and China. It estimates that it faces the following price elasticities of demand for its holidays in these countries is shown in Table 1.

a Discuss the possible reasons why the PED may vary between the three holiday destinations.

b Explain what the travel agent should do in terms of its pricing strategy to increase the revenue of the business.

Table 1

Holiday destination	PED
Spain	−2.0
Greece	−1.1
China	−0.6

Summary

In this unit you have learned that:

- **Elasticity** is the extent to which one **variable** responds to a change in another variable.

- **Price elasticity of demand (PED)** measures the responsiveness of the quantity demanded of a product to a change in its price.

- Price elasticity of demand is calculated by using the formula:

$$PED = \frac{\text{percentage change in quantity demanded}}{\text{percentage change in price}}$$

- PED is usually negative as price and demand are inversely related.

- Demand can be elastic, inelastic, unit, perfectly inelastic or perfectly elastic.

- A rise in the price of products with **elastic demand** will cause a greater percentage change in quantity demanded.

- A rise in the price of products with **inelastic demand** will result in a smaller percentage change in quantity demanded.

- The main factor influencing the type of PED of a product is the availability or otherwise of close substitutes. Other factors include what proportion of income is spent on the product, whether the product is addictive, whether its purchase can be postponed, whether it is a luxury or a necessity and the time period under consideration.

- A rise in price usually causes demand to become more elastic.

- When demand is elastic, price and total revenue move in the opposite direction. When demand is inelastic, price and total revenue move in the same direction.

- A tax on a product with inelastic demand will increase government revenue but will not be very effective in lowering demand.

Multiple choice questions

1 A product has inelastic demand. What effect will a rise in its price have?

A a shift of the demand curve to the left

B a shift of the demand curve to the right

C a decrease in total expenditure on the product

D an increase in total expenditure on the product

2 A product falls in price by an amount which stimulates a 6% rise in demand. The change in quantity demanded leaves total expenditure on the product unchanged. What is the price elasticity of demand?

A 0

B greater than 0 but less than 1

C equal to 1

D greater than 1 but less than infinity

3 Table 2 shows a demand schedule for a product. Within what price range is PED −2.5?

A $10–9

B $9–8

C $8–7

D $7–6

Table 2	
Price ($)	Quantity demanded
10	40
9	50
8	60
7	70
6	80

4 Which of the following is most likely to make demand for a product elastic?

A people spend a low proportion of their income on the product

B there are a number of close substitutes for the product

C the product is viewed as a necessity

D the product is habit forming

Multiple choice questions continued

5 Which diagram in Figure 6 illustrates zero price elasticity of demand?

6 The price of a product rises from £12 to £18. This causes demand to fall from 480 to 360. What is the price elasticity of demand?

A −0.5

B −0.67

C −1.0

D −2.0

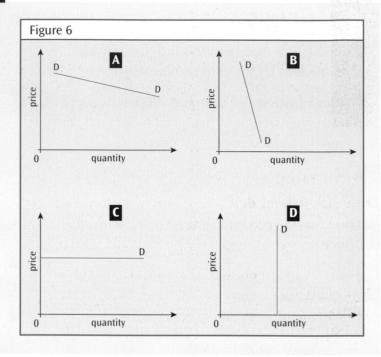

Figure 6

Data response question: demand for Strovers' wrapping paper

Strovers is a small company which produces gift wrapping paper. It operates in a competitive market with a high number of other companies. Table 3 shows the demand schedule for Strovers' wrapping paper based on the firm's research.

Table 3: Weekly demand schedule for Strovers' wrapping paper	
Price per roll (£)	Quantity demanded (number of rolls)
4.20	500
3.60	1,000
3.00	2,000
2.40	4,000
1.80	7,000
1.20	9,000
0.60	10,000

a i Use the information in Table 3 to draw the demand curve for Strovers' wrapping paper. [3]

ii Explain what this curve indicates. [2]

b i Define price elasticity of demand. [2]

ii Use the information in Table 3 to calculate the price elasticity of demand for Strovers' wrapping paper as the price falls from £2.40 to £1.80. [2]

iii Comment on the degree of price elasticity of demand you have found. [3]

c Explain what use Strovers' can make of the PED estimate you calculated. [4]

d Discuss two factors that could shift the demand curve for Strovers' wrapping paper to the right. [4]

4 Cross elasticity of demand

In this unit you will examine how the price of one product affects demand for another product. You will see that demand can be affected in different ways and to different extents.

The meaning of cross elasticity of demand

Cross elasticity of demand measures the extent to which demand for one product changes in response to a change in the price of another product. The formula used is:

$$\text{Cross elasticity of demand} = \frac{\text{percentage change in quantity demanded of product A}}{\text{percentage change in price of product B}}$$

This can be abbreviated to:

$$\text{XED} = \frac{\%\Delta\text{QD of A}}{\%\Delta\text{P of B}}$$

XED can be positive, negative or zero, indicating an increase, decrease or no change in demand. The numerical value of XED indicates the extent of the change in demand.

Positive cross elasticity of demand

Substitute products have **positive cross elasticity of demand**, so a rise in the price of one product is likely to cause demand for its substitute or substitutes to increase. For example, a 10% rise in the price of fish may cause demand for chicken to increase by 2%. In this case the cross elasticity of demand is:

$$\text{XED} = \frac{\%\Delta\text{QD of chicken}}{\%\Delta\text{P of fish}} = \frac{2\%}{10\%} = 0.2$$

The relationship between fish and chicken can be shown in a cross elasticity of demand diagram. For simplicity, the demand curve is drawn as a straight line. Figure 1 shows that a rise in the price of fish from P to P1 causes demand for chicken to increase from Q to Q1. With positive cross elasticity of demand, the demand curve slopes upwards from left to right.

The effect of a rise in the price of fish on demand for chicken can also be shown on an ordinary demand curve.

Activity 1

Work out the formula to show:

a the cross elasticity of demand for apples with respect to pears.

b the cross elasticity of demand for newspapers with respect to train tickets.

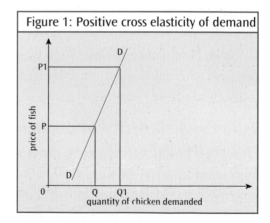

Figure 1: Positive cross elasticity of demand

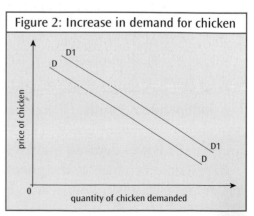

Figure 2: Increase in demand for chicken

Figure 2 shows demand for chicken increasing, but it does not show the cause of the change in demand.

If two products are close substitutes, with consumers switching easily between them, they will have a high cross elasticity of demand. Two brands of sugar, for example, are likely to have a high cross elasticity of demand. In contrast, the cross elasticity of demand between a sports car and a family saloon is likely to be low as the two are not close substitutes.

Negative cross elasticity of demand

Complementary products have **negative cross elasticity of demand**. A rise in the price of air travel, for example, causes a fall in demand for foreign holidays.

Negative cross elasticity of demand is illustrated by a downward sloping cross elasticity of demand curve. Figure 3 shows that a fall in the price of paper results in a rise in demand for pens.

The effect of a fall in the price of paper on demand for pens can also be illustrated on an ordinary demand diagram as shown in Figure 2.

If a 20% fall in the price of paper causes demand for pens to increase by 5%, the cross elasticity of demand will be:

$$\text{XED} = \frac{\%\Delta\text{QD of pens}}{\%\Delta\text{P of paper}} = \frac{5\%}{-20\%} = -0.25$$

Close complements have high negative cross elasticity of demand whereas distant complements have low negative cross elasticity of demand.

Zero cross elasticity of demand

Unrelated products have **zero cross elasticity of demand**. For example, a rise in the price of cheese is unlikely to have any effect on demand for bicycles. So a 10% rise in the price of cheese will leave demand for bicycles unaffected, giving a cross elasticity of:

$$\text{XED} = \frac{\%\Delta\text{QD of bicycles}}{\%\Delta\text{P of cheese}} = \frac{0\%}{10\%} = 0\%$$

Products with zero cross elasticity of demand are referred to as **independent goods**. Figure 4 shows that apples and gloves are independent goods. The rise in the price of apples from P to P1 leaves demand for gloves unchanged at Q.

In practice, a change in the price of a product may affect demand for products that appear to be unrelated. This is

Activity 2

A 20% rise in the price of ice cream causes demand for sweets to increase by 4%.

a Calculate the cross elasticity of demand for sweets with respect to ice cream.

b Does your answer suggest ice cream and sweets are close or distant substitutes?

Figure 3: Negative cross elasticity of demand

Activity 3

A 12% fall in the price of air fares leads to a 30% rise in demand for foreign holidays.

a Calculate the cross elasticity of demand for foreign holidays with respect to air fares.

b Does your answer suggest air fares and foreign holidays are close or distant complements?

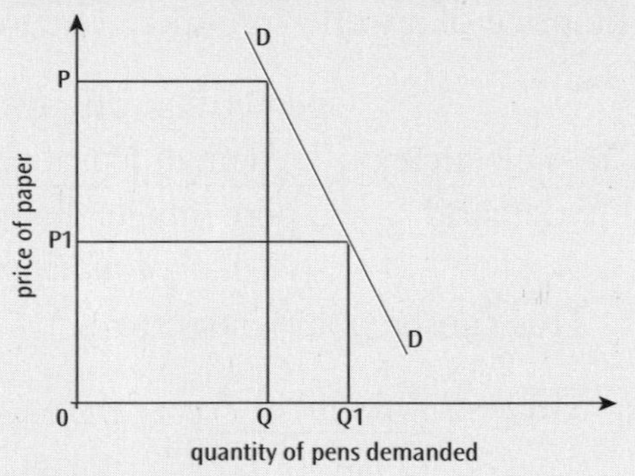

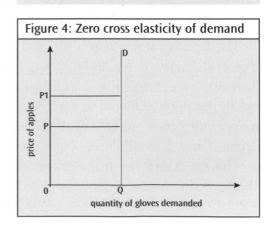

Figure 4: Zero cross elasticity of demand

because the change in the price of a product, especially one on which consumers spend a high proportion of their income, influences households' purchasing power. For example, in the past a rise in the price of bread reduced people's demand for magazines. This is because people sought to buy almost the same amount of bread and to do this they cut purchases of other items.

The significance of cross elasticity of demand

Cross elasticity of demand is of particular significance to firms. A firm may discover, from past experience and from surveys, that its product has a high positive cross elasticity of demand with other firms' products. It will therefore have an incentive to cut its price since a lower price will attract a high proportion of its rivals' sales. However, a high positive cross elasticity of demand also limits the firm's ability to raise the price of its product.

In contrast, a low positive cross elasticity of demand gives a firm more power to raise its price but less opportunity to benefit from cutting its price.

A high negative cross elasticity of demand also has implications for firms. This may occur between two or more of a firm's own products or between its own product and the products of other firms. If a firm finds that there is a high negative cross elasticity of demand between two of its own products, it can increase the sales of the more expensive item by lowering the price of the cheaper item. For example, a retailer may make a special offer on its DVD players and video recorders to encourage sales of its digital televisions. If a firm discovers that there is a high negative cross elasticity of demand between its own product and another firm's product, it will expect a rise in demand for its product following a fall in the price of the other firm's product. In contrast, there will be a fall in demand should the other firm raise the price of its product.

Activity 4

Decide whether the following pairs of products are likely to have positive, negative or zero cross elasticity of demand:

a tea and milk

b paint and paint brushes

c cod and plaice

d car travel and public transport

e satellite and cable television

f bread and butter

Activity 5

A supermarket researches the cross elasticity of demand for a particular brand of cheese, Oxfordshire Mild, with respect to a range of products. Its findings are shown in Table 1.

a Identify the relationship between Oxfordshire Mild and:
  i the supermarket's own brand of mild cheddar
  ii cream crackers

b If the supermarket wants to raise the revenue it earns from French wine, what should it do to the price of Oxfordshire Mild?

c Compare the cross elasticity of demand of Oxfordshire Mild with respect to:
  i the supermarket's own brands of mild and mature cheddar
  ii Spanish and French wine

Table 1	
Product	Cross elasticity of demand
Own brand of mild cheese	3.0
Own brand of mature cheese	0.6
Spanish wine	−0.2
French wine	−0.8
Cream crackers	−1.2

Current issue: demand in world markets

Advances in technology and communications and reductions in trade barriers between countries are increasing the degree of positive cross elasticity of demand in world markets.

For example, the internet enables consumers to compare prices between airlines, insurance companies and suppliers of CDs and books, and to place orders more easily. This makes the firms more effective competitors. It reduces each firm's ability to raise its price above that of its rivals and puts pressure on each firm to keep quality high.

Increasing use of the internet has also increased the degree of negative cross elasticity of demand between products and delivery services. People are now buying from further afield. If the price of wine decreases, for example, demand for the services of road haulage firms is likely to rise by a greater percentage than it used to.

Summary

In this unit you have learned that:

- **Cross elasticity of demand** is a measure of the responsiveness of demand for one product with respect to a change in the price of another product.

- The formula for cross elasticity of demand is:

$$XED = \frac{\text{percentage change in quantity demanded of product A}}{\text{percentage change in the price of product B}}$$

- Substitutes have **positive cross elasticity of demand**. A high positive cross elasticity of demand indicates that the two products are close substitutes.

- Complements have **negative cross elasticity of demand**. A high negative cross elasticity of demand indicates that the two products are close complements.

- Unrelated products have **zero cross elasticity of demand**.

- A high positive cross elasticity of demand with its competitors' products may encourage a firm to cut the price of its product but is likely to discourage it from raising its price.

- A high negative cross elasticity of demand between two of a firm's own products may encourage it to lower the price of the cheaper item.

Multiple choice questions

1 Table 2 shows the price and demand for two products, Y and Z. What is the cross elasticity of demand between Z and Y when the price of Y rises from £4 to £5?

A −1
B −2
C 2
D 5

Table 2		
Price of Y (£)	Quantity of Y demanded	Quantity of Z demanded
4	80	100
5	60	50

2 Which diagram illustrates the relationship between two products which are substitutes?

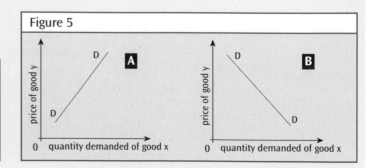

Figure 5

Multiple choice questions continued

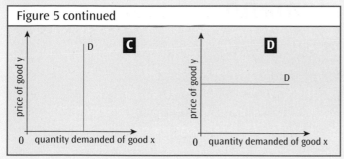

Figure 5 continued

3 What is the cross elasticity of demand for two products which are complements?

A zero

B positive

C negative

D infinity

4 What is the formula for the cross elasticity of demand for good X with respect to good Y?

A $\dfrac{\text{percentage change in quantity demanded of good X}}{\text{percentage change in price of good Y}}$

B $\dfrac{\text{percentage change in quantity demanded of good X and good Y}}{\text{percentage change in their joint prices}}$

C $\dfrac{\text{percentage change in quantity demanded of good X}}{\text{percentage change in quantity demanded of good Y}}$

D $\dfrac{\text{percentage change in price of good X}}{\text{percentage change in price of good Y}}$

5 The price elasticity of demand for cream cakes is –2.0 and the cross elasticity of demand between cream cakes and fruit cakes is 0.8. What effect will a 10% increase in the price of cream cakes have on demand for cream cakes and fruit cakes?

	Cream cakes	Fruit cakes
A	fall by 50%	rise by 18%
B	fall by 20%	rise by 8%
C	rise by 10%	fall by 18%
D	rise by 20%	fall by 8%

6 It is found that the cross elasticity of demand between beef and pork is positive and below 1. As a result it follows that:

A a rise in the price of pork will cause a smaller percentage rise in demand for beef

B a rise in the price of pork will cause a greater percentage rise in demand for beef

C a fall in the price of pork will cause a greater percentage rise in demand for beef

D a fall in the price of pork will cause a smaller percentage rise in demand for beef

Data response question: the luxury car market

In spring 2000 a price war broke out in the UK luxury car market. It was triggered by the government ordering major manufacturers to offer ordinary buyers the discounted prices enjoyed by fleet buyers, and by competition from similar, cheaper models in Ireland and other European countries.

In May 2000 Porsche cut the prices of its cars by 10% and as a result experienced a 40% rise in sales. Mercedes also cut its prices by 10%. Some car companies, however, did not respond. Rolls-Royce, for example, decided not to lower its prices. This may have been because officials at Rolls-Royce believed that works of art and race horses were stronger competitors than other cars. Nevertheless, demand for Rolls-Royce cars fell by 3% in June.

a i Calculate the price elasticity of demand for Porsche cars. [2]

   ii Comment on your findings. [3]

b i What is the relationship between Mercedes cars and Porsche cars? [2]

   ii Draw a diagram to illustrate the relationship between the two products. [4]

c i Calculate the cross elasticity of demand between Porsche cars and Rolls-Royce cars. [2]

   ii Comment on your findings. [3]

d Explain what determines the cross elasticity of demand between two products. [4]

5 Income elasticity of demand

This unit concentrates on the relationship between demand and income. You will examine the meaning, the different types and degrees, and the significance of **income elasticity of demand**.

The meaning of income elasticity of demand

Income elasticity of demand measures the extent to which demand for a product changes in response to a change in income. The formula used is:

$$\text{Income elasticity of demand} = \frac{\text{percentage change in quantity demanded}}{\text{percentage change in income}}$$

This can be abbreviated to:

$$YED = \frac{\%\Delta QD}{\%\Delta Y}$$

The sign will indicate the nature of the product and the numerical value will show the extent of the relationship between income and demand for the product.

Activity 1

What do you expect will happen to the market demand for the following products if income rises?

a cider

b French wine

c water

d cosmetics

Positive income elasticity of demand

Most products have **positive income elasticity of demand**, so a rise in income will cause an increase in demand and a fall in income will result in a decrease in demand. So common is this relationship that products which exhibit it are known as normal goods.

It has been estimated, for example, that a 10% increase in income results in a 2.3% increase in demand for coffee. This gives an income elasticity of demand of:

$$YED = \frac{\%\Delta QD \text{ of coffee}}{\%\Delta Y} = \frac{2.3\%}{10\%} = 0.23$$

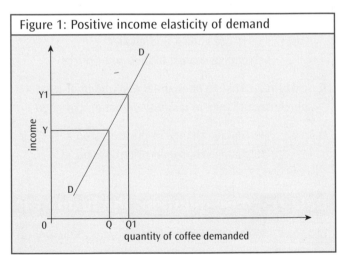

Figure 1: Positive income elasticity of demand

Figure 1 illustrates this positive relationship with a rise in income from Y to Y1 causing an increase in demand for coffee from Q to Q1.

The effect of an increase in demand for coffee could also be shown on an ordinary demand curve. In this case it would be illustrated by a shift in the demand curve to the right (see Figure 2, Unit 4, p73).

A figure of 0.23 indicates that demand for coffee is not very responsive to a change in income. Products with an income elasticity of demand between 0 and 1 (whatever the sign) are said to be **income inelastic**. This means that a percentage change in income causes a smaller percentage change in demand.

UK citizens' demand for holidays to South Africa also has a positive relationship with income. When demand increases, demand for South African holidays also rises. However, this time demand is **income elastic**. This means that demand changes by a greater percentage than the percentage change in income. It has been estimated that the income elasticity of demand for South African holidays is 2.0.

Products with a positive income elasticity of demand greater than 1 are sometimes called **superior** or **luxury goods**. Figure 2 illustrates positive, income elastic demand. The rise in income from Y to Y1 causes a greater percentage increase in demand.

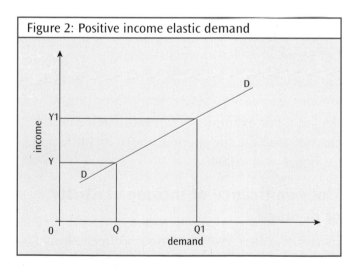

Figure 2: Positive income elastic demand

Activity 2

The income elasticity of demand for fruit juices in the UK in 2001 was estimated at 0.94.

a Explain what this estimate means.

b Discuss whether the relationship is one you would expect.

Negative income elasticity of demand

Some products have **negative income elasticity of demand**. This means that an increase in income will result in a decrease in demand and a fall in income will cause an increase in demand. Products with negative income elasticity of demand are known as inferior goods. These products usually have higher quality, higher priced substitutes which people will switch to if their incomes rise.

It has been estimated, for example, that fresh potatoes have an income elasticity of demand of −0.48. The inverse relationship between income and demand is illustrated in Figure 3. This shows that a rise in income from Y to Y1 causes a decrease in demand for potatoes from Q to Q1.

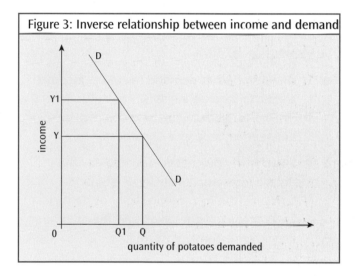

Figure 3: Inverse relationship between income and demand

The decrease in demand for potatoes could also be shown on an ordinary demand diagram. This time the demand curve will shift to the left (see Figure 5, Unit 2, page 57).

As with normal goods, inferior goods can exhibit income elastic or income inelastic demand. If an inferior good has income inelastic demand, a percentage rise in income will cause a smaller percentage decrease in demand. The numerical value of the income elasticity of demand will be between 0 and 1 (ignoring the sign).

If the inferior product has income elastic demand, the numerical value of the elasticity will be between 1 and infinity (again ignoring the sign).

A percentage rise in income will lead to a larger percentage decrease in demand (see Figure 4).

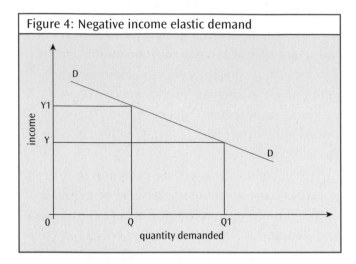

Figure 4: Negative income elastic demand

Activity 3

The income elasticity of demand for tea in the UK in 2001 was estimated at −0.56 and processed vegetables at −0.17.

a i Decide whether demand for tea is income elastic or income inelastic.
   ii Draw a diagram to illustrate the relationship between income and demand for tea.

b i Explain why processed vegetables have negative income elasticity of demand.
   ii Compare the income elasticity of demand for processed vegetables and the income elasticity of demand for tea.

Zero income elasticity of demand

Zero income elasticity of demand occurs when a change in income has no effect on demand, which remains unchanged (see Figure 5). For example, a rise in income of 5% in a rich country may leave demand for toothpaste unchanged at 10,000 tubes a week. This gives an income elasticity of demand of:

$$\text{YED} = \frac{\%\Delta \text{QD of toothpaste}}{\%\Delta Y} = \frac{0\%}{5\%} = 0\%$$

Over a certain income range, some products have or come close to zero income elasticity of

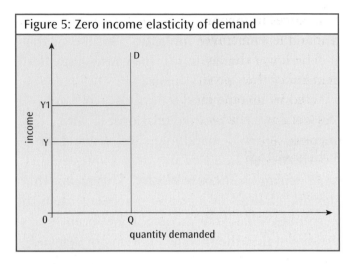

Figure 5: Zero income elasticity of demand

Activity 4

Decide whether the following products are likely to have positive, negative or zero income elasticity of demand:

a bus travel

b swimming pools

c pepper

d books

e wine

demand. For example, it was estimated that in the UK in 2001 the income elasticity of demand for butter was −0.04.

The significance of income elasticity of demand

Income tends to rise over time, so in the long run firms that produce products with positive income elasticity of demand usually do best. This is why some firms producing inferior products seek to change consumers' perception of their goods and services. It is also why poor countries, seeking to raise the living standards of their inhabitants, try to produce more normal and fewer inferior goods.

However, during a recession firms producing inferior products may benefit. In this situation firms that supply products with high positive income elasticity of demand are the most vulnerable. For example, air travel is susceptible to changes in income. When incomes fall, people demand less air travel.

The lower the level of income elasticity of demand of their products, the less firms are affected by income changes, but they also gain less from any changes in income.

Activity 5

The firms in a town include a funeral director, a beauty salon, a coal merchant and a bookseller. Table 1 shows the income elasticities of demand for their products.

a Decide whether each of the products is a normal, inferior or superior good.

Table 1

	YED
Funeral services	0.01
Beauty salon treatments	3.60
Coal	−0.40
Books	2.20

b What effect would a rise in income of 10% have on the revenue earned by:
  i the funeral director
  ii the bookseller

c Draw a diagram to show the effect of a fall in income on demand for:
  i beauty salon treatments
  ii coal

Current issue: government spending

Income elasticity of demand has significance for governments. Education and health care have high positive income elasticity of demand. This puts pressure on the government to increase its spending on both services. As households become richer they demand better standards of education and more of their children want to progress to higher education.

As a society gets richer its inhabitants demand higher standards of health care and expect more ailments to be treated. This is because a rise in income raises people's expectations of improved living standards. They are less willing to put up with aches and pains, they are better informed about what treatments are available and they live longer. Elderly people place the greatest burden on the NHS.

Summary

In this unit you have learned that:

- **Income elasticity of demand** is a measure of the responsiveness of demand to a change in income.

- The formula for income elasticity of demand is:
$$YED = \frac{\%\Delta QD}{\%\Delta Y}$$

- Normal goods have **positive income elasticity of demand**. This means that as incomes rise, demand for these products increases. Normal goods with **income elastic** demand are sometimes referred to as **superior goods**.

- Products which have **negative income elasticity of demand** are called inferior goods. As incomes rise demand for these products decreases.

- It is possible for products to have, over a given income range, zero income elasticity of demand. This means that a rise in income leaves demand unchanged.

- Demand can be income elastic or **income inelastic** in the case of both normal and inferior products. Income elastic means that a percentage change in income will cause a greater percentage change in demand. Income inelastic means that a percentage change in income will cause a smaller percentage change in demand.

- Over time firms producing normal and superior goods do best, but a recession is likely to benefit firms selling inferior goods.

- Education and health care have positive income elasticity of demand, which puts pressure on the government to raise its spending.

Income elasticity of demand

Multiple choice questions

1 Which of the following diagrams illustrates negative income elasticity of demand?

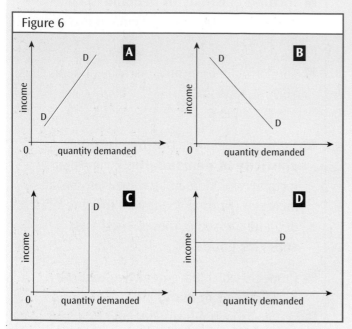

Figure 6

2 A person's disposable income is $400 a week and she spends $50 on food. It is known that her income elasticity of demand for food is 0.4. If her income rises to $500, what will be her new spending on food?

A $40

B $55

C $90

D $200

3 Demand for a product is observed not to increase as rapidly as income. What is income elasticity of demand for this product?

A negative

B zero

C greater than zero but less than one

D greater than one but less than infinity

4 Table 2 shows a person's demand for four different products, A, B, C and D at two different income levels. Over the income range shown, for which product does the person have an income elasticity of demand of unity?

A   B   C   D

Table 2				
Income (£)	Number of products demanded			
	A	B	C	D
20,000	100	100	100	100
25,000	100	105	125	150

5 The income elasticity of demand for a product is 0.7. What will be the effect of a rise in income?

A a proportionately greater rise in demand

B a proportionately smaller rise in demand

C a proportionately smaller fall in demand

D a proportionately greater fall in demand

6 Table 3 shows a household's income elasticity of demand for soft drinks. The household's income rises by 10%. Which of the following will result from this increase?

A no change in demand for grapefruit juice

B a 0.6% rise in demand for lemonade

C a fall in demand for cola

D a 20% rise in demand for orange squash

Table 3	
Soft drink	YED
Lemonade	0.6
Orange squash	2.0
Cola	0.3
Grapefruit juice	1.0

Data response question: income elasticity of demands in a recession

In the boom period of the late 1990s luxury products enjoyed high and increasing sales. But as the USA entered a recession in 2001, sales of luxury goods fell. For example, sales of expensive Burberry raincoats fell by 15%. Foreign tourism, management consultancies, advertising agencies and other business services also experienced steep falls in business.

However, some US firms continued to do well and some even increased their sales. US holiday resorts catering mainly for domestic holiday makers saw an upturn in business. Food sales remained largely unchanged, although the effect on different items varied, partly because different items have different income elasticities of demand. One US supermarket estimated in 2001 the income elasticities of demand for a small range of its products (see Table 4).

a Define income elasticity of demand. [2]

b Discuss what type and degree of income elasticity of demand you would expect luxury goods to have. [3]

c i Compare the income elasticity of demand of apples and whisky. [3]

Table 4: Income elasticity of demand for five products

Product	YED
Box of luxury chocolates	2.4
Whisky	4.1
Digestive biscuits	0.6
Apples	0.2
Own-brand baked beans	−0.4

ii From the information in the passage, explain whether the income elasticity of demand in 2001 for the following products was positive, negative or zero:
– Burberry coats [2]
– US domestic holidays [2]
– Food [2]

d i Estimate the effect of a 5% fall in income on demand for the supermarket's box of luxury chocolates and its own brand of baked beans. [4]

ii Apart from a change in income, discuss one other factor that could affect demand for whisky. [2]

6 Price elasticity of supply

In this unit you will examine the meaning of **price elasticity of supply** and how to calculate it. You will investigate the different degrees of price elasticity of supply, the influences on it and its significance.

The meaning of price elasticity of supply

Price elasticity of supply is a measure of the responsiveness of supply to a change in price. The formula is:

$$\text{Price elasticity of supply} = \frac{\text{percentage change in quantity supplied}}{\text{percentage change in price}}$$

This can be abbreviated to:

$$PES = \frac{\%\Delta QS}{\%\Delta P}$$

For example, the price of a product may rise from £5 to £7, causing an extension in supply from 800 to 1,000. This means that:

$$PES = \frac{25\%}{20\%} = 1.25$$

In most cases, price and supply are directly related so price elasticity of supply is positive. Economists usually concentrate on the responsiveness of supply to a change in price, so price elasticity of supply is often referred to as just elasticity of supply.

Activity 1

In the following cases calculate the price elasticity of supply, if appropriate to two decimal places:

a The price of a product falls from 60p to 40p causing supply to contract from 120 to 100.

b A product's price is reduced from $45 to $40. As a result supply falls from 6,000 to 5,000.

c The price of a product rises from €50 to €60, causing supply to extend from 100 to 200.

d A product's price rises from £12 to £13 but supply remains unchanged at 2,000.

e Supply extends from 900 to 1,200 because of a rise in price from £10 to £11.

Degrees of price elasticity of supply

In most cases, supply is elastic or inelastic. **Elastic supply** is where a percentage change in price results in a greater percentage change in supply. The numerical value of price elasticity of supply is greater than 1 and less than infinity. Elastic supply is usually illustrated by a shallow upward sloping supply curve (see Figure 1). The rise in price from £10 to £14 causes a greater percentage extension in supply from 10 to 60.

Inelastic supply arises when the supply of a product is not responsive to a change in its price. A percentage change in price will result in a smaller percentage change in quantity supplied. The numerical value is between 0 and 1 and is illustrated by a steep upward sloping supply curve. Figure 2 shows that a rise in price from £10 to £18 causes a smaller percentage rise in supply from 20 to 30.

Unit price elasticity of supply occurs when a percentage change in price causes an equal

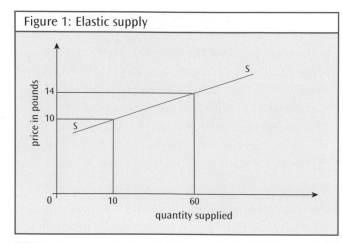

Figure 1: Elastic supply

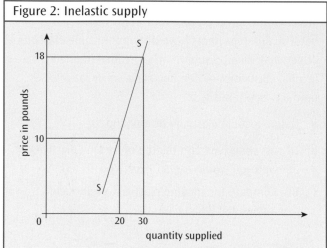

Figure 2: Inelastic supply

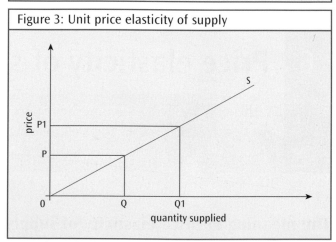

Figure 3: Unit price elasticity of supply

percentage change in quantity supplied. It gets its name from the fact that its numerical value is 1. Any straight line, such as that shown in Figure 3, which passes through the origin illustrates unit price elasticity of supply. The rise in price from P to P1 causes an equal percentage rise in supply from Q to Q1.

For a period of time some products can exhibit perfectly inelastic supply. A change in price has no effect on supply, leaving the quantity offered for sale unchanged. The numerical value is 0 and it is illustrated by a straight downward sloping supply curve (see Figure 4 (a)). Here the rise in price from P to P1 has no effect on supply, which remains at Q.

Perfectly elastic supply occurs in markets with a high level of competition. A change in price will cause an infinite change in supply. For example, if one of the many suppliers of copper raises its price, it is likely to lose all its customers. The numerical value of perfectly elastic supply is infinity (see Figure 4 (b)). At a price of P the firm is willing to sell any quantity, for example Q or Q1, but a change in price will cause an infinite change in the quantity supplied.

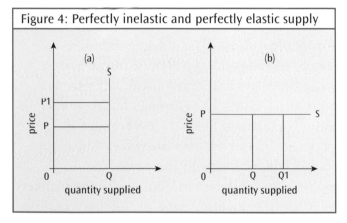

Figure 4: Perfectly inelastic and perfectly elastic supply

Activity 2

Decide in the case of each of your answers to Activity 1 whether supply is elastic, inelastic, unity, perfectly inelastic or perfectly elastic.

Influences on price elasticity of supply

The main influence on price elasticity of supply is the extent to which resources are flexible and mobile. If it is possible to adjust the production of a product quickly and easily, and/or products can be moved in and out of storage easily, supply will be elastic. If it is not possible to alter production and adjust stocks quickly and easily when price alters, supply will be inelastic.

Various factors influence the ability to adjust supply and so determine price elasticity of supply.

■ If resources can be used for a number of purposes supply will be elastic. If the price of one product rises, resources can be moved from making another product to making the one that has risen in price.

■ The level of capacity in the industry concerned. If the industry is working with spare capacity, in the form of underemployed workers and underused or unused machines and factory or office space, it should be easy to adjust supply. This will make supply elastic.

■ The level of employment. When unemployment is low, it can be difficult to recruit new workers. Firms will have problems in responding to a rise in price by extending supply, so supply will be inelastic.

■ The time it takes to produce the product. The supply of pens, for example, is much more elastic than the supply of oil tankers. It takes a few seconds to produce a pen but several years to construct an oil tanker. If the price of pens rises, given some spare capacity, more pens can be produced quickly. In contrast, it is difficult to adjust the supply of oil tankers quickly in response to a change in price. If the price fell there would be problems in stopping the construction of a tanker, and extending the supply following a price rise would take a considerable time.

■ The nature of the product also influences the length of the production period. This is why agricultural products generally have more inelastic supply than manufactured products. For example, it would be difficult to supply significantly more beef in the short run because more cattle would have to be bred and given time to mature. Similarly, it takes years for newly planted rubber trees to reach maturity.

Price elasticity of supply is also influenced by whether the product can be stored or not. For example, the supply of tinned carrots is elastic. If their price falls, some cans can be moved into storage, and if price rises, some can be taken out of storage. The supply of fresh carrots is more inelastic. Because they are perishable, they cannot be stored. Some services are perishable. For example, if a seat on an aeroplane is not sold today, that sale is lost forever.

The supply of products is more elastic in the long run. This is because there is more time for firms to alter their productive capacity, either increasing or reducing it. For example, if airline seats are not sold, their price will fall. In the very short run the supply will be perfectly inelastic. The planes will fly with some seats empty. After a short period the airline may keep some planes idle and in the longer run fewer or smaller planes will be operated.

Activity 3

Decide in each of the following cases whether supply is likely to be elastic or inelastic:

a pork

b paper clips

c fresh strawberries

d ties

e tinned peas

f aeroplanes

The significance of price elasticity of supply

Firms have a profit incentive to make their supply as elastic as possible. They want to respond to a price rise that they think will last by selling more of the product. This will raise their revenue. It will also raise their profits, provided they keep their unit costs the same or reduce

them as a result of being able to take greater advantage of economies of scale. In contrast, they want to move resources away from making products whose prices are falling. Failure to do so is likely to result in losses.

To increase the elasticity of supply of their products, firms seek to keep their resources flexible and to keep appropriate stock levels, but these can be difficult to estimate. High stocks can impose costs of storage and low stocks can reduce the elasticity of supply and result in dissatisfied customers. Some products cannot be stored and some resources are immobile. It can be difficult to retrain some workers and some capital goods, such as nuclear power stations, do not have an alternative use.

Current issue: governments and elasticity of supply

Governments seek to increase the elasticity of supply of products. The quicker and more fully supply can respond to a change in price, the more the allocation of resources will reflect consumers' tastes. For example, if duvets become more popular and blankets less popular, the price of duvets should rise and the price of blankets should fall. This should encourage the reallocation of resources from producing blankets to producing duvets.

To increase the responsiveness of supply to changes in price, governments attempt to raise the mobility and flexibility of resources. The measures they use include encouragement and provision of training for workers and provision of information about markets.

Nevertheless, the lack of mobility and flexibility of resources continues to cause problems. For example, despite falling prices the UK continued to produce relatively high quantities of steel and coal in the 1980s. In 2001, there was a shortage of teachers in the UK and there were some unemployed former bank workers.

Summary

In this unit you have learned that:

■ **Price elasticity of supply** is a measure of the responsiveness of supply to a change in price.

■ The formula for price elasticity of supply is:

$$PES = \frac{\Delta QS}{\Delta P}$$

■ Most products have either elastic or inelastic supply. **Elastic supply** means that a percentage change in price causes a greater percentage change in quantity supplied. **Inelastic supply** occurs when a percentage change in price causes a smaller percentage change in quantity supplied.

■ The main influences on price elasticity of supply are the flexibility and mobility of resources and the ability, or otherwise, to store products. These in turn are influenced by the level of capacity in the industry, the level of employment in the country, the production time, whether the product is agricultural or manufactured and the perishability of the product.

■ To earn high profits firms seek to achieve a high degree of price elasticity of supply.

■ Governments seek to promote price elasticity of supply in order to ensure an efficient allocation of resources.

Multiple choice questions

1 What does price elasticity of supply measure?
A the responsiveness of supply to changes in demand
B the responsiveness of supply to changes in price
C the percentage change in price divided by the percentage change in supply
D the percentage change in the supply of one product divided by the percentage change in the supply of another product

2 The price of a product falls from €50 to €40. As a result supply contracts from 200 to 168. What is the product's elasticity of supply?
A 0.16
B 0.2
C 0.8
D 1.25

3 Supply of a product will be more inelastic:
A the shorter the production period is
B the longer the time period under consideration
C the more stock firms in the industry hold
D the more difficult it is for firms to enter or leave the industry

4 Figure 5 shows a straight line supply curve which passes through the origin. What price elasticity of supply does it have?
A elastic
B inelastic
C infinity
D unity

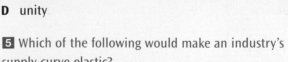

Figure 5

5 Which of the following would make an industry's supply curve elastic?
A firms use highly skilled workers
B firms have spare capacity
C the product produced is a luxury item
D the product produced takes up a large part of consumers' income

6 The price elasticity of supply of a product is 0.8. Its price is initially £10 and 2,000 units are sold. If its price rises to £20, what will be the new quantity supplied?
A 400
B 1,200
C 2,800
D 3,600

Data response question: the price elasticity of supply of gold

The price of gold fluctuates considerably, but over the past 20 years its value has been on a downward trend. It reached its peak in 1980 when gold was sold at $850 an ounce. At the start of 2001 its price was $290 an ounce, and by June it had fallen to $250 an ounce. The supply of gold to the world's bullion markets fell by 2%. AngloGold, the world's biggest gold-mining firm, sold off two mines and closed a shaft in South Africa in a bid to cut its costs and make its operations viable in the long run. There was an upturn in gold prices in the second half of 2001 as increasingly uncertain political and economic conditions encouraged some speculators to buy gold. Nevertheless, analysts remained concerned about the future of gold prices.

Purchasers of gold include not only speculators but also coin makers, jewellers, the electronics sector and central banks, which keep gold in their reserves. During 2000 demand for gold fell by over 200 tonnes to 3,946 tonnes, largely as a result of a collapse in demand from coin makers.

a Define price elasticity of supply. [2]

b **i** Estimate the price elasticity of supply of gold in the first half of 2001. [2]

   ii Comment on your findings. [3]

c Identify three causes of a change in the supply of gold. [3]

d Explain why the supply of gold is slow to respond to changes in price. [4]

e **i** Explain the type and degree of income elasticity of demand you would expect gold to have. [4]

   ii Explain the type of cross elasticity of demand you would expect to find between gold and silver. [2]

7 Market price and output

Why are some products more expensive than others? This unit seeks to answer this question. You will consider how prices and output are determined. You will then explore what happens if demand and supply are not equal and consider why the prices of products differ.

Determinants of market price and output

When there is no government intervention, the price and output of a product are determined by the demand of consumers and the supply of producers. The **equilibrium price** and output exist where demand and supply are equal. The equilibrium price is also sometimes referred to as the market clearing price, because at the equilibrium price the quantity that consumers want to buy equals the quantity that producers want to sell. There are no unsold products and no unsatisfied demand. So there is no reason why price should change.

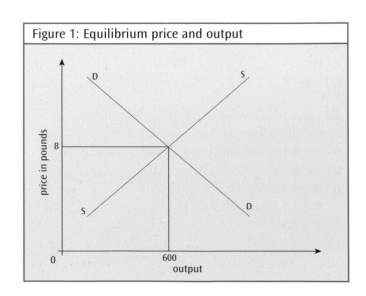

Figure 1: Equilibrium price and output

Figure 1 shows that the equilibrium price of a product is £8. At this price demand and supply are equal, giving an **equilibrium output** of 600.

Activity 1

The schedule (Table 1) shows the demand and supply of a product. Calculate:

a the equilibrium price

b the equilibrium output

Table 1		
Price $	Quantity demanded	Quantity supplied
1	100	5
2	95	35
3	85	50
4	70	70
5	50	100
6	20	140

Market forces and equilibrium price

Markets are not always in equilibrium. When demand and supply are not equal, markets are in **disequilibrium**. Market forces, however, should move price to its equilibrium level.

If the price is initially set too high, supply (QS) will exceed demand (QD) as shown in Figure 2. There are unsold stocks of QD – QS.

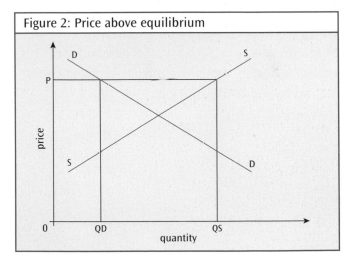
Figure 2: Price above equilibrium

In this situation producers will have to lower their price in order to sell their output. As price falls the quantity demanded will extend and the quantity supplied will contract. This fall in price

will continue until the price level is reached at which demand and supply are equal. In Figure 3 this is at a price of P1.

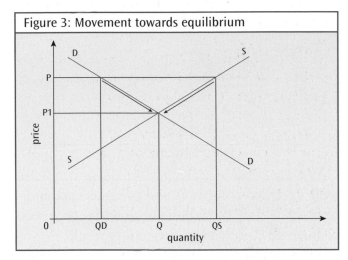
Figure 3: Movement towards equilibrium

A market experiencing such downward pressure on price is sometimes known as a buyers' market.

Market forces should also move the price back to the equilibrium level if price is initially too low. In this case, sometimes known as a sellers' market, the quantity demanded exceeds the quantity supplied. This is shown in Figure 4.

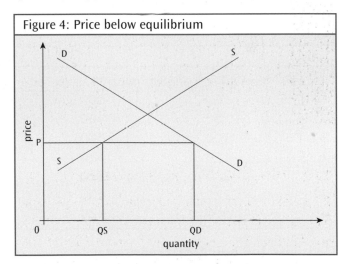
Figure 4: Price below equilibrium

The shortage, illustrated by the distance QS – QD, will push the price up to P1 as consumers compete with each other to buy the product. Figure 5 shows that as price rises the quantity demanded contracts and the quantity supplied extends to Q.

How smoothly and how quickly price moves to the equilibrium level is influenced by how

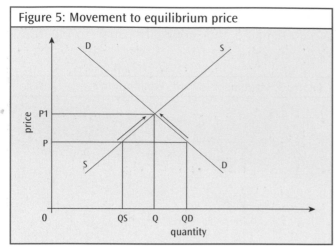

Figure 5: Movement to equilibrium price

well-informed consumers and producers are and how easily they can adjust the quantity they seek to buy and the quantity they offer for sale.

Activity 2

The schedule (Table 2) shows the demand and supply of a product. Calculate:

a the shortage of the product if price is €5

b the amount by which demand will contract if price rises from €5 to the equilibrium level

c the amount by which supply will extend if price rises from €5 to the equilibrium level

Table 2

Price €	Quantity demanded	Quantity supplied
10	20	500
9	50	450
8	100	390
7	160	320
6	220	220
5	270	100
4	300	20

Reasons for price differences

Market forces are a significant factor in explaining the differences in price between different products and factors of production. Products and resources that have a high demand relative to their supply usually have a high price and those with a low demand relative to their supply usually have a low price.

Mobile phones have become cheaper in recent years because advances in technology have reduced the cost of producing them. So the supply of mobile phones has increased at a greater rate than demand. In contrast, demand for rail travel in the UK has been increasing more rapidly than supply. This increasing demand has enabled train companies to raise their prices.

Current issue: demand for football match tickets

The popularity of Manchester United Football Club has significantly increased demand for tickets to watch matches at the club's ground, Old Trafford. For most games, demand exceeds supply, so many supporters are unable to buy tickets. This excess demand has meant that the club has been able to raise ticket prices. But this has not restored equilibrium, and demand is still greater than supply. The club could raise prices further and/or seek to provide more seats by either enlarging its current ground or building a new, larger stadium.

A football club, or any other business, has to consider not only current but also future demand. If it overestimates future demand it will supply too much, which may drive price down. Oxford United's new stadium, the Kassim Stadium, was completed just as demand for tickets fell with the club's relegation from the second to the third division.

Summary

In this unit you have learned that:

■ In a market without government intervention, price and output are determined by demand and supply.

■ **Equilibrium price** is where demand and supply are equal.

■ If price is initially above the equilibrium the excess supply will push the price down to the equilibrium level.

■ If price is below the equilibrium level the excess demand will push the price up to the equilibrium level.

■ Price is high when demand is high relative to supply.

■ Price is low when supply is high relative to demand.

Multiple choice questions

1 Equilibrium price is the price at which:
A the number of consumers is equal to the number of suppliers
B consumer surplus is maximised
C stock levels are minimised
D the quantity demanded is equal to the quantity supplied

2 If demand exceeds supply, what will happen to price and output?

	Price	Output
A	rise	rise
B	rise	fall
C	fall	fall
D	fall	rise

3 Price is initially set above the equilibrium and then falls towards the equilibrium level. During this fall what is happening to demand and supply?

	Demand	Supply
A	contracts	extends
B	contracts	contracts
C	extends	contracts
D	extends	extends

4 If price is initially set below the equilibrium price, what will happen?
A price will be pushed down even lower
B stocks of unsold products will rise
C some consumer demand will be unsatisfied
D more firms will enter the industry

5 Disequilibrium occurs in a market when:
A price is unchanged
B price is high
C the market clears
D demand and supply are not equal

6 Figure 6 shows the demand and supply for a product. What price would give rise to unsold stocks of 22,000?
A $10
B $20
C $30
D $40

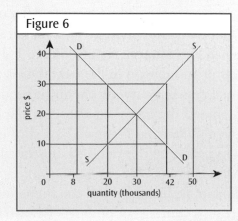
Figure 6

91

Data response question: cardamom production

India is the world's second largest producer and exporter of small cardamom, an aromatic spice. Demand comes from the country's inhabitants and from dealers in Saudi Arabia, Bangladesh, the UK and Japan, among other countries.

In November 2001 the country's producers faced a high demand, largely because of the approach of the Eid festival, which marks the end of the Ramadan fast. India's producers experienced problems meeting the demand, mainly because of a lack of rain during the growing season. The crop fell to 9,000 tonnes, 1,500 tonnes less than the previous year. Demand was approximately

10,500 tonnes in 2001. To satisfy this the producers took 900 tonnes out of their stocks. This left hardly any stocks.

a Using a diagram, explain the state of the market for Indian cardamon in 2001. [9]

b Explain what you expect would have happened to the price of cardamon in December 2001. [4]

c Identify three factors that could cause an increase in the supply of cardamon. [3]

d Explain what you would expect to happen to the level of stocks Indian cardamon sellers will decide to keep in the future. [4]

8 Changes in price and output

In this unit you will examine the impact on price and output of changes in demand and supply. You will discover why the prices of some products fluctuate more than the prices of others.

Changes in demand

Equilibrium prices and output change frequently because demand and supply change frequently. Economists predict that, in the **short run**, an increase in demand for a product will cause its price to rise, provided that other influences on the market do not change. This higher price will cause an extension in supply. Figure 1 shows the effects of an increase in demand. DD is the original demand curve, P the initial equilibrium price and Q the initial equilibrium output. The increase in demand is shown by a shift of the demand curve to the right, as illustrated by the demand curve, D1D1.

The immediate effect of the higher demand is to create a shortage of products (shown by the dotted line) at the initial equilibrium price of P. This pushes up the price to P1. The higher price

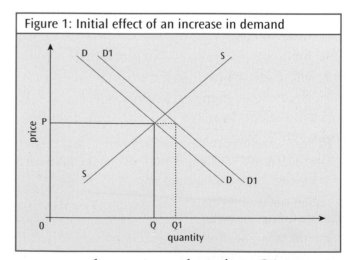

Figure 1: Initial effect of an increase in demand

encourages firms to extend supply to Q1 (see Figure 2).

So an increase in demand is expected to raise price and cause an extension in supply. In contrast, a decrease in demand is expected to lower price and cause a contraction in supply.

Figure 3 shows that the immediate effect of a decrease in demand from DD to D1D1 is to cause a surplus at the equilibrium price (equal to the horizontal distance line between the two demand curves).

The excess supply will cause firms to lower the price to P1 in order to clear their stocks. The lower price will cause supply to contract from Q to Q1 (see Figure 2).

Activity 1

As Christmas approaches, demand for gift-wrapping paper increases.

a Draw a demand and supply diagram to illustrate the effect of this change in demand on the market for wrapping paper.

b Explain what will happen to the price of gift wrapping paper and why.

c Explain what will happen to the supply of gift wrapping paper.

Changes in supply

Economists also make predictions about what will happen when supply conditions change. They expect that in the short run, other things being equal (**ceteris paribus**), an increase in supply will lower the price of a product and cause an extension in its demand. Figure 4 illustrates the immediate effect of an increase in supply. The supply curve shifts to the right from SS to S1S1. This creates a surplus (shown by the dotted line) at the equilibrium price P.

The surplus or excess supply will force prices down to P1. This will lead to an extension in demand. The short run outcome is shown in Figure 5.

A decrease in supply will also have an immediate and short run effect. Initially, a fall in supply from SS to S1S1 will result in excess demand (equal to the horizontal distance between the supply curves), as shown in Figure 6.

The shortage of products at the initial equilibrium price will cause price to rise to P1. The higher price causes demand to contract and market equilibrium to be restored (see Figure 5).

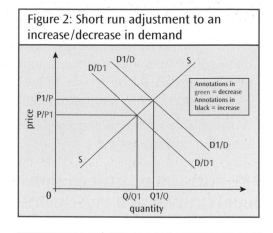

Figure 2: Short run adjustment to an increase/decrease in demand

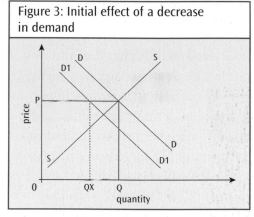

Figure 3: Initial effect of a decrease in demand

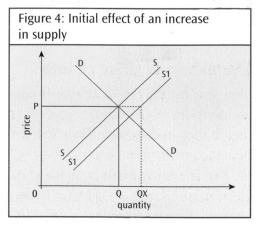

Figure 4: Initial effect of an increase in supply

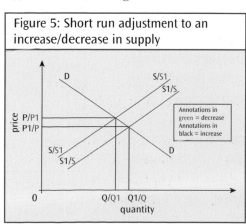

Figure 5: Short run adjustment to an increase/decrease in supply

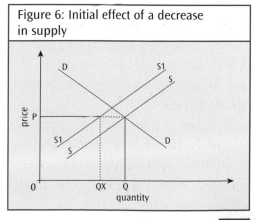

Figure 6: Initial effect of a decrease in supply

Activity 2

Over the last 30 years, stocks of cod in the North Sea have declined by more than two-thirds. In the 1970s there were approximately 1 million tonnes of cod, but by 2001 the number had fallen to 290,000 tonnes.

Draw a diagram to show the likely effect of the decline in cod stocks on the market for cod.

The distinction between shifts in demand and supply curves and movements along the curves

In analysing changes in market prices, it is important to consider what has caused the change in price. For example, if there has been an increase in demand, a higher price will be associated with higher demand. But if the cause of the price rise is a decrease in supply, a higher price will be associated with lower demand. So it is important to recognise the cause of the change in price and the order of events, and to use unambiguous terms. An economist reading a report stating that supply has increased, price has fallen and demand has extended will recognise certain key points. These are that a change in an influence on supply other than a change in price of the product shifted the supply curve to the right and pushed the price down. Demand has risen in response to the lower price, as shown by a movement along the demand curve.

The extent of price changes

How much the price of a product rises or falls when conditions of either demand or supply alter depends crucially on the size of the change in demand or supply and the price elasticities of demand and supply.

The greater the extent to which demand or supply conditions change, the greater is the impact on price. Price elasticities of demand and supply also play a key role in determining the outcome of demand and supply changes.

For example, if demand is elastic, an increase in supply will cause a relatively small fall in price and a greater percentage change in quantity demanded. In this case total revenue will rise. Figure 7 shows the effect of an increase in supply when demand is elastic.

If demand is inelastic, an increase in supply will cause a relatively large fall in price and a smaller percentage change in quantity demanded. In this case total revenue will fall. Figure 8 shows the effect of an increase in supply in a market where demand is inelastic.

Activity 3

In each case decide whether the change in the market described would have been caused by (i) an increase in demand, (ii) a decrease in demand, (iii) an increase in supply or (iv) a decrease in supply:

a   the price of a product rises and the quantity bought and sold rises.

b   the price of a product falls and the quantity bought and sold rises.

c   the price of a product falls and the quantity bought and sold falls.

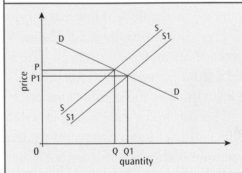

Figure 7: Increase in supply in a market with elastic demand

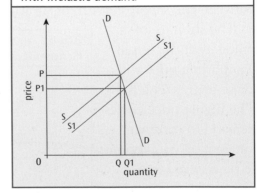

Figure 8: Increase in supply in a market with inelastic demand

If supply is elastic, an increase in demand will cause a relatively small rise in price and a greater percentage change in quantity supplied (see Figure 9).

If supply is inelastic, an increase in demand will cause a relatively large rise in price and a smaller percentage change in the quantity supplied (see Figure 10).

In markets where both demand and supply are inelastic, a shift in demand and/or supply will have a significant effect on price but not much impact on quantity. Figure 11 illustrates the effect of a decrease in supply.

In markets where both demand and supply are elastic, a change in demand and/or supply will have a significant impact on output but only a small impact on the equilibrium price. Figure 12 shows the effect of a decrease in supply.

Prices of primary products, also known as **commodities**, fluctuate more than prices of manufactured products because they experience larger shifts in demand and particularly supply, and demand and supply are generally more inelastic. For example, the supply of agricultural products can be reduced by disease or bad weather and the supply of minerals increased by new discoveries or changes in methods of extraction.

Current issues: production of primary products

Developing countries are major producers of primary products. Fluctuations in the prices of primary products have caused economic instability in these countries, so schemes have been set up to create price stability. Most of these seek to control the supply of these products by creating **buffer stocks**. Buffer stock managers buy the product when the market price is low and sell when price is high. The aim is to smooth out price changes and give producers more stable incomes. However, buffer stocks face major problems. In 2001, for example, the Association of Coffee Producing Countries gave up its struggle against low coffee prices and closed down.

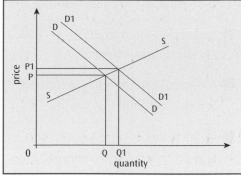

Figure 9: Increase in demand in a market with elastic supply

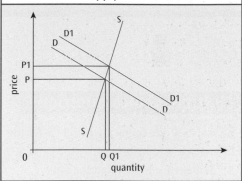

Figure 10: Increase in demand in a market with inelastic supply

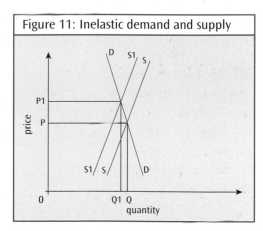

Figure 11: Inelastic demand and supply

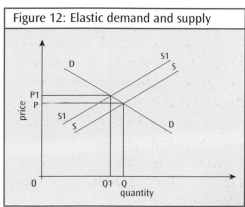

Figure 12: Elastic demand and supply

Activity 4

Between 1991 and 2001, favourable weather conditions and a rise in the number of coffee producers caused the supply of coffee to world markets to increase by 15% .

a Draw a diagram to show the effect of this rise in supply on the market for coffee.

b Discuss what effect the rise in supply is likely to have had on the revenue of coffee producers.

Summary

In this unit you have learned that:

- An increase in demand will cause a rise in price and an extension in supply.

- A decrease in demand will cause a fall in price and a contraction in supply.

- An increase in supply will result in a fall in price and an extension in demand.

- A decrease in supply will cause a rise in price and a contraction in demand.

- The more elastic demand and supply are the more a change in demand and/or supply will affect quantity rather than price.

- The more inelastic demand and supply are the more a change in demand and/or supply will affect price rather than quantity.

- The prices of primary products fluctuate more than the prices of manufactured products.

Multiple choice questions

1 Which of the following could cause the supply of milk to increase and its price to fall?

A   an increase in demand for milk
B   a subsidy given to diary farmers
C   a fall in the productivity of farm workers
D   a rise in the profitability of arable production

2 Which of the following could have caused the fall in the price of restaurant meals illustrated in Figure 13?

A   a reduction in the cost of food used to produce restaurant meals
B   a cut in the price of theatre and cinema tickets
C   a fall in incomes
D   a rise in the wages of restaurant workers

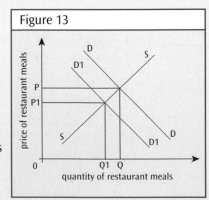

Figure 13

3 Which combination of events could cause the equilibrium price of eggs to change from X to Y (see Figure 14)?

A   a fall in the price of bacon and a subsidy given to chicken producers
B   a disease affecting chickens and a fall in population size

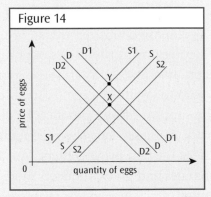

Figure 14

C   a report stating that eating eggs is beneficial to health and an increase in the price of chicken feed
D   an increase in the number of chicken farmers and a successful advertising campaign for eggs

Multiple choice questions continued

4 What would be the effect on the price and output of apples of a rise in the price of oranges?

	Price	Output
A	rise	fall
B	rise	rise
C	fall	rise
D	fall	fall

5 What effect will a 5% increase in both demand and supply have on price and the quantity bought and sold?

A increase both price and the quantity bought and sold

B increase price but reduce the quantity bought and sold

C leave price unchanged but increase the quantity bought and sold

D reduce both price and the quantity bought and sold

6 The market is initially in equilibrium at point X (see Figure 15). Incomes rise and advances in technology reduce the cost of producing washing machines. What will the new equilibrium position be as a result of these changes?

A   B   C   D

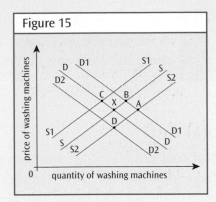

Figure 15

Data response question: the PC market

In 2001 there was the first worldwide decline in the sales of personal computers. Individual customers started to wait for significant new developments in software before buying a new machine and companies were upgrading less frequently.

The five biggest PC makers laid off thousands of employers because of the increasing need to stay price competitive. In the past, computer makers themselves offered innovations such as portable and then notebook-sized PCs portable and added accessories such as modems. By 2001 the computer makers were leaving much of the important technology to software and chip giants such as Microsoft and Intel, which were increasingly just refining existing technology rather than developing anything new. For example, Windows XP, launched in 2001, was able to handle digital photos, music and movies, but many people already had these facilities through add-on software and services.

The absence of new breakthroughs meant that firms were waiting an average of more than four years to buy new PCs. In the 1990s the average waiting period was three years.

Individual customers already had enough for sending email and cruising internet retailers. There were also fewer first-time buyers.

Source: Adapted from 'Time to reboot: PC makers say farewell to 15-year boom', by Don Clark and Rebecca Buckman, *Wall Street Journal Europe*, 24 August 2001.

a **i** Using a demand and supply diagram, explain what happened to sales of PCs in 2001. [4]

ii Explain the likely effect of these market changes on the price of PCs. [2]

b Using a demand and supply diagram in each case, explain the effect on the market for PCs of:

i the development of a new PC with substantial new features [4]

ii a significant improvement in technology involved in producing PCs [4]

c Discuss whether individuals' price elasticity of demand for PCs is likely to be higher or lower that that of firms. [4]

9 Costs of production

In the previous unit you examined how changes in demand and supply affect price and quantity. A significant cause of a shift in the supply curve is a change in the costs of production. In this unit you will examine **total**, **average** and **marginal costs** and distinguish between **short** and **long run costs**.

Total cost

Total cost (TC) is, as its name suggests, the total cost of producing a product. For example, the total cost of making a film will include the pay of the actors, cameramen and other workers, the rent of studios and equipment, and interest on loans.

As output rises, total cost rises, because more factors of production have to be employed. So as more cars are produced, for instance, the total cost rises.

Average cost

Average cost (AC), also called unit cost, is the cost, on average, of producing each unit. It is found by dividing total cost by output. As output rises, average cost often falls at first as resources are used more efficiently and more specialised production methods are employed. However, once output rises beyond a certain level, average cost may increase.

Marginal cost

Marginal cost (MC) is the change in total cost when output is changed by one unit. For example, if the total cost of making 10 cars is £30,000 and the total cost of making 11 cars is £32,800, the marginal cost of the eleventh car is £2,800 (£32,800 − £30,000).

Economists and producers are particularly interested in calculating marginal cost because firms are often considering whether to alter their current output by a small amount. For example, if price rises, producers will have to decide by how much they are willing and able to extend supply.

When a firm expands its output its marginal cost often falls at first as the firm's resources work more efficiently, but after a certain level of output is reached, marginal cost may

Activity 1

In 2001 Tesco, a supermarket chain, increased the volume of its sales by opening new branches.

Identify three of Tesco's costs which would have risen in 2001.

Activity 2

Using the information in Table 1 below, calculate the average cost of producing 1, 2, 3, 4 and 5 units.

Table 1	
No. of units	Total cost (£)
1	100
2	180
3	240
4	280
5	400

Table 2: Marginal cost		
Output (no. of units)	Total cost (£)	Marginal cost (£)
1	80	
2	150	70
3	210	60
4	260	50
5	320	60
6	390	70

begin to rise. Table 2 shows how marginal cost alters as a firm expands its output.

The relationship between marginal and average costs

Changes in marginal costs influence average costs. A fall in marginal cost will lower average cost. For example, when four units are produced the total cost may be £36. The marginal cost of producing an extra unit may be £4. This would give an average cost of £8 at five units of output (£40/8). If marginal cost falls to £2 when six units are produced, average cost will be reduced to £7 (£42/6).

A rise in marginal cost will push up average cost. So if the marginal cost of producing a seventh unit increases to £3.50, average cost will rise to £6.50 (£45.50/7).

This relationship between the marginal and average applies in everyday life. So, for instance, the average height of a group of people in a room will be lowered by the arrival of someone shorter than the average. Similarly, the average earnings of a firm's workers will rise if the last worker employed is paid more than the previous average.

Short and long run costs

In analysing costs, economists distinguish between short run and long run costs. **Short run costs** are the costs incurred when there is not enough time to change the quantity of at least one factor of production. For example, in the short run it may be possible to change the quantity of labour and raw materials used, but there may not be sufficient time to change the size of the factory, office or farm. **Long run costs** are the costs experienced over a period of time when it is possible to change all the factors of production.

Activity 3

From the following information in Table 3, calculate the marginal cost.

Table 3	
Output (no. of units)	Total cost (£)
1	30
2	45
3	55
4	60
5	70

Activity 4

From the information in Table 4:

a calculate average and marginal costs

b identify where marginal cost is in relation to average cost when:
  i average cost is falling
  ii average cost is rising

Table 4	
Output (no. of units)	Total cost (£)
1	50
2	90
3	120
4	140
5	200
6	270

Activity 5

A clothes shop in a town experiences a significant rise in demand which the two owners believe will last. Initially, they open the shop for an extra two hours each weekday and for four hours on Sunday. After six months of continuing high demand, the owners decide to move into new, larger premises.

Identify two costs which will rise:

a in the short run

b in the long run

Fixed and variable costs

Short run costs can be divided into fixed and variable costs. **Fixed costs** (FC) can also be called indirect costs or overheads. As the name suggests these costs are fixed in the short run. They do not change as output changes and have to be paid even when output is zero. For example, if a factory is closed over Christmas and so does not produce anything, its owners will still have to pay rent on its premises, business rates to the government, interest on past loans, and wages to its permanent workers on long-term contracts.

Variable costs (VC) include the cost of raw materials, fuel and power, overtime payments, the pay of workers on short-term contracts and transport costs. Variable costs are also called direct costs because they are directly related to the amount produced.

It is possible to estimate variable costs if the total cost at different levels of output including at zero output is known. For example, in Table 5 the value of the fixed costs can be identified by examining the costs that the firm incurs when output is zero, in this case £200 a week. The fixed costs including, for instance, rent and insurance will stay constant at £200 as output rises. Variable costs can be found by subtracting fixed costs from total cost.

Table 5: Variable costs			
Output (no. of units)	Total cost (£)	Fixed costs (£)	Variable costs (£)
0	200	200	–
1	600	200	400
2	1,100	200	900
3	1,500	200	1,300
4	1,800	200	1,600
5	2,200	200	2,000
6	2,800	200	2,600

As Table 5 shows, fixed costs plus variable costs equal total cost, and total cost minus variable costs equals fixed costs.

Activity 6

Decide whether the following costs incurred by an airline company are fixed or variable:

a the cost of food used to prepare in-flight meals

b aircraft maintenance costs

c the rent of hangers

d pensions paid to former employees

e fuel

Short run marginal, average and total costs

In the short run, marginal cost usually falls at first as output rises because the variable resources can be combined in more productive combinations. The resulting rise in efficiency is sometimes referred to as **increasing returns**. However, after a certain level of output is reached, output may rise more slowly than the volume of variable resources and so marginal cost will rise. This is sometimes known as **diminishing returns**.

Increasing and diminishing returns can be illustrated by examining a car repair shop. It initially employs five mechanics. The average waiting time for customers to have their car serviced is four hours. If demand is high, the shop may employ an extra mechanic. This enables the staff to work more efficiently and so reduces the waiting time by ten minutes. As more people are employed the mechanics are able to specialise more and to work in teams. This lowers waiting time and improves the quality of the service further. However, once a certain level of employment is reached, the workers take longer to service cars and the quality of their work falls because they have to wait to use a fixed quantity of tools, equipment and workshop space. Marginal cost will rise because the combination of workers, equipment and workshop space is not efficient.

Short run average costs also fall and then rise as output expands. This is because as more variable resources are employed they can initially be used in a more efficient and specialised way, but after a certain point is reached the combination of resources will become inefficient. Average costs also fall at first because fixed costs are spread over a higher number of units.

If marginal and average costs fall as output expands and then rise, the marginal and average cost curves will be U-shaped. The marginal cost curve is initially below the average cost curve, as falling marginal cost reduces average cost. The marginal cost curve cuts the average cost curve at its lowest point and then rises above it as the higher marginal cost pulls up average cost. The shape and relationship between the marginal and average cost curves are shown in Figure 1. The lowest point on the average cost curve is sometimes referred to as the **optimum output.**

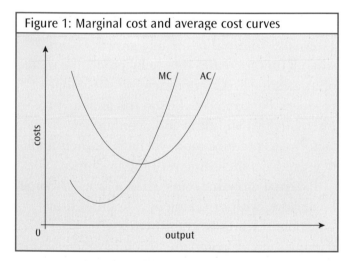

Figure 1: Marginal cost and average cost curves

When output is zero, total cost will not be zero as there will be some fixed costs. In Figure 2 fixed costs are £10,000. When output expands, total cost increases as variable costs rise with, for example, the use of more raw materials and fuel. However, because returns first increase and then diminish, total cost rises slowly and then more quickly. This is illustrated in Figure 2, which also shows how short run total cost is composed of both fixed and variable costs.

At 5,000 units the total cost is £25,000, consisting of £15,000 variable costs and £10,000 fixed costs.

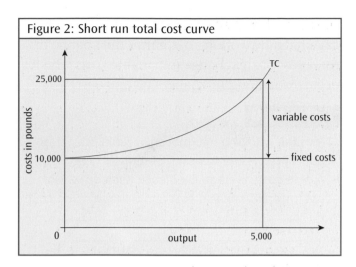

Figure 2: Short run total cost curve

Activity 7

During the Christmas period, the Post Office takes on extra staff and hires extra vehicles to cope with the Christmas rush.

a   Identify what will happen to the Post Office's total cost.

b   Explain what may happen to the Post Office's average cost.

c   Identify a fixed factor of production the Post Office is likely to have at this period.

Average fixed and variable costs and marginal fixed and variable costs

Average fixed cost (AFC) is fixed cost divided by output. For example, if the fixed cost of producing ten units is £200, the average fixed cost is £20. As fixed cost remains constant, average fixed cost must fall as output rises. The overheads are spread over more units.

Average variable cost (AVC) will fall if there are increasing returns and rise if there are diminishing returns. This gives the AVC curve its common U-shape. Average variable cost, as its name suggests, is variable cost divided by output.

Marginal cost is a measure of changes in total cost as output changes, so it is influenced by changes in variable costs but not fixed costs. Marginal fixed cost (MFC) is always zero as fixed costs do not change with output. So marginal cost is the same as marginal variable cost

(MVC). This means that marginal cost can be calculated by working out either the change in total cost or the change in variable costs which occurs when output changes by one unit.

Activity 8

From the following information in Table 6 on total cost, calculate the marginal cost, fixed cost, variable cost, average fixed cost, average variable cost, marginal variable cost and marginal fixed cost.

Table 6	
Output	Total cost (£)
0	60
1	140
2	240
3	270
4	280
5	450
6	660

Long run total, average and marginal costs

In the long run, all costs are variable as this is the time period when the scale of operation can be changed and the quantities of all the factors of production can be altered.

The shapes of the total, average and marginal cost curves are influenced by economies and diseconomies of scale. The long run average cost curve falls when economies of scale are dominant but rises if diseconomies of scale become dominant. In this situation the long run average cost curve will be U-shaped. In practice, it is thought that industries such as oil production, chemicals, car production and pharmaceuticals have average cost curves which slope down from left to right (see Figure 3). This is because in these industries, technical and research and development economies are so significant that they outweigh any managerial and administrative diseconomies of scale.

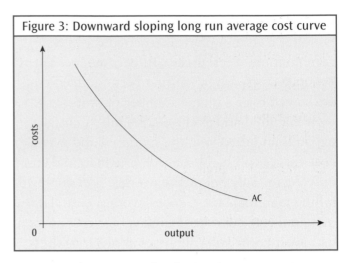

Figure 3: Downward sloping long run average cost curve

Current issue: reducing average costs

Firms are always seeking to reduce their average costs in order to increase their price competitiveness. Producers and economists disagree about whether a firm is more likely to lower its average cost by growing internally or externally. Internal or organic growth occurs when a firm increases its size by producing more of its existing product or increasing its range of products. For example, Dyson has grown internally by extending and opening new factories to produce more vacuum cleaners and new products including washing machines.

External growth occurs when a firm gets larger by merging with or taking over another firm. GlaxoSmithKline is a multinational pharmaceuticals company which has increased its size through mergers.

Internal growth enables a firm to achieve what it considers to be its optimum size, where its average cost is minimised, by moving towards a specific output. External growth can be achieved quickly but it is unlikely that the new firm will be the size at which average cost is minimised. It may be able to experience further economies of scale by getting even larger or it may have become too large. Studies have shown that average costs often rise after a merger owing to problems of co-ordination.

Summary

In this unit you have learned that:

■ **Total cost** rises with output.

■ **Average cost** and **marginal cost** may fall initially and then rise.

■ Changes in marginal cost influence changes in average cost and total cost.

■ The short run is the period of time when at least one factor of production is fixed. The long run is the period when all factors of production are variable.

■ In the short run, costs can be divided into **fixed** and **variable costs**.

■ Short run marginal, average and total costs are influenced by increasing and diminishing returns.

■ Marginal cost is below average cost when marginal cost is falling and above it when average cost is rising. The marginal cost curve cuts the average cost curve at its lowest point.

■ **Average fixed cost** has to fall with output as fixed costs are spread over more units.

■ Long run marginal, average and total costs are influenced by economies and diseconomies of scale.

Multiple choice questions

1 Marginal cost is:
A the change in total cost when output changes by one unit
B the change in total cost when one more worker is employed
C total cost divided by output
D total cost divided by price

2 Which of the following is a variable cost?
A insurance
B pensions
C raw materials
D rent

3 A firm's fixed costs total £2,400. The average cost of its output is £10 and the average variable cost is £6. What is the firm's total output?
A 150 units
B 240 units
C 400 units
D 600 units

4 Table 7 shows a firm's total cost at different units of output. What is the average fixed cost of producing six units of output?
A £2
B £10
C £12
D £60

Table 7	
Output (units)	Total cost (£)
0	12
1	22
2	30
3	36
4	40
5	48
6	60

5 When average cost is increasing:
A average cost must equal marginal cost
B average cost must be greater than marginal cost
C marginal cost must be greater than average cost
D marginal cost must be falling

6 The short run is the period of time when:
A at least one factor of production is fixed
B all factors of production are fixed
C it is not possible to increase output
D it is not possible to alter costs of production

Data response question: profits increase at Go

Go, a low-cost airline that is now part of easyJet, experienced a 51% increase in profits to £16.9 million and a 41% increase in passengers in 2001, compared with the previous year. This resulted in more of its planes operating with full, or near full, passenger loads and some potential customers being turned away.

The rising demand, allowed Go to add extra flights on some of its routes, including between London and Belfast. It also raised its target for passenger numbers in 2002. It stated that it was planning to double passenger numbers from 2 million to 4 million. To cope with these extra numbers it intended to increase its staff by 1,000. The firm, which already had bases at Stansted and Bristol, also announced that it would open a third base in 2002

and would add at least seven more aircraft to its fleet of 18 Boeing 737s during 2003.

a Explain two causes of an increase in demand for tickets on low-cost airlines. [4]

b What would have happened to Go's total cost in 2002? [2]

c Identify one variable and one fixed cost an airline may experience. [2]

d Explain why the marginal cost of carrying one more passenger may be lower in the short run than in the long run. [6]

e Discuss what may have happened to Go's average cost in 2002. [6]

10 Revenue

In this unit you will examine the meaning of **total revenue**, **average revenue** and **marginal revenue**. You will explore the relationship between price elasticity of demand and revenue and the significance of the relationship between revenue and cost.

Total, average and marginal revenue

Total revenue is the amount received from the total amount sold. It is equal to the number of units sold multiplied by the selling price. **Average revenue** is total revenue divided by the amount sold. For example, if total revenue earned from selling 600 units is £1,800, the average revenue is £3 (£1,800/600). Average revenue is another name for price as it is equal to revenue per unit sold. **Marginal revenue** is the change in total revenue when sales are altered by one unit.

Revenues when price is unaffected by changes in a firm's output

A firm's price will remain constant as it changes the number of products it sells if its output is too small

Activity 1

A firm was selling 19 units a week and receiving £171 in revenue. Its sales rise to 20 units and its revenue to £180. Calculate:

a the average revenue received when 20 units are sold.

b The marginal revenue of the 20th unit sold.

to affect price. In this case demand for the firm's product is perfectly elastic.

The firm's marginal and average revenue will be equal and both will be constant because when the firm sells an extra unit it will receive the same price. As its price is unchanged, its total revenue will rise by constant amounts as the firm sells more units.

This relationship between average, total and marginal revenue is shown in Table 1.

Table 1: Revenues when price is constant			
Average revenue (price) £	Quantity demanded units	Total revenue £	Marginal revenue £
6	1	6	6
6	2	12	6
6	3	18	6
6	4	24	6
6	5	30	6

What happens to a firm's revenues as sales change can also be illustrated in diagrams. Figure 1 shows that the marginal revenue curve is equal to the average revenue curve and both stay constant at £6.

Note also that the average revenue curve is equivalent to the demand curve. This is because both plot the quantity demanded against different prices.

When demand is perfectly elastic, a firm's total revenue curve rises consistently with quantity as shown in Figure 2.

Activity 2

In the following case (Table 2), complete the total revenue and marginal revenue columns.

Table 2			
Average revenue (price) £	Quantity demanded units	Total revenue £	Marginal revenue £
4	1		
4	2		
4	3		
4	4		
4	5		
4	6		

Revenues when price changes with output

In most cases a firm has to lower its price in order to sell more and will experience a contraction in demand if it raises its price. Where this occurs, average and marginal revenue fall as sales rise. Initially, marginal revenue is equal to average revenue but falls below it after one unit. This is because to sell more the firm has to lower the price not just of the extra unit but also of the other units. So, for example, if a firm was originally selling four units a day for £6 its total revenue would be £24. If it decides to sell five units at £5 each, its total revenue would be £25. At five units its average revenue is £5 but its marginal revenue is £1. The decision to lower the price to £5 would result in £5 being gained from the fifth unit but a £1 being lost on each of the previous four units. This gives a net gain of £1 (£5 – £4).

Marginal revenue can even be negative. This occurs when a fall in price causes demand to rise by a smaller percentage and so total revenue falls. For example, a shop may sell ten birthday cards a

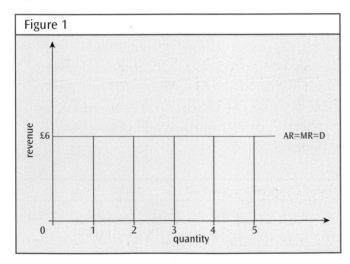

Figure 1

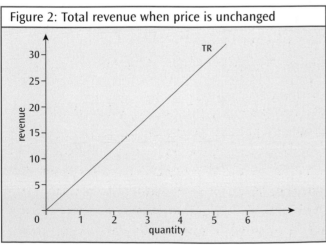

Figure 2: Total revenue when price is unchanged

day for £2 each. To raise its sales, it may cut the price of its cards to £1.70 each. If sales rise to only eleven, its total revenue will change from £20 to £18.70 and so its marginal revenue will be minus £1.30.

Figure 3 shows the relationship between average revenue and marginal revenue in a market where price varies with output.

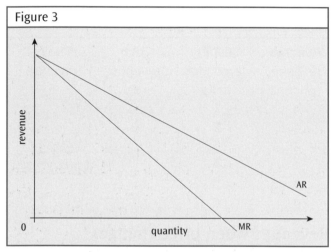

Figure 3

Total revenue usually rises initially as sales increase, but beyond the point when marginal revenue becomes negative it will fall. Table 3 shows the average revenue, total revenue and marginal revenue of a firm facing a variable price.

Table 3: Revenues when price varies			
Average revenue (price) £	Quantity demanded units	Total revenue £	Marginal revenue £
16	1	16	16
14	2	28	12
11	3	33	5
9	4	36	3
7	5	35	−1
5	6	30	−5

Price elasticity of demand and revenue

The responsiveness of demand to a change in price influences what happens to a firm's total revenue when it alters price. As it influences total revenue, price elasticity of demand also influences marginal revenue.

Activity 3

In Table 4, complete the total revenue and marginal revenue columns.

Table 4			
Average revenue (price) £	Quantity demanded units	Total revenue £	Marginal revenue £
6	1		
5	2		
4	3		
3	4		
2	5		
1	6		

When demand is elastic, a fall in price will cause a greater percentage rise in demand, so total revenue rises and marginal revenue is positive. At the point where PED becomes unity, total revenue reaches its peak and is constant and marginal revenue is zero. After this point, as sales increase demand becomes inelastic. Now the sale of an extra unit will cause total revenue to fall and so marginal revenue will be negative. Table 5 shows the relationship between average, total and marginal revenue and price elasticity of demand.

Table 5: Revenues and PED				
Average revenue (price) £	Quantity demanded units	Total revenue £	Marginal revenue £	PED
10	1	10		
			8	1
9	2	18		
			6	1
8	3	24		
			4	1
7	4	28		
			2	1
6	5	30		
			0	−1
5	6	30		
			−2	1
4	7	28		
			−4	1
3	8	24		

The relationship between revenue and price elasticity of demand can also be illustrated using diagrams. Figure 4 shows that demand becomes more inelastic as average revenue falls and the quantity demanded extends. It also shows that when demand is elastic marginal revenue is positive, when it is unity marginal revenue is zero and when it is inelastic marginal revenue is negative.

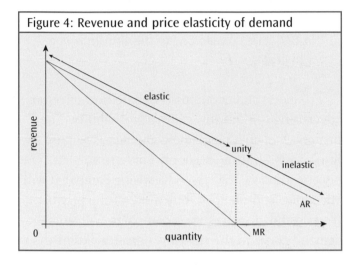

Figure 4: Revenue and price elasticity of demand

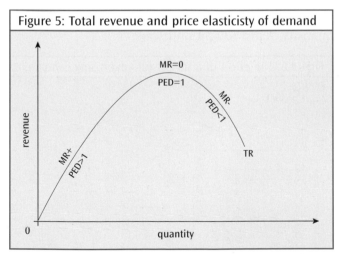

Figure 5: Total revenue and price elasticisty of demand

Figure 5 shows the relationship between total revenue and price elasticity of demand and marginal revenue.

Revenue and cost

When considering whether to change the price of their products, firms take into account the effect not only on their revenue but also on their costs. For example, a coach operator may calculate that the price elasticity of demand for

coach tickets is 3. He may currently sell 80 tickets in an hour at a price of £8 each (giving a total revenue of £640). Cutting his price to £6 would raise sales to 140 tickets and increase total revenue to £840. It would appear to be beneficial for the coach operator to implement the price reduction. However, he will also have to consider the effect of carrying more customers on his costs. If his coaches currently run with a high number of empty seats, carrying more passengers is likely to raise total costs by less than total revenue. If, however, extra coaches would have to bought or rented and extra drivers hired to cope with the rise in passengers, total costs may rise by more than total revenue. This may discourage the coach operator from cutting the price.

The relationship between revenue and cost

The relationship between revenue and cost determines whether a firm makes a profit or a loss. Economists include in costs of production a payment to entrepreneurs known as **normal profit**. This is the minimum amount that has to be received to keep a firm in the industry in the long run. If normal profit is not earned in the long run, the firm will switch its resources to the production of alternative products. When total revenue equals total cost (and so average revenue equals average cost), normal profit is earned.

If total revenue exceeds total cost, a profit greater than normal profit is earned. Economists refer to this as **supernormal profit**. If total revenue is less than total cost, a firm will experience a **loss**. This loss may mean that the firm is making less than normal profit but covering its other costs (a situation sometimes described as subnormal profit). But it may be more serious with the firm not earning enough to make any normal profit and not covering some of its other costs.

A firm will leave the industry in the long run if it cannot cover all of its costs, including normal profit. In the short run it is likely to continue to produce the product, even if it is making a loss, provided its variable costs are covered and it is covering some of its fixed costs. If it is covering its variable costs, it is paying the direct costs of production and making some contribution towards, for example, its rent and business rates. If it is closed down, it will have no revenue to pay any of its fixed costs, which it would still have to pay in the short run. If its revenue is insufficient to cover even its variable costs, it will not be able to pay for, say, raw materials and will leave the industry.

Current issue: advertising

Concerns about the slowdown in the growth of UK economic activity and the US recession caused some UK and US firms to cut their spending on advertising in 2001.

Activity 6

In November 2001 analysts were forecasting that British Airways would experience a loss of £600 million in the period March 2001 to March 2002. To try to improve its trading position, BA cut its fares.

a Explain two causes of a firm moving from earning a profit to experiencing a loss.

b Explain what would determine whether the cut in BA's fares would cause the firm to move into profit.

Producers and economists debate how effective advertising is in raising a firm's profitability. The first effect of an advertising campaign is to raise a firm's costs, shifting its supply curve to the left. The hope is, though, that the advertising campaign will encourage consumers to buy more of the product. If successful, an advertising campaign will shift the demand curve to the right by a greater extent than the decrease in supply. Figure 6 shows that a successful advertising campaign results in a greater quantity being bought and sold.

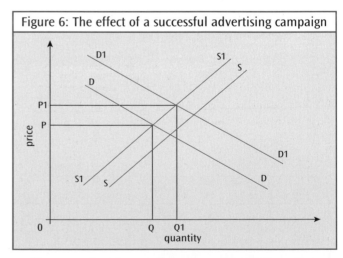

Figure 6: The effect of a successful advertising campaign

Firms undertaking advertising campaigns expect that their revenues will rise by more than their costs and so they will earn more profit. An advertising campaign may also benefit a firm by increasing brand loyalty for its product. In this case demand will become more inelastic and will give the firm greater power to raise its price and increase its revenue.

Summary

In this unit you have learned that:

- **Total revenue** is price multiplied by the number of units, **average revenue** is total revenue divided by the amount sold, and **marginal revenue** is the change in total revenue when sales are altered by one unit.

- If a firm's output does not affect price, its average revenue and marginal revenue will be equal and will be constant as its sales rise. Its total revenue will increase by constant amounts.

- In most cases, firms have to lower their prices in order to sell more. Average and marginal revenue fall as the quantity sold rises and average revenue exceeds marginal revenue.

- Total revenue rises when demand is elastic and marginal revenue is positive. It reaches its peak when demand is unity and marginal revenue is zero. It falls when demand is inelastic and marginal revenue is negative.

- If total revenue equals total cost, **normal profit** is earned.

- If total revenue exceeds total cost, **supernormal profit** is earned.

- If total revenue is less than total cost, a **loss** is made.

Multiple choice questions

1 Average revenue is equal to:

A price

B total revenue divided by price

C total revenue divided by total cost

D the change in revenue resulting from selling one more unit

2 Table 6 shows the relationship between a firm's sales and the price it obtains from each unit sold. What is the marginal revenue earned from the sixth unit sold?

A −£1.33

B −£2

C £8

D £48

Table 6	
Quantity	Price per unit (£)
1	20
2	18
3	15
4	12
5	10
6	8

3 When is total revenue maximised?

A when average revenue equals average cost

B when sales are maximised

C when marginal revenue is zero

D when total cost is minimised

4 A firm's total revenue changes from £200 to £209 when it increases its sales from 10 to 11. What is the marginal revenue?

A £9

B £19

C £20

D £209

Revenue

Multiple choice questions continued

5 The average revenue of a firm changes from £50 to £48 when its sales increase from 22 to 23. What is the marginal revenue?

A −£2

B £1

C £4

D £48

6 A firm faces perfectly elastic demand for its product. Which of the diagrams in Figure 7 illustrates its total revenue curve?

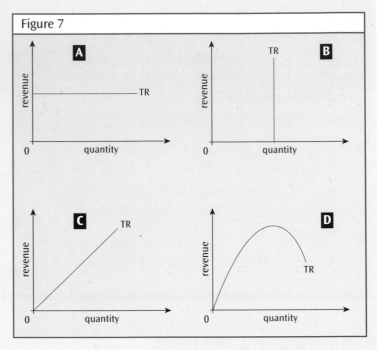

Figure 7

Data response question: reversal of fortune at Bhs

Bhs (British Home Stores), a clothes retail chain store, made a loss of £16 million in 1999. Philip Green, a retail entrepreneur, bought the company and turned its fortunes round. In 2001 it announced profits of £80 million.

The reversal in the fortunes of the company was achieved by radical cost cutting, merchandise streamlining and taking the company back to its roots. One of Mr Green's first actions was to reduce the labour force by hundreds through merging the company's two head offices. He then introduced rigorous cost controls, including checking that, given quality standards, materials are purchased from the cheapest sources.

Sales rose between 1999 and 2001 as the company refocused on its traditional market of women aged 40–55.

a What is meant by loss? [2]

b Explain why Bhs moved from earning a loss in 1999 to earning a profit in 2001. [6]

c Explain what is likely to have happened to Bhs's average cost in 2001. [3]

d Discuss what may have happened to Bhs's total revenue in 2001 as its sales increased. [6]

e Discuss one way a clothing retail chain store could seek to attract more customers. [3]

11 Market structures

The way firms behave is influenced by the **market structure** in which they operate. In this unit you will examine the main categories of market structure. You will explore their characteristics, how they compete and their advantages and disadvantages for consumers.

Market structures

In analysing how firms behave, economists examine both actual and potential competition. Actual competition is influenced by how many firms are currently in the market. Potential competition is determined by how easy it is for firms to enter and leave the market.

Economists identify four main categories of market conditions, which they call **market structure**: perfect competition, monopolistic competition, oligopoly and monopoly. Figure 1 shows that perfect competition is the most competitive market structure and monopoly the least competitive.

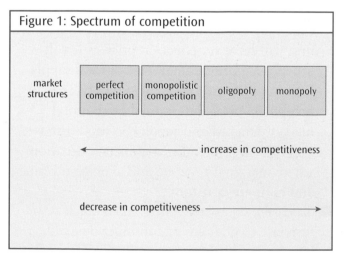

Figure 1: Spectrum of competition

market structures: perfect competition | monopolistic competition | oligopoly | monopoly

⟵ increase in competitiveness

decrease in competitiveness ⟶

The more competitive a market is, the more power consumers have; conversely, the less competitive the market, the more power producers have. Producers also have more power if there are obstacles, or barriers, to firms entering and leaving the market.

Activity 1

Identify in which market structure:

a consumers are most powerful

b producers are most powerful

Barriers to entry and exit

When there are significant barriers to entry into and exit from a market, the firm or firms in the market will have considerable market power. They will be able to raise prices without fear that new competitors will be attracted into the market by higher profits.

Barriers to entry are obstacles or restrictions which make it difficult for firms not currently making the product to start producing it. **Barriers to exit** are obstacles or restrictions which make it difficult for existing firms to stop producing the product.

Barriers to entry include the following.

■ Legal barriers, such as franchises, licenses, patents and copyrights. The Post Office has a franchise to deliver post, and television and mobile phone companies are licensed. Patents, which encourage invention and innovation, prevent other firms selling the same product for a period of time. Copyright gives people like artists, musicians and writers exclusive rights to profit from their ideas for a limited period.

■ Access barriers to resources and outlets. The soil and climatic conditions for cultivating wine exist only in certain parts of the world, and the principal diamond mines are owned by De Beers. The main tour operators in the UK own many of the country's travel agents, making it difficult for new tour operators to find suitable outlets for their products.

- Cost barriers. It can be expensive to set up in an industry and where economies of scale are important, new entrants will find it difficult to compete. Where transport costs are high a local firm may not face much competition.
- Advertising and reputation. Large-scale advertising expenditure and a well-known name and good reputation can make it difficult for a new firm to become established in a market. To compete against the household names in the vacuum cleaner market, a new firm would have to come up with an improved or cheaper version. This is sometimes possible, as James Dyson has proved.

A firm will also be discouraged from entering a market if it believes that, should market conditions alter, it will be difficult to leave it. There are two main barriers to exit.

- **Sunk costs.** These are forms of expenditure that cannot be recovered if the firm leaves the industry, such as spending on advertising campaigns and specialised capital equipment.
- Long-term contracts. Firms may decide not to supply a product if they are required to sign such contracts. For example, a university may ask firms to tender for a five-year catering contract. Catering firms must consider carefully if they can make a profit from such a contract.

Perfect competition

Perfect competition is the highest degree of competition possible. In this market structure there are no barriers to entry and exit. It is easy for additional firms to start producing the product if demand increases and for existing firms to switch resources to producing something

Activity 2

In 2001 independent petrol stations complained that oil companies, including BP Amoco, Esso and Royal Dutch Shell, were selling them fuel at higher prices than they were charging their own outlets. They argued that this made it difficult for them to compete against the oil companies' outlets.

a What type of barrier were the independent petrol stations complaining about?

b Discuss two barriers to entry that are likely to exist in the oil industry.

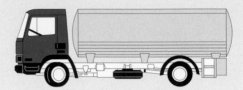

else if demand falls. The market is thus very responsive to changes in consumer demand and firms will earn only normal profit in the long run.

Other conditions are required for perfect competition to exist.

- There must be a large number of buyers and sellers each acting independently, so that no one buyer or seller can influence price. For example, a rise in the quantity supplied by one firm will have no effect on price as it will account for only a small part of total supply. Each supplier and each consumer has to accept the price determined by the total market demand and supply. So each firm is said to be a price taker and faces a situation where marginal revenue and average revenue and both are constant.
- To ensure competitiveness and a quick response to changes in consumer demand, current and potential consumers and suppliers must be fully informed about market conditions. Other suppliers must know what profits are made to decide whether they want to enter the market, and consumers must be aware of the prices charged by all the suppliers.

Consumers must not mind whom they buy from and suppliers whom they sell to. This ensures that one supplier cannot raise its price above that of its rivals. For consumers, the products sold by the suppliers must be identical (sometimes called homogeneous) and there must be no advertising or any other form of product differentiation.

In such a highly competitive market, there are advantages for consumers: costs are driven down to their lowest viable level as suppliers seek to gain a competitive edge by cutting costs; suppliers are responsive to changes in consumer tastes; and there is a wide choice of suppliers.

However, perfect competition is not necessarily as perfect as its name suggests. Although consumers have a choice of sellers, they do not have a choice in terms of variations of the product. Some consumers may not have the time or inclination to 'shop around' and may prefer to buy from the same supplier, and some may actually enjoy advertisements. Furthermore, although costs are driven down to their lowest level, it may not be that low. This is because the relatively small size of the firms means that they are less able to take advantage of economies of scale than firms operating under other market conditions.

It is difficult to think of markets that fit the model of perfect competition. For example, buyers and sellers rarely have perfect knowledge. But some, such as the foreign exchange market and some agricultural products markets, come close to it. In the US dollar market, for instance, there are many buyers and sellers, the product is identical, buyers and sellers have access to a considerable amount of information via computers, there is little attachment between buyers and sellers and the price charged for dollars is similar throughout the world. However, even in this foreign exchange market, some buyers and sellers are more powerful than others.

Perfect competition also serves as a model against which markets can be assessed.

Activity 3

Coffee beans are grown by millions of farmers in countries such as Brazil, Ethiopia, Ivory Coast, Mexico, Peru, Uganda and Vietnam. The coffee market is a world market. Large volumes of coffee beans are traded on international markets. The main purchasers of coffee are a few large companies, including Nestlé and Volcafe.

a What features of a competitive market does the coffee market exhibit?

b Identify a feature that is not consistent with perfect competition.

c Identify two other pieces of information that would be useful to help assess the extent to which the coffee market matches that of perfect competition.

Monopoly

At the other end of the competitive spectrum is **monopoly**. A pure monopoly is a single seller of a unique product. In Germany, Deutsche Post has a monopoly of first-class postal deliveries, and in England and Wales, the Bank of England is the only supplier of bank notes. The legal definition of a monopoly is any firm that has a 25% or greater share of the market. Such a firm is sometimes said to enjoy a scale monopoly.

A monopoly firm faces a downward sloping demand curve. It is a price maker, as the quantity it offers for sale affects the market price. Its average revenue exceeds its marginal revenue and both decline with output.

There is some controversy about the effects monopolies have on consumers. Traditionally, this market structure has been heavily criticised. Monopolists have the market power to restrict supply and drive price above cost. This enables them to earn supernormal profits, and the high barriers to entry and exit, which usually exist in monopoly markets, allow them to continue to enjoy them in the long run. Thus consumers may suffer from high prices and income may be redistributed from consumers to firms, with consumer surplus falling and producer surplus rising.

The lack of competition may reduce a monopolist's incentive to keep costs low and innovate. If so, consumers may pay higher prices than they need to and may not enjoy high-quality products. In the absence of competition, the quality and range of products on offer may even decline over time. The monopolist may become complacent, knowing that consumers have no choice.

However, these disadvantages may not occur and it can be argued that there are potential benefits of monopoly.

■ Even if a firm has no direct competitors and there are high barriers to entry and exit, there is still the threat posed by potential competitors and takeover by other firms. The existence of supernormal profits may encourage a firm to seek to overcome the barriers by developing a superior version of the product. If a firm is being run inefficiently, another firm may be tempted to buy it in the belief that it could run it more efficiently.

■ Far from discouraging innovation, a monopoly market structure can encourage it. The supernormal profits a monopoly can earn and its ability to protect any further rise in profits will provide funds to undertake research and development and investment and to employ skilled workers, and the incentive to innovate.

■ In a market where economies of scale are significant, costs may be lower and, even with a high **profit margin**, prices may be lower than under any other market structure. There are some industries in which economies of scale are so great that one firm can supply the entire market at a lower cost than two or more smaller firms. These are referred to as **natural monopolies**. For example, it would be inefficient and potentially dangerous to have more than one firm being responsible for the laying and maintenance of gas pipelines.

■ A monopoly can provide some stability of output and price for consumers. The monopolist may have wide experience of estimating market trends and the confidence to make long-term plans.

Activity 4

Bus passengers in West Oxfordshire have protested after being hit by some of the highest fares increases in the country.

Ms Graham, who relies on the X3 service from Eynsham to Witney, said Stagecoach's monopoly on rural routes forced people to accept the new fares.

She said: 'I have no other way of getting to work, so I have no choice. We really are over a barrel. It's a lot more money, especially if you're a low paid worker.' ('Customers protest against new Stagecoach fares', Witney Gazette, *Roseena Parveen, 12 December 2001)*

a Explain what is meant by Stagecoach being a monopoly on rural routes.

b Identify two disadvantages of a monopoly identified in the extract.

c Explain one possible advantage to society of Stagecoach having a monopoly on rural routes.

Monopolistic competition

Monopolistic competition describes a market structure with features of both perfect competition and monopoly. As with perfect competition, each firm acts independently. There are also many small firms, although not as many as under conditions of perfect competition.

An important difference, and one of the main characteristics of monopolistic competition, is **product differentiation**. The firms make products that are similar but not exactly the same as their rivals' products. For example, all the public houses in a city sell alcohol, but they differ in quality of service, location, opening hours, atmosphere, whether they offer food and the pub games available. To differentiate their products further to create customer loyalty, monopolistically competitive firms undertake small-scale advertising. Public houses advertise in local papers and on notice boards outside their premises, for instance. They also compete by differences in price.

As their products are similar but distinct from their rivals' products, firms operating under monopolistic competition have a degree of market power. They are price makers, so their average revenue exceeds marginal revenue and both fall with output. If a firm raises its price it will lose some but not all of its customers, as brand loyalty will ensure that some continue to buy the product.

However, market power is more limited under monopolistic competition than under monopoly. There are two main reasons: each firm's product is in competition with close substitutes produced by other firms in the market and it is easy to enter and leave the industry. In most monopolistically competitive industries there are no or low barriers to entry. For example, usually it is not difficult to get a loan to set up a hairdressing business and if the business is unsuccessful the premises can be sold. However, a new hairdresser may experience problems initially as it will have to attract some consumers away from established hairdressers. The ease of entry and exit means that the firms earn only normal profits in the long run.

Monopolistic competition can provide benefits for consumers. The competitive nature of the market protects consumers from exploitation by sellers and the product differentiation provides them with choice. However, the firms in this market structure are not efficient as they do not produce at the lowest possible average cost.

Monopolistic competition is the most common market structure. Examples of monopolistically competitive markets in the UK include hairdressers, public houses, restaurants and shoe shops.

The main way of assessing what type of market structure exists is to calculate a **concentration ratio**. It is possible to calculate, for example, the proportion of workers employed by the largest two, three, four or five firms in the market or the proportion of output accounted for by the largest firms. However, the most commonly used concentration ratios focus on the sales revenue of the largest two to five firms relative to the total sales revenue earned in the market. In monopolistic competition there is a low concentration ratio.

Activity 5

You are considering opening a restaurant in a city that has more than 80 restaurants. Identify five ways in which you could seek to make your restaurant distinct from the other restaurants.

Oligopoly

Oligopoly is a market structure dominated by a few large firms. There may be many firms in the market but the concentration ratio is high. For example, in the UK tobacco market in 2001 there was a two-firm concentration ratio of 80%. Imperial Tobacco had a 41% share of the market and its main rival, Gallaher, had a 39% share.

Some important industries operate under conditions of oligopoly. Some produce identical products, such as copper, oil, salt and steel. Others produce differentiated products, such as breakfast cereals, cars, detergents and sportswear.

These and other oligopolistic markets have high barriers to entry, particularly in terms of economies of scale. These high barriers enable oligopolistic firms to earn supernormal profits in the long run.

The market conditions facing oligoplistic firms are more complex and uncertain than under pure monopoly or any other market structure because the firms are interdependent.

They are aware that their actions are likely to bring a response from their rivals, and when making decisions they take into account the possible reactions of their rivals.

The firms may decide to try to attract more customers by cutting their prices. However, this is a risky strategy because it may tempt their rivals to cut their prices. A price war may develop, with prices being driven down to a point where some firms are unable to cover their costs. For a firm to start a price war, it must believe that its costs are lower than its rivals' costs, that it has funds to cover any losses, or that it can be cross-subsidised by another connected firm.

Some economists argue that fear of a price war and awareness that rivals may not follow a price rise mean that prices remain stable for some time under conditions of oligopoly. This price rigidity is illustrated by the **kinked demand curve** shown in Figure 2.

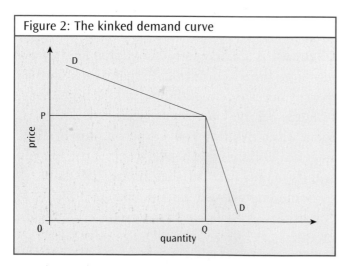

Figure 2: The kinked demand curve

Above the current price of P demand is elastic. If the firm raises its price and its rivals do not follow suit, it is likely to experience a greater percentage fall in demand. If it lowers its price its rivals are likely to cut theirs, so the firm will experience a smaller percentage rise in demand.

Because of the risks of price competition, some firms concentrate on non-price competition. This includes large-scale spending on advertising (a common feature of oligopolistic markets), brand names, packaging, free gifts,

competitions and sponsorship of sports events.

Even non-price competition can be risky. It can involve considerable expenditure, and if rivals adopt similar policies it may not noticeably increase demand. For example, a newspaper may launch a fantasy football competition with £1 million prize money in a bid to raise readership. However, its rivals are likely to launch their own competitions. The newspapers may end up with the same readership but higher costs.

The risks associated with price and non-price competition can encourage some oligopolists to collude, either formally or informally. Formal **collusion** involves the firms forming a **cartel**. This involves the firms acting as a monopoly, agreeing on the price to charge and the output to produce.

As formal collusion is illegal in many countries, including the UK, informal collusion (often referred to as tacit collusion) is more common. The main form of tacit collusion is **price leadership**. This involves one firm setting the price and the other firms following its lead. The price leader may be the firm that has the largest share of the market, the lowest-cost firm or the firm with the most experience in setting price.

The economies of scale that oligopolists often enjoy mean costs can be low in an oligopolistic market and consumers can benefit from non-price competition. However, oligopolists have considerable market power. They can push price above average cost and so enjoy supernormal profits and may disadvantage consumers by restricting competition among themselves through collusion.

A comparison of market structures

Table 1 shows the main features of the four main market structures.

Current issue: monopolies

Economists and governments continue to debate whether monopolies act in the public interest. In recent years there has been controversy about

	Perfect competition	Monopolistic competition	Oligopoly	Monopoly
Number of sellers	very many	many	dominated by a few	one
Barriers to entry and exit	non-existent	very low	high	very high
Degree of concentration	very low	low	high	very high
Type of product	identical	differentiated	identical or differentiated	unique
Long run profits	normal	normal	supernormal	supernormal

Table 1: A comparison of market structures

whether Microsoft, the US software giant, acts in the best interest of consumers. More than 90% of personal computers run on the firm's software.

In 1999 the US courts accused the company of abusing its monopoly power. It claimed that Microsoft prevents the entry of new competitors to the market by adding more applications to be run on Windows. Its actions were also alleged to stifle innovation and to give the firm the power to charge a higher price for Windows than would be possible in a competitive market.

Four years earlier, in 1995, the US courts had accused Microsoft of tying its own internet browser to its Windows operating system and distributing it free to stop consumers and computer makers buying the products of its software rival, Netscape Communications.

In its defence, Microsoft claimed that its market power was limited by the threat of potential competitors and that it needs to be able to innovate and add new features and functions to Windows. At the beginning of the twenty-first century it was developing a voice-recognition software system to add to Windows so that PCs would respond to spoken commands. Other software firms argued that voice recognition software should be sold separately so as to allow competition to develop in the market.

Activity 6

Procter and Gamble, a US detergent, cosmetic and washing powder company, set up a competitive intelligence unit to discover the secrets of its rival, Unilever, an Anglo-Dutch cosmetics giant. It employed Vietnam veterans to find out Unilever's plans for its haircare business, including what shampoos it was developing and its marketing strategy, by searching through the company's rubbish bins. Procter and Gamble's industrial espionage was discovered in August 2001 and Unilever demanded millions of pounds in compensation.

a What use might Procter and Gamble have made of the information it obtained?

b Discuss two strategies Procter and Gamble could use to increase its profits.

Summary

In this unit you have learned that:

- There are four main **market structures**: **perfect competition**, **monopolistic competition**, **oligopoly** and **monopoly**.

- The amount of market power a firm has is influenced by whether there are **barriers to entry** and **exit** into the market. Where high barriers exist, firms have considerable market power and are in strong position to protect any supernormal profits earned.

- Perfect competition is characterised by many buyers and sellers, an identical product and no barriers to entry and exit.

- Perfect competition can benefit consumers as the high level of competition puts pressure on firms to keep their costs low and there is a wide choice of sellers. However, it does not provide consumers with variations of the product and there is likely to be little opportunity to take advantage of economies of scale.

- A pure monopoly exists when there is one seller in the market. Other characteristics are very high barriers to entry, a unique product and the ability to earn supernormal profits in the long run.

- Consumers may suffer from high prices, low quality and a lack of choice under monopoly. However, they may benefit from low costs and so low prices as a result of the monopolist's incentive and ability to innovate, the threat of takeover and the possibility that a firm may overcome the barriers to entry.

- Monopolistic competition is characterised by many sellers, differentiated products and easy entry and exit.

- The competitive nature of monopolistic competition keeps profits to the normal profit level in the long run and provides consumers with choice, but the firms in this market structure do not produce at the lowest possible average cost.

- One way of assessing the degree of market power in a market is to calculate the market share of the largest firms.

- In oligopoly the market is dominated by a few large firms, there are high barriers to entry and exit, and the firms can sustain supernormal profits in the long run. It is difficult to predict how oligopolistic firms will behave. They may engage in price and non-price competition or collude.

- Consumers may benefit from low costs and non-price competition in oligopoly, but they can use their market power to push up price above average cost and earn supernormal profit. They may also restrict competition by colluding.

- Among the main distinguishing features of market structures are the number of sellers in the market, whether there are barriers to entry and exit, the degree of concentration, the type of product, and whether supernormal profits can be earned in the long run.

Multiple choice questions

1 Which of the following may be found under conditions of perfect competition?

A   advertising of different brands

B   differentiated products

C   free entry and exit

D   supernormal profits in the long run

2 Oligopoly is a market structure:

A   dominated by a few large firms

B   containing many firms making slightly different products

C   in which a firm's behaviour is independent of that of its rivals

D   in which firms can make only normal profits in the long run

3 Which of the following is a characteristic of monopolistic competition?

A   a homogeneous product

B   small-scale advertising

C   long run supernormal profits

D   significant barriers to entry and exit

4 In which market structures is a firm's average revenue greater than its marginal revenue?

A   perfect competition and monopolistic competition

B   oligopoly and monopoly

C   perfect competition, monopolistic competition and oligopoly

D   monopolistic competition, oligopoly and monopoly

5 In which market structures can firms earn supernormal profits in the long run?

A   perfect competition and monopolistic competition

B   monopolistic competition and oligopoly

C   oligopoly and monopoly

D   monopoly and monopolistic competition

6 Why may a firm operating in a oligopolistic market be reluctant to lower its price?

A   it may be concerned that such a move will encourage new firms to enter the market

B   it may consider that rival firms will match any of its price reductions

C   its demand will become more elastic the lower the price it charges

D   it may think that such action would increase its long run profits

Data response question: competition among supermarkets

Supermarket chains try to gain more customers in a variety of ways. In 2000 Tesco and Sainsbury launched a campaign to poach Safeway shoppers, offering them special deals and free points if they surrendered their Safeway ABC loyalty cards. This was, in part, a reaction to Tesco and Sainsbury losing market share to Safeway. Table 2 shows the market share of the UK's top five supermarkets in 2000.

Table 2	
Supermarket chain	Market share (%)
Tesco	24.4
Sainsbury	18.4
Asda	16.2
Safeway	10.5
Somerfield	6.9

A year later, a price war broke out among the supermarkets. Tesco introduced a wide-ranging price-cutting campaign. It backed up the move by conducting the UK's largest ever poster campaign and publishing details of the price cuts on the internet. Sainsbury, Asda, Safeway and Somerfield followed suit by cutting their prices. Competition also rose in non-food areas. Tesco and Asda, in particular, increased the range of items on sale by including clothing, health and beauty products in most of its branches.

a   Calculate the three- and the five-firm concentration ratios for the supermarket industry in 2000. [4]

b   Explain, using evidence from the data, in what market structure UK supermarkets operate. [6]

c   Discuss two ways, not mentioned in the passage, that a supermarket may seek to increase its market share. [4]

d   Discuss the possible advantages and disadvantages a supermarket may experience as a result of cutting its prices. [6]

12 Objectives of firms

Achieving high profits, satisfying consumers and shareholders and pursuing environmental objectives are among the possible objectives that a firm may set itself. In this unit you will examine some of the main objectives, including **profit maximisation**, **sales revenue maximisation**, **sales maximisation** and **profit satisficing**.

Profit maximisation

Traditionally, it has been thought that a firm will seek to achieve as high a level of profit as possible. A firm will maximise its profit if it produces where marginal cost equals marginal revenue (MC = MR), as shown by an output of Q in Figure 1. Any output below this level, such as output Q1, will mean that marginal revenue is greater than cost. More profit could be gained by raising output and sales. Any output greater than this, such as output Q2, will mean that marginal cost is greater than marginal revenue and so the extra output reduces the firm's profit.

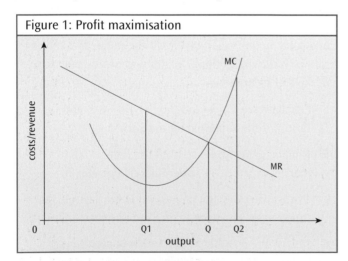

Figure 1: Profit maximisation

Some economists claim that it can be difficult for firms to calculate marginal cost and marginal revenue and so to calculate the profit maximising price and output. In practice, many firms estimate their long run average cost and then add a profit margin. However, this does not invalidate the

profit maximisation theory if firms are still seeking to earn as much profit as possible and are moving towards the output where MC = MR.

More significant reasons for questioning whether firms always aim for maximum profits are that in many firms ownership is divorced from control and that high profits can bring risks. Many large companies are owned by shareholders and run by managers, including chief executives. Shareholders are interested in high profits, as these are likely to lead to high **dividends**. Managers may have other objectives as their status, prestige and pay are often more closely linked to the size of the firm than its profitability. High profits can also attract unwanted attention from the government, concerned that the firm may be exploiting consumers, or from other firms keen to acquire profitable assets.

Activity 1

Airbus, an aircraft manufacturer, threatened by falling demand in 2001, was expected to cut its labour force. However, in December 2001 it announced a deal to cut hours and overtime to save jobs. Unions accepted the deal and praised the company for taking a long-term perspective by putting job security and protecting the skills base and capacity at the top of the agenda.

a Explain why Airbus's profits are likely to have fallen in 2001.

b Discuss whether Airbus's strategy will raise or lower profits in the long run.

Sales maximisation

Managers may be more interested in maximising sales than maximising profits because if the size of the firm grows their pay will rise. However, they are unlikely to be indifferent to profits even when pursuing sales maximisation because they will not usually increase output beyond a point where average cost equals average revenue. Only when a firm has large funds or can cross-subsidise from other activities is it likely to be willing to push sales to a point where it experiences a loss.

Sales maximisation and profit maximisation and the interests of managers and shareholders may conflict, especially in the short run. To increase sales a firm may spend a large amount on advertising and/or cut prices, which may initially lower profits. Shareholders are likely to want a high proportion of profits distributed as dividends, whereas managers, concerned about growing the firm, will want to reinvest most of the profits in equipment and buildings. However, in the long run the two objectives may be compatible and both shareholders and managers may be happy if the actions taken in pursuit of sales maximisation increase market share and raise long run profits.

Activity 2

At the end of November 2001 Intelligent Finance, the online and telephone banking division of HBoS, a banking group, reported that it should break even in 2003. However, it had attracted only half the number of customers it had aimed for during its first year of operation.

a What objective does it appear that Intelligent Finance sacrificed in the short run?

b Why might seeking to attract customers initially conflict with the objective you identified in (a)?

Sales revenue maximisation

Managers' actions may also be influenced by the level of sales revenue. High sales revenue can make it easier for a firm to raise loans from banks.

If a firm is aiming to achieve **sales revenue maximisation** it should produce where marginal revenue is zero since at this point total revenue will be at a peak. The level of output is likely to be beyond the profit maximisation point, but whether the firm earns supernormal or normal profit or makes a loss will depend on the relationship between total revenue and total cost at this point.

Activity 3

From the information in Table 1 calculate:

a the profit maximising output

b the highest output at which the firm can break even

c the sales revenue maximisation output

Table 1		
Output	Price (£)	Average cost (£)
1	12	8.00
2	11	7.00
3	10	6.00
4	9	5.00
5	8	4.80
6	7	5.33
7	6	6.00
8	5	6.75

Profit satisficing

Studies of firms' activities have suggested that rather than trying to maximise profits, managers aim for a profit level that will keep shareholders happy. This may be because they are reluctant to accept the increased risks and pressures associated with fiercely competitive policies, or because they are seeking to satisfy not only shareholders but also other **stakeholders** in the firm. Stakeholders are people with a direct interest in the actions of the firm, including (in addition to managers and shareholders) workers, consumers, suppliers, the local community and environmentalists. These groups may have different objectives: consumers want low prices and high quality; workers want high wages, job satisfaction and security; suppliers want a high price; the local community want employment but an absence of congestion; and environmental groups want a clean environment and the conservation of flora and fauna.

Some of the objectives that may appear to conflict in the short run may be compatible in the long run. For example, showing concern for the environment, say by not selling genetically modified food or diverting a pipeline away from an area of natural beauty, is likely to raise a firm's costs. However, it may also provide it with good publicity and may increase demand for its products. In the long run revenue may rise by more than costs and so profit may increase. Similarly, raising workers' wages will increase costs in the short run but may reduce labour costs in the long run if the higher wages increase labour productivity and reduce labour turnover.

Some claim that seeking to please all the stakeholders can distract a firm from its main function of providing profits for shareholders. Others argue that firms have a responsibility to pursue not only profits but also high labour, environmental and ethical standards. They also claim that with increasing consumer power such an approach, far from conflicting with profit maximisation, can contribute to it. If the public perceives that a firm is not following ethical policies, its sales and profits can suffer. In 2000 Nike's profits were adversely affected by a consumer boycott organised to protest about the firm's use of sweatshops in developing countries.

Current issue: executives' pay

To increase incentives for chief executives and to make them more concerned about their firms' profit position, firms are increasingly giving them shares and share options. However, some city commentators, trade unionists and economists argue that executives' pay should be linked more closely linked to performance. Some high-profile cases in 2000 and 2001 appeared to give weight to this argument. For example, in 2000 Christopher Gent, chief executive of Vodafone, was paid nearly £6 million, despite the fact that shareholders suffered a decline of almost 20% in the value of their investment. John Browne, BP's chief executive, was paid £4.1 million, despite an 11% fall in the value of shareholders' investment.

In 2001 chief executives' pay increased by 14.8% while sales lost value. In the same year Peter Bonfield, BT's chief executive, left his job. The firm was performing badly but, nevertheless, he left with a £1.5 million cash settlement.

Activity 4

Many firms are becoming more environmentally aware. In the USA Dupont, a chemicals group, has set itself the target of cutting its 1990 levels of greenhouse gas emissions by 65% by 2010.

United Technologies, a producer of products ranging from air conditioners to helicopters, is seeking to reduce its energy and water consumption by 25% of sales by 2007. In 2000 it saved $200,000 by instructing its 1,600 employees in Florida to turn off their computers each night.

Some religious groups in the USA that hold shares are putting pressure on firms such as Ford Motor Company and Exxon Mobil to adopt more green policies.

a What may be motivating the US firms to adopt more environmentally friendly policies?

b Discuss whether pursuing environmentally friendly policies will conflict with profit maximisation.

Summary

In this unit you have learned that:

- It has traditionally been thought that firms will seek to maximise profits and so will aim to produce where MC = MR.

- In practice, a firm may not produce at the profit maximising output because it can be difficult to calculate MC and MR, it may attract attention from a predatory firm and the government, or it may be pursuing another objective.

- As managers' pay is often linked to the growth of the firm, they may seek to achieve **sales maximisation** subject to the constraint that the firm earns at least normal profit.

- Maximising sales revenue is another possible objective. This is because high sales revenue can lead to an increase in managers' pay and can make it easier to raise loans.

- Rather than seeking to maximise profits, a firm may aim for a satisfactory level of profits. This may be because managers want to avoid stress or because they want greater flexibility to pursue other objectives which will benefit some of the firm's other stakeholders.

Multiple choice questions

1 Profits are maximised where:
A a high price is charged
B output is maximised
C marginal revenue equals marginal cost
D supply exceeds demand

2 The manager of a firm decides not to launch a new product because she believes that, although it would probably increase profits, developing and promoting it would involve a lot of work and stress. Which of the following describes the objective she is following?
A profit maximisation
B profit satisficing
C sales maximisation
D sales revenue maximisation

3 A perfectly competitive firm produces an output which maximises both its profit and its total revenue. What does this indicate?
A marginal cost is zero
B total cost is maximised
C marginal cost is less than marginal revenue
D marginal revenue is equal to average cost

4 A perfectly competitive firm is producing where marginal cost is greater than marginal revenue. What should it do if it wishes to increase its profits?
A lower its output
B reduce its price
C increase its price
D increase its output

5 When a firm is earning supernormal profits it is achieving a level of profits above that:
A required to cover the cost of launching new products
B earned on average in the industry over the long run
C needed to keep the firm in the industry in the long run
D earned on average by the other firms in the industry

6 A firm wants to increase its share of the market but it does not want to experience a loss. It should therefore produce at a level of output where:
A marginal cost equals marginal revenue
B marginal revenue is zero
C average total cost is maximised
D average cost equals average revenue

Data response question: sales and profit maximisation

Cramer Systems, a telecoms software firm based in Bath, was founded in 1996. It competes against large firms such as BT and Cegeted, a French mobile-phone operator. Its sales increased by 169% a year from £321,000 in 1997 to £6.2m in 2000. Its target for 2001 was to double its sales.

In the same year Alastair George, chief executive of Littlewoods, a high-street retailer, stated that the firm's main objective was to move the business from loss to profit. The firm was experiencing some difficulty in maximising its profits. The year before it had cut 250 jobs when its involvement in a price war with other high-street retailers proved to be unsuccessful. Sales had risen, but not enough to move the firm back into profit. In 2001 the firm stated that it was going to focus on its more profitable customers and home shopping.

a Distinguish between the objectives of sales maximisation and profit maximisation. [4]

b Discuss two ways a firm could seek to increase its sales. [4]

c i Identify in which market structure price wars are a feature. [2]

 ii Explain why price competition may not always be successful in this market structure. [4]

d Discuss whether the objectives of sales maximisation and profit maximisation will conflict. [6]

3 Market failure

1 Efficiency

The existence of unemployed workers, overcrowded trains and unsold mobile phones indicates that markets are not working efficiently. This is market failure. To understand its causes and consequences, it is first useful to understand what would happen if markets worked efficiently. In this unit you will examine the meaning of efficiency, distinguishing between **productive** and **allocative efficiency**, and consider the conditions necessary for **Pareto efficiency** to be achieved.

Economic efficiency

Economic efficiency occurs when markets operate in a way which most benefits consumers. To achieve this, markets must make best and fullest use of resources. Labour and other resources should be fully employed in producing the products that reflect consumers' tastes, in the quantities they want and at the lowest possible cost. This means that economic efficiency consists of both productive and allocative efficiency.

Activity 1

As demand switches from videos to DVDs, firms are producing more DVDs and fewer music and film videos. Retailers, including Virgin and WH Smith, are devoting more shelf space to DVDs and less to videos.

a Explain why the changes outlined could be described as increasing efficiency.

b What is the incentive for firms to be more efficient?

Productive efficiency

Productive efficiency is achieved when firms produce at the lowest point on the lowest possible average cost curve as shown in Figure 1.

When firms are producing at the lowest cost, they are using the smallest quantity of resources possible. When firms are productively efficient and there is full employment of resources, the

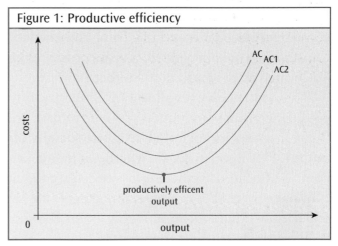

Figure 1: Productive efficiency

country is producing as much as it can with existing resources. So productive efficiency can also be illustrated on a production possibility curve. Points A, B, C and D in Figure 2 are all productively efficient. At these points it is not possible to produce any more of one product without reducing the output of the other. Points E and F are productively inefficient, since they indicate production points where resources are not being used fully and efficiently.

If firms are not productively efficient, they could cut costs by using fewer resources. This would free resources, which could be used to produce other goods and services.

Allocative efficiency

Allocative efficiency is achieved when resources are allocated in a way which maximises

125

consumers' satisfaction. The products produced are the ones that consumers want and they are made in the right quantities.

Firms achieve allocative efficiency when they produce an output at which marginal cost equals price (average revenue). At this output the cost of producing the last unit is equal to the value that consumers place on the product reflected in the price they are prepared to pay. Figure 3 shows that the allocatively efficient output is at point Q.

Any output below Q, such as Q1, is allocatively inefficient as the value consumers place on the product is less than the cost of producing it. The product is being underproduced. A rise in output to Q would increase consumer satisfaction. Any output beyond Q, such as Q2, is also allocatively inefficient, because the cost of producing the last unit exceeds the value consumers place on it and it is being overproduced. Consumers would benefit from some of the resources being reallocated to production of another product.

If a country achieves allocative efficiency, it will be producing on the production possibility curve and achieving the best results for society. This is the **socially optimum output**. However, to decide whether a particular production point is allocatively efficient it is necessary to know what consumers want. For example, in Figure 4, if most of the population value education highly, point B is more likely to be allocatively efficient than point C.

It is unlikely that points A and D are allocatively efficient as most economies will not want to devote all their resources to producing one type of product.

Pareto efficiency

Pareto efficiency is named after Vifredo Pareto, an Italian economist. He stated that an economy is economically efficient when it is not possible to change the existing allocation of resources in a way that will make one person better off without making someone else worse off.

For Pareto efficiency to exist it is necessary for an economy to achieve both productive and allocative efficiency. In other words, it must be economically efficient. On Figure 5, for example, point A could not illustrate Pareto efficiency because more could be produced with existing resources, so it would be possible to make some people better off without having to divert products away from other people. Point B may not be allocatively and Pareto efficient if consumers prefer a higher output of luxuries and a lower output of

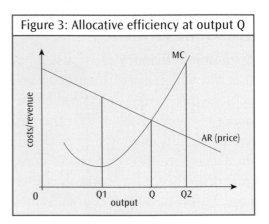

Figure 2: Productively efficient and inefficient points

Figure 3: Allocative efficiency at output Q

Activity 2

In the 1980s and 1990s high street banks introduced more advanced technology to improve the quality of their services and to reduce their average costs. Through the introduction of, for instance, cash point machines and telephone banking, the banks were able to reduce their staffing levels and wage costs.

a Discuss another way a firm could become more productively efficient.

b Would the need for fewer workers in the banking sector necessarily make an economy more productively efficient?

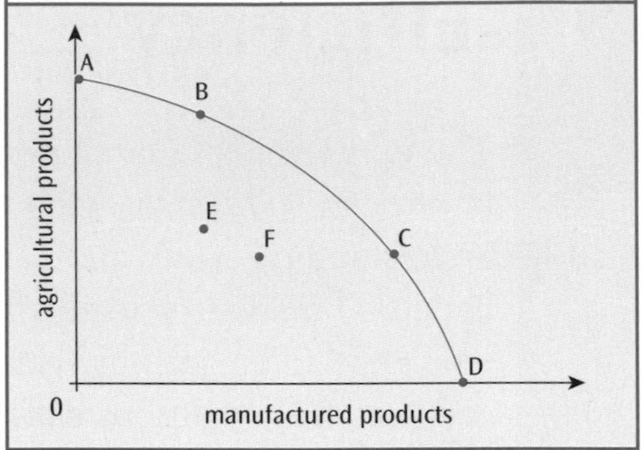

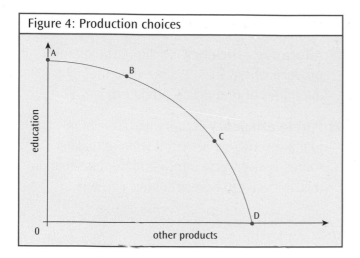

Figure 4: Production choices

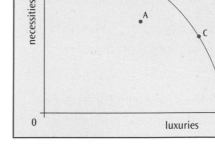

Figure 5: Assessing allocative efficiency

Activity 3

When the Public Record Office decided to put details of the 1901 census on the internet it anticipated there would be considerable interest from historians and people seeking to trace their family trees. As a result, it created a website that could cater for 1.2 million people a day. However, even this proved inadequate. On its first day of operation in January 2002, more than 50 million people tried to access the site, at a rate of more than 1 million an hour. This led to millions of frustrated people being unable to access.

a What evidence is there of allocative inefficiency in the passage above?

b What would have been the implication for allocative efficiency if only 250,000 people had sought to log on to the website?

Activity 4

Decide whether the following will lead towards:
- productive efficiency
- allocative efficiency
- economic efficiency

a A firm saves money by encouraging its staff to cut down on using the firm's facilities to make personal phone calls and to access internet chat lines and other non-business sites.

b Previously unemployed workers are recruited to work in the health service in order to cut waiting lists.

c Following an improvement in international relationships, a country switches resources from defence to health care.

d A firm replaces its out-of-date machinery with new, cheaper machinery which embodies new technology and produces a higher output.

e Sportswear firms in the UK produce more tennis rackets and fewer rugby balls in the summer.

necessities. Point C may be Pareto efficient, but it would be necessary to know the exact combination of luxuries and necessities that would give consumers maximum satisfaction.

Current issue: increasing efficiency

Markets do not often operate efficiently. This results in an opportunity cost, as people do not enjoy as many goods and services as they could. Governments seek to increase the efficiency of markets in order to increase their international competitiveness and raise the living standards of their inhabitants.

For decades UK governments have sought, by various means, to increase both productive and

allocative efficiency. If a country is not producing products at their lowest possible cost and is not making the products people want to consume in the right quantities, it will experience problems selling its goods and services both at home and abroad.

Efficiency will rise if employment of resources increases, productivity rises and resources move quickly to reflect changes in consumer preferences.

Summary

In this unit you have learned that:

- **Economic efficiency** involves producing the products people want at the lowest possible cost.

- **Productive efficiency** occurs when firms produce at the lowest point on their lowest average cost curves.

- An economy achieves productive efficiency when it cannot make more of one product without making less of another product. It will be producing on its production possibility curve.

- **Allocative efficiency** is achieved when firms produce where MC = P, since then the right quantities of products is produced.

- **Pareto efficiency** occurs when it is not possible to make someone better off without making someone else worse off. To achieve this situation it is necessary to have economic efficiency.

Multiple choice questions

1 When does an economy achieve productive efficiency?

A when its firms earn supernormal profits in the long run

B when its firms produce at the lowest point on their lowest average cost curves

C when it produces inside its production possibility curve

D when it is able to produce more of one good without producing less of another

2 Which point on the production possibility curve in Figure 6 illustrates productive efficiency?

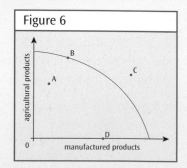

Figure 6

3 Which of the following would indicate a country is not achieving allocative efficiency?

A when there is an absence of shortages and surpluses

B when there is an absence of barriers to entry and exit into the country's markets

C when it is not able to make one person better off without making someone else worse off

D when the allocation of the country's resources do not reflect consumers' tastes

4 Allocative efficiency occurs when a firm produces where:

A marginal cost equals average cost

B marginal cost equals average revenue

C average cost equals average revenue

D average cost equals marginal revenue

5 Which of the following would move an economy towards Pareto efficiency?

A a rise in unemployment

B an increase in output beyond where marginal cost equals price

C a reduction in the mobility of factors of production

D a shift of resources from declining towards expanding industries

6 For Pareto efficiency to occur it is necessary to achieve:

A allocative efficiency only

B productive efficiency only

C allocative efficiency and productive efficiency

D allocative efficiency, productive efficiency and concentration of market power

Data response question: General Motors

At the start of 2002 General Motors (GM), the world's largest car maker, announced that it was seeking to achieve more cost reductions. It wanted to make savings in the materials used, reduce overheads and raise productivity.

In the previous three years, GM had reduced costs by approximately $3 billion a year by reducing administrative staff, renegotiating contracts with suppliers and cutting back on the materials used.

GM also stated that it would reduce costs by cutting its productive capacity. It started the year with the ability to produce 17.5 million vehicles but expected demand to be approximately 15.5 million vehicles. It was planning to reduce its capacity not by closing car factories but by reducing shifts and cutting overtime. It was also aiming to concentrate its resources on areas with the highest market demand.

a   Distinguish between productive efficiency and allocative efficiency. [2]

b   What evidence is there in the passage that at the start of 2002 GM was seeking to move towards:
   i   productive efficiency [6]
   ii   allocative efficiency? [4]

c   Draw a production possibility curve diagram to illustrate the planned change in GM's productive capacity in 2002. [3]

d   Discuss the possible effect of a rise in its efficiency on GM's market share. [5]

---

2   Efficiency and competition

In this unit you will consider how the level of competition in a market is influenced by its market structure and why a high level of competition may promote efficiency.

Influences on efficiency

The level of efficiency achieved in a market is influenced by its market structure. The more competitive a market is, the more pressure there is for it to be both productively and allocatively efficient.

Perfect competition and efficiency

One of the benefits claimed for perfect competition is that it leads to efficiency. The high level of competition should provide firms with the pressure and incentive to produce at their lowest average cost. If a firm fails to keep its costs low, it will lose custom to its rivals and be driven out of the industry. However, if a firm manages to push its average cost below that of its competitors, it may gain some market power. In the model of perfect competition it is assumed that firms will produce at their lowest average cost in the long run and so be productively efficient.

Activity 1

Supermarkets are devoting more shelf space to organic fruit and vegetables and less shelf space to non-organic fruit and vegetables in response to changes in consumer preference.

a   What type of efficiency, productive or allocative, might the action of supermarkets outlined above lead towards?

b   What may have motivated the supermarkets to make the change?

Perfectly competitive firms also produce where marginal cost is equal to price (average revenue) in both the short and long run, because they have the competitive pressure and incentive to be allocatively efficient. If they do not produce what consumers want and do not respond to changes in consumer demand, they will go out of business. However, if firms respond to changes in consumer demand they will make supernormal profits in the short run. These supernormal profits will provide an incentive for new firms to enter the market. The absence of barriers to entry and exit assists the smooth and quick reallocation of resources following changes in consumer demand.

The high level of information that consumers and suppliers are assumed to have in perfect competition and the absence of any consumers or suppliers with market power can also contribute to Pareto efficiency. Consumers and suppliers will only enter into transactions that will benefit both of them. If consumers and suppliers are happy with the outcome of their transactions, Pareto efficiency will be achieved. It will not be possible to make someone better off without making someone else worse off.

Current issue: perfect competition and Pareto efficiency

Perfect competition may lead to efficiency, but there is a possibility that even this high level of competition may not in practice achieve efficiency. A high level of competition does provide pressure and incentives for firms in this market structure to produce where marginal cost equals price and at its lowest average cost. However, private-sector firms are likely to take into account only costs and benefits that affect them directly.

Production and, indeed, consumption can impose costs on and provide benefits to people not directly involved. For example, producing chemicals may generate pollution. This may have harmful effects on those living nearby which the firm will not pay for. In deciding what level of output to produce, the firm will not take into account these costs to third parties. So perfect competition will ensure that Pareto efficiency is achieved, but only if there are no costs or benefits to third parties.

Activity 2

In January 2002 Philip Fletcher, the water industry regulator, stated that the industry would benefit from more competition. He argued that prices would be likely to fall if more water companies were to bid to supply water outside their monopoly areas.

a Explain why more competition may result in lower prices.

b Discuss one other benefit consumers may gain from a rise in competition.

Summary

In this unit you have learned that:

■ The more competitive a market is, the more likely it is to achieve Pareto efficiency.

■ The conditions formed in a perfectly competitive market provide the pressure and incentives for firms to achieve productive efficiency and allocative efficiency.

■ The high level of information which consumers and suppliers have under conditions of perfect competition should ensure that transactions benefit both parties.

Multiple choice questions

1 Which of the following market structures is the most competitive?

A perfect competition

B monopolistic competition

C monopoly

D oligopoly

2 A firm producing under conditions of perfect competition always achieves allocative efficiency because it produces where:

A MC = MR

B MC = AR

C MC = AC

D AC = AR

3 What will happen if a perfectly competitive firm's costs rise above that of other firms in the industry?

A it will make only normal profit in the short and long run

B it will make a loss in the short run but normal profit in the long run

C it will have to leave the industry

D it will lose some of its customers to rival firms

4 What is meant by an efficient allocation of resources?

A one which ensures firms earn supernormal profits

B one where it would be possible to make someone better off without making someone else worse off

C one where firms produce at the lowest point on their highest average cost curve

D one which makes the fullest use of resources to produce the right products in the right quantities

5 Why does the absence of barriers to entry and exit promote efficiency in a market?

A it enables supernormal profits to be earned in the long run

B it makes it easier for firms to gain market power

C it enables the allocation of resources to change quickly in response to a change in consumer demand

D it puts pressure on firms to produce at the point where marginal cost equals marginal revenue

6 Which of the following is a characteristic of perfect competition?

A advertising

B differentiated products

C low barriers to entry and exit

D full information about market conditions available to consumers and suppliers

Data response question: the Post Office

The Post Office has been criticised for failing to meet its targets for first-class mail and for the price it charges for delivering letters within towns and cities.

The government is considering introducing competition into the market for the delivery of letters. The Post Office has a monopoly in the delivery of letters priced at less than £1 and weighing less than 350 grammes. If the government cuts the threshold to 50 grammes or even 30 grammes, many of Europe's postal services and privately owned express and courier companies are likely to be interested in competing with the Post Office.

The Post Office is resisting such a move, claiming that it could threaten its ability to deliver mail throughout the country at a uniform price. Those in favour, however, argue that increased competition would stimulate innovation, improve quality and reduce price.

a Identify two disadvantages of a monopoly suggested in the passage. [4]

b Why might companies be interested in competing with the Post Office? [3]

c Explain why increasing competition may threaten the Post Office's ability to deliver mail throughout the country at a uniform price? [5]

d Explain why increased competition may stimulate innovation, improve quality and reduce price. [8]

3 Market failure

In this unit you will examine the nature of market failure and its main causes.

Market failure

Market failure arises when free market forces, using the price mechanism, fail to produce the products that people want, in the quantities they desire and at prices that reflect consumers' satisfaction. In other words, market failure occurs when productive, allocative and thus economic and Pareto efficiency are not achieved.

An example of a market failing to produce an equitable outcome occurred in March 2001, when the South African government took the world's major drug manufacturers to court. It argued that the firms were putting their profits before the needs of those suffering from AIDS and other devastating diseases in the developing world. The drug companies were seeking to stop other firms producing cheaper versions of their medicines. This use of the companies' patents was preventing millions of people having access to cheaper medicines to fight Aids, tuberculosis and malaria.

Activity 1

Which of the following would provide evidence of market failure?

a shortages

b unemployment

c unfilled job vacancies

d output occurring inside the production possibility curve

Causes of market failure

Market forces may not result in the best use of resources for various reasons.

- The existence of costs and benefits that do not go through the price mechanism.
- The lack of a financial incentive to produce certain important products.
- Underconsumption or overconsumption of products if left to market forces.
- If consumers, workers and suppliers have insufficient or incorrect information, they may make choices that do not maximise their satisfaction, income or profits.
- Even if suppliers are fully informed, they may still not produce the most allocatively efficient output at the lowest average cost because some firms may exploit their market power and some may experience problems attracting appropriate quantities of resources.
- Difficulties can arise in moving resources, particularly labour, from one use to another.

The free operation of markets may also result in what society regards as an unfair distribution of income and wealth.

Current issue: blood transfusions

There is a debate about whether using the market mechanism is the best way of getting blood for transfusions.

In the USA blood is bought and sold. The buyer is the blood transfusion service. Many sellers are low-paid workers and unemployed people. The service seeks to buy healthy blood.

Activity 2

In December 2001 in the USA, a former chairman of Sotheby's was found guilty of price-fixing. He was convicted of conspiring with Christie's to eliminate competition between the two firms by fixing the commissions paid by sellers. The two auction houses control 90% of art auctions. The prosecution's case claimed that the price-fixing had cost their clients approximately $400 million between 1993 and 1999.

a In what market structure do the two auction houses operate?

b Explain how consumers were suffering as a result of the auction houses' actions.

It does not want blood from people with HIV, hepatitis or other diseases that are transmitted through blood, or from people who have sold blood recently. However, some of the sellers, desperate for money, lie and sell contaminated blood. This has led to people becoming HIV positive and developing other illness as a result of blood transfusions. The screening of blood is improving all the time, but the quality of blood sold in the USA remains lower than that of blood donated free in the UK. When people are not being paid for their blood, they have no financial incentive to lie about their medical condition or when they last gave blood. A voluntary donation system does, however, depend on enough people being willing to give blood regularly.

Activity 3

In a Carlisle hospital, domestic cleaners earn £7,505 a year for a 39-hour week. A large part of this poorly paid but essential job is mopping floors. In the same hospital other cleaners – 'wall washers' – earn £9,995 for a 37-hour week. The lower-paid jobs are done by women and the higher-paid positions are held by men.

Despite the introduction of the Equal Pay Act in 1990, the gap between men's and women's pay is still 19%.

Mrs Kingsmill, the lawyer commissioned by the government to conduct a review of women in work, said: 'This is not simply a matter of equal treatment and social justice. It is about wanting a pool of talented individuals who are outperfoming men during their education. It is therefore important for the future productivity and competitiveness of the UK.' ('Waging war on sex bias', Jill Treanor, Guardian, 6 December 2001)

a What was the pay differential between male and female cleaners in the Carlisle hospital in 2001?

b Explain how discrimination against female workers could lead to inefficiency.

Summary

In this unit you have learned that:

- **Market failure** occurs when productive, allocative and thus economic and Pareto efficiency are not achieved.

- Market failure occurs for a variety of reasons including the failure of demand and supply to be based on full costs and benefits, the absence of a financial incentive to produce some products, other products being underconsumed and overconsumed, lack of information, the exploitation of market power and immobility of resources.

- Free market forces may also result in an inequitable distribution of income and wealth.

Multiple choice questions

1 Market failure occurs when:

A prices fluctuate

B firms make a loss

C resources are not allocated efficiently

D the economy produces on the production possibility curve

2 Which of the following is a cause of market failure?

A a lack of information

B a lack of barriers to entry to and exit from markets

C a high level of mobility of factors of production

D the existence of costs and benefits that go through the market mechanism

3 Market failure would be reduced by:

A a decrease in consumer sovereignty

B an increase in average costs above the minimum level possible

C an increase in market concentration ratios

D an increase in the occupational mobility of labour

4 Market failure would be increased by:

A an increase in the number of firms in the market

B an increase in the incentive for firms to be productively efficient

C a reduction in the inaccuracy of information available

D a reduction in the pressure on firms to be allocatively efficient

5 What is the main benefit of a reduction in market failure?

A higher consumer satisfaction

B higher unit costs

C reduced choice

D reduced use of resources

6 Which point on Figure 1 illustrates the highest degree of market failure?

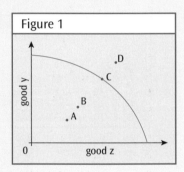

Figure 1

Data response question

A judge accused London Underground yesterday of sacrificing safety in favour of profits after it emerged that employees were forced to work beside live rails as trains rattled past centimetres away.

The company was fined £225,000 for failing to stop a manager nicknamed 'Dangerous Dave' even though some of his team suffered electric shocks and one was treated in hospital.

Judge John Samuels said LU had paid little more than 'lip service' to safety issues and expressed concern that it would take 'years' for the situation to be corrected.

He said: 'This was a case in which safety was sacrificed for the dominant demands of management to keep trains
running at all costs and thus to support the profitability of the system.' ('Tube put profit before safety – judge', Steven Morris, Guardian, 11 January 2002.)

a In making its decisions, what harmful effects was London Underground not taking into account? [4]

b i Why might a firm see a conflict between profit and the safety of its employees? [5]

 ii Explain why, in practice, the two may not conflict. [5]

c What information would you need to decide whether London Underground is achieving:

 i allocative efficiency [3]

 ii productive efficiency? [3]

4 Externalities

In this unit you will see how the costs and benefits to those consuming and producing products can diverge from the total costs and benefits to society. You will examine the nature of **private costs** and **benefits**, **negative** and **positive externalities** and **social costs** and **benefits**. You will also explore the significance of externalities and the nature of **welfare loss**.

Economic decisions and market performance

Markets work most efficiently when the people making economic decisions are the ones affected by those decisions. In this case consumers and suppliers will only enter into transactions which will benefit them. A consumer will only buy a product if the value to him or her is equal to the price charged for it. A supplier will only sell a product if the revenue received is at least equal to the cost of production.

However, people other than those directly involved in the decision to consume or produce a product are often affected. For example, an airport's decision to increase night flights into and out of its terminus will create noise, disturbance and possibly a fall in property prices for those living nearby.

Activity 1

A public house is permitted to stay open all weekend over the May bank holiday. Identify one group of people not directly involved in running or visiting the pub who may:

a benefit from this decision

b suffer as a result of this decision

Private costs and benefits

Private costs and benefits are those experienced by the people directly involved in the decision to consume or produce a product.

Private costs, which can also be called internal costs, are the costs incurred by those who consume and those who produce products. For example, if a person buys a litre of petrol, the cost (in the form of the price charged) may be £1. If a firm produces 50 cars a day, the cost (in terms of wages, components, rent and other costs) may be £40,000.

Private benefits, also known as internal benefits, are the benefits received by those who consume and those who produce products. The private benefit people receive from a litre of petrol is the pleasure and convenience they gain from driving their cars. The private benefit a car firm receives from selling cars is the revenue it earns.

Activity 2

Identify:

a three private costs a bus company may incur when operating a bus route

b two private benefits a newspaper company can gain from selling its newspapers

Externalities

There would be more chance of achieving an efficient allocation of resources if there were only private costs and benefits. However, the consumption and production of some products have effects on people who are not directly involved. These effects are known as **externalities**, or sometimes spillover effects.

135

Those who benefit or suffer as a result of the consumption and production activities of others are known as third parties.

Those affected by externalities, sometimes known as third parties, do not pay for the benefits they receive and are not financially compensated for the harmful effects they suffer as a result of the consumption and production decisions of others.

Activity 3

Identify a benefit the other residents of a street could gain from one household holding a firework party to which they were not invited.

Negative externalities

The costs imposed on third parties by the economic activity of others are called **negative externalities**, or external costs.

When people drive their cars they impose costs on other people. These negative externalities include congestion, noise pollution, air pollution, damage to buildings and injuries to pedestrians and other car drivers.

Production can also impose costs on third parties. The production of cars, for instance, may cause noise, air and visual pollution in the area where the factory is located.

Activity 4

Identify three negative externalities which villagers may experience as a result of a bypass being built through their village.

Positive externalities

Positive externalities, also called external benefits, are the benefits which third parties gain from the consumption and production decisions of others. Car travel makes some out-of-town shopping and leisure complexes viable.

Other positive externalities include the following.

- If I spend time and money improving my garden and house, other people may take pleasure from looking at my garden and my neighbours' properties may appreciate in value. These people will benefit from my actions without paying for the advantages they gain.
- If a firm spends money on training staff who leave when their training is completed, rival firms gain the benefit. These firms are unlikely to compensate the firm which undertook the training.
- The production of cars, through creating employment in an area, will benefit the shops and places of entertainment in which car workers spend their money.
- The provision of improved rail services between London and Birmingham, for instance, would encourage more people to travel by train. This would reduce road congestion, accidents and pollution.

Activity 5

Decide whether the following are positive or negative externalities.

a the trees in a farmer's orchard being pollinated by bees kept by a neighbour

b the construction of a motorway reducing the biodiversity of an area

c a person talking in a loud voice on their mobile phone on a crowded train

d a firm discovering a new, cheaper process by reading about the results of another firm's research and development

e a taxi firm's takings being affected by the introduction of a new bus service

Social costs and benefits

Social costs are the total costs to society of an economic activity. They consist of both private costs (in terms of the price paid or expenditure on factors of production) and negative externalities (such as pollution and congestion).

In some cases the costs to society as a whole are greater than the costs to those who pay to consume and produce the products. Where social costs exceed private costs, there are negative externalities. For example, the social cost of smoking exceeds the private cost of the price that smokers pay for the cigarettes. This is because smoking has harmful effects on others. The negative externalities include passive smoking and the burden on the national health service.

Social benefits are the total benefits to society from an economic activity. They consist of both private benefits and positive externalities. So where social benefits exceed private benefits, there are positive externalities.

Health care and education give rise to positive externalities. People undertaking education can receive both private consumption and investment benefits. They may enjoy the courses they undertake and their studies may stimulate lifelong interests. Qualifications also raise people's earning capacity – for example, graduates earn considerably more than non-graduates. There are also benefits for third parties. The positive externalities include higher output, resulting from a more informed and inventive labour force, and a more educated electorate.

In health care the private benefits can also be divided into consumption and investment benefits. Receiving preventative or curative health care can improve the quality of people's lives. They may also receive higher lifelong earnings because they are able to perform better at work and have fewer days off ill. The positive externalities again include higher output, resulting from a healthier labour force, and a reduction in the risk of disease which people enjoy through others being inoculated against and treated for infectious diseases.

The allocatively efficient output

The **allocatively efficient output** occurs where the marginal social cost (MSC) equals the marginal social benefit (MSB) as illustrated in

Activity 6

The construction of a new rail link between Oxford and Witney, a town 12 miles away, is being considered. The main route between Witney and Oxford is the A40 which, for most of its distance, is a single-lane road that is heavily congested at peak hours. Stagecoach operates a regular bus service on this route.

Many people who live in Witney work in Oxford, and many regularly visit Oxford for shopping and entertainment.

Identify:

a the social costs of building and operating a rail link between Witney and Oxford, distinguishing between private and external costs

b the social benefits of building and operating the rail link, distinguishing between private benefits and external benefits

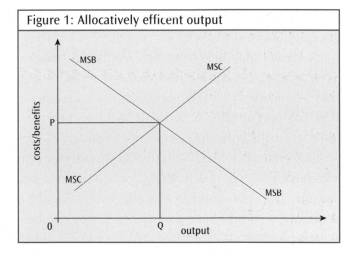

Figure 1: Allocatively efficent output

Figure 1. This output can also be called the socially optimum output, as it is the output which most benefits society.

At output Q the value that consumers place on the last unit produced is equal to the full cost of producing that unit.

The allocatively efficient output can also be illustrated on a demand and supply diagram. It occurs where demand and supply are equal, as then the right quantity of resources is allocated to the production of the product. However, this happens only if demand and supply reflect the full social costs and benefits involved.

The effect of externalities

The existence of externalities results in an inefficient allocation of resources. Products are overproduced where there are negative externalities and underproduced where there are positive externalities.

When firms and consumers make their production and consumption decisions, they usually take into account only marginal private cost (MPC) and marginal private benefit (MPB). This does not create a problem if there are no externalities, since then private costs and benefits will equal social costs and benefits. However, Figure 2 shows that where there are negative externalities, MSC exceeds MPC. Output (Q) is greater than the allocatively efficient output of QX and the price charged (P) is below that of PX, which reflects the full cost of producing the product.

This can also be illustrated on a demand and supply diagram. In Figure 3 the supply curve SS reflects private costs and the curve SXSX shows the full cost of producing the product, or social costs. The price, P, is again shown below the allocatively efficient price of PX and there is overproduction of Q – QX.

A market also fails to be efficient when there are positive externalities. Figure 4 shows that where MSB is greater than MPB, consumers will demand less than the allocatively efficient output of QX. So firms will not allocate sufficient resources to the production of the product.

The price, P, which is charged is lower than the value, PX, which society receives from the product. To persuade consumers to demand QX amount, they would have to be encouraged to take into account not only the benefits to themselves but also to others, or the price would have to be lowered to P1.

The failure of a market to allocate resources efficiently in the presence of externalities, in this case positive externalities, can be illustrated on a demand and supply diagram. In Figure 5 DD represents demand based on private benefits and DXDX is demand based on social benefits. Output Q is shown to be below the allocatively efficient output of QX.

Activity 7

Explain why allocatively efficient output is not achieved where:

a MSC exceeds MSB

b MSB exceeds MSC

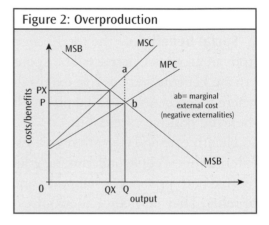

Figure 2: Overproduction

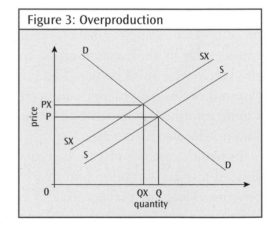

Figure 3: Overproduction

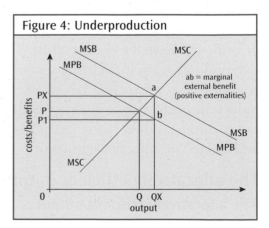

Figure 4: Underproduction

Activity 8

It has been argued that too many resources are devoted to the production of alcoholic drinks.

a What does this statement indicate about the relationship between marginal social cost and marginal social benefit in the market for alcohol?

b Identify three negative externalities which can arise from people drinking alcohol.

Welfare loss

When output is undertaken where marginal social cost and marginal social benefit are not equal, consumers will experience a **welfare loss**.

Figure 6 shows output taking place where MSC exceeds MSB. The value that consumers place on the extra unit of output at Q is less than the cost to society of producing that output. A reduction in output to QX would increase the welfare of consumers.

A welfare loss also arises when MSB is greater than MSC. Figure 7 shows the welfare loss arising when consumers value the product more than the cost of producing the last unit. Society would benefit from an increase in output from Q to QX.

Current issue: achieving a socially optimum output

To achieve a socially optimum output, it is necessary to calculate the costs and benefits involved as accurately as possible.

In the case of externalities, this is not always easy. Some externalities can be calculated by assessing the financial benefits and costs that third parties experience. For instance, the building of a football stadium will increase the revenue earned by nearby public houses and places of entertainment.

It is harder to estimate the non-monetary externalities. Economists seek to find out how much people who benefit from positive externalities would be prepared to pay for them, and how much people who suffer from negative externalities would need to be paid to compensate them for putting up with them. Surveys can be undertaken, asking people about the extent to which they are affected. However, some people may be uncertain about how much they will be affected before the stadium is built. Others may exaggerate harmful effects, thinking they may be compensated, and play down benefits, fearing that they may have to pay for them in the future.

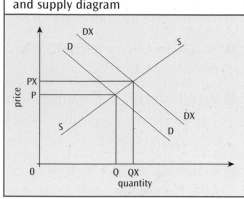

Figure 5: Underproduction on a demand and supply diagram

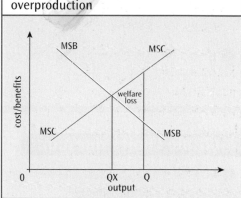

Figure 6: Welfare loss from overproduction

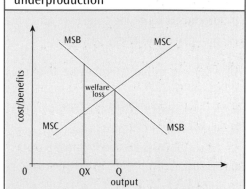

Figure 7: Welfare loss from underproduction

Summary

In this unit you have learned that:

- People are often affected by the economic decisions of others.

- **Private costs** and **benefits** are those experienced by people directly involved in the decisions to produce and consume products.

- **Externalities** are effects on people resulting from the production and consumption decisions of others.

- **Social costs** are the total costs to society of an economic decision.

- If social costs exceed private costs, there must be negative externalities.

- **Social benefits** are the total benefits to society of an economic decision.

- If social benefits exceed private benefits, there are positive externalities.

- The existence of **negative externalities** results in overproduction and hence market failure.

- The existence of **positive externalities** results in underproduction and hence market failure.

- The **allocatively efficient output** is where MSC equals MSB.

- When output is undertaken where MSC and MSB are not equal, consumers experience a **welfare loss**.

Multiple choice questions

1 What does a gap between the social and private costs of producing a product imply?

A underproduction

B the existence of negative externalities

C the divergence between private and social benefits

D producers pursuing objectives other than profit maximisation

2 Why does training tend to be underproduced if left to market forces?

A it gives rise to external benefits

B it gives rise to external costs

C its social costs exceed its private costs

D its social costs equal its private costs

3 Which of the following is an external cost of production?

A the bad publicity a firm receives from dumping waste in a beauty spot

B the rise in a firm's average costs resulting from the firm growing too large

C the emission of an unpleasant smell during the production process

D the cost of buying raw materials from another firm

4 What is another name for negative externalities?

A external costs

B private costs

C social costs

D unit costs

5 In Figure 8, which area illustrates the welfare loss that occurs if production is at Q?

A RST

B RSQQX

C PXPSR

D OPXRQX

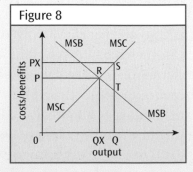

Figure 8

6 Socially optimum output is achieved where:

A MPC equals MPB

B MEC equals MEB

C MSC equals MSB

D MSC equals MPC

Data response question: the costs of driving cars

When people drive their cars they generate more costs than they pay for. This is particularly true when they drive on congested roads. In this case the gap between marginal social cost and marginal private cost of an extra road user can be very high.

Most car drivers are unaware of the size and range of the externalities they cause. They think that the cost of driving is high and that the taxes they pay in terms of road tax and fuel tax more than cover the costs their driving imposes on society. This is why they think that taxes on car ownership and driving should be reduced, not increased.

Economists, however, argue that car drivers pay less through taxation and other costs for using roads than the real costs of their use. As a result, there is an inefficient allocation of resources. Society would benefit from allocating fewer resources to road use and more resources to other forms of transport, including rail and bus travel.

a Explain what is meant by marginal social cost of an extra road user. [3]

b Explain why the gap between the marginal social cost and the marginal private cost of an extra road user can be very high on a congested road. [3]

c Identify:
  i two private costs of driving [2]
  ii three external costs of driving [3]

d Using a diagram, explain how the allocation of resources devoted to car driving may be inefficient. [6]

e Identify three external benefits arising from people deciding to travel by bus. [3]

5 Public goods

In this unit you will discover the essential characteristics of a public good, how to distinguish between **public** and **private goods**, the nature of **mixed** and **quasi public goods** and the significance of the existence of public goods.

Definition of public goods

There are some products which, if left to free market forces, would provide benefits for consumers but would not be produced. These products are called **public goods**.

Public goods have two defining characteristics: they are non-rival and non-excludable.

■ Non-rival means one person's consumption of the product does not prevent anyone else consuming the product. For example, if I walk down a street at night, the benefit I receive from the light provided by the streetlights does not prevent anyone else taking advantage of that light.

■ Non-excludable means that consumption of the product cannot be restricted to those who have paid for it. Once it is made available for a few it is made available for all. There can be free riders in the sense of people enjoying the product without paying for it. For example, some people in an area threatened by flooding may say that they do not want to contribute to paying for a flood defence system in the knowledge that if the system is built their house will be protected.

Non-rivalry and non-excludability are the principal characteristics of public goods, but there are others that most public goods share.

Some, such as a vaccination programme, have large external benefits relative to private benefits. Once provided, the marginal cost of supplying some public goods to one more person is zero. An extra person walking down the street does not add to the cost of providing street lighting. Some public goods cannot be rejected in the sense that people cannot stop consuming them even if they want to. For example, some people may not want the police patrolling their neighbourhood but they are given no choice.

Activity 1

Public libraries are state-financed. Anyone can join a public library and make use of its facilities, including borrowing books, videotapes and CDs and using its reference sections. Public libraries are, however, not public goods.

Explain why public libraries are not public goods.

The distinction between public and private goods

To understand the nature of public goods, it is useful to distinguish between public and **private goods**. Most products are private goods. This means that they are both rival and excludable. For instance, if I buy a television someone else cannot buy it, and if I am not willing and able to pay for a television, the shop will not allow me to take one. Similarly, the enjoyment of food items, clothing and most other goods and services can be made dependent on direct payment to the supplier.

Activity 2

Decide whether the following are public or private goods:

a newspapers

b pavements

c public drainage

d public transport

e retirement homes

Mixed and quasi public goods

Some products have some of the characteristics of both private and public goods. These are sometimes called **mixed goods**. For example, up to a certain volume of traffic, one more driver on a road will not affect the driving experience of others. It is also difficult, but not impossible, to exclude drivers from a road with many entry and exit points.

Products that have some of the characteristics of private goods but come closest to a public good can be called **quasi public goods**. For example, the enjoyment a person derives from visiting the New Forest, which covers an area of 376 square km in the south of England, may not be reduced by more visitors unless they are concentrated in the same part. It would also be difficult to exclude non-payers, and attempts to do so would reduce the natural beauty of the area, the very feature that encourages people to visit it.

Some public and quasi public goods are moving closer to private goods through advances in technology. The development of smart cards, for instance, has made it possible to charge drivers according to which city roads they drive on and at which times.

Activity 3

Explain why a large beach may be regarded as a quasi public good.

The significance of public goods

The principal characteristics of public goods mean that their consumption cannot be made dependent on direct payment. Many people are unlikely, for example, to be prepared to pay for updating the country's sewage system. They know that everyone will benefit from any improvements and that if they do not pay they cannot be excluded from them.

As suppliers cannot withhold public goods if people do not pay for them, a free market is unlikely to provide them. Government intervention can solve the problem since the government can make people pay for public goods by taxing them. Some public goods, including the provision of defence by central government and street lighting by local authorities, are provided directly by the state. Others, including flood control, are provided by the government giving contracts to private-sector firms.

Current issue: environmental problems

Environmental problems increasingly feature in the news. These problems arise largely as a result of three market failures.

- The quasi public good nature of the environment. It is difficult to exclude people from using large parts of the environment, particularly the air and the sea. This makes it difficult to charge for its use. However, after a certain point the use of the environment becomes rival. For example, only so much waste can be buried in a landfill site and only so much timber can be obtained from a tropical rainforest.

- The use of the environment generates externalities. When car drivers create pollution through exhaust fumes and firms create pollution by emitting poisonous gases during production, they are imposing costs on third parties.

- Lack of information. People may be unaware or not fully informed of the extent to which their activities are harming the environment. For example, many people do not realise that the coolants used in fridges can create chlorofluorocarbons (CFCs), which are released into the atmosphere.

Summary

In this unit you have learned that:

- The two defining characteristics of **public goods** are that it is not possible to exclude non-payers from enjoying them and one more person enjoying them does not reduce other people's enjoyment of them.

- Most products are **private goods**. They are both excludable and rival.

- **Mixed goods** have some of the characteristics of both private and public goods. A product which comes close to being a public good can be called a **quasi public good**.

- As people can act as free riders, it is unlikely that a free market will provide public goods. They have to be financed through taxation.

Multiple choice questions

1 What is a public good? One which:

A involves no externalities

B is supplied by the government

C if consumed by one person is still available for consumption by others

D if people do not pay they can be excluded from consuming

2 Which of the following is a public good?

A air traffic control

B education

C health care

D postal services

3 Which of the following is a defining characteristic of a pure public good?

A it is rival in consumption

B it has to be produced by the state

C no one can be excluded from enjoying it

D there is no opportunity cost involved in its production

4 Why can public goods not be supplied through the price mechanism?

A some people would not be able to afford to buy them

B they would be overconsumed and so overproduced

C the benefits enjoyed cannot be restricted to the buyers as they are automatically made available to non-buyers

D private-sector firms would use their market power to charge a price in excess of the marginal cost of production

5 A public good is non-rival. What does this mean?

A it is produced by a monopoly

B the resources used to produce it have no alternative uses

C people not willing to pay for it cannot be excluded from enjoying it

D consumption of it by one person does not reduce the quantity available to other consumers

6 Which of the following is a public good?

A a car

B car insurance

C petrol

D traffic lights

Data response question

Plans by ministers to privatise the prison regarded as Britain's worst have collapsed because no company was prepared to run the troubled jail.

The refusal of any private security firm to take on HMP Brixton in South London is an embarrassment to the Home Office, which decided in the summer of last year to 'market-test' the prison.

A year after the former prisons minister, Paul Boateng, announced that the 'failing' prison was to be the first public penal institution to face privatisation, the Prisons Service admitted that no company had submitted a tender.

The only offer to run the jail was a bid by the present prison staff, led by the new governor, Stephen Twinn, to continue running the prison within the public sector.

The outcome is a blow for ministers, who had hoped that turning Brixton prison over to the private sector would send a warning message to other underperforming jails. ('Private firms refuse to run 'Britain's worst jail', Ian Burrell, Independent, *2 August 2001)*

a Discuss why the government was seeking a private security firm to run Brixton prison. [5]

b Explain why private security firms may have been reluctant to tender for the contract to run Brixton prison. [5]

c Explain why the Prison Service can be regarded as a public good. [6]

d Discuss one positive and one negative externality arising from a new prison being opened in a town. [4]

6 Merit and demerit goods

In this unit you will examine the nature of products that governments seek to encourage people to consume more of and products that governments seek to discourage people from consuming. You will see why market forces may fail to allocate the appropriate quantity of resources to producing these products.

Merit goods

Merit goods are more beneficial for consumers than they realise. For example, people may not fully appreciate the advantages of regular health check-ups and studying. Merit goods also usually have positive externalities. As noted in Unit 3, health care and education provide benefits for third parties.

Health care and education are merit goods. They are not public goods since it is possible to make consumption of them dependent on payment. They are rival as one person undergoing a hip operation or gaining a university place stops someone else having the operation from the same staff at the same time or taking up the same university place. In the UK and many other countries, some health care and education services are sold in the private sector.

However, the UK government believes that if left to market forces, education, health care and other products including training, insurance, inoculation and seat belts would be underconsumed and so underproduced. This, of course, involves a value judgement. The government is acting on the assumption that it knows better than individuals what is best for them. A few economists argue that individuals are the best judges of what to consume and that the government is taking a paternalistic approach in promoting the consumption of these goods.

Activity 1

In 1998 grants were replaced by interest-free loans. Now students from families that earn more than £20,000 have to pay tuition fees. They also face other costs including rent, books and travel. In 2001 it was estimated that the annual cost per student outside London was £7,011. This means that many students have to work during the academic year. Money problems cause some students to drop out of their courses.

Employers find that graduates have higher productivity levels than non-graduates. Graduates can expect to earn 56% more over their working life than non-graduates, on average £1,071,114 compared with £685,616.

a Identify a private benefit of education.

b Explain why higher education may be underconsumed.

Demerit goods

Demerit goods are more harmful for consumers than they realise. For example, smokers may not be fully informed of the health risks of smoking or may underestimate the chances of being affected by smoking-related illnesses.

Demerit goods also usually have harmful effects on third parties, or negative externalities. The consumption of alcohol, for instance, can have an adverse effect not only on drinkers but also on others. The negative externalities created may include drunks creating a disturbance in public places, workers who drink heavily making mistakes at work and heavy drinkers placing a burden on the health service.

145

What are viewed as demerit goods varies over time and among countries. For example, the Dutch government has a more liberal attitude to the use and sale of cannabis than the UK government.

Activity 2

Clubbers who take drugs have more health problems.

Regular ecstasy users are 25% more likely to suffer a mental health disorder than the rest of the population, according to what is believed to be the most extensive survey of clubbers published yesterday [14 January 2002].

One in four had a potentially serious psychiatric disorder, compared to the national average of less than one in five, the survey of 1,000 clubbers, in the dance culture magazine Mixmag, *revealed.*

Respondents were also twice as likely to have seen a doctor about mental health issues, with half of those being concerned about depression.

The findings – gleaned after respondents completed a mental health questionnaire used to diagnose psychological disorders – tally with a wealth of recent research suggesting ecstasy is linked to mental health problems such as paranoia, panic attacks and depression. ('Mental health warning to ecstasy users', Sarah Hall, Guardian, *15 January 2002)*

a What information may clubbers lack about the effects of taking ecstasy tablets on a regular basis?

b How does the UK government seek to discourage the consumption of ecstasy tablets?

The significance of merit and demerit goods

If people do not fully appreciate the beneficial and harmful effects of some of the products they consume, then resources will not be allocated efficiently. Merit goods will be underprovided if left to market forces. Figure 1 shows why. Demand, represented by the demand curve DD, is based on an underestimate of private benefits. The full benefit to consumers and third parties is represented by the demand curve D1D1. So society would gain from increasing output from Q to Q1.

In the case of demerit goods, too many resources will be allocated to their production without government

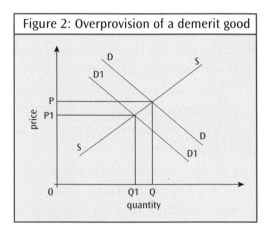

Figure 1: Underprovision of a merit good

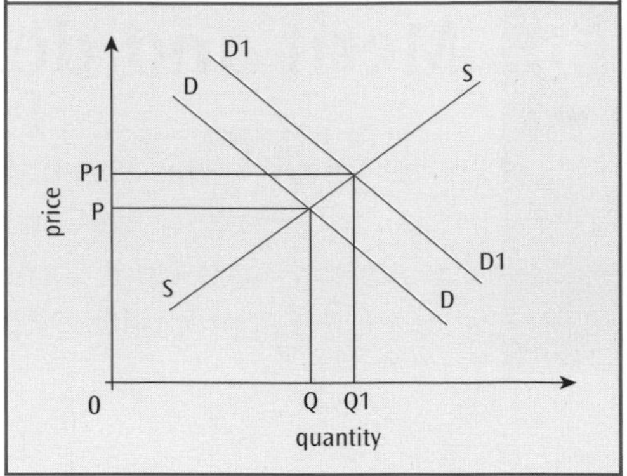

Figure 2: Overprovision of a demerit good

Activity 3

Decide which of the following are merit goods and which are demerit goods and explain why:

a heroin

b catalytic converters

c insurance

d MOT tests

e public libraries

intervention. Figure 2 shows that people's perception of the benefits of a demerit good, shown by demand curve DD, is greater than the true benefits.

A reduction in output from Q to Q1 would be a move towards a more efficient allocation of resources.

Current issue: cannabis

In July 2002 the government reclassified cannabis as a class C drug. This means that the police no longer automatically arrest people for smoking it. However, in certain circumstances people can be arrested, such as when they are causing a disturbance, and its sale is still an arrestable offence. Some argue that the use and sale of the drug should be fully legalised.

Those in favour argue that cannabis use can be less harmful than drinking alcohol and that people are fully informed about the effects of cannabis use. They also argue that legalising its use would reduce crime and reduce the pain of people suffering from medical complaints such as multiple sclerosis.

Those who oppose legalisation are concerned about the harmful effects of cannabis use on people's health and the risk that people who take it may go on to take, and become addicted to, hard drugs. They believe that there is a serious information failure and regard cannabis as a demerit good, with many people failing to appreciate the adverse effects its use can have. They also think that cannabis use causes negative externalities, including car accidents and accidents and underperformance at work.

Summary

In this unit you have learned that:

- **Merit goods** have more private benefits than consumers realise.

- If left to market forces, merit goods would be underconsumed and hence underproduced.

- Merit goods usually have positive externalities.

- **Demerit goods** have more harmful effects than consumers realise.

- If left to market forces, demerit goods would be overconsumed and hence overproduced.

- Demerit goods usually have negative externalities.

- The decision as to what constitutes merit and demerit goods and the extent to which they generate private benefits and private costs that consumers do not recognise is a value judgement.

Merit and demerit goods

Multiple choice questions

1 What is a merit good?

A a good that is both non-excludable and non-rival

B a good that the government considers people will buy too little of if it is provided by market forces

C a good where the social costs of consumption exceed the private costs of consumption

D a good where there are significant benefits to those firms which produce it

2 Which of the following is a merit good?

A defence

B health care

C radio transmissions

D street lighting

3 What is a demerit good?

A a good that has positive externalities

B a good that is produced at a loss by private-sector firms

C a good that will be overconsumed if provided by private-sector firms at market prices

D a good where the social benefits of consumption exceed the private benefits

4 Which of the following is a demerit good?

A an economics textbook

B fresh fruit

C security locks

D tobacco

5 A market provides a demerit good. If there is no government intervention, how will the market outcome compare with the allocatively efficient outcome?

	Market price	Market output
A	too high	too high
B	too high	too low
C	too low	too high
D	too low	too low

6 A merit good is one which is:

A underconsumed and underproduced

B underconsumed and overproduced

C overconsumed and underproduced

D overconsumed and overproduced

Data response question: drinking health risk for young women

Women are drinking themselves into early graves, with some consuming so much alcohol they are developing serious liver disease in their early 20s, doctors warn.

Advanced cirrhosis of the liver, traditionally found in hard drinking men in their 40s and 50s, is now being diagnosed in young women, the Royal College of Physicians said.

The warning that more women are damaging their health through drink came as the college said that alcohol-related problems were costing the nation up to £6bn a year. Drink-related illnesses accounted for up to 12% of NHS funding for hospitals, or £3bn a year, with extra costs to the taxpayer from the knock-on effects of absenteeism, unemployment and loss to business.

One in five women and one in three men are known to drink more than the recommended sensible levels regularly. Teenagers are also drinking substantially more and starting at a younger age, with the danger they will turn into heavy-drinking adults.

The college recommends that a national alcohol director should be appointed to give the problem as much

importance as drug abuse and change the nation's relaxed attitude to overdrinking.

Ian Gilmore, the chairman of the college working party that produced the report, said the change in drinking patterns now meant doctors were treating young women who had developed life-threatening cirrhosis over six months rather than 10 years of heavy drinking as expected. ('Drinking health risk for women in their 20s', Lorna Duckworth, Independent, *2 February 2001*)

a What evidence is there in the extract that alcohol is a demerit good? [6]

b Discuss the negative externalities which result from the consumption of alcohol. [8]

c What does the extract suggest is happening to the quantity of resources devoted to producing alcohol? [3]

d To increase efficiency, what should happen to the quantity of resources devoted to producing alcohol? [3]

7 Information failure

Misleading advertising can persuade consumers to make purchases that do not maximise their satisfaction. Misleading or a lack of information can cause suppliers and workers to make inappropriate choices. For markets to work efficiently, it is necessary for all participants to have adequate and accurate information. In this unit you will examine the three main forms of information failure.

Lack of information

Consumers' ability to maximise their welfare by buying the highest-quality and lowest-priced products is influenced by the amount of information they have about products and suppliers. Advances in technology, particularly the internet, are increasing the information available, but it still takes time to make comparisons, full and up-to-date information is not available on all products and not everyone has access to the internet.

Workers may be unaware of job opportunities outside their current employment and may fail to recognise the benefits of training and education. Suppliers may lack information about the availability and productivity of different factors of production and so may not produce at the lowest possible average cost.

Inaccurate information

Consumers, workers and suppliers may make inefficient choices because they have inaccurate information. They may then enter into transactions which leave them worse off, and so Pareto efficiency is not achieved.

Persuasive advertising may mean that consumers operate on the basis of incorrect information. For example, some people may be persuaded to buy a cream that will not cure their acne, and some may buy lottery tickets thinking their chances of winning are greater than they really are. Some workers may be misled about

promotion chances and fringe benefits when they are offered a job, and some may not be given the right instructions about how best to undertake their tasks.

Suppliers may have an incentive to provide inaccurate information to their rivals. For instance, a firm moving into an area may ask other firms in that area what wages they pay. These firms may state that they pay less than they really do, hoping that the new firm will offer low wages and so have difficulty attracting labour.

Consumers may not always provide suppliers with accurate information. People with a history of illness or a genetic susceptibility to illness may lie when completing applications for health insurance.

Activity 1

In January 2002 GlaxoSmithKline, a British pharmaceuticals company, was found guilty of misleading the public about its anti-depressant drug, Seroxat. One of its executives said on television that reports of withdrawal symptoms were 'very rare'. It was forced to issue a new warning to patients and doctors, acknowledging that some people might become addicted and suffer severe side effects when they try to stop taking it.

a What information did consumers lack about Seroxat before January 2002?

b Explain what effect the lack of information would have on the consumption and production of the drug.

Activity 2

In February 2002 some credit card companies and retailers were banned from using 'misleading' sales tactics for credit agreements. Many companies attract customers with the promise of a low interest rate for the first six months of a credit agreement. However, after this introductory period, the cost of such loans can rise quickly and steeply.

a What risk do 'misleading' sales tactics for credit agreements pose for consumers?

b Why do companies make special introductory offers?

Asymmetric information

In some transactions information is unlikely to be shared equally between the two parties. This is known as **asymmetric information**. For example, a person visiting a doctor is unlikely to have the medical knowledge to question a doctor's diagnosis and recommendations for treatment. Similarly, a car mechanic, possessing more knowledge of cars than most consumers, may be able to persuade customers to pay for work that has not actually been done or for more extensive work than was needed.

Activity 3

Some private-sector dentists have been accused of giving their patients more dental treatment than necessary.

a What enables some dentists to give their patients more treatment than they need?

b What effect does such action have on the efficiency of the dental health market?

Current issue: the internet

The internet provides people with a wealth of information, enabling them to make more informed choices. People who have been told they have an illness can find out more about it, check the records of hospitals treating it and learn about the side effects of any medication.

People wanting to buy a train ticket can check out the cheapest offers; people wanting to buy a book can find out the price charged in various countries; and people planning a holiday can search for information about different destinations.

Increased access to information gives consumers more market power and puts pressure on firms to achieve productive and allocative efficiency.

Summary

In this unit you have learned that:

■ Lack of information may result in consumers, workers and suppliers making decisions that do not maximise their welfare.

■ Inefficient choices may be made as a result of inaccurate information.

■ Information is not always equally shared between the two parties of a transaction which may mean that the transaction does not equally benefit both parties.

Multiple choice questions

1 A lack of information about job vacancies in the south of the country while there is unemployment in the north can result in:

A falling house prices in the south

B geographical immobility of labour

C occupational immobility of labour

D wage rises in the north of the country

2 A firm buys components from one supplier, unaware that components of the same quality can be purchased from another supplier at a lower price. What will this result in?

A higher profit for the firm

B lower price for the firm's consumers

C productive inefficiency

D allocative efficiency

Multiple choice questions continued

3 A poor person buys a large number of scratch cards each week. He or she is likely to be:

A underestimating the chances of winning a large sum
B estimating accurately the chances of winning a large sum
C overestimating the chances of winning a large sum
D indifferent to the chances of winning a large sum

4 What occurs when a transaction does not benefit both parties?

A allocative efficiency
B Pareto inefficiency
C productive inefficiency
D socially optimum output

5 When people visit a restaurant, which piece of information are they most likely to be lacking?

A the price of the different meals served
B when the restaurant is open
C how clean the kitchen is
D the type of food served

6 A pet owner is persuaded by an unscrupulous vet to spend more on medication for his dog than necessary. This a case of market failure arising from:

A asymmetric information
B inaccurate information held by the vet
C veterinary treatment being a public good
D negative externalities arising from veterinary treatment

Data response question: Botox

Botox is a treatment derived from a purified form of toxin released by the botulinum *bacterium which can cause chronic food poisoning.*

It was the discovery of the toxin's ability to eliminate wrinkles and fine lines, by paralysing the facial muscles that cause them, which saw the beginning of the Botox revolution. Soon word was spreading of the 'miracle treatment' that would smooth furrowed brows and iron out awkward imperfections.

… poorly administered doses have led to reports of patients temporarily losing the ability to swallow or speak normally.

Of further concern is the way in which Botox is marketed. It is part of a new group of non-surgical treatments, including 'skin-peel' and collagen 'fillers' which, while not as extreme or potentially hazardous as traditional facelifts and surgery, require continued use to maintain the result.

Most users of Botox repeat the 10-minute procedure every three months which, at between £200 and £500 a treatment, makes it a nice earner for the clinics cashing in on the boom. The profits of Allergan, the treatment's manufacturer, have soared, with revenue from Botox growing from £12 million 10 years ago to more than £190 million last year [2001], with some analysts predicting that this figure could quadruple within the next two years should the drug be declassified for cosmetic use. (Declassification would mean no medical qualifications would be necessary to administer the treatment.)

In America, the Food and Drug Administration is understood to have requested that Allergan's marketing plans, which include advertisements for billboards, magazines and buses, should not feature models under the age of 40.

In the United Kingdom, some practitioners appear willing to overlook the age or appearance of a potential client, playing instead on vanity and insecurity. (Extracts from 'It's developed from a deadly bacterium that paralyses muscles. So why are so many women willing to take the Botox plunge?', Jane Mulkerruns and Lois Rogers, The Sunday Times, *17 February 2002)*

a What does the passage suggest is happening to the demand for Botox treatment? [3]

b i   In what sense is there likely to be asymmetric information in the market for Botox? [3]
   ii What evidence is there in the passage to suggest that inaccurate information about Botox may be being provided to consumers? [3]

c Identify three forms of information about Botox which consumers may lack. [3]

d Explain what is likely to happen if declassification is introduced in the UK to:
   i   the price charged for Botox treatment [4]
   ii the quality of Botox treatment? [4]

8 Market power

In most markets in the UK firms have a degree of market power, but there is a danger that this can result in market failure. In this unit you will examine how market power arises and how it can result in market failure.

Growth of market power

Over time the number of firms in any market declines, giving the remaining firms greater market power. This is because firms have a profit incentive to grow and eliminate rivals. If a firm can gain a competitive edge, it can grow and, by taking advantage of economies of scale, reduce other firms' ability to stay in the market. It can also increase its market power by taking over or merging with other firms in the market.

In most markets firms do not operate under conditions of perfect competition. They operate under conditions of monopolistic competition, oligopoly or monopoly – all markets with some degree of market power.

The existence of market power reduces the competitive pressure on producers and shifts the influence on the use and allocation of resources from consumers towards producers. This can lead to market failure for the reasons listed below.

Activity 1

The big four banks, Barclays, Royal Bank of Scotland/NatWest, HSBC and Lloyds TSB, account for 83% of the small business banking market.

a What is the market structure of small business banking?

b How would you expect firms in this market to compete?

Prevention of entry into and exit of firms from the market

There are barriers to entry and exit in both oligopoly and monopoly (see Section 2, Unit 11). This means that markets operating under these conditions may not respond quickly or fully to changes in consumer demand. For example, the existence of barriers means that if consumer demand for a product increases, the entry of new firms will be blocked and the capacity of the industry will not expand sufficiently to meet the higher consumer demand.

Activity 2

Silentnight Beds ran a successful advertising campaign for its 'miracoil' spring mattress featuring a hippopotamus and a duck as husband and wife. The advert was supported by sponsorship of an ITV drama, *Where the heart is*.

a What would be considered to be a successful advertising campaign?

b In what sense may Silentnight Beds' advertising campaign and sponsorship act as a barrier to entry?

Restricting output and raising price

To generate higher profits, firms with market power may push up the price by restricting supply. This means that they will produce at a level of output where price is greater than marginal cost. As a result they will fail to achieve allocative efficiency and consumers may have to pay more and be able to buy less than if the market was more competitive.

Activity 3

In February 2002 government watchdogs ruled that Nationwide, a building society, had been overcharging some of its customers. In response to the ruling, Nationwide agreed to pay out an average windfall of £250 each to 400,000 mortgage customers.

a Building societies operate in an oligopolistic market. Identify three characteristics of an oligopolistic market.

b Explain the effect a rise in the interest charged by a building society on mortgage loans given to its customers may have on:
   i the revenue of the building society
   ii the profits of the building society
   iii consumer surplus

Failure to keep costs low

The lack of competition in monopoly or oligopoly markets where firms collude may mean that firms do not seek to minimise average costs. They may become complacent and not make efficient use of scarce resources. For example, there may be overstaffing and the use of out-of-date production techniques. This tendency for firms in monopoly and oligopoly markets to produce at higher than minimum average cost is known as organisational slack or **X-inefficiency**.

Activity 4

In January 2002 bus companies Arriva and FirstGroup were found guilty of operating a **cartel**. It was proved that staff of both companies had met in a hotel room and agreed Arriva would withdraw five buses on two local routes. This left FirstGroup with no competition on either route. In return, FirstGroup agreed to withdraw from two routes that Arriva took on.

a What would be the likely effect on bus fares of the bus companies' action?

b What would have motivated the two companies to form a cartel?

Restricting the introduction of new products

Firms with market power may delay or stop the introduction of new or improved products if they believe this would reduce their profits. For instance, pharmaceuticals firms may prevent a cure for the common cold coming on to the market as they earn a considerable amount from selling cough medicines, throat lozenges and other medication for colds.

There is also a debate about whether the existence of market power encourages or discourages innovation (see Section 2, Unit 11).

Current issue: market power in oligopolistic markets

In oligopolistic markets, the dominant firms can exercise considerable market power. Theory suggests that in these markets, such as those for cars, detergents and processed food, price is higher and output is lower than is socially ideal.

However, in some oligopolistic markets the firms have large capital equipment and thus high overhead costs. In this case the firms have an incentive to sell a high output so that they can take full advantage of economies of scale and so lower costs. If the firms are more concerned with growth than short-term profit maximisation, they may set low prices. The car industry, for example, is criticised not for underproducing but for overproducing.

Summary

In this unit you have learned that:

- Market power develops because firms have a profit incentive to grow and capture a larger share of the market.

- Market power can be consolidated by taking advantage of economies of scale and taking over or merging with competitors.

- Market power shifts the influence over the use and allocation of resources from consumers to producers.

- Barriers to entry into and exit from markets reduces the degree and speed of response to changes in consumer demand.

- To increase profits, firms with market power may push up price by restricting supply and produce where price is greater than marginal cost.

- The lack of competition may mean that firms in monopoly markets and oligopoly markets, where collusion occurs, become complacent and produce at higher than minimum average cost.

- Firms with market power may block the introduction of new or improved products if they believe they will reduce their profits.

Multiple choice questions

1 Which of the following can give rise to monopoly power?

A a patent

B low transport costs

C diseconomies of scale

D the entry of new firms into the industry

2 Which of the following features is found in monopoly but not perfect competition?

A an absence of barriers to firms entering and leaving the industry

B all the firms in the industry produce a homogeneous product

C the ability of a firm to earn supernormal profit in the short run

D the ability of a firm to influence price

3 In which market structure will a firm have most market power?

A perfect competition

B monopolistic competition

C oligopoly

D monopoly

4 Which of the following would reduce the level of competition in a market?

A mergers between the firms

B a fall in start-up costs

C a reduction in firms' advertising expenditure

D an increase in information available about the profits earned in the market

5 Why, in practice, may innovation be greater in a market where firms have market power than in one where firms are unable to influence price?
The existence of:

A X-inefficiency

B competitive pressure

C perfect knowledge

D large profits to finance research and development

6 Firms having market power reduces:

A consumer surplus

B producer surplus

C barriers to entry

D barriers to exit

Data response question: fixing the price of vitamins

The European Commission levied record fines of 855m euros (£530m) on eight chemical and pharmaceutical companies yesterday for operating a cartel that fixed the price of vitamins used in a huge range of consumer products.

The firms are thought to have cost shoppers millions of pounds, by carving up the market and rigging prices for vitamins included in everything from cereals, biscuits and drinks to animal feed, pharmaceuticals and cosmetics.

Mario Monti, the EU competition commissioner, described the case as 'the most damaging series of cartels the Commission has ever investigated, due to the sheer range of vitamins covered which are found in a multitude of products'.

Consumer groups in Britain welcomed the fines, which they hoped would hasten the implementation of laws proposed in the Enterprise Bill to curb anti-competitive behaviour. The Consumers' Association described the secret vitamin cartel as 'corporate mugging'.

Phil Evans, principal policy adviser at the Consumers' Association, said: 'Any time a cartel jacks up the costs of legitimate business, they jack up the prices that the consumer ultimately pays.'

Mr Monti said the firms were able 'to charge higher prices than if the full forces of competition had been at play, damaging consumers and allowing the companies to pocket illicit profits'. ('Drug firms fined £530m for fixing price of vitamins', Stephen Castle and Matthew Beard, Independent, *22 November 2001*)

a Explain in what market structure pharmaceuticals companies operate. [3]

b What anti-competitive behaviour were the eight chemicals and pharmaceuticals companies found guilty of? [3]

c Explain how consumers suffered as a result of the anti-competitive behaviour of the firms. [4]

d Explain two barriers to entry which are likely to exist in the pharmaceutical market. [4]

e Discuss the effect that anti-competitive behaviour can have on efficiency. [6]

9 Factor immobility

In this unit you will examine how geographical immobility and occupational immobility of resources can lead to market failure. You will focus particularly on the immobility of labour.

Geographical immobility

All resources may be subject to geographical immobility, although land is the most geographically immobile and the entrepreneur probably the most mobile (see Section 1, Unit 11).

When there is difficulty in moving resources from one area to another, there will be a shortage of resources in some areas and a surplus in other areas. For example, in 2002 there were unfilled vacancies in the south-east of the UK and high unemployment in some areas of Northern Ireland and the north-east of the UK. Economists refer to the unemployment which exists in one area while there is unfilled demand for workers in other areas as **regional unemployment**. The existence of unemployment means that an economy is producing inside its production possibility curve.

Factor immobility

Activity 1

There are job vacancies in fast-food restaurants in the south of the UK and unemployed low-skilled workers in the north of the country.

Identify three reasons why low-skilled workers may not move to take up the vacancies in the fast-food restaurants.

Occupational immobility

Occupational immobility arises when it is difficult to move resources from one use to another. Land and entrepreneurs are relatively occupationally mobile. However, some capital can be used only for specific purposes and some workers find it difficult to switch from one occupation to another.

The result of occupational immobility is a shortage of resources in some industries and a surplus in other industries. In the UK in 2001 some former bank and building society workers remained unemployed and there was a shortage of teachers and telecommunications workers. The unemployment which arises when workers are unable to move from a declining to an expanding industry is known as **structural unemployment**. Occupational immobility means that producers do not make as many products as possible or the right quantities of different products.

Activity 2

Intelligent Finance, the HBOS internet and phone bank, created 800 jobs in a new branch on a former Royal Naval base in the Firth of Forth. Some of these were filled by staff relocating from the bank's other offices in Edinburgh and Livingston. However, some of the jobs were unfilled because of the shortage of workers in the area with financial sector skills.

a The relocation of staff from the bank's other offices to the new office is an example of what type of mobility?

b The shortage of workers with a particular skill is an example of what type of factor immobility?

Problems caused by factor immobility

Geographical and occupational immobility of resources result in a misallocation of resources. Markets are unable to respond fully to changes in consumer demand. Products which are declining in popularity are likely to be overproduced and others which are rising in popularity are likely to be underproduced. Some resources are not used at all.

The inappropriate use and unemployment of some resources means that allocative, productive and Pareto efficiency are not achieved.

Activity 3

As well as a shortage of highly skilled workers, there is also a shortage of low-skilled workers. Some call centres have relocated to the north-east of the UK, which suffers the highest unemployment in the country, in search of workers. However, they are experiencing problems recruiting staff as some of the people applying for the jobs do not know how to use computers.

a What form of immobility of labour were the call centres trying to overcome by moving to the north-east?

b i What form of labour immobility are the call centres experiencing?
   ii How could they try to overcome this problem?

c Explain the effect of a shortage of workers with the right skills on:
   i allocative efficiency
   ii productive efficiency

Current issue: the geographical mobility of labour

Concerns about shortages of skilled and unskilled workers in some occupations and their ageing populations have led the UK, the rest of the EU and the USA to make it easier for workers to enter their countries on a temporary or permanent basis. In 2000 the UK, for instance, recruited 5,000 nurses from Spain and Germany and 20,000 software specialists from India and Eastern Europe.

156

Nevertheless, barriers to the geographical mobility of labour still exist. People from outside the EU must have work permits or permanent residence in order to work in the UK. Other barriers include lack of knowledge of job opportunities, high housing costs, cultural differences and lack of recognition of some foreign qualifications.

Efforts to overcome some of these barriers are likely to accelerate as the working populations of the EU and the USA decline. Without any change in net immigration, the ratio of working-age people to pensioners in these regions is likely to fall from 4:1 in 2000 to 2.5:1 in 2050.

The EU and the USA may lack workers, but parts of Latin America, Africa and Asia have surplus workers. This suggests an inefficient allocation of resources. World output and the welfare of the world's population are likely to be raised by an increase in the international geographical mobility of workers.

Summary

In this unit you have learned that:

- Geographical immobility of resources refers to the difficulty of moving resources from one area to another.

- Geographical immobility of labour results in **regional unemployment**.

- Occupational immobility of resources occurs when there are problems moving resources from one use to another.

- Occupational immobility of labour results in **structural unemployment**.

- Geographical and occupational immobility of resources leads to a misallocation of resources.

Multiple choice questions

1 Which of the following would increase geographical immobility of labour?
A a reduction in transport costs
B a reduction in the differences in house prices in different areas of the country
C abolition of the national minimum wage
D abolition of the national curriculum in schools

2 Regional unemployment occurs when:
A the number of people voluntarily unemployed differs between regions
B there are job vacancies in one area and unemployed people in another area
C there are fewer jobs available in some parts of the country than in other parts
D people in one region are in between jobs

3 Which of the following is an example of structural unemployment?
A the unemployment of car workers resulting from the closing of a loss-making car company
B workers losing their jobs in one area when a bank transfers its headquarters from one city to another
C the unemployment of shop workers in one area while there are job vacancies in other parts of the country
D unemployed people unable to take up jobs in another part of the country because of family ties

4 Which of the following would increase the occupational mobility of labour?
A an increase in spending on training
B an increase in the qualifications required for skilled jobs
C an increase in the availability of rented accommodation
D a decrease in information about job vacancies

Multiple choice questions continued

5 The greater the degree of factor immobility:

A the nearer the economy is to producing on its production possibility curve

B the greater is the level of competition in factor markets

C the lower is the level of unemployment

D the longer it takes for markets to adjust to changes in consumer demand

6 Which movement in production points on Figure 1 could illustrate a reduction in the immobility of resources?

A R to S

B T to V

C T to S

D V to U

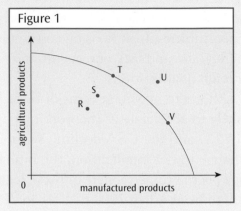

Figure 1

Data response question: recruitment difficulties

A council is struggling to fill key posts due to very low levels of unemployment and the high cost of housing.

The council's head of human resources, Mrs Tracy Madgwick, said: 'The council has recently struggled or failed to recruit for several key posts.

'The county as a whole has very low levels of unemployment and as a result, many employers are struggling to fill key posts within their organisations. One of the results of such low levels of unemployment is that salaries are pushed up as employers, in effect, compete with each other to attract and retain their staff.

'As a district council, we are competing with other local authorities and private industry to attract staff in several different labour markets.'

At the moment the council, which employs around 300 people, has 34 vacancies.

A recent campaign to recruit environmental health officers had ten strong applicants after interviews, but six did not accept the offer of a job due to house prices in the area.

Councillors will be considering a package of measures including increasing salaries, spending more on recruitment, advertising, mortgage subsidies and buying houses for employees to rent. ('Recruitment crisis hits council posts', Suzanne Huband, Witney Gazette, *28 November 2001)*

a Why was West Oxfordshire Council experiencing difficulty recruiting new staff in 2001? [3]

b What particular form of immobility of labour is outlined in the passage? [4]

c What measures were the Council planning to take to overcome this form of immobility of labour? [4]

d Explain how three of these measures might help to make labour more mobile. [9]

10 Inequalities in the distribution of income and wealth

In this unit you will examine how market failure in labour markets can result in inequalities in **income** and **wealth** and how the operation of free market forces can lead to an unacceptable allocation of resources.

Market forces and the distribution of income and wealth

The free operation of market forces should, in theory, ensure that people whose skills are in most demand and who are prepared to innovate should receive the highest incomes. The possibility of earning high incomes and being able to accumulate wealth should act as an incentive for people to work hard and take responsibility and risks.

However, not everyone has an equal opportunity to earn a high income and accumulate wealth, and society may view too unequal a distribution of income and wealth as undesirable.

Income inequality

Under free market forces there are two main sources of **income**. One is earned income, which is income from employment, and the other is unearned income, which includes dividends and interest received on shares and savings.

The ability to earn a high income can be distorted by market failure. One cause of labour market failure is discrimination. Some employers seek to pay lower wages to, and to employ, fewer workers from certain groups. Figure 1 shows the effect on the pay and employment of women in a market where employers discriminate against female workers.

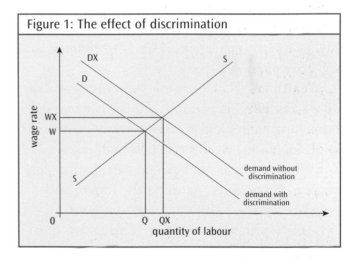

Figure 1: The effect of discrimination

Other groups that may experience discrimination include older workers, disabled workers and workers from ethnic minorities.

There are other influences on people's ability to earn high incomes. Richer people can afford to keep their children in full-time education for longer and to pay for private education or extra tuition. They can also afford to undertake more courses and training than poorer people. The resulting skills and qualifications increase richer people's earning potential. People with good health also have higher earning capacity than those who experience long periods of illness.

Wealth inequality

One cause of wealth inequality is differences in income, which mean that people have different opportunities to save and to buy assets. The higher the income a person has, the easier it is to accumulate wealth.

Wealth is a stock of assets. A person's wealth may consist of, for example, the net value of her home, car, shares and savings accounts. As well as accumulating wealth through high incomes and saving, people can become wealthy through chance, for example, winning the lottery and marriage. However, the main reason for a person's wealth is inheritance. This means that people do not have the same opportunity to accumulate wealth.

The consequences of inequalities in the distribution of income and wealth

The inequality of income and wealth means that some people have more influence over the allocation of resources than others and are able to buy more goods and services. People with low incomes and wealth are unable to buy many goods and services and may be unable to purchase basic necessities, including an adequate quantity of nutritious food and adequately heated housing. They are also less able to spend money on their children's education, their own education and training, and their family's health care.

Society may be unhappy with a very uneven distribution of income and wealth. It is likely to consider that everyone should have access to basic necessities, education and health care. It may also be concerned that such inequalities will widen over time because wealth generates income and higher wealth, which enables people to enjoy better education, training and health care, which further increases their earning capacity. Society may also recognise that if some workers are not well educated and not very fit, owing to poor nutrition, housing and health care, their productivity will be low.

Of course, people disagree about what is an acceptable degree of inequality of income and wealth distribution. It is a value judgement.

Current issue: reducing child poverty

The UK government is committed to reducing child poverty. In 2002 more than 15% of children lived in families that were below the official poverty line, which is judged to be household income below 60% of median (average) earnings. The UK has one of the worst records in child poverty in Europe. In 2002 less than 5% of children were living in poverty in Sweden, Norway and Finland.

Children are likely to experience poverty if they live in families with unemployed parents, lone parents or parents earning low wages.

Children who are bought up in poverty experience worse nutrition, worse housing, worse education and reduced lifetime prospects. For example, some children eat mostly food of a low nutritional value, live in houses with damp running down the walls and with little heating, do not wear new clothes and have low expectations about their future.

Activity 4

Poverty and class differences are an important influence on educational attainment. An Office for National Statistics report says high levels of children eligible for free school meals generally correspond with lower GCSE attainment levels.

When it comes to social class, the differences are even more striking. In 1998 only a fifth of those whose parents were in unskilled manual jobs achieved five GCSE passes at grades A to C. In contrast, more than two-thirds of children of the professional and managerial classes got five GCSEs at this standard. ('How gap between rich and poor has grown', Alan Travis, Guardian, 11 May 2000)

a Why do children from poor families, on average, do worse at school than children from richer families?

b What implications do differences in educational achievement have for the future distribution of income and wealth?

Summary

In this unit you have learned that:

■ Market forces can result in a distribution of **income** and **wealth** which society regards as too unequal.

■ Under market forces, the sources of income are income from employment and income from shares and savings.

■ Some groups' employment chances and earning potential may be adversely affected by discrimination.

■ People's ability to earn high incomes is influenced by their education and health.

■ People with high incomes find it easier to accumulate wealth than do poor people.

■ The main way people become wealthy is through inheritance.

■ The inequality of income and wealth means that some people have more influence over the allocation of resources than others.

■ Society may be unhappy with a very uneven distribution of income and wealth as it may mean that poor people do not have adequate access to basic necessities, education and health care.

■ What constitutes a desirable distribution of income and wealth is a value judgement.

Multiple choice questions

1 Free market forces should mean that workers will receive high wages if:

A   demand for their labour is high and the supply of their labour is high

B   demand for their labour is high and the supply of their labour is low

C   demand for their labour is low and the supply of their labour is high

D   demand for their labour is low and the supply of their labour is low

2 Which of the following would increase the efficiency of labour markets?

A   a reduction in the geographical immobility of labour

B   a reduction in the information available about job opportunities

C   an increase in discrimination

D   an increase in unemployment

3 Which form of wealth is the most evenly distributed in the UK?

A   houses

B   government bonds

C   shares

D   yachts

4 What is the main source of wealth?

A   chance

B   enterprise

C   inheritance

D   savings

5 What would be expected to increase as a result of a redistribution of income from the rich to the poor?

A   the production of necessities

B   the ownership of second homes

C   demand for luxury products

D   poverty

6 Which of the following statements is a normative statement?

A   A major cause of poverty is unemployment.

B   Black Caribbean men earn £115 a week less than white men.

C   Wealth is more unevenly distributed than income.

D   It is not fair that the richest 50 million people in the world have the same income as the 2.7 billion poor people.

Data response question: children in poverty

Margaret's youngest daughter "celebrated" her fourth birthday yesterday. But Margaret won't be able to get to the shops to buy her anything as simple as a present until tomorrow's money rolls in. Her daughter's shoes are falling apart, and she sleeps on a mattress some friends had thrown out. Her children sometimes eat pizza and sausages, but mostly live on beans and toast.

Theresa, a mother of three from Acomb in York, remembers the moment when she felt most hopeless, about a year ago. She and her three children had just moved into a long-awaited council house. There were no carpets, and the walls were filthy. Her son, Lewis, nine at the time, was too scared to sleep in the room, the walls defaced with graffiti and stained black from a recent house fire. He clambered into his mother's bed for comfort. Theresa found it hard to soothe him; she was just as scared herself. Theresa's family have lived on the breadline since her husband left six years ago.

Two hundred miles away in the shadow of London's Canary Wharf, a group of four tower blocks are known collectively as Will Crock Estate. On the top floor of Devitt House lives Moriom Begum. She is 44 and was born in Bangladesh. In 1991, her family of five moved into a two-bedroom flat. Her son, 21, and daughter, 16, share one room, and the youngest, who is six, sleeps with her husband in their bed. The room was not even big enough for a cot. Her husband has recently become unemployed and the family claim a Jobseekers Allowance. ('Hope is a luxury she can't afford', Kamal Ahmed and Nick Walsh, Observer, 11 June 2000)

a Explain two causes of poverty touched on in the extract. [4]

b What basic necessities does the extract suggest the three families lack? [4]

c Discuss three reasons why Margaret, Theresa and Moriom's children may perform badly at school. [6]

d Discuss what evidence there is in the extract to suggest that a socially optimum allocation of resources had not been achieved. [6]

4 Government intervention in markets

1 Remedies for market failure

All governments have always intervened in the economy of their country, but the extent to which they intervene differs among countries and over time. In this unit you will examine why governments intervene in markets and consider some of the methods they employ.

Reasons for government intervention

Governments intervene in markets to correct market failure and to create a more equitable, that is fairer, distribution of resources. How much a government intervenes is influenced by the extent to which, among other things, it:

- believes market failure exists;
- thinks the distribution of resources is unfair;
- believes that government intervention will improve the performance of markets and create a fairer distribution of resources.

Activity 1

Since 1979 the number of houses rented out by councils has fallen dramatically. As former council houses and flats have been sold to residents and non-profit housing associations, owner occupation has risen from more than half of all tenures to more than two-thirds, and renting from councils has fallen from one-third to one-fifth.

a What has happened to the level of state intervention in the housing market since 1979?

b What does this change indicate about the perceived level of market failure in housing in 1979 compared with now?

Methods of government intervention

The methods governments use can be described as market-based and non-market based policies.

- Market-based policy measures include indirect taxes, subsidies, the provision of information and the creation of **property rights**. These are the rights to use, change and transfer assets and products. As you will see in the following units, these measures are aimed at altering demand or supply in such a way as to bring about an efficient allocation of resources.
- Non-market based policy measures involve more direct government intervention in markets. They include state provision, government-set market regulations and standards, competition policy and price controls.

Activity 2

In February 2002 Ken Livingstone, the mayor of London, approved a scheme to charge motorists £5 to drive into the capital between 7am and 6.30pm. The plan was implemented in February 2003. An extra 200 buses, providing 9,000 more seats, were being provided to carry the 7,500 people who were expected to switch to public transport.

a Does the action outlined above suggest pre-2003 car use in central London was above, at or below the socially optimum level? Explain your answer.

b Identify two other policies that could be used to discourage people from driving their cars into central London.

Activity 3

The government does not provide IVF treatment in every region of the country, and where it is available it is often limited to women under 36 and those with no children from previous relationships.

This means that couples often use private IVF clinics. This part of the private sector has been expanding rapidly in recent years and is worth billions of pounds. It has been criticised for creating too many multiple births and therefore costing the NHS more at the time of delivery. (Ruth Deech, head of the Human Fertilisation and Embryology Authority, suggested a figure of £60 million a year.)

a Why does the government not provide IVF treatment in every region?

b Does the passage suggest NHS health care treatment is a substitute or a complement to private IVF treatment?

Summary

In this unit you have learned that:

■ Governments intervene in markets to correct market failure and to create a more equitable distribution of resources.

■ Among the policy measures the government can use to correct market failure are indirect taxes, subsidies, the provision of information, the creation of property rights, state provision, government-set market regulations and standards, competition policy and price controls.

Current issue: tobacco advertising

There is increasing pressure on the government to ban tobacco advertising. As far back as 1962, a report from the Royal College of Physicians established that smoking caused heart disease. It urged the government to take action to reduce smoking, including banning tobacco advertising. Since that date 5 million people have died prematurely from smoking. In 1962 approximately 70% of men and 43% of women smoked. By 2001, the figures had fallen to 29% of men and 25% of women.

However, smoking still causes 120,000 deaths each year, and more young women are starting to smoke. Television advertising of tobacco was banned in the mid-1960s. The tobacco companies responded by sponsoring televised sport. In 2002 they spent £130 million on promoting smoking.

Multiple choice questions

1 Which of the following is a reason for government intervention in the economy?

A output occurring at the socially optimum levels in markets

B a high level of geographical and occupational mobility of resources

C an inequitable distribution of income and wealth

D full employment of resources

2 Which of the following forms of government intervention could correct market failure?

A the granting of a subsidy to firms producing demerit goods

B the taxation of merit goods

C the provision of public goods

D the banning of the consumption of inferior goods

3 A government is more likely to intervene in a market if:

A MC is greater than AR

B MC is equal to MR

C MR is equal to AR

D AC is at a minimum

4 A government may intervene in a market if it believes that:

A firms are achieving productive efficiency

B firms are price takers

C consumers lack accurate information

D consumers' tastes are reflected in the allocation of resources

5 An objective of government intervention is to:

A increase producer surplus

B increase firms' profits

C decrease factor mobility

D decrease allocative inefficiency

6 A government may seek to make the distribution of income and wealth more equal if it believes that:

A poor people lack sufficient purchasing power to buy basic necessities

B poor people are too geographically and occupationally mobile

C rich people have sufficient purchasing power to buy luxury products

D rich people are being rewarded for their effort and enterprise

Data response question: road pricing

Every car could be fitted with a satellite tracking device so drivers could be charged for journeys on Britain's most congested roads, under plans revealed to ministers today. The report from the government's independent transport advisers warns of gridlock, longer and more unpredictable journeys and spiralling pollution if the plan is not implemented.

The scheme from the Commission for Integrated Transport (CFTI) could see drivers getting a monthly bill for journeys on congested hotspots, but the sweetener for motorists is that gridlock would be cut by 44%.

The scheme's authors do not want it until the end of the decade when public transport will have been improved by the government's promised £180bn overhaul.

The CFTI says the financial burden for drivers would remain the same. In return for road pricing the car tax disc would be scrapped and the duty on vehicle fuel cut.

Under the proposals Global Positioning System (GPS) satellites would track vehicles via electronic 'black boxes' fixed to car dashboards.

This information would be beamed back to computers and drivers would be charged with the average weekday tariff set at 3.5p per mile on motorways and 4.3p per mile on other roads. Charges could be varied according to the level of congestion and travel would be free off peak and on quiet roads.

David Begg, who devised the plan, said the alternatives of more roads or expanding public transport would do little or nothing to slash congestion. 'We either decide to continue without this type of measure and we continue to queue and congestion continues to rise, or we road price.'
('Tracking devices urged as drivers face charges to use busy roads', Vikram Dodd, Guardian, 25 February 2002)

a Describe two negative externalities caused by road use. [4]

b Explain what is meant by road pricing. [4]

c What is the aim behind road pricing? [6]

d Discuss what is likely to happen if the government does not introduce road pricing. [6]

2 Taxes, subsidies and benefits

In this unit you will examine how taxes and subsidies can be used to affect the output of merit and demerit goods. You will consider some of the advantages and disadvantages of using taxes and subsidies for this purpose.

Taxes and subsidies

Income tax was introduced in the UK in 1799 as a temporary measure to help fund the Napoleonic war effort. Taxes had been levied before, on items such as windows, female servants, dogs and watches, also to raise the finance to defend the country. Financing public goods, including defence, is still a function of taxes, but they are now used, with subsidies and benefits, to correct a variety of forms of market failure and to reduce inequalities in income and wealth distribution.

Taxes are charges imposed by a government on people and firms. **Indirect taxes**, also known as sales and outlay taxes, are taxes on expenditure on goods and services, for example VAT (value added tax). **Direct taxes** are taxes on the income of individuals and firms and include income tax and corporation tax.

An indirect tax has the same effect as an increase in the cost of production. Firms have to pay what is in effect an extra cost. As a result supply decreases, price rises and demand contracts. How much price rises depends on how much of the tax a firm passes on to the consumer. When demand is inelastic, it is likely to be a high proportion, since a rise in price will result in a smaller percentage contraction in demand. When demand is elastic, it is likely to be a low proportion, because producers know that if they try to pass on most of the tax in the form of a higher price their sales will decrease.

Direct taxes imposed on individuals reduce their disposable income and thus their purchasing power. They also affect people's incentives to work and save. Corporation tax, which is a tax on firms' profits, leaves firms with lower income and influences their ability and incentive to reinvest and distribute dividends.

Subsidies are payments by the government to producers and consumers. Subsidies to producers reduce the costs of supplying products so supply increases, price decreases and demand extends.

When a subsidy is given to consumers, to help poor people and/or to encourage the consumption of a product, the demand curve rather than the supply curve shifts to the right.

Activity 1

Using a demand and supply diagram, explain the likely effect of a rise in income tax on the market for whisky.

Merit and demerit goods

A government can provide a subsidy when a market allocates too few resources to the production of a product, and it can impose a tax when a market allocates too many resources to the production of a product.

For example, a government may decide that, if left to market forces, people may fail to appreciate the true value of installing smoke detectors in their homes. It could then choose to subsidise either the production or the consumption of smoke detectors. Both would increase the quantity of smoke detectors bought and sold.

A government may also decide that people are not fully aware of the health risks involved in, for example, eating high-fat foods, underestimating the full cost to them of consuming the product. To move output to the socially optimum level, a government may impose a tax on the producers of high-fat foods. Figure 1 shows that the socially optimum output of butter is QX. If left to market forces, however, output will be Q.

Figure 2 shows that a tax which shifts the supply curve to S1S1 will result in the market reaching the socially optimum level.

Some economists refer to taxes which are designed to discourage unhealthy living as **sin taxes**.

Reaching the socially optimum output of merit and demerit goods is not as easy as it appears. This is because the government must be able to calculate both the socially optimum output and the level of subsidy or rate of taxation needed to achieve it.

Activity 2

The tax on cigarettes (excise duty) rose by 30% between 1997 and 2001. The anti-smoking group ASH (Action on Smoking and Health) argues for higher increases in excise duty as part of the policy to discourage smoking.

a Explain why cigarettes are considered to be a demerit good.

b Discuss whether a rise in excise duty is likely to be effective in reducing smoking.

Externalities

Governments use taxes and subsidies to try to make markets take into account externalities. The intention is to turn external costs (negative externalities) into private costs and external benefits (positive externalities) into private benefits. If successful, this will move output to the socially optimum level.

One significant cause of negative externalities is pollution. For example, a firm which creates air pollution will reduce the quality of life and health of people living nearby and may also reduce the value of their properties. To make the firm take into account these harmful effects on third parties, a government could impose a tax. For this tax to succeed in moving output to the socially optimum level, it must be equal to the marginal external cost.

Figure 3 shows the market for a product, the production of which causes pollution. The market output is Q and the price charged is P. The socially optimum output is QX and the

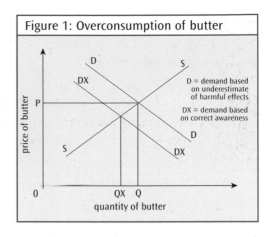
Figure 1: Overconsumption of butter

D = demand based on underestimate of harmful effects

DX = demand based on correct awareness

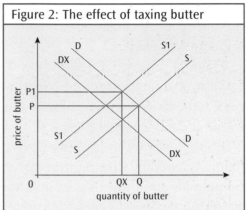
Figure 2: The effect of taxing butter

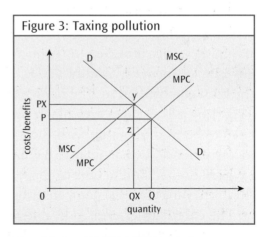
Figure 3: Taxing pollution

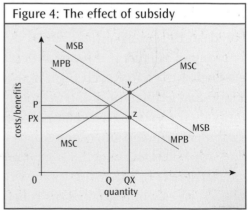
Figure 4: The effect of subsidy

price is PX. The tax per unit should be YZ as the gap between marginal social cost and marginal private cost is marginal external cost.

When considering changing output to reflect the existence of positive externalities, it is necessary to calculate marginal external benefit. The government subsidises some rail companies because it believes that the revenue which can be earned from selling tickets does not reflect the true benefits which arise from rail travel. The social benefits exceed the private benefits because there are positive externalities. These include reduced congestion, pollution and accidents on roads.

Figure 4 shows that a subsidy of YZ, which is equal to marginal external benefit, will lower price, encourage consumption and move output to the socially optimum level.

Using taxes and subsidies to overcome market failures caused by externalities forces individuals, households and firms to take into account the full social costs and benefits of their actions. However, it is not easy to measure externalities accurately since, by their very nature, they do not have a price attached to them. A government may, for example, seek to calculate the costs imposed on nearby residents of an airport by asking them how much they would need to be paid to put up with the inconvenience. Residents may be tempted to exaggerate the harmful effects, especially if they think they may receive compensation.

The externalities created by different firms, households and individuals differ. Although it is relatively easy to levy a tax or grant a subsidy based on the externalities created by an industry or group of people, it is more difficult and expensive to charge each firm, household or individual a different rate based on its own individual creation or receipt of externalities.

If a government imposes a tax to reduce the output of products which, for example, emit CO_2 gases, there is risk that the total world emissions of CO_2 gases will not fall. This is because the price of the products produced in the country will rise, causing demand for them to fall. However, consumers may switch demand to products made by firms in other countries, and some of the home country's firms may move abroad to avoid the tax. So there is a possibility that the government's action will reduce employment in the country but merely shift the source of the pollution elsewhere.

There is also a risk that a tax may fall more heavily on poor people, taking a larger proportion of their income than that of rich people. This may be considered to be inequitable.

Granting subsidies may reduce the incentive for firms to be efficient. Some recipients may become reliant on the subsidies, and the government may find that it is supporting firms and organisations which are not striving to achieve productive efficiency and do not respond quickly or fully to changes in consumer demand.

Activity 3

In March 2002 the government's railway agency, the Strategic Rail Authority, agreed to give a net extra subsidy of £56 million to National Express for its ScotRail and Central Trains franchises. It was thought that if the SRA had not stepped in, the company would have cut services and put up fares.

a Explain why a cut in rail services and a rise in rail fares may be considered disadvantageous for society.

b On what basis should a government decide the amount of subsidy to give?

Public goods

One reason for levying taxes is to raise the revenue to finance public goods. Public goods would not be produced if left to market forces since people would seek to act as free riders (see Section 3, Unit 5). The government, though, can make people pay for public goods by imposing taxes on them. Government tax revenue is also used to finance, in whole or part, merit goods and state benefits.

There is debate about whether taxes should be levied according to the benefits people receive from the goods and services financed by taxation or according to their ability to pay. The benefit principle links the amount of tax people pay to the quantity they consume. However, this is difficult to apply when it is hard to calculate who benefits and by how much from particular services, such as defence. The ability to pay principle is based on fairness. Those with the highest incomes will pay the most. However, they are not always the ones who benefit most from government spending. For example, rich people make considerable use of the National Health Service and university education, but they do not benefit significantly from the largest item of government expenditure, social security payments, which include jobseeker's allowance, pensions, income support and housing benefit.

Activity 4

In February 2002 the government published plans to cope with the threat of flooding and freak weather and the impact of climate change on river and sea levels. These included requiring households in flood risk areas to pay at least £60 a year in special taxes designed to raise cash for flood defences. It was also suggested that developers might be subject to a large connection charge if they build on flood plains.

People in areas prone to flooding already pay higher taxes to finance flood defences, but the government believes that £200 million more needs to be spent. It expects to provide 80% of this out of central taxes and the rest from extra taxes on people living in the areas at risk.

a Explain why flood defences have to be paid for out of taxation.

b Using a demand and supply diagram, analyse the effect of the imposition of a large connection charge on the housing market in flood areas.

Distribution of income and wealth

Governments use progressive taxes and benefits to redistribute income from rich people to poor people. **Progressive taxes** are those, including income tax, which take a higher proportion of rich people's income than of poor people's income. Imposing progressive taxes reduces the gap in income and wealth between rich and poor people. This gap is further reduced and the living standards of poor people are improved by the provision of subsidies in the form of benefits.

There are both cash benefits and benefits in kind. Cash benefits, as their name suggests, are financial payments to particular groups; benefits in kind are the provision of goods and services free to particular groups. Both types of benefits can be either means-tested or universal. **Means-tested benefits**, such as income support, are given to people who prove that their incomes are below a certain level. **Universal benefits**, such as state pensions, are given to everyone in a certain category, in the case of state pensions to people aged over 65, irrespective of income. Free eye tests for children is a universal benefit in kind and free school dinners for children from low-income families is a means-tested benefit in kind.

Progressive taxes combined with means-tested benefits and universal benefits targeted at groups prone to poverty will redistribute income from rich to poor people. However, such measures do cause problems. Progressive taxes may act as a disincentive to work and effort. Means-tested benefits are often expensive to administer and have low take-up rates because some people find forms difficult to fill in or feel embarrassed to apply. Universal benefits are more straightforward to administer and do not have a stigma attached to them, but some of the money may go to those who do not need it. For example, the Duke of Westminster, who has a personal fortune of £4 billion, receives child benefit.

Activity 5

Between 1997 and 2001 the incomes of the poorest 10% of the population rose by 13% as a result of changes to the tax and benefit system, and the next poorest group gained a 10% increase. Meanwhile, the average gains for the richest group were 3%.

In 2002 in the UK a person could earn £4,535 before they paid any income tax. After that tax rates were: (Table 1)

a Explain how changes to the tax and benefit system could raise the incomes of poor people.

b Compare the pre-tax income and post-tax income of a barman earning £199 a week and heart surgeon earning £5,288 a week in 2002.

Table 1	
Taxable income (£)	Rate (%)
0 – 1,880	10
1,881 - 29,400	22
Over 29,400	40

Factor mobility

A government can encourage mobility of factors of production by taxing resources in declining uses and areas and subsidising them in expanding uses and areas. For example, unemployed people can be given financial assistance to help them move to an area where there are jobs or to undertake training. Subsidies and tax reductions can also be given to firms which relocate or set up in areas of high unemployment.

UK **regional policy** is largely based on taking work to workers. This means that it seeks to encourage firms to move to where there are unemployed people rather than moving the people. This is because capital is usually more mobile than labour and moving people out of a depressed area can cause further problems there. In many cases location does not significantly influence firms' costs, whereas moving can be difficult for people because of family ties and differences in housing costs in different parts of the country. If people move out of a depressed area it can further reduce job opportunities there, because demand for food from supermarkets, cinema tickets, school places and so on will decline. People who leave a depressed area in search of employment or promotion may be the most skilled and enterprising. Their departure is likely to make the area less attractive for prospective employers.

Activity 6

In the 2001 budget, the chancellor of the exchequer announced a £1 billion package of tax cuts to help rundown areas of the country. To enable people to move more easily he stated he was abolishing stamp duty (a tax on the sale of property) on property sales in the most blighted areas. His measures also included extra relief on corporation tax for firms investing in urban regeneration in areas such as the centre of Middlesbrough, where in 2002 over 60% of households lived on incomes of less than £10,000 a year.

a i What form of mobility of labour was the abolition of stamp duty in blighted areas designed to promote?

ii Why, despite this help, may people still find it difficult to move?

b Discuss why the mobility of labour may be low in an area like the centre of Middlesbrough.

Market power

A government can impose a **lump-sum tax** if it believes that monopolists or oligopolists are earning excessive profits. In 1997 the UK government imposed a lump-sum tax, referred to as a windfall tax, on the profits of privatised utilities.

A lump-sum tax raises a firm's average cost but does not change its marginal cost, so price and output are not altered – consumers do not suffer a rise in price or a fall in output.

Current issue: a tax on plastic bags

On 5 March 2002 the Irish government introduced what became known as a 'plastic' levy of 15 euro cents (9p) for every plastic bag a person takes home from all retail outlets including bookshops, record shops and supermarkets. Small bags used for bread, fish, fruit, meat, and vegetables are exempt.

The aim is to reduce a growing litter problem. In the year before the measure was introduced approximately 1.2 million plastic bags had been given free to Irish shoppers. This amounted to one bag per person per day or 14,000 tonnes of plastic.

In the months up to the introduction of the levy, retailers noted a change in customers' behaviour. There was a marked increase in the sales of reusable plastic carrier bags which cost about €1 in most supermarkets.

If the initiative proves to be a success, there are likely to be increased calls for such a levy in the UK, where plastic bags are also a major source of litter.

Summary

In this unit you have learned that:

■ Taxes and subsidies are widely used to correct market failure.

■ The imposition of an **indirect tax** decreases supply, raises price and causes demand to contract. The more inelastic demand is, the more of any tax a consumer will bear.

■ **Direct taxes** affect incentives to work and purchasing power.

■ **Subsidies** to producers are designed to increase supply, and subsidies to consumers are designed to increase the consumption of a product and/or to help poor people.

■ To increase the output of a merit good to the socially optimum level, a government may subsidise its production or its consumption.

■ To reduce the output of a demerit good to the socially optimum level, a government may impose an indirect tax on it.

■ To achieve the socially optimum level, a government must calculate the level accurately and the level of subsidy or the rate of taxation needed to achieve it.

■ Taxes and subsidies can be used to change externalities into private costs and benefits and so move output to the socially optimum level.

■ Taxes and subsidies force consumers and producers to take into account the full social costs and benefits of their decisions. However, it is difficult to measure externalities accurately and to charge different tax rates to different groups. The imposition of environmental taxes by one country may not reduce world pollution levels, and such taxes may fall more heavily on poor people.

■ Taxes raise revenue to finance state provision of public goods, merit goods and benefits. There is some debate as to whether taxes should be levied according to the benefits people receive or according to their ability to pay.

■ **Progressive taxes** and benefits given to poor people can be used to redistribute income from rich to poor people.

■ Factor mobility can be increased by means of subsidies and tax incentives.

■ A government can impose a **lump-sum tax** if it believes that monopolists or oligopolists are earning excessive profits.

Multiple choice questions

1 A tax is imposed on a product which has inelastic demand. Who will bear the tax?

A consumers and producers will share the burden of the tax

B consumers will bear most of the tax

C producers will bear most of the tax

D producers will bear all of the tax

2 Figure 5 shows that market output is Q. Government intervention then moves output to QX, the socially optimum output. What form of government intervention could have caused this movement?

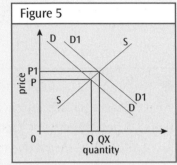

Figure 5

A a subsidy given to consumers

B a subsidy given to producers

C a direct tax imposed on consumers

D an indirect tax imposed on the product

3 A tax is an appropriate measure to convert:

A external costs into private costs

B private costs into external costs

C private benefits into external benefits

D external benefits into private benefits

4 Public goods have to be financed by taxation. This is because, if left to market forces, public goods would:

A be underconsumed and so underproduced

B not be produced as people will act as free riders

C be overconsumed and so overproduced

D not be consumed as consumers will lack information about their true benefits

5 Which of the following is an appropriate measure to increase the occupational mobility of labour?

A a subsidy given to firms to relocate to areas of high unemployment

B a subsidy given to workers to undertake training

C a reduction in income tax

D a reduction in corporation tax

6 Left to market forces the output of a product is Q as shown in Figure 6. To achieve the socially optimum output, a government should impose a tax per unit of:

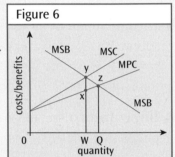

Figure 6

A WX

B XY

C YZ

D ZQ

Data response question: VAT on food

Some economists argue that VAT should be imposed on high-fat foods. A few advocate the imposition of VAT on all food.

The case for imposing VAT on fatty foods, including whole milk and cheese, is that consumption of fatty foods is thought to result in 1,000 premature deaths a year. Supporters of such a move argue that healthy foods such as fruit, fresh vegetables and low-fat foods should remain free of the 17.5% tax. This, they claim, would lead people to substitute healthy, low-fat foods for high-fat foods. However, it would not be easy to decide whether a food should be classified as a high-fat or low-fat food. There is also concern that such a tax would disproportionately affect poor people, who buy more high-fat foods as they are relatively cheap and filling.

This is also the reason some economists oppose the imposition of VAT on all food. This would be a regressive tax since it would take a higher proportion of the income of poor people than that of rich people. However, supporters of the measure argue that zero-rating of most food provides an unintended subsidy to the rich, and that imposing VAT on food would raise a considerable amount of revenue as demand for food is inelastic.

a Explain why fatty foods may be regarded as demerit goods. [3]

b Using demand and supply diagrams, analyse the effect of the imposition of a tax on high-fat foods on the market for:
  i cheese [5]
  ii low-fat yoghurt [5]

c Explain why demand for food is inelastic. [2]

d Discuss the arguments for and against imposing VAT on fatty foods. [5]

3 State provision

Governments provide goods and services when they think markets will fail to produce them or will fail to produce an appropriate quantity of them. In this unit you will examine the decisions that governments have to make in connection with state provision, the reasons for providing products free or nearly free and the relative merits of the state or private-sector firms producing the products.

Government decisions

The government (the state) finances the production of a range of products through taxation and then provides them free or nearly free to consumers. What products and what quantities of products it provides and who produces them is influenced by four main factors:

■ the degree of market failure the government perceives to exist;
■ its views on the socially optimum levels of output;
■ the amount of taxation it feels it can raise;
■ its assessment of the relative efficiency of the public and private sectors in producing the products.

Activity 1

The government has promised to increase the amount of national income spent on health care by £12 billion a year. There are several ways of achieving this objective, such as reducing spending on other public services, raising taxes or introducing some charges for NHS health care including, for example, charging for seeing a general practitioner and imposing 'hotel' charges for hospital stays.

a Identify one possible opportunity cost of increasing government spending on health care.

b Discuss one argument for and one against charging for visits to a GP.

Public and merit goods

The government has to provide public goods and finance them through taxation. Deciding on the quantity of public goods to provide, however, is not straightforward, because the price mechanism will not reveal the true level of consumers' demand. The government, in aiming to achieve the socially optimum level of output, has to

Activity 2

The government significantly increased the number of university places in the 1980s and 1990s and wants to increase them further. Its target for 2010 is for 50% of all 18–30 year olds to have experience of HE. It also wants universities to find more low-income students with high academic potential. The universities argue that teaching and retaining students from poorer households costs more money, so they need extra funding to enable them to do this.

a Does the information in the passage indicate that the government thinks the provision of HE is at, above or below the socially optimum level?

b Identify:
  i a private benefit of HE
  ii an external benefit of HE

c Why may students with high academic potential from low-income families not apply for HE places?

d Why may it cost more to teach and retain students from poor households?

estimate marginal social benefit. It could do this by asking people the maximum amount they would be willing to pay for an additional unit of the good, and then totalling each individual's marginal private benefit at different quantities of provision. It would have to estimate any marginal external benefit.

In deciding the quantity of merit goods to provide, the government has to consider the extent to which consumers fail to appreciate their full private benefits, the positive externalities they create and the benefits poor people can gain from their provision.

Free provision

Free, or near free, provision of products by the state can be justified on a number of grounds.

One is that it will stimulate consumption. If a price is charged, output for merit goods will be below the socially optimum level because consumers do not fully appreciate their full private benefits or take into account the positive externalities generated. Also private-sector firms with market power may overcharge.

Another is equity. It can be argued that there are basic necessities to which everyone should have access. For example, health care should be provided on the basis of need rather than purchasing power.

Free state education overcomes the problems of lack of awareness of true benefits, failure to take into the account the positive externalities created, lack of income to buy it and lack of willingness of some parents to spend on their children's education.

Production

When a government has decided which products to provide free or nearly free to consumers, it can either produce them itself or pay private-sector firms to produce them. The source of production it uses is influenced by its views on the relative efficiency of firms in the two sectors. If it believes that private-sector firms will produce

higher-quality products at a lower cost, it will probably use the private sector.

Governments also produce some products to sell in the market.

The arguments for governments to run what are known as state-owned or **nationalised industries** include: protecting consumers from high prices in the case of natural monopolies; taking a long-term perspective; and ensuring that social costs and benefits are taken into account when production decisions are made. However, in recent decades some industries have been moved from the public to the private sector in the belief that subjecting firms to market forces will make them produce what consumers want at low cost. If they do not, they will lose customers to rival firms and go out of business. In a more competitive market, consumers may have more choice and experience lower prices and higher quality.

Activity 3

Some 85% of prescriptions are free. People on means-tested benefits, all children and everyone over retirement age are exempt, despite that fact that 20% of pensioners have income above the national average and children are as likely to be in high-income as in low-income households.

a Explain why prescribed medicines may be regarded as a merit good.

b Consider one argument for and one against rich pensioners receiving free prescriptions.

Current issue: using private-sector health care

The government is using the private sector to provide extra capacity to meet its targets for waiting time and residential medical care. In 2000 an agreement was signed with the Independent Healthcare Association for the NHS to use the private sector for routine operations, provision of critical care and help with rehabilitation.

Even before the agreement, the NHS had been buying some waiting list operations and, to a much greater extent, residential care for mentally ill and elderly people from private hospitals. For example, in 1999 it bought about 40,000 procedures and more than half the secure places for people with serious mental illness. Over 60% of places in private and residential nursing homes were also publicly funded.

Summary

In this unit you have learned that:

■ The government provides a range of goods and services free or nearly free.

■ In deciding what quantity of a public good to provide, governments take into account social costs and benefits.

■ In deciding the quantity of merit goods to provide, governments take into account the extent of consumer ignorance about their full private benefits, the positive externalities they create and the benefits they give to poor people.

■ Free provision of products can be justified on grounds of correcting market failure and equity.

■ The products a government decides to provide can be produced by itself or by the private sector.

■ The arguments for **nationalised industries** include protecting consumers from high prices, taking a longer-term perspective and ensuring that social costs and benefits are taken into account.

■ The arguments for privatisation include increased efficiency, more choice, lower prices and higher quality.

Multiple choice questions

1 Which of the following has to be provided by the state?
A defence
B education
C postal services
D transport

2 The socially optimum level of output of public goods occurs where:
A average revenue equals average cost
B the output of public goods is maximised
C marginal social cost equals marginal social benefit
D costs are minimised and profits are maximised

3 What is an advantage of the NHS providing free visits to the doctor?
A demand for health care will equal supply
B demand for health care will outstrip supply
C some people will seek medical help before conditions become serious
D some people will take into account the positive externalities of health care

4 Which of the following is provided by the government free at the point of consumption?
A liposuction
B train travel
C services of public libraries
D MOT tests

5 Why does the state provision of public and merit goods redistribute income from rich to poor people?
A free access to all public and merit goods is means-tested
B public and merit goods are not consumed by rich people
C public and merit goods are sold at a lower price to poor than to rich people
D the contribution poor people make to the costs of public and merit goods through taxation is less than the benefits they receive

6 Public goods:
A have to be produced by the state
B have to be financed out of taxation
C are made by nationalised industries
D are provided by public limited companies

Data response questions: road tolls

Road tolls would make our roads flow again. That would be good for firms' profitability, for people's marriages and stress levels, for the environment and especially for our grandchildren's wellbeing.

The money raised could be spent in useful ways, such as reducing other taxes – including those on fuel – and improving public services and infrastructure. Our present fuel tax is a blunt instrument: it penalises those on empty lanes as much as those on the M25, and it does little to change the amount of traffic.

Building roads is not the answer. In the past 20 years car traffic has doubled. The rise shows no sign of flattening. Yet Britain still has far fewer cars per head than the US. Something has to be done if the next generation of Britons is not to be overwhelmed by jams, smog and concrete.

Although we pay petrol and road fund taxes, we are free to use any particular British road. Imagine what would happen if supermarkets gave away their products for free or nearly free. There would be queues outside every store. People would have to get up early and allocate periods in their diaries just to buy food.

It would be no use building wider front doors to these supermarkets (the let's build more roads approach), or having special paths into supermarkets that only certain people could use (the bus lane approach). As soon as the queue started to shorten, other consumers would notice and come to the new wide entrance supermarkets.

The supermarkets would be better advised to put prices on their goods. That is what they do – and it works. Britain's roads could be like this. They could flow without queues.

Every economist knows that a queue forms when a demand and supply mechanism fails. Using the price system to ration things is the most sensible way. That is what we do for steel ingots, newspapers, cream teas and everything else. It is especially necessary on roads because drivers do not bear in mind when they make a journey that their presence on the road creates an 'externality' for others. ('If only Britain would manage roads in the way it does supermarkets', Andrew Oswald, Guardian, 9 October 2000)

a Does the extract suggest that the provision of road space free to users leads to a socially optimum level of use? Explain your answer. [3]

b In what sense could it be argued that roads are changing from a public into a private good? [4]

c Identify one public service which would benefit from increased public finance. Explain your answer. [3]

d **i** Explain the advantage claimed in the text for the price mechanism. [3]

   ii Does use of the price mechanism always ensure a socially optimum output level? [3]

   iii Explain two externalities that drivers create. [4]

4 Regulations and standards

In this unit you will examine how regulations and standards can be applied to markets and assess how effective they are in correcting market failure. You will see how a system of **tradable permits** is one way of operating regulations that restrict permitted pollution levels.

The nature of regulations and standards

Government-set standards and regulations, enforced by law, seek to correct market failure by overruling market forces. The extent of market failure will control the number and severity of the restrictions a government is likely to impose. For example, for years the UK government tried, with little success, to persuade people to wear car seat belts by running campaigns to inform them of the dangers of not wearing them. So it decided to make it compulsory for people to wear seat belts and for companies to fit them. This measure removed consumer and producer choice.

Setting standards of desired consumer and producer behaviour and then regulating them has advantages and disadvantages. One advantage is that they can be easy to understand. For example, most parents know that they must educate their children, by sending them to school or otherwise, and that failure to do so will result in legal action being taken against them.

Regulations and standards allow a government to influence the activities of consumers and producers. This can be important when there is a high risk of market failure or where market failure will have serious consequences. For example, the UK government requires anyone who practices surgery in the country to be appropriately qualified. In an unregulated market, some unqualified people may carry out operations with potentially disastrous consequences for their patients.

However, regulations and standards must be monitored, which can be difficult and expensive. For example, checking that restaurants are following hygiene laws requires an adequate supply of trained environmental health officers.

Regulations are unlikely to be effective if they do not have a reasonable level of support from the general public. If most producers and/or consumers seek to flout them, they will become impossible to enforce. Widespread bootlegging led the US government to abandon the prohibition of drinking alcohol in 1933.

Regulations also do not usually directly compensate those who suffer from market failure. Restrictions on the amount of CO_2 gases that firms can emit, for example, do not compensate third parties who are harmed by the gases.

Activity 1

In the UK it is illegal to drive with more than 80 milligrams of alcohol per 100 millilitres of blood. Some campaigners want to drop the limit to 50 milligrams of alcohol because they believe that a single pint of beer or a double scotch can seriously reduce the ability of the brain to co-ordinate the movements of eyes and hands and so to drive safely.

a Why is a law needed to stop people drink-driving?

b Discuss the social cost of drink-driving.

Regulations and different forms of market failure

Regulations are widely used to overcome different forms of market failure.

- A lack of information, or inaccurate information, may result in people making decisions which endanger their lives. So, for example, in the UK it is illegal for motorcyclists not to wear crash helmets and for people to drive cars that are not roadworthy.
- Children may suffer from a lack of information and/or a lack of maturity to make rational decisions as well as inappropriate decisions made by their parents. So there are laws to protect children, including preventing them buying alcohol and restricting the number of hours they can work.
- Behaviour that imposes negative externalities can be banned, for example drug dealing, and restricted, for example the amount of pollution that firms can generate and the volume of noise that households can create.
- Laws prevent suppliers and consumers from providing misleading information and stop firms abusing their market power (see Unit 6).
- Legislation sets controls on shop opening hours, how food for sale is prepared and stored, working hours and conditions, and the minimum wage employers can pay their workers (see Unit 7).

Tradable permits

Tradable permits, which can also be called marketable permits, are designed to reduce pollution. They are a form of government control which also makes use of the market.

A government or governments set a limit on the amount of pollution which firms or countries can discharge. The firms or countries are then issued with permits which they can trade. So the level of pollution is determined by government intervention, and the market decides who creates it.

Activity 2

A Witney company has been fined for polluting a stream and a river with 1,000 litres of oil in what was described as 'an accident waiting to happen'.

Baker Brothers, of Buttercross Works, Station Lane, admitted contaminating Queen Emma's Dyke.

The pollution flowed downstream into the river Windrush the court heard.

Environment Agency enforcement officer, Mr Rod Gould, said: 'This incident was entirely predictable and in the absence of any maintenance it was an accident waiting to happen.

We hope that this sends a clear message to companies that they are entirely responsible for their premises and that they have a duty to maintain them in order to prevent such incidents.

For the sake of basic maintenance checks the company has landed itself with a bill for the lost oil, thousands of pounds of clear-up costs, the agency's bills, fines, costs and a criminal conviction.'

The company was fined £1,500 and ordered to pay £2,417 in costs. ('Firm is fined for stream pollution', David Home, Witney Gazette, 13 February 2002)

a Explain why river pollution is regarded as an external cost.

b Explain the effect that the fine would have had on:
  i the private cost of producing Baker Brothers' products
  ii the external cost of producing Baker Brothers' products

A firm which can reduce its pollution below the permitted level can sell some of its emissions rights to firms which have high pollution levels. The idea is that overall pollution levels will be reduced, because the low-polluting firms will have lower costs than the firms that have to buy pollution permits. This will give the low-polluting firms a competitive advantage and is likely to drive some of the high-polluting firms out of business.

The advantages of the system are that it provides firms with a financial incentive to reduce pollution and is relatively simple to design. The use of tradable permits is thus increasing both nationally and internationally.

The disadvantages of the system are that it may not reduce pollution but merely change its source, it is expensive to monitor and it does not directly compensate the victims. At international conferences developing countries, in particular, have expressed concern that using tradable permits on an international scale may reduce the pressure on the main polluters, notably the USA, to reduce pollution and that their inhabitants will continue to suffer the effects of pollution. Industrialised countries are likely to be able to afford to buy up other countries' rights to pollute while many of the worst effects of air pollution, including droughts and floods, are experienced in developing countries.

Current issue: mobile phones and driving

A report by the Transport Research Laboratory published in March 2002 stated that talking on a mobile phone while driving is more dangerous than being drunk. Research showed that motorists using their mobile phones react much more slowly to hazards, and their braking distance at 70 mph is 46 feet more than a normal driver's and 33 feet more than a drunk driver's.

The report has increased pressure on the government to introduce a ban on using hand-held phones at the wheel.

More than 30 countries have already introduced a ban, including Austria, Germany, Ireland, Poland, Singapore and Switzerland. In the USA, 14 cities, including New York, have prohibited the use of mobile phones. Japan introduced a ban in 1999, which led to a 53% reduction in the number of people injured in accidents involving the use of mobile phones.

The UK police claim that a ban is not required because they believe that existing laws against careless and dangerous driving cover the problem. However, very few drivers have been prosecuted for careless and dangerous driving while using a mobile phone and there has been a significant increase in the number of people using a mobile phone while driving.

Summary

In this unit you have learned that:

■ Regulations and standards are widely used to correct market failure.

■ Regulations and standards overrule market forces and reduce consumer and producer choice.

■ Regulations have the advantages of being relatively easy to understand and can provide a government with significant power in cases where market failure will have serious consequences.

■ Regulations must be monitored, require a reasonable level of support from the general public and do not directly compensate those who suffer from market failure.

■ Regulations are used to correct market failure arising from, among other things, lack of information, inappropriate decisions, negative externalities and firms abusing their market power.

■ **Tradable permits** combine use of government control and market forces. The government sets the level of permitted pollution and then allows firms to buy and sell the tradable permits.

■ The tradable permit system provides an incentive for firms to reduce pollution and is relatively easy to design.

■ Tradable permits may not reduce pollution but merely shift its source, they can be expensive to monitor and they do not directly compensate victims.

Multiple choice questions

1 Which of the following is prohibited by law in the UK?
A parents smacking their children
B cyclists riding a bicycle without a helmet
C consumers buying aspirins without a prescription
D employers discriminating among their employees on the basis of gender

2 Which of the following is a shortcoming of using regulations as a way of dealing with negative externalities?
A they turn external costs into private costs
B they allow market forces to work unhindered
C they seek to reduce output to the socially optimum level
D they do not compensate those who experience negative externalities

3 In the UK the formation of a cartel is illegal. What form of market failure is this measure designed to overcome?
A externalities
B factor immobility
C abuse of monopoly power
D overconsumption of demerit goods

4 The UK government has made MOT tests compulsory. This is because if left to market forces:
A MOT tests would be underconsumed
B garages would overcharge for MOT tests
C MOT tests would not be provided as they are a public good
D there would be a shortage of garage mechanics to carry out MOT tests

5 Tradable permits affect the level and distribution of emissions of greenhouse gases. What mechanism or mechanisms does the system rely on?

	Level of emissions	Distribution of emissions
A	market forces	market forces
B	government-set limits	market forces
C	government-set limits	government-set limits
D	market forces	government-set limits

6 Which of the following is a possible advantage of tradable permits?
A they do not require any monitoring
B they convert private into external costs
C they result in pollution becoming less geographically widespread
D they allow a target level of pollution to be set and provide incentives for firms to reduce pollution

Data response question: carbon trading

London is set to become the world's international trading centre for a multibillion pound new industry, providing a potential spur to British technology and jobs.

Under the agreement reached in Bonn, companies that save carbon by installing new technology or renewables will be able to sell the carbon dioxide saved to a company unable or unwilling to do so.

The new scheme will mean that every tonne of carbon dioxide saved in the UK by energy efficiency, renewable energy, or new technology becomes an asset.

Every tonne of carbon saved could earn £10 on the international carbon market – a new system of global trading specifically designed to cut the world's emissions of greenhouse gases through trade.

With the US having written itself out of the Kyoto protocol, analysts believe London has the potential to dominate the new trading system in which tonnes of carbon dioxide will be sold on the commodity markets much in the same way as cocoa or rice. Several companies have already begun forward trading in the hope that the Kyoto proposals would become reality, and a Europe-wide trading scheme could come into operation as early as 2005. ('UK may take lead in carbon trading', Paul Brown, Guardian, 24 July 2001)

a Explain what is meant by carbon trading. [4]

b Discuss one negative externality caused by the emission of greenhouse gases. [4]

c Explain how firms could benefit from carbon trading. [6]

d Discuss the effectiveness of a global system of carbon trading which does not include the USA. [6]

5 Provision of information and creation of property rights

In this unit you will examine how the provision of information can be used in an attempt to correct market failure. You will consider how the extension of property rights may increase market efficiency and examine some of the advantages and disadvantages of this measure.

Provision of information

A government may seek to correct market failure arising from inadequate or inaccurate information either by providing the information itself or by requiring suppliers and consumers to provide full and truthful information. For example, there is a legal requirement that producers of processed food provide information to consumers about the contents of their products.

Activity 1

The government has set itself a target of reducing the number of people, particularly young people, who smoke. In pursuit of this objective, it publishes information in its anti-smoking campaigns. In 2002 it said: 120,000 people a year die prematurely from smoking; 17,000 under 5s are admitted to hospital each year with illnesses caused by their parents smoking; and smoking causes 5,400 property fires each year.

a What information may some smokers lack?

b Why may the provision of information about the effects of smoking not stop some people smoking?

Provision of information and different forms of market failure

The provision of information by the government can be used to combat some of the causes of market failure.

■ Where there is asymmetrical information, such as in the health care market, it is likely to increase the chance of trade being mutually beneficial.

■ It can tackle the problems arising from the lack of and inaccurate information. As well as providing information itself, the government seeks to ensure that producers and consumers provide accurate information. For example, details about job vacancies are available in government job centres, and the Office for National Statistics (ONS) publishes information about the economy which enables producers to make more informed decisions. It is illegal for firms to make false claims about their products and for consumers to make false statements on insurance forms.

■ It is widely used in the case of merit and demerit goods. For example, the government requires cigarette producers to print a health warning on their cigarette products and it runs campaigns to encourage parents to vaccinate their children.

■ It may also be used in an attempt to reduce negative externalities. By naming firms which pollute and giving details about the nature and extent of their pollution, the government is seeking to put pressure on them to reduce the pollution they create.

Activity 2

Each year the government's Environment Agency publishes a list of the worst 20 polluters in England and Wales. Companies are listed on the basis of how much they have been fined for polluting during the year.

Companies which regularly appear in the list include chemicals, oil, construction, waste management, nuclear fuels and water companies.

The list is intended to shame industry into doing more to stop toxic and hazardous chemicals seeping into rivers, underground aquifers and lakes.

a What form of pollution does the Environment Agency's list appear to concentrate on?

b Explain the possible effect that an appearance in the list may have on a firm's profit and output.

Property rights

The provision of information is designed to help consumers and producers make more informed choices and so increase efficiency. The extension of property rights is also designed to empower people and to make sure that economic activity results in mutually beneficial outcomes.

Property rights are concerned with ownership. They determine who owns what and how ownership can be transferred. Market failure can occur when property rights do not exist or are unclear. For example, they do not exist over large areas of air space, the sea, some rivers and some areas of land. Where property rights do exist, the owners can protect their property and either prevent others imposing costs on them or charge them for doing so. However, where they do not exist, property can be overused and negative externalities can

occur. For example, waste material may be dumped in rivers causing environmental damage and health problems, and aircraft may fly low at night keeping some people awake.

Activity 3

In the late nineteenth century in the USA, there were flocks of millions of passenger pigeons. People reported that they blacked out the sun as they flew past. Hunters shot them in their tens of thousands, unaware of the impact they were having. By the 1870s their numbers were in decline and the last passenger pigeon, called Martha, died in Cincinnati Zoo in 1914.

a What evidence is there in the passage that property rights did not exist in the case of the passenger pigeon?

b Explain how the existence of property rights might have saved the passenger pigeon from extinction.

c How do governments and international organisations now seek to prevent rare animals becoming extinct?

Advantages and disadvantages of extending property rights

Ronald **Coase** developed a theory in 1960 which suggests that extending property rights is an effective way of tackling externalities. He argued that the problem of externalities arises because of a lack of property rights. Where they do not exist or are unclear, as in much of the environment, people cannot be excluded from using the products so they can be overused. Extending property rights to, for example, rivers and the atmosphere, would restrict access, internalise externalities and should prevent overuse.

Coase claimed that ensuring that property rights exist enables the market to determine the socially optimum level of output. For example, if the inhabitants of a town are given ownership rights over the river running through it, they can either stop a firm polluting the river by taking legal action or negotiate to charge it for the pollution. The level of pollution that occurs should be where the amount of compensation is equal to the marginal external cost.

Extending property rights also has the advantage of compensating victims directly.

However, extending property rights is not straightforward. It is particularly difficult where there are many people adversely affected and possibly several firms responsible for generating negative externalities. This is because people have different views on the extent to which they have been adversely affected and the amount of compensation they require, so it is likely to be hard to achieve agreement.

There is also the question of equity. Rich people or firms are in a stronger position than poor people or firms to take legal action because they are able to afford the legal fees.

Current issue: insurance markets

Insurance markets encounter problems because of both a lack of and inaccurate information. It is difficult for insurance companies to get full information, and some people may withhold information in the belief that it will reduce their premiums. For example, someone with a history of heart disease may not mention this when filling in an application form for health insurance. This could lead to what is known as **adverse selection**, where an insurance company charges the same premium to people who have different chances of claiming.

There is also the risk of **moral hazard**. When people are insured they may take less care, knowing that, for example, if their car is stolen the insurance company will replace it. If insurance companies base their premiums on the behaviour of people who are not insured, they will charge too low a price.

Adverse selection and moral hazard could result in insurance becoming unprofitable and the market failing. To overcome these problems insurance companies adopt various strategies. In the case of adverse selection, they use information

about their customers, including age, occupation and location, to estimate risks. To deal with moral hazard, they offer no-claims bonuses, require customers to pay, for example, the first £100 of any claim and charge lower premiums for people who take precautions to reduce risks, such as fixing a burglar alarm to a house and keeping a guard dog. Soon more detailed information is expected to become available about people's genetic make-up, including their susceptibility to various illnesses and medical conditions. There will then be the question of how much of this information people will be required to reveal to insurance companies.

Summary

In this unit you have learned that:

- Information failure may be corrected by a government providing information directly or requiring suppliers and consumers to provide full and truthful information.

- Provision of information can help to increase market efficiency in the cases of merit and demerit goods where negative externalities exist.

- Where property rights do not exist, property can be overused and negative externalities can occur.

- Extending property rights has the advantages of internalising externalities and so achieving the socially optimum level of output. The measure also compensates directly third parties suffering any harmful effects.

- Extending property rights is difficult where many people are affected and its is likely to benefit rich people and firms more than poor people and firms since taking legal action can be expensive.

Multiple choice questions

1 What effect is the government provision of information about the harmful effect of a demerit good designed to have on its price and output?

	Price	Output
A	increase	increase
B	increase	decrease
C	decrease	decrease
D	decrease	increase

2 What is the publication by the government of details about firms which pollute designed to achieve?

A a reduction in demand for the products the firms produce

B a reduction in the firms' average and marginal costs

C a increase in the firms' output

D an increase in negative externalities

3 What does Coase's theory recommend?

A government provision of information

B the extension of property rights

C the taxation of demerit goods

D the subsidising of merit goods

4 Which of the following is an advantage of the extension of property rights?

A the removal of restrictions on the use of property

B an increase in output beyond the socially optimum level

C a reduction in social costs

D the internalising of external costs

5 Which of the following is a potential difficulty involved in extending property rights?

A the problem rich people will encounter in gaining access to the law

B the adverse effect the existence of property rights has on efficiency

C the inability to extend property rights to the environment

D the problem of reaching agreement about the level of compensation required by those adversely affected by the actions of others

6 The extension of property rights is designed to achieve:

A a more even distribution of income and wealth

B an increase in long-run supernormal profits

C a move towards the socially optimum level of output of products

D a reduction in the consumption of products whose marginal social costs equal their marginal private costs

Data response question: excessive consumption of alcohol

It is thought that excessive consumption of alcohol is costing the NHS £3 billion a year. It has to deal with binge drinkers, car crashes caused by drunk drivers and alcohol-related illnesses, including coronary heart disease, mental health problems and liver damage. It also has to pay for security at A & E (accident and emergency) departments and loss of staff from departments because of the aggressive behaviour of drunken patients.

The increase in binge drinking, especially among young people, has led the government to consider requiring firms to place health warnings on alcohol. It is particularly keen to warn young people that getting into a habit of heavy drinking is likely to lead to medical problems. Cirrhosis of the liver, for example, is now killing more men than Parkinson's disease and more women than cervical cancer. It has also been estimated that one person in 13 is dependent on alcohol, twice as many as are hooked on other drugs, including prescription drugs.

Government health officials recommend that men should not drink more than 21 units of alcohol a week and women 14 units. (A unit of alcohol is half a pint of beer, a small glass of wine or a measure of spirits.) They do not think it is realistic to curb advertising, but they want to change its nature to emphasise healthier patterns of drinking.

a What evidence is there in the passage that alcohol is a demerit good? [4]

b Discuss two negative externalities created by 'binge' drinking. [4]

c Explain how health warnings on alcohol may move the output of alcohol towards the socially optimum level. [4]

d Discuss two other methods of achieving a more allocatively efficient output of alcohol. [8]

6 Competition policy

In this unit you will examine the role and nature of competition policy. You will assess the impact of competition policy in tackling the problems created by the abuse of market power.

Role of competition policy

Competition policy seeks to protect consumers' interests and to increase economic efficiency. It aims to control firms' use of market dominance and to promote competitive pressures.

When the government considers how a firm is using its market power or how a proposed merger would result in the new firm using its market power, it takes into account what is sometimes referred to as the public interest. A firm is thought to be acting against the public interest if it charges high prices, produces low-quality products, restricts output, does not innovate, colludes and/or prevents the entry of new firms into the industry. When firms are not acting in the public interest, economic efficiency is not achieved.

The nature of competition policy

The UK government tackles the abuse of market power in various ways. It:

- prevents mergers that it thinks will not be in the public interest because of their effect on competition;
- makes uncompetitive practices illegal;
- regulates privatised utilities;
- removes artificial barriers to entry and exit into markets.

In implementing its competition policy, the government relies on regulatory agencies, including the Office of Fair Trading (OFT), the Competition Commission (CC), the Office for Gas and Electricity Regulation (Ofgem) and the Office for Communications (Ofcom), which covers telecommunications, television and radio.

The **Office of Fair Trading** administers government competition policy. It seeks to prevent the abuse of market dominance by, for example, breaking up cartels and prosecuting firms that engage in price fixing.

Activity 1

The cost of making calls from a land line to a mobile phone is due to fall after Oftel, the telecoms watchdog, forced the biggest operators to cut their charges over the next four years.

Furthermore, David Edmonds, Oftel's director general, said he wanted the four operators to provide 'much clearer information' to consumers on prices and services so they could more easily decide which operator to use.

While Mr Edmonds said the review of the mobile market found increasing competition, he said he could not yet conclude that the mobile market was 'effectively competitive'. ('Oftel orders cuts in price of mobile phone calls', Liz Vaughan-Adams, Independent, *27 September 2001)*

a Identify two forms of market failure which the extract indicates existed in the telecoms industry in 2001.

b Explain how the measures that Oftel took may have increased economic efficiency.

c Discuss three benefits consumers may gain from a market becoming 'effectively competitive'.

The **Competition Commission** investigates mergers which are likely to lead to dominance in a market and firms which are considered to be abusing their market power. It also acts as a final arbiter on appeals from OFT and regulatory agencies' decisions. Ofgem and other agencies, including Orr (Office of Rail Regulator), Oflot (Office of the National Lottery) and Ofwat (Office of Water Supplies), check the performance, prices and profits of privatised utilities to ensure that they do not abuse their market power. In these industries, which contain large natural monopoly elements, there is a risk that they will exploit their customers.

Activity 2

In 2001 the OFT stopped the merger of two banks, Lloyds TSB and the Abbey National. It was concerned that such a merger would significantly lessen competition, and in particular that it would result in the closure of a significant number of bank branches.

a What motivates firms to merge?

b Explain how the merger of Lloyds TSB and Abbey National might have:
 i benefited their customers
 ii disadvantaged their customers.

Competition policy in practice

Mergers that are likely to result in the new firm gaining a 25% or larger share of the market may be referred to the CC. If, after investigation, the CC reports that the proposed new firm will disadvantage consumers through, for example, charging higher prices or producing low-quality products, the OFT will prohibit the merger.

The CC also investigates firms that already have a dominant market position and are suspected of abusing their market power. Lacking competitive pressure, a firm may restrict output by charging a price above marginal cost, produce low-quality products and not keep costs to a minimum. It may also seek to reduce competition

and potential competition further by engaging in anti-competitive practices. The government has made some practices illegal, including collusion, predatory pricing, limit pricing, bundling and resale price maintenance.

Collusion occurs when firms restrict competition by jointly fixing prices and market shares (see Section 2, Unit 12). **Predatory pricing** involves a firm or firms setting prices below costs in order to drive rivals out of the market, whereas **limit pricing** is setting price low to discourage the entry of new firms into the market. **Bundling** is the practice of requiring a customer to buy another complementary product when one product is purchased. For example, a building society may require that someone seeking to take out a mortgage also has to buy building insurance from it. **Resale price maintenance** (also called retail price maintenance) involves a producer of a product fixing the price retailers can sell it at. The objective is to maintain a range of outlets and thereby give manufacturers more power than retailers do in setting the amount that retailers have to pay manufacturers. If a firm is found guilty of engaging in any of these anti-competitive practices, it can be fined by the OFT and/or have price controls imposed on it.

Price controls can also be used in the regulation of privatised utilities, some of which enjoy natural monopolies. Government agencies seek to apply the competitive pressure that can be lacking in these markets by setting limits on price rises and in some cases instructing the firms to make price cuts. They also target improvements in quality and, where considered necessary, take action to make it easier for other firms to enter the market.

A government may also use privatisation and deregulation to increase competition. Moving firms from the public to the private sector exposes them to the competitive pressures arising from the need to earn revenue from consumers and to raise finance from shareholders.

Deregulation involves the removal of laws and regulations that restrict competition. For example, in recent years the government has been removing the barriers protecting the Royal Mail's monopoly.

Activity 3

In 2001 the OFT found Napp Pharmaceuticals, a Cambridge-based company, guilty of abusing its dominant market position. It had nine-tenths of the hospital market for supplying MST, a sustained release morphine drug. As GP's prescriptions are strongly influenced by the brands used in hospitals, this was encouraging a growth in the company's sales to the community.

The OFT found that Napp had been engaging in predatory pricing when supplying the tablets to hospitals. In cases where it faced a rival, it was giving discounts of up to 90%. In contrast, it was charging considerably higher prices for tablets prescribed by GPs.

The OFT fined Napp £2.2 million and ordered it to reduce community-based prices. It was thought that the resulting lower prescription charges would save the NHS around £2 million a year.

a What evidence is there in the passage that Napp Pharmaceuticals had a dominant market position?

b Explain what is meant by predatory pricing.

c How may the community have benefited from the OFT's action?

Assessment of competition policy

A successful competition policy will put pressure on firms to produce in a more efficient way. It should result in lower prices, higher output, more innovation and higher consumer surplus than would exist in its absence. However, in cases where market power enables firms to take advantage of economies of scale and encourages them to innovate, there is a risk that economic efficiency may be reduced by measures that reduce their dominance.

It can also be difficult to design and implement the appropriate policies. For example,

it is thought there is a risk that regulatory agencies may fall prey to **regulatory capture**. This is the danger that such agencies may become too influenced by the executives of the industries they are regulating. An agency is likely to have more and closer contact with the industry's executives than with its customers. This, combined with the high level of technical knowledge that the executives are likely to possess, may result in the regulatory agency treating the industry too leniently.

Current issue: tightening up UK competition policy

In 2003 it was decided that UK competition policy was not stringent enough. Before 2003, firms that had been found guilty of abusing their market power could be fined an amount equal to 10% of their turnover for three years. A competitor that had been injured by a rival's illegal activities could also sue and the guilty party had to pay back any ill-gotten gains. A firm's executives may have considered that this was a gamble worth taking. Any anti-competitive practices they engaged in, such as collusion, may not have been discovered; injured parties may have chosen not to sue; and even if they were found out, the fines and damages would have been paid for out of the firm's profits, not the executives' personal resources.

At the start of 2003 the competition authorities were given new powers. They would be able to seek imprisonment for business people involved in price-fixing cartels and impose heavier fines.

Competition policy

Summary

In this unit you have learned that:

- The aims of competition policy are to protect consumer interests and to increase economic efficiency.

- It is in the public interest to have low prices, high quality, a sufficient output, a high level of innovation and consumer surplus.

- Competition policy tackles the abuse of monopoly dominance by preventing mergers that are against the public interest, makes anti-competitive practices illegal and removes artificial barriers to entry and exit.

- The government bodies which implement competition policy include the **Office of Fair Trading**, the **Competition Commission** and other regulatory agencies.

- The CC will investigate mergers that are likely to result in the new firm gaining a 25% or larger share of the market and are thought to be against the public interest.

- Examples of abuse of market power include collusion, **predatory pricing**, **limit pricing**, **bundling** and **resale price maintenance**.

- Government regulatory agencies seek to make privatised utilities act in a competitive way.

- Other measures included in competition policy are privatisation and **deregulation**.

Multiple choice questions

1 Which of the following would be against the public interest?
A innovation
B an absence of barriers to entry and exit into a market
C firms setting price equal to marginal cost
D firms producing at the lowest point on the highest average cost curve

2 What is the organisation which regulates telecoms and cable TV industries known as?
A OFT
B Ofcom
C Ofgem
D Ofwat

3 Limit pricing is setting price at a level designed to:
A drive competitors out of the market
B discourage the entry of new competitors into the market
C restrict increases in average costs
D control the amount of long-term profits earned

4 What is the aim of competition policy?
A to increase market power
B to increase economic efficiency
C to reduce consumer sovereignty
D to reduce competitive pressures

5 Which of the following is designed to increase competition?
A bundling
B deregulation
C predatory pricing
D resale price maintenance

6 What is meant by regulatory capture?
A an industry becoming dominated by a regulatory agency
B a government influencing the actions of a regulatory agency
C a regulatory agency becoming too influenced by the industry
D one regulatory agency merging with another regulatory agency

Data response question: resale price maintenance on children's toys

The makers of Monopoly, the board game where players are encouraged to 'own it all', is being investigated amid allegations of murky monopolistic practices. The Office of Fair Trading is exploring accusations that the UK arm of the American toy giant Hasbro has tried to use its financial muscle to fix the price at which games are sold on the high street. The pricing of Monopoly, the world's most famous board game where players attempt to build up huge financial power and force competitors out of business, is one of the areas understood to be under scrutiny.

The investigation is one of the highest profile since the OFT was recently handed greater power to protect consumers' interests and encourage competition.

Whilst punishment for errant players in Monopoly includes going straight to jail, fines and exorbitant rents for nights in hotels, the penalty for Hasbro could be much tougher. If the complaint is upheld the firm could be fined up to 10% of turnover for three consecutive years – a sum of £25 million.

Hasbro also produces Scrabble and Trivial Pursuit and toys including Action man and My Little Pony. Some retailers are

understood to be unhappy that they cannot offer some Hasbro toys at a discount in an effort to encourage more customers into their shops.

A spokesman for the OFT said the watchdog is 'conducting a formal investigation into alleged resale price maintenance on children's toys'. US-based Hasbro is the UK's largest toy company with about 15% of the annual £1.7 billion market for toys, games and associated merchandise. ('Monopoly inquiry more than a trivial pursuit', John Cassy, Guardian, 13 December 2001)

a Why may price fixing be against consumers' interests? [4]

b Explain two ways a firm could drive competitors out of business. [6]

c What measures can the OFT take against firms which engage in anti-competitive practices? [3]

d Explain what is meant by resale price maintenance. [3]

e Would Hasbro have been regarded as a monopoly in 2001? Explain your answer. [4]

7 Price control and minimum wage

Price controls are a non-market based measure to tackle market failure. In this unit you will examine why a government may impose maximum and minimum prices and their effects. You will then focus on one form of minimum price, the national minimum wage.

The nature of price controls

Price controls involve a government setting limits on the price that can be charged in a market. It will do this when it believes that the market-determined price reflects an abuse of market power or is inequitable. The use of price controls is likely to influence output. It may also redistribute income from rich to poor people, from suppliers to consumers, from

employers to employees and from taxpayers to certain groups of suppliers.

Maximum prices

The introduction of a **maximum price** sets a limit or ceiling above which the market price is not allowed to rise. There is no point introducing a maximum price unless it is set below the current market price because it would have no effect. For example, if the current market price is

£10, setting a maximum price of £12 will not change the price that suppliers charge. If, however, a maximum price of £8 is imposed, then price will have to fall.

Activity 1

Decide in each of the following market situations whether a government is likely to seek to lower or raise price:

a firms are earning high long-run supernormal profits

b the product is a merit good

c the product is a basic necessity and most consumers of it are poor

d output of the product is lower than is regarded as desirable

A government may set a maximum price to promote equity and to enable poor people to purchase basic necessities including, for example, housing and food. Figure 1 shows the effect of setting a maximum rent below the market equilibrium. Price falls from the market price of P to the maximum price of PZ.

Figure 1 also shows that when a maximum price is set below where demand and supply are equal, a major problem occurs: a shortage will be created. The lower price causes demand to extend to Qd and supply to contract to Qs. Demand exceeds supply and there is a shortage of Qs – Qd amount. This means that the product will have to be allocated in some way, perhaps on the basis of first come, first serviced (queuing) or a ballot. However, whatever method is used, a **black market** is likely to develop. In this case the welfare of those who are able to buy the product will rise as they will purchase it for less than the market price. However, some others who are willing to pay the price, or even a higher price, will lose out because of the shortage.

The problems of shortages and a black market led to the removal of rent controls in the UK in 1988.

However, setting a maximum price below the current market price will not always lead to shortages. A firm operating under conditions of monopoly or oligopoly may restrict supply in order to raise price above marginal cost and earn supernormal profits. In this case a government may want to impose a maximum price to prevent the abuse of market power and increase economic efficiency. A lower price will cause demand to extend and move output closer to the allocatively efficient output where AR = MC, as shown in

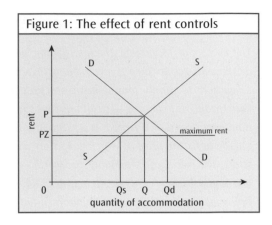

Figure 1: The effect of rent controls

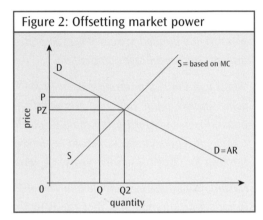

Figure 2: Offsetting market power

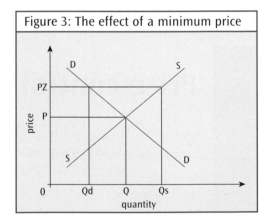

Figure 3: The effect of a minimum price

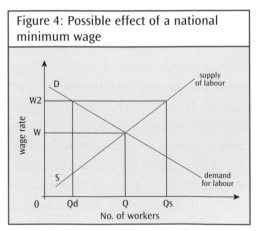

Figure 4: Possible effect of a national minimum wage

Figure 2. It will also redistribute some of the supernormal profit to consumers.

Avoiding excessively high prices is the objective of price controls imposed on the privatised utilities by the government's regulatory agencies.

Activity 2

In 2002 Ofgem, the energy industry regulator, introduced price cuts of 1.5% for electricity transmission. Oftel, the telecommunications regulator, went further and lowered telecommunication prices by 13%. In the same year firms in the two industries achieved improved efficiency.

a What may the passage indicate about the relative profit levels achieved by the firms in the two industries in 2001?

b Explain what is meant by improved efficiency.

Minimum prices

When a government sets a **minimum price** it is setting a floor below which price is not allowed to fall. This action has an effect only if the minimum price is set above the market price.

A government will introduce a minimum price if it believes that the market price is too low. In the European Union (EU) a minimum price is set on agricultural products to ensure the continued existence of an EU agricultural sector and to protect and stabilise the incomes of farmers.

Operating a minimum price, though, can lead to surpluses. Figure 3 shows that setting a minimum price of PZ causes supply to extend to Qs and demand to contract to Qd. Supply exceeds demand and there is a surplus of Qd – Qs amount.

To maintain the price of PZ, a government would have to buy the surplus. This can be expensive and it is not the only possible cost of operating a minimum price. As the EU has found with its **Common Agricultural Policy (CAP)**, additional costs can arise from storing the surplus and, in some cases, later destroying some of it. Storing and destroying surpluses is obviously a

wasteful use of resources. Another possible disadvantage is that minimum prices may protect inefficient producers.

Activity 3

British families are paying £16 a week extra in taxes and high food prices because of the common agricultural policy, according to a study by the Consumers' Association. Its research shows that the CAP cost the UK £5 billion last year [2000] or the equivalent of 2p on the rate of income tax.

Sheila McKechnie, director of the association, said: 'The CAP has led to appalling levels of waste, inflated food prices, and a market rigged against consumers, and for the interests of producers.' ('Watchdog puts cost of CAP to UK at £5 billion', Felicity Lawrence, Guardian, 12 February 2001)

Using a diagram, assess the statement made by Sheila McKechnie.

National minimum wage

A well-known example of a minimum price is a national minimum wage (NMW), which is the minimum price paid for labour. The main objective of a NMW is to reduce poverty by raising the living standard of low-paid workers. It also seeks to prevent the exploitation of workers by employers who have stronger bargaining power.

Many national governments set a minimum wage that employers have to pay for the services of workers. In the UK, the NMW was introduced on 1 April 1999. It became illegal for any organisation to pay employees aged 22 and over less than £3.60 per hour and those aged 18–21 less than £3 per hour. The legislation does not apply to anyone aged under 18. Since its introduction, the NMW has been raised in most years to take account of rises in the average national wage.

At the time of its introduction, some economists and Conservative politicians warned that it would result in a rise in unemployment. Figure 4 shows how this might happen.

The market wage rate is initially W and Q workers are employed. Introducing a NMW of W2 encourages more people to seek employment and the supply of labour extends to Qs. However, the higher cost of employing labour causes demand for workers to contract to Qd. Unemployment of Qd – Qs amount is created. The workers who may be made redundant are likely to come from the groups most prone to poverty, including disabled and less skilled people.

Those who had previously been paid just above the minimum wage may press for a wage rise and set off a string of wage claims intended to maintain **wage differentials**. If granted, these could raise firms' costs, reduce their international competitiveness and further increase unemployment.

However, a minimum price does not always result in a surplus. In an uncompetitive market where buyers have considerable market power, prices may be kept low. In some markets firms earn high supernormal profits and, in terms of labour, they are price makers, determining the wage rates they pay. They can afford to pay higher wages, and the introduction of a NMW may offset their strong bargaining power in the market for labour.

Another reason the introduction of a NMW may not result in a rise in unemployment is that it may increase the demand for labour by cutting labour costs per unit. Paying low-paid workers more may increase their motivation and productivity. It may also lower costs of training and recruitment by reducing labour turnover.

Current issue: price controls and economic efficiency

Some companies claim that price controls imposed by the government's regulatory agencies have a harmful effect on economic efficiency. They argue that price cuts reduce their ability to finance large investment programmes to improve quality and, in the long term, lower their costs of production and hence their ability to keep prices low.

However, the government argues that if there was no regulatory intervention, there would be a danger that in a situation of pure monopoly or strongly dominant market position, firms would be able to charge excessive prices and/or provide a low-quality product. The agencies set price limits every four or five years. They use a formula that permits firms to increase prices in line with inflation less allowances for efficiency improvements and after providing for future investment.

Summary

In this unit you have learned that:

- Price controls can be used to reduce the abuse of market power, to reduce poverty and to encourage the production of certain products.

- A **maximum price** will have an impact on a market only if it is set below the market price.

- A maximum price may be set to promote equity and to enable the poor to purchase basic necessities.

- A maximum price may result in a shortage and a **black market**, but this may not happen if it offsets the abuse of market power.

- A **minimum price** will have an impact on a market only if it is set above the market price.

- A minimum price may result in a surplus, but not if it offsets the abuse of market power.

- One example of the use of a minimum price is the EU's minimum price for agricultural products, designed to protect and stabilise farmers' incomes and to ensure the continued existence of a strong EU agricultural sector.

- Another example is the national minimum wage, which is intended to reduce poverty and to avoid the exploitation of workers by employers with strong bargaining power.

- A national minimum wage may benefit employers by raising labour productivity and reducing labour turnover.

Multiple choice questions

1 A government sets a minimum price of P as shown in Figure 5. What will be the effect of setting this minimum price?

A price and quantity will remain unaffected

B there will be excess supply

C demand will exceed supply

D price and quantity will fall

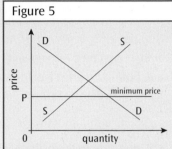

Figure 5

2 Figure 6 shows the demand for and supply of wheat in a market. A government sets a minimum price of PZ. To maintain this price, what quantity of the product will the government have to buy?

A OX

B XY

C YZ

D XZ

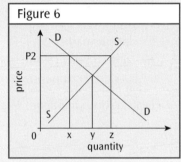

Figure 6

3 Which of the following is a possible objective of setting a maximum price for bus travel below the market equilibrium price?

A equity

B a reduction in the shortage of bus travel

C an increase in demand for transport by private car

D increased competitive pressure on bus companies

4 A government decides to intervene in the market for private rented accommodation. It fixes a maximum rent of PZ as shown in Figure 7. What will be the outcome of the government's action?

A a surplus of unsold rented accommodation

B a reduction in the number of rooms available for rent

C an increase in the willingness of people to rent out accommodation

D a decrease in the number of people wanting to rent

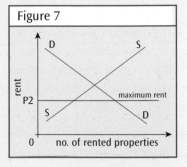

Figure 7

5 Price controls may be imposed on a privatised utility in order to:

A create greater price stability

B ensure it earns high supernormal profit

C prevent abuse of its market power

D stop it engaging in price cutting

6 Which of the following is a reason for the EU setting a minimum price for agricultural products?

A to reduce surpluses of agricultural products

B to promote a low price of agricultural products

C to ensure a reasonable income for farmers

D to redistribute income from farmers to taxpayers

Data response question: introduction of a minimum wage

Dire predictions that the minimum wage would cost millions of jobs have proved erroneous, say economic researchers.

A comprehensive study of workers affected by the introduction of the £3.60 minimum introduced in 1999 shows it had no impact on their chances of losing their job.

In the run-up to the 1997 election Conservative ministers warned that Labour's plan to introduce a wage floor would cost millions of jobs, and pointed to research from economists such as Patrick Minford at Liverpool University to back their claim.

But Mr Stewart told the Royal Economic Society Conference at Warwick University that the predictions of massive job losses were based on a simplistic idea of how the labour market works. 'If you take the textbook model of the labour market and you use it to predict the impact of the minimum wage, you would expect it to cause job losses,' he said.

'But that assumes that the labour market is perfectly competitive and that the market sets wage rates not firms.' In fact, in practice, firms have a lot of discretion about the wage rates they set, according to Mr Stewart. Some

evidence suggests that it may actually be more efficient for firms to pay above the going rate because it reduces staff turnover which is costly.

'The introduction of the minimum wage may reduce recruiting costs, reduce staff turnover and cut training, and improve employee morale and increase productivity,' he said. ('Labour market weathers minimum wage', Charlotte Denny, Guardian, 28 March 2002)

a Define a minimum wage. [2]

b Using a diagram, explain why the introduction of a national minimum wage might be expected to cause large job losses. [6]

c Discuss:
   i what would be meant by a perfectly competitive labour market [4]
   ii why, in practice, the labour market is not perfectly competitive [4]

d Explain why a minimum wage may cut labour costs. [4]

8 Cost-benefit analysis

In this unit you will examine the nature of **cost-benefit analysis**, its uses and the stages of a cost-benefit analysis. You will assess its advantages and limitations and the criterion on which decisions are made.

The nature of cost-benefit analysis

Cost-benefit analysis (CBA) is a way of assessing an investment project by considering its full costs and benefits. It can be applied in cases where market failure occurs and a government has to make a decision about the use of resources. For example, a government may conduct a CBA to help it decide the quantity of a public good to provide. It is also a useful approach when determining the desirability of a project which may generate significant externalities.

Whereas a private-sector firm is likely to take into account only private costs and benefits when deciding whether to go ahead with a project, a CBA considers both private and external costs and benefits, that is, the social costs and benefits. So it aims to estimate the full opportunity cost of a project and whether it will provide a net benefit to society.

Activity 1

British Energy and British Nuclear Fuels, the UK's two atomic power operators, are planning to build nine nuclear stations to replace the country's ageing advanced gas-cooled reactors.

Identify:

a a private cost and a private benefit

b an external cost and an external benefit of operating a new nuclear station

The stages of a cost-benefit analysis

There are several stages involved in conducting a CBA.

- Identifying the relevant costs and benefits, including both private and external costs and benefits.
- Assigning a monetary value to each cost and benefit. This is not always straightforward, particularly in the case of external costs and benefits but even in the case of some private costs and benefits.
- Estimating the chances of the costs and benefits occurring. It may be calculated, for example, that there is only a 0.2% chance of a radiation leak from a new nuclear power station.
- Making adjustments to take into account the timing of costs and benefits. For example, revenue received today is worth more than revenue earned in several years' time because it can be placed in a bank or other financial institution to earn interest. So future costs and benefits are adjusted (discounted) downwards.
- Considering the likely distribution of the costs and benefits identified – who is losing and who is gaining. A sensitivity analysis may also be undertaken. This involves placing a range of possible values on the uncertain costs and benefits and seeing if the different values affect the desirability of the project.
- Adding up the monetary value of all the costs and benefits, interpreting the results and

making a recommendation as to whether the project should go ahead or not. If social costs exceed social benefits, the project will not be recommended. If social benefits are greater than social costs the project will have passed the first hurdle, but whether it is recommended or not will depend on whether its net benefit is greater than other projects under consideration.

Activity 2

A government is considering four possible capital investment projects. It has the finance to go ahead with one of the projects. Table 1 shows estimates of the private and external costs and benefits of each of the projects.

a Decide which project would be given the go-ahead if a private-sector approach were taken to investment analysis.

b Decide which project would be recommended by a CBA

c Identify three possible external costs arising from building a new motorway.

Table 1				
	2 new hospitals	4 new shools	A new motorway	A new airport
	£M	£M	£M	£M
Private benefits	180	60	240	350
Private costs	200	80	180	200
External benefits	280	240	100	90
External costs	80	60	120	130

The advantages and limitations of a CBA

The overwhelming advantage of a CBA is that it seeks to ensure that the total costs and benefits to society of a project are considered. This increases the chances of achieving a socially optimum level of output and maximising economic welfare.

However, it is not an easy process to carry out. Many private costs and benefits will have a price attached to them but some may not. For example, it can be difficult to estimate the consumer surplus that passengers using a train service on a new rail line may gain and the value that should be placed on the time they may save in making their journeys.

It may appear to be easy to attach a monetary value to some external costs and benefits. For example, the effect of a new rail line on rival transport firms could be assessed by examining what happens to their profits. However, the problem of deciding the cut-off point for considering external costs and benefits makes it difficult, in practice, to attach a monetary value to most of them. The operation of a train service on a new rail line will generate noise pollution. It is obvious that the disturbance caused to people living close to the rail line should be considered, but what about the effect on people living ten miles away?

To place a value on a negative externality such as noise, economists may conduct a survey. This would ask people how much they would have to be paid to put up with any harmful effects they suffer, and how much they would be willing to pay for any external benefits they experience. However, their answers may not provide an accurate reflection of these costs and benefits because they may be tempted to exaggerate external costs, hoping they will receive compensation, and to understate external benefits, fearing they may be charged for them. They may also have difficulty in estimating the effects on themselves and they may be seeking to influence the outcome of the survey.

Economists may, in addition to a survey, use information obtained about the costs and benefits generated by a similar project. For example, a year after a new rail line had opened elsewhere, how much had house prices, employment, spending on double glazing and the number and variety of wild birds in the area changed?

Valuation problems also occur in relation to particular items, when the costs and benefits occur and the distributional consequences. In transport projects, a decision has to be made on how to value time. Generally, the value of time is based on the national average wage. For instance, if the building of a new rail line results in a reduction in congestion on nearby roads, the external benefit to drivers could be estimated by multiplying the time saved by the average wage rate.

It is also difficult to place a monetary value on lost lives and injuries. Economists do this in various ways, including calculating potential lost earnings and the cost to the NHS and the emergency services, and asking people how much they would be prepared to pay to reduce the risk of injury and death.

As noted above, it can be difficult to value costs and benefits. If it is decided to value revenue and costs paid in the future at less than current revenue and costs, some form of **discounting technique** has to be used.

The distributional effects of project decisions must also be considered. The external costs in terms, for example, of air, noise and visual pollution and congestion, are likely to be concentrated in a small geographical area. In contrast, the external benefits may be more widespread. The costs of some projects based in city centres may also fall most heavily on poor people while the main beneficiaries may be firms and rich households.

Activity 3

In 2001 a traffic study conducted by Trafficmaster, a travel data company, found that the M25 orbital road is the UK's most dangerous and congested motorway. It reported that peak-time journeys take four times as long as off-peak journeys, and that congestion and 'bunching' contribute to the high number of road accidents.

Identify the costs to society of:

a congestion

b road accidents

The Hicks-Kaldor criterion

If projects were judged on the basis of moving to Pareto efficiency, it is unlikely that many would be given the go-ahead. To achieve an improvement in Pareto efficiency, there would have to be gainers and no losers. So those who benefit from the project would have to be able to compensate those who have been made worse off and still have a net gain. This does not happen in reality. Any compensation for those who have been adversely affected is likely to come from taxpayers, and some people are still likely to feel worse off.

So some economists suggest that rather than applying a Pareto criterion, use should be made of the **Hicks-Kaldor criterion**. According to this, the desirability of a project should be judged on its potential to lead to a Pareto improvement, that is, whether in theory those who benefit could compensate those who lose and still receive a net gain even if they do not actually offer any compensation. This is the approach adopted by most CBAs.

Current issue: protecting SSSIs

Economists, politicians and environmentalists debate how much protection areas of natural beauty and Sites of Special Scientific Interest (SSSI) should have.

In 2002 a public inquiry was held into plans for a new port on an important maritime wildlife site and SSSI at Dibden bay on the edge of the New Forest, near Southampton.

Associated British Ports (ABP), which owns the land, wanted to build a container terminal covering 500 acres. It argued that this would create up to 3,000 jobs and would ensure that Southampton would remain one of the world's most important ports. ABP promised to compensate for the loss of the mudflats by building an artificial creek around the southern end of the site and a new mudflat for birds nearby. Its case was supported by the city's two MPs and Southampton City Council.

Opposing the plans were English Nature, the government's conservation agency, the Countryside Agency, the government's main adviser on rural matters, Hampshire County Council, the New Forest District Council and local residents. They claimed that it would adversely affect the environment in an area which is a winter home to 50,000 birds.

Summary

In this unit you have learned that:

■ A **cost-benefit analysis (CBA)** is a method of assessing an investment project that takes into account social costs and benefits.

■ The key stages of a CBA include identifying the relevant costs and benefits involved, placing a monetary value on them and then making a recommendation on a project's desirability depending on the relationship between its social costs and benefits.

■ A CBA has the benefit of ensuring that all costs and benefits are taken into account, but it is difficult to place a monetary value on some costs and benefits, particularly external costs and benefits.

■ The **Hicks-Kaldor criterion** suggests that a project should be recommended if there is net social benefit.

Multiple choice questions

1 What is the most common use of a CBA?

A to calculate the private costs and benefits generated by the output of state-owned companies

B to determine the balance between taxation and government spending

C to decide on the appropriate level of private-sector investment

D to assess public-sector investment projects

2 What benefits is the recommendation of a CBA based on?

A external benefits

B financial benefits

C private benefits

D social benefits

3 Which of the following statements about a CBA is correct?

A it is based on an assessment of private costs and benefits

B it takes into account only monetary external costs and benefits

C it involves placing a monetary value on all relevant costs and benefits

D it recommends that an investment project should go ahead if social cost equals social benefit

4 Economists find, after carrying out a CBA, that the social benefits of an investment project exceed the social costs. What recommendation would they make?

A to proceed with the project

B not to proceed with the project

C to proceed with the project only if its net social benefit exceeds that of rival project proposals

D not to proceed with the project unless the number of gainers equals the number of losers

5 How does a CBA differ from private-sector investment appraisal?

A it takes into account both external and private costs and benefits

B it values external costs and benefits more highly than private costs and benefits

C it includes future costs and benefits

D it excludes non-monetary costs and benefits

6 In which of the following cases would a CBA be most likely to be applied?

A the proposed purchase of a new piece of capital equipment by a private-sector firm

B the proposed building of a new NHS hospital

C the decision by consumers on how to allocate their expenditure

D the decision by foreigners on whether to purchase UK or home-produced products

Data response question: expansion of Heathrow airport

The idea of building a new Heathrow terminal as large as Gatwick, which will attract thousands of extra flights a year, was greeted in west London with widespread resignation, but some strong feelings, too.

Mike Walsh, hurrying through the centre of Hounslow as planes passed 3,000 feet overhead at 8.45am, was almost lost for words. 'It's dia-bloody-bolical. The traffic is already horrific, the pollution is terrible,' he said. 'You sit in the garden and you feel you are in the damned aeroplane.'

But S Choban, from Ealing, who works in the Hounslow benefits agency, believes it will provide many jobs. 'I used to live under the flight path and it was really quite horrific,' she said. 'I would have preferred the terminal to have been built well outside London, but I can see that it will bring more money to the area. It's good for the councils and for the unemployed.'

George Francis also used to live near the flightpath at Heston. He moved, but he still works in west London. 'The planes, you might say, ate my family's brain. I can never prove that I became ill because of the noise, or that my children suffered at school, but we're all much better since we left.'

Paul Majors, a teacher living in Hounslow, believes Heathrow is the most dangerous airport in Britain in terms of risk to people living nearby. 'It's only a matter of time before there's a major crash,' he said.

Julia Holland, in her 70s, lives just to the west of Heathrow. 'I've seen west London become more and more congested and more polluted. It's horrible here now,' she said. 'They call it progress, but it seems like sheer greed to me. Few people have any idea how big this development is going to be, they really can't comprehend the effects it will have on people. If I had the money I'd move out, but I've lived here all my life.' ('Suffering residents ponder price of extra jobs', John Vidal, Guardian, *21 November 2001)*

a Identify a private cost and a private benefit of operating the new terminal at Heathrow. [4]

b Discuss the external costs and benefits of Heathrow airport and the new terminal mentioned in the extract. [6]

c Explain how the CBA into the proposed terminal would have been carried out. [6]

d Discuss two policies the government could use to reduce the potential negative externalities which could be created by the operation of the new terminal. [4]

9 Government failure

In this unit you will discover the meaning of **government failure** and examine its main causes.

The nature of government failure

Government failure occurs when government intervention, instead of reducing market distortions and so improving economic efficiency and welfare, increases market distortions and reduces economic efficiency and welfare. For example, keeping the Millennium Dome standing empty in 2002 cost nearly £30 million of public money. This was higher than the government had predicted and was widely condemned as a misuse of resources.

Government intervention may increase economic inefficiency for various reasons, including information problems, bureaucracy,

Which of the following indicate government failure?

a a government tax moving output away from the socially optimum output

b a subsidy on a merit good equalling marginal external benefit

c the provision of government information about the dangers of smoking encouraging some young people to smoke

d the social costs of providing a public good exceeding the social benefits

A government decides to set a maximum price on a product produced by a pure monopolist.

a Decide what information the government needs to find or estimate before it sets the maximum price.

b Discuss the possible consequences of basing a maximum price on inaccurate information.

time lags, abuse of government power, lack of continuity of policies, reduction in incentives and distributional problems.

Information problems

It is not easy to obtain much of the information the government needs to correct market failure, such as the extent of externalities and the social benefit gained from public goods. If the government is using inaccurate or inadequate information, it risks increasing economic inefficiency, not reducing it.

Figure 1 shows that if left to market forces, output, based on marginal private costs, would exceed the socially optimum level by $Q - QX$. However, placing a tax of ab, based on an overestimate of marginal external cost, moves output further from the socially optimum level.

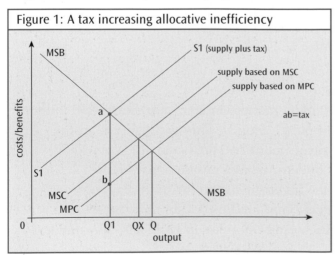

Figure 1: A tax increasing allocative inefficiency

Bureaucracy, time lags and abuse of government power

Government policymaking and intervention requires the use of resources in the form of labour, land and capital. If the state employs too many resources or uses them inefficiently, this will reduce economic welfare. High numbers of government officials and civil servants, for example, may result in inflexible and bureaucratic procedures and slow response to changing economic circumstances.

Indeed, time lags are a possible cause of government failure. It takes time for a government to recognise that market failure is occurring, to draw up an appropriate policy measure and to implement it. By the time policy measures are introduced, the problems may have become acute, requiring more radical measures, or economic circumstances may have changed, necessitating different measures.

There is also a risk of politicians and civil servants abusing their power. They may pursue their own financial and career interests rather than seek to increase the public good. For example, a government minister may try to increase the size of her department in the hope that it will increase her profile and political power even if she suspects that such an expansion will not be a good use of resources. Politicians' views and actions may be influenced by their outside business interests. For example, someone with shares, a directorship or hopes for a future job in a tobacco company may be inclined to oppose measures to reduce smoking.

Activity 3

It was revealed in April 2002 that John Bercow, the shadow chief secretary to the Treasury, had cost the taxpayer £552,672 between June 2001 and March 2002 by tabling thousands of parliamentary questions to ministers in order to 'expose government waste'. A large number of staff had worked on providing the answers to the questions. The information requested was for use in a Conservative campaign, Wastewatch, in which Mr Bercow details alleged government excesses.

a Identify a possible opportunity cost of answering John Bercow's questions.

b Discuss two ways a society could benefit from a reduction in government waste.

Lack of continuity of policies, reduction in incentives and distortionary effects

If there are frequent changes in government policy measures, it will be difficult for firms and households to plan ahead. For example, if investment subsidies and **corporation tax** keep changing, firms may not have the confidence to go ahead with investment projects.

Government intervention may reduce economic efficiency by having an adverse effect on incentives. Setting minimum prices and buying up surpluses may enable some inefficient producers to survive. The existence of unemployment benefit (jobseeker's allowance) may discourage some people from seeking employment. Taxes may reduce the incentive to work (but see Current issue) and corporation tax may reduce firms' ability and willingness to invest.

There may also be a lack of incentives in the public sector. The lack of the carrot (the profit motive) and the stick (risk of bankruptcy) provided by competition may mean that public-sector workers do not strive to keep costs low and raise quality.

Government intervention may create unintended distortionary effects. Taxing demerit goods, for instance, is likely to increase income inequality since poor people spend proportionately more on alcohol and cigarettes than rich people. A government requirement that public-sector organisations reach certain targets and provide information about their progress may mean that the organisations change their priorities and manipulate data.

Current issue: work and taxes

Economists debate what effect a rise in income tax rates has on the number of hours people work. Some argue that such an increase will reduce the incentive to work and encourage people to work fewer hours and take more leisure time.

Others claim that workers will be forced to work longer hours. This is because higher tax rates will mean that workers will have less

Activity 4

Stuart Emslie, a risk assessment expert at the Department of Health, claimed that some £9 billion (almost 20% of the entire NHS budget) is either wasted or unnecessarily spent; £9 billion is more than 3p on the rate of income tax.

His figure included £100 million on avoidable management and legal costs; £1.4 billion on hospital acquired infections and clinical negligence (from which 40,000 people die every year in the NHS, and which has cost it nearly £4 billion in compensation); £2 billion (just under 1p on income tax) on beds needlessly blocked because patients cannot be relocated; £2 billion on staff absences and sickness; £1.3 billion on fraud; and £300–600 million on wasteful prescriptions. ('The £325 light bulb', John Laughland, Mail on Sunday, *17 March 2002)*

a Discuss two costs of economic inefficiency in state health care provision.

b Discuss two ways in which economic efficiency in the provision of state health care could be increased.

disposable income. If they want to maintain their living standards, they will have to work more hours than before the tax rise.

Most studies indicate that tax rate increases have little effect on the number of hours people work. This is because many people cannot alter the hours they work and of those who can, about as many choose to work more hours as choose to work fewer hours. The main impact is likely to be on those who are considering whether to enter the labour force.

Summary

In this unit you have learned that:

■ **Government failure** arises when government intervention increases economic inefficiency.

■ If a government lacks information or has inaccurate information it may move output further away from the socially optimum level.

■ Bureaucracy wastes resources, time lags can result in policy measures being implemented too late and the abuse of government power can cause economic inefficiency.

■ Frequent changes in government policy measures make it difficult for firms and households to plan. There is also a risk that government failure can arise as a result of the distortionary and disincentive effects that government intervention can have.

Multiple choice questions

1 Why might government intervention to correct market failure make the situation worse?

A information about market conditions is easy to obtain

B significant negative and positive externalities exist

C public goods are non-rival and non-excludable

D incentives are distorted by taxes and subsidies

2 Which of the following would not cause government failure?

A excessive red tape

B taxes based on marginal external costs

C civil servants following their own interests

D time lags in implementing policy measures

3 Which of the following is a possible source of government failure?

A adequate information

B high administrative costs

C continuity of appropriate government policy measures

D an absence of disincentive effects arising from government policy measures

4 How might government subsidies reduce economic efficiency?

A they may prevent the exit of high-cost firms from the industry

B they may be based on marginal external benefit

C they may be placed on products which if left to market forces would be underconsumed

D they may be financed by taxes placed on firms which produce products at a level where marginal social cost exceeds marginal social benefit

5 Which of the following government measures would reduce economic efficiency?

A welfare payments which result in scarce resources not being used

B regulations which limit the abuse of market power

C deregulation which leads to a more competitive market

D marketable permits which turn external costs into internal costs

Multiple choice questions continued

6 Which of the following would reduce government failure?

A an increase in information about the extent of externalities

B an increase in the time it takes to design and implement government policies

C a decrease in the accountability of politicians

D a decrease in the accuracy of information about the demand for public goods

Data response question: manipulation of hospital waiting lists

Systematic fiddling of hospital waiting lists, driven by intense pressure on mangers to meet ministers' targets, is exposed in a report by the National Audit Office. It found that a culture of waiting list 'adjustment' was so ingrained that six hospital chiefs who left with generous payoffs after irregularities were found were promptly re-employed by the NHS. One chief executive received nearly £100,000.

About 6,000 patients were affected by waiting list manipulation at nine hospital trusts investigated by the audit office, hundreds of them having to wait longer for operations as a result. The watchdog said that another 13 hospitals should be examined as a matter of urgency because of suspiciously high levels of patients suspended from the official waiting list. Waiting list fiddles were a major breach of public trust, the audit office said, and 'inconsistent with the proper conduct of proper business'.

Sir John Bourne, the Comptroller and Auditor General, concluded that many of the manipulations followed the 'very strong message' that waiting time targets were key government priorities. He added: 'The adjustments were made in the context of pressure on trusts and particularly chief executives to meet key departmental targets.' Meeting waiting list targets has been one of the biggest problems for hospital managers. The Government's NHS Plan stipulated that no one should be waiting more than 18 months for an operation; this would fall in stages to 15, 12 and then six months by 2005.

Hospitals which manipulated lists used a variety of methods: their names were not added to the lists; or they were taken off the lists even though they had not been treated.

The Department of Health pledged to create a new code for managers, and to prevent those who broke it from being re-employed by the NHS. ('Hospitals "betray trust" by fiddling waiting lists', Nigel Hawkes and David Charter, The Times, 19 December 2001)

a Explain the effect that government-set targets appear to have had on the six hospitals referred to. [4]

b Discuss the impact the effect is likely to have had on economic welfare. [4]

c Explain how a free market would respond to waiting lists. [4]

d Identify, from the extract, one measure to reduce government failure. [2]

e Discuss how government targets for examination performance set for schools may affect their priorities and the quality of the data they provide. [6]

1 Housing

In this unit you will examine the nature of the housing market and explore the factors that influence house prices and regional differences in house prices. You will consider market failure in the housing market, assess different types of government intervention and examine the relationship between the housing market and developments in the national economy.

The nature of the housing market

There are various types of dwellings and of tenure in the housing market. Dwellings include houses and bungalows (detached, semi-detached and terraced), flats, maisonettes and mobile homes. Some are owner occupied, either owned outright or owned with a mortgage. Others are rented, from either the social sector (the council or a housing association) or the private sector (furnished or unfurnished). Ownership and rental are forms of tenure.

Activity 1

Using the information in Table 1 from 1998–99, assess:

a which was the most common type of tenure

b which ethnic group was the most reliant on renting from the social sector

Table 1: Ethnic group of head of household: by tenure, 1998–99					
	Owned Outright	Owned with mortgage	Rented from social sector	Rented privately [1]	All tenure (=100% millions)
White	27	43	21	10	19.2
Black	9	31	50	10	0.4
Indian	22	54	11	13	0.3
Pakistani	17	53	12	18	0.2
Bangladeshi	5	31	54	10	0.1
Other groups [2]	11	35	27	27	0.3
All ethnic groups [3]	26	43	21	10	20.4

[1] Includes rent free accommodation
[2] Includes those of mixed origin.
[3] Includes those who did not state their ethnic group.

Source: Survey of English Housing, Department of the Environment, Transport and Regions

Activity 2

In 1950, councils undertook 85% of the construction of new dwellings; now they build very few new houses. Housing associations build some new houses, but these account for only 13% of new completions.

In the last 50 years there has also been a move away from building terraced houses to building detached and semi-detached houses and purpose-built flats and maisonettes.

a What has happened to the proportion of new dwelling construction by the private sector in the last 50 years?

b Give one reason for the move away from building terraced houses.

Changes in the pattern of tenure

In recent decades there have been major changes in the pattern of tenure. One of the most significant is the growth in owner occupation and the decline in renting. Between 1960 and 2000, the number of owner-occupied dwellings more than doubled to 17.1 million and the number of rented dwellings fell by a sixth. In 1998, 68% of dwellings were owner-occupied. This compares with an average of 60% in the EU, 82% in Ireland and 42% in Germany. Owner occupation is more popular in Ireland and the UK than in most EU countries, where there is more of a tradition of renting.

In the social sector there has been a decline in council (municipal) rented accommodation. There are two reasons for this. One is the privatisation of council housing stock, encouraged in the 1980s by the Conservative government's 'right to buy' legislation, which gave council tenants the right to buy their homes at a discount depending on the length of the tenancy. In 1996 this right was extended to housing association tenants. The other is the significant decline in council house construction.

At the same time there has been a rise in rented accommodation provided by **housing associations**. Since 1988, 125 English councils, owning a total of 620,000 houses, have sold some or all of their houses to housing associations. In 1992 housing associations, financed partly by the state and party by the private sector, became the main providers of new social housing. They charge what are referred to as 'affordable' rents. These are usually below the market equilibrium level.

The number of households has also been increasing, partly because more people are living alone. There are several reasons for this, including younger people taking out **mortgages** on their own, an increasing divorce rate and more elderly people living alone.

Demand and supply in housing

Demand for houses is influenced by several factors. A crucial one is changes in real disposable income. Demand for houses has a high income elasticity of demand. Another is the availability and cost of mortgages. Most people who buy a house have to take out a mortgage. Building societies and other mortgage lenders are usually willing to lend three or four times the borrowers' gross annual earnings. Other influences include government policy, expectations, changes in population size and changes in household structure.

There is a large stock of housing in the UK, but net additions each year are small. The supply of houses at any time consists of new houses and houses which are put on to the market by their owners.

The building of new houses is a speculative process. Builders have to estimate what demand and prices will be in, for example, three months' time. Other factors influencing the supply of new houses include changes in wages, since house building is a labour-intensive industry, planning permission and weather conditions. If it is easier to gain planning permission, the supply of new houses will increase. In contrast, a prolonged period of bad weather would hold up building and reduce supply.

Sales of older houses are influenced by, for example, the level of economic activity, changes in household structure and the time of year. When the economy is doing well and incomes are rising some people are likely to trade up, selling their homes to buy more expensive property. More houses generally come on to the market in spring than during the Christmas period.

House prices

The prices of houses and other dwellings change with changes in demand and supply. In the 1980s, increased competition between banks, building societies and other financial institutions to provide loans and rising incomes led to a rise in house prices. This accelerated in 1987 and 1988, when financial institutions were lending more than five times annual earnings, unemployment was falling and expectations were rising.

Between 1989 and 1993 average house prices fell by 8% because of a doubling of interest rates, rising unemployment, pessimism about future economic prospects, fears that prices would fall in the future and repossessed houses being put on the market at reduced prices. Many people got caught in a **negative equity trap**, with their homes being worth less than they owed on their mortgages.

After 1996 the market started to pick up. In 2001 house prices rose by 16.8%, the largest annual rise since July 1989. This was a result of strong growth in average earnings, low unemployment, low mortgage interest rates and a reduction in the number of new houses built.

There were marked regional differences. Between 1991 and 2001, house prices in Thames Ditton, in the south-east of England, rose by 206% to an average of £342,262. Thames Ditton is 20 minutes by train from Waterloo, and close to the M25 and the A3. In contrast, prices in the Scottish town of Ardrossan fell by 6% to an average of £47,000. Ardrossan had 15% unemployment in 2001, five times the national average and a low average wage rate.

Activity 3

In April 2002 the Centre for Economics and Business Research (CEBR) predicted that the average UK house price would rise to £300,643 in 2020, an average annual growth rate of 6.2%.

The first half of 2002 saw the fastest rise in house prices since 1999, fuelled by record mortgage borrowing and a shortage of property.

a Explain one reason why the average UK house price may not rise as much as predicted by CEBR.

b Explain two reasons why mortgage borrowing may have increased in the first half of 2002.

Market failure in the housing market

The UK housing market is not economically efficient. Evidence of market failure includes the following.

■ **Homelessness**. Between 1979 and 2000 homelessness more than doubled, partly because of a decrease in house building by the social sector, the sale of council accommodation and a rise in private rents. Although there are more dwellings than households, there is still a national shortage of housing because some is lying empty, some is undergoing conversion and some is used as second homes. There has also been a growth in the number of households. In 2002, 40,000 more new households were created than homes built.

■ **Regional imbalances**. There are shortages in some areas and surpluses in others. For example, London and the south-east are short of homes, but 20% of homes in the north-west are empty and derelict.

■ **Reduction in mobility of labour**. Differences in the availability and cost of property in different parts of the country reduce the mobility of labour. When areas become depressed it can become difficult to sell property, and in rundown parts of old industrial towns in the north-west some people are trapped in negative equity. In contrast, in the prosperous south-east housing is difficult to find and is likely to be expensive.

■ **Damage caused by high house prices**. There is concern that public services in London and the south are being damaged by high house prices. In 2001 a report by the Labour Research Department found that people employed in occupations considered essential to a functioning community, including ambulance personnel, local government staff, nurses and teachers, were finding it difficult to buy a new house.

■ **Lack of equilibrium**. The housing market does not always move smoothly towards equilibrium because some people buy houses for the purposes of both consumption (as places to live in) and investment (as financial assets). When demand for houses outstrips supply, price rises. The higher price, instead of restoring equilibrium, can push price even higher if it encourages more people to buy houses in the belief there will be a financial gain. Similarly, a fall in house prices can lead to a downward spiral. Demand may fall as people switch from buying houses as investments to alternative financial assets. This can contribute to housing booms and slumps.

Activity 4

Social workers, care assistants and others on low public-sector wages are finding it difficult to buy a home. In turn, that is making it more difficult for local authorities in the south-west to attract staff, and putting pressure on them to increase salaries.

Labour shortages have not reached the proportions facing London and the south-east, where council leaders say there are severe recruitment problems.

The south-east branch of the Local Government Association says average house prices in the south-west are six times higher than average wages. In the north-west, for example, the ratio is just four. ('Property boom puts high price on public services', Jim Pickard, Financial Times, *10 June 2002)*

a What evidence is there in the extract that house prices are higher in the south-west than the north-west?

b Using the information in the extract, explain how regional price differences can result in labour market failure.

Government intervention in the housing market

In the last 30 years there has been a reduction in state intervention in the housing market. The government has moved away from rent controls because if rents are kept below the market equilibrium price, the quantity and quality of rented accommodation are likely to decline. The emphasis of policy has also shifted away from supplying housing towards helping poor people and other groups afford housing. The government provides:

■ Through local authorities, accommodation for households classified as being in priority need. These include families with children, pregnant women and mentally ill, elderly and handicapped people.
■ Help for the homeless, such as the 1990 'Rough sleepers' initiative', which provides finance for extra hostel places and 'move-on' accommodation for non-priority homeless.
■ Housing benefit to help unemployed people and low-income families cover their housing costs. This is becoming an important way of subsidising the rented sector.
■ For owner occupiers, tax relief on any profit made on the sale of a household's main home.
■ Finance for housing association investment (through the Housing Association Grant), so housing association rents remain below the market level. However, the importance of private-sector funding, through bank and building society loans, is increasing.
■ Cash top-ups for councils in London and the south-east so that they can offer higher salaries to make up for the high cost of living, including high housing costs.
■ Interest-free loans for key private-sector workers to help them buy property.

Activity 5

[The latest] spending review promises that housing spending will rise by 4.2% for the next three years, reaching £5.9 billion in 2005–06. Mr Prescott, the deputy prime minister, told MPs that the crisis had been compounded by an economic boom, putting houses beyond the reach of teachers, nurses and other key workers. The average house price in London is £200,000, nine times the pay of many nurses.

With 150,000 fewer houses being built than 30 years ago, Mr Prescott told MPs: 'No wonder prices are rocketing.' ('Housing cash goes into new towns in south', Peter Hetherington, Guardian, 19 July 2002)

a Why were nurses finding it difficult to buy a house in London in 2002?

b Explain why fewer houses being built would be likely to lead to a rise in house prices.

c Identify two ways in which a rise in government spending on housing could make housing more affordable.

The housing market and the national economy

The housing market is extremely important. It has a significant influence on people's living standards, and changes in the housing market affect other markets and the national economy.

When the economy is doing well, the housing market usually does well. People are more likely to enter the housing market and to trade up to more expensive property when their incomes are rising and they are optimistic about the future.

A buoyant housing market also promotes increases in national output. When people move home they often buy new curtains, carpets and white goods (such as refrigerators) and spend more on DIY materials. For most people their home is their main asset, and higher house prices make them wealthier. This encourages them to spend more and enables them to borrow more, as they have a more valuable asset to use as security.

Activity 6

In mid-2002 some building societies expressed concern that house prices were rising at an unsustainable rate. They warned that house prices could fall in the future.

a Explain the effect that a fall in house prices would be expected to have on total spending in the economy.

b Identify two industries that are likely to suffer from a fall in house prices.

Current issue: mortgage debt

In April 2002 there was a record level of new mortgage debt. This led some commentators to highlight the risk that some people were taking out mortgages that they might not be able to afford in the future. They thought that low interest rates and the expectation that wages would continue to rise were tempting people to take out high mortgages. There was concern that if interest rates were to rise and/or wage rises to slow down, some people would default on their mortgage payments and have their houses repossessed. The mortgage lenders would then sell the houses, often at reduced prices, which would depress the housing market.

Summary

In this unit you have learned that:

- The housing market consists of a variety of dwellings including houses, bungalows, flats, maisonettes and mobile homes.

- Some dwellings are owner occupied and some are rented.

- In recent decades there has been a move away from renting to buying dwellings, a decline in council house accommodation, a rise in the importance of **housing associations** and an increase in the number of households.

- The supply of houses is influenced by the level of economic activity, changes in household structure and the time of year.

- The demand for houses is influenced by changes in real disposable income, **mortgage** rates, government policy, change in population size and change in household structure.

- House prices rose in the second half of the 1990s and at the start of the 2000s because of higher disposable income, falling unemployment, low interest rates and a reduction in the number of new houses built.

- House prices vary throughout the country, being particularly high in London and the south-east.

- Evidence of market failure in the housing market includes homelessness, shortages and surpluses in different parts of the country, reduction in labour mobility and slow adjustment to the equilibrium level.

- The government intervenes in the housing market to offset market failure by providing accommodation for the homeless, housing benefit, finance for housing association investment, tax relief for mortgage lenders and free loans for key workers.

- A buoyant housing market promotes higher national output and higher national output encourages more activity in the housing market.

Multiple choice questions

1 A house price:earnings ratio is 3:1 means that:

A average house prices are rising three times more rapidly than gross annual earnings

B average house prices are three times gross annual earnings

C labour costs form a third of total housing costs

D the supernormal profit earned on house sales is a third of the sales price

2 Which of the following would be likely to increase house prices?

A a fall in employment

B a fall in interest rates

C a rise in income tax

D a rise in house construction

3 Which of the following is a possible adverse effect of negative equity?

A a rise in consumer spending

B an increase in house prices

C a reduction in labour mobility

D a decrease in consumer debt

4 In which circumstance would the imposition of rent controls lead to a shortage of rented accommodation?

A when maximum rents are set above the equilibrium level

B when maximum rents are set below the equilibrium level

C when minimum rents are set below the equilibrium level

D when minimum rents are set at the equilibrium level

5 Why does a government provide accommodation for homeless people?

A for equity

B to reduce house prices

C to make income more unevenly distributed

D to overcome the problem of non-excludability in the housing market

6 What is the relationship between houses and mortgage loans?

A they are in joint supply

B they are in competitive supply

C they are in competitive demand

D they are in joint demand

Data response question: the housing boom

The general picture of sharp price differentials between north and south is widely appreciated. Of course a house in central London is going to be worth more than a similar one in the north of Scotland, for incomes in the south on average are higher.

What is less widely appreciated is that this gap has been widening rapidly over the past couple of decades, driven by population movements. London in particular has outpaced the rest of the country, as its rising population puts pressure on the existing housing stock. Scotland has experienced a small fall in population, and has seen a correspondingly small rise in house prices.

These broad regional trends conceal 'hot spots' and 'cold spots' towns where property has been in special demand or where it is unusually depressed. For example, Edinburgh has seen a surge in prices, despite the relatively small rises elsewhere in Scotland, because the market has been driven by two factors: the strength of the financial services industry and the creation of the new Scottish Parliament. By contrast, Hastings, despite being in the generally prosperous south-east, has seen only slow growth in prices, largely because it has poor road access both to London and east–west along the south coast.

It is easy to predict strong demand for houses that suit older people; as the population ages it is inevitable that smaller property will do well. ('The housing boom must end, but 1988 won't be repeated', Hamish McRae, Independent, 2 August 2001)

a Discuss two reasons, mentioned in the extract, why house prices are higher in London than Scotland. [4]

b Explain:
  i why Edinburgh is a property hot spot [3]
  ii one factor which could turn Hastings into a property hot spot [3]

c Identify two reasons why demand for smaller property is likely to increase. [4]

d Discuss two influences on demand for houses not mentioned in the extract. [6]

2 Sport and leisure

In this unit you will examine the nature of **leisure**, the leisure market including sport, leisure industries, market failure in leisure, government intervention and the link between the leisure industry and the national economy.

The nature of leisure

People's time can be divided into three main categories: work and education; maintenance; and leisure. Maintenance is the time spent on maintaining the home, family and self – for example, cleaning, child-care and sleeping. **Leisure** is the time people have left after fulfilling their work and maintenance commitments.

It is not always easy to decide in which category to put an activity. For example, cooking may be regarded as a leisure activity or as maintenance. People taking an evening A level English class may be doing it for interest or to gain a qualification for university entrance.

The amount of leisure time people have varies. Among adults, women who work full time and have a family have the least leisure time and retired people have the most.

People have to make choices about how they spend their time. If they are offered an extra hour of work, the opportunity cost is likely to be lost leisure time. So they will have to compare the income they will earn with the value they place on the leisure time.

As income rises, demand for normal goods increases. Leisure is a normal good, and as incomes have risen in the UK, people have devoted more of their time to leisure. Technological developments have also increased leisure time by reducing the time people spend on cleaning and washing clothes.

The leisure market

Leisure is a large and growing market. It includes sport, tourism, TV and the media, the theatre, film and gaming industries. Leisure activities can take place in the home, for example watching TV, or outside, for example visiting the theatre.

Activity 1

In April 2002 a survey on how people in the UK spend their time found that on average people spend 29% of their time sleeping, 10% in paid work, 11% on child-care, 9% on personal care, 9% on social life, 15% watching TV and 17% on other activities including travelling, cooking, hobbies and studying. It also found that residents of affluent households were more likely to take part in sport or spend time on cultural activities than residents of poor households.

a What is the main leisure activity in the UK?

b How does the time people spend pursuing leisure activities compare with the time they spend in paid employment?

Activity 2

In the 1990s there was a growth in membership of golf clubs and more golf clubs were opened.

a Identify two possible reasons why membership of golf clubs increased.

b Identify a substitute and a complement to membership of a golf club.

Leisure activities are supplied by the private, public and voluntary sectors. Private-sector firms run cinemas, bingo halls and hotels. Local authorities and government agencies run museums, public libraries and sports centres. The voluntary sector includes angling clubs, astronomy clubs and youth hostels.

Demand for a particular leisure activity is influenced by various factors. One is obviously price. For example, as foreign holidays have become cheaper, demand has extended. Prices of substitutes and complements also have an influence. For example, in the case of playing tennis, the price of playing golf and the price of tennis rackets and tennis sportswear affect the demand for membership of tennis clubs and the hiring of tennis courts.

A few leisure activities, such as bingo, have negative income elasticity of demand, but most have positive YED. Some, such as theatre visits, are superior goods.

Other influences on demand for particular leisure activities include changes in tastes, advertising, and the gender and age structure of the population.

Sport

People can play and watch sport. When they play sport they may gain both a consumption and an investment benefit. A consumption benefit is the enjoyment they gain. An investment benefit is raised income potential if a person becomes fitter and more socially skilled as a result of playing sport.

Watching sport provides mainly a consumption benefit. In some sports, such as squash, more people actively participate in it than watch it; in others, such as football, more people watch it than play it.

Some sports have become big business. For example, in the mid-1980s football was declining as a spectator sport, but by the early 2000s it was generating millions of pounds of revenue. This turnaround resulted from a decline in

hooliganism, increased TV coverage and the creation of a more glamorous image. Premier League clubs can earn vast amounts of money. Manchester United, for example, generates some income from ticket sales but even more from TV contracts and the sale of merchandise ranging from football shirts to duvet covers. Indeed, Manchester United is the world's richest football club. It has the most valuable brand in Europe and the second most valuable global sports brand, behind Dallas Cowboys American football team.

There has also been an increase in the number of people joining fitness clubs and gyms. In 2002 more than 3 million UK citizens were members.

Activity 3

Explain two benefits to society of more people playing sport.

Tourism

Tourism involves people travelling from where they live to another place, where they make use of facilities and undertake activities. It takes place at both home and abroad.

Tourism is the world's fastest-growing industry. The number of people travelling abroad increased from 25 million in 1950 to 670 million in 1999. The World Tourism Organisation estimates that by 2020 1.6 million people will travel abroad. In 2001 tourism accounted for 11% of world output and employed directly and indirectly more than 200 million people.

The tourism market is volatile. There can be large changes in demand as a result of weather conditions, income, and terrorism and war.

UK citizens are now spending more on holidays, particularly foreign holidays, because of increases in income, higher expectations and improved transport.

Activity 4

Tourism does not always bring in as much income as might be expected. This is because some foreign firms build all-inclusive resorts which mainly employ staff and use food and materials imported from their own countries and not from the countries in which they are based. In Thailand, 60% of the £4 billion earned from tourism in 2001 left the country.

a Give two reasons why a foreign firm might decide to open a holiday complex in Thailand.

b Explain two ways in which Thailand could benefit from the presence of foreign holiday complexes.

Other leisure activities

The gaming industry, which covers casinos, gaming machines, the national lottery, bingo clubs and betting (race course, spread, football pools), has been growing in recent years. The national lottery, introduced in November 1994, has made betting more acceptable, although it has led to a reduction in spending on the football pools. The removal of restrictions on casinos, including the abolition of the rule that customers must have been members for 24 hours before playing, is transforming some seaside resorts, most noticeably Blackpool.

Also expanding are the film, TV, radio and music industries. The USA and the UK both have the advantage of producing products that use the global language of English. The USA has

Activity 5

Attendance at cinemas has been increasing, partly because of the release of some family blockbusters.

a Are videos and DVDs of a film substitutes or complements of viewing the film at a cinema?

b Identify two other factors which could influence demand for cinema tickets.

the advantage of not only producing for a large home market but also selling internationally. Making a TV programme, for example, may have a high fixed cost, but selling it to another country costs very little. US broadcasters can, in many cases, cover their costs at home and then sell a programme cheaply abroad. For most European broadcasters, making their own programmes costs over three times more than buying programmes from the USA.

Market failure

Leisure markets experience market failure for various reasons. One is because in some cases there is a fixed supply and price is set below the equilibrium. For instance, there is a fixed number of seats on Wimbledon's centre court. The price for tickets is set in advance and usually demand exceeds supply (see Figure 1).

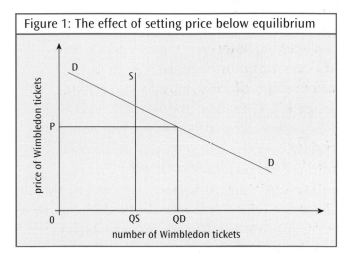

Figure 1: The effect of setting price below equilibrium

The shortage leads to a black market, with ticket touts selling the tickets at high prices.

A similar problem occurs at some football matches, most noticeably the FA cup final. Football clubs, though, have become more sophisticated in their pricing strategies. Most Premier League clubs now charge higher prices for watching the most popular teams.

There is also the problem of a surplus occurring if price is set above what turns out to be the equilibrium price. At some theatre performances there is a high number of empty

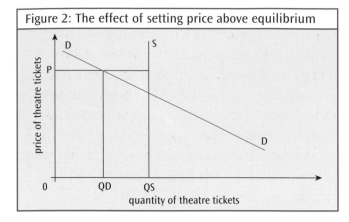

Figure 2: The effect of setting price above equilibrium

seats. Figure 2 shows supply exceeding demand and so a misallocation of resources.

A misallocation of resources can also arise from a lack of information and the existence of externalities. Many people, especially children, do not appreciate the full benefits they can gain from participating in sport and visiting the theatre. External costs arise from tourism. For instance, more tourists visiting a popular holiday destination can generate congestion and the opening up of new tourist resorts can damage the environment.

Firms can exercise considerable market power in the leisure market. An example is Premier League football clubs – Arsenal has monopoly control over the sale of tickets to its stadium and much of the merchandise it sells.

Leaving leisure activities to market forces would mean that poor people may not be able to afford to participate in some leisure activities which would be beneficial for their physical and mental health.

Activity 6

In 2001 Channel 5 made a substantial loss; in 2002 it performed much better. It increased both its share of audiences and its advertising revenue, which rose by 23.3%. This was thought to be largely because of soaps and a new emphasis on arts and documentaries.

a In what sense does it appear that Channel 5 became more allocatively efficient in 2002?

b Explain how a loss might be eliminated by a rise in productive efficiency.

Activity 7

Manchester United, the Football Association and some of the high street's best known retailers face fines totalling tens of millions following an investigation into the price of replica football kits that include the England strip.

The Office of Fair Trading said yesterday that it had found evidence that 11 groups entered into anti-competitive agreements to fix the price of shirts made by the sportswear manufacturer Umbro.

Parents and consumer groups have long complained that at £30 to £45 each the shirts are too expensive, particularly when most clubs introduce a new strip each or every other year. Retail experts say replica shirts cost as little as £7 to make. ('Man Utd face fine over 'deal' on soccer kit prices', John Cassy, Guardian, 17 May 2002)

a What two concerns do parents have about replica football shirts?

b What evidence is there in the extract of market failure?

Government intervention in the leisure market

The government intervenes in various ways to try to correct market failure.

■ It has made the sale of tickets for sports and other events by ticket touts illegal in a bid to reduce the problem of black markets.

■ To overcome problems of lack of information and the failure of market forces to take externalities into account, state schools provide physical education to ensure that all children have the opportunity to participate. The government also fully finances or partially subsidises leisure industries that it regards as producing merit goods, such as museums, ballet companies, sports centres, art galleries and public libraries.

■ It provides free, or subsidises private-sector firms to provide free or at reduced prices, sports facilities and cultural activities to promote equity and to ensure that everyone has the opportunity to keep fit and take part in cultural activities.

■ Through the Office of Fair Trading and the Competition Commission, it regulates the behaviour of firms with market power in leisure industries to ensure they do not abuse their position. It also assesses whether mergers between, for example, media companies, will be in the public interest.

Leisure and the national economy

When the economy is doing well, with output and income rising, most leisure activities also do well. This is because most leisure activities have positive income elasticity of demand.

Thriving leisure industries also help the national economy by generating tax revenue and employment opportunities. Employment opportunities are created directly and indirectly. For instance, tourism generates jobs not just in hotels and theme parks but also in transport and other firms supplying, for example, food, insurance and souvenirs for tourists. Some jobs in leisure activities, including tourism, funfairs and theme parks, are low skilled and low paid. However, in areas such as TV and film there are some high-quality, well-paid jobs.

Leisure goods and services, including tourism, TV programmes, films and sports equipment, are both exported and imported. A fall in the exchange rate will boost export revenue and reduce import expenditure. For instance, it will make UK holidays cheaper for foreigners and foreign holidays more expensive for UK citizens.

Successful leisure industries attract tourists. Many people visit the UK because of its national heritage and theatre productions. Hosting a major sports event is also likely to generate revenue from both domestic and foreign citizens. Whether it makes a profit or not will depend on how the revenue compares with the costs involved. It will, nevertheless, create other benefits for the country, including the building of facilities which can be used after the event, either for its original or another purpose. For instance, the main stadium used to host the Manchester Commonwealth Games is now used as Manchester City's football ground. People who visit the country for the sports event may also return in future years as tourists.

Of course, hosting a major sports event may also impose external costs, including congestion, pollution and destruction of the natural environment.

Activity 8

In June 2002 Japan and South Korea co-hosted the football World Cup. Economists estimated that it generated revenue of 800 billion won ($6.8 billion) and 350,000 lasting jobs in South Korea.

Explain how hosting the World Cup could have generated revenue and 'lasting jobs' in South Korea.

Current issue: water supply

There is increasing concern about the effect that the booming tourism industry is having on water supplies, particularly in developing countries. Hotel complexes, swimming pools and golf clubs use vast amounts of water. The UN Food and Agriculture Organisation has estimated that 100 tourists use an amount of water in 55 days that would grow rice to feed 100 villages for 15 years. In Goa, India, for instance, the water table is critically low and wells are running dry to feed the tourism industry's demands. In the Caribbean, hundreds of thousands of people are having to go without purified water during the tourism season as spring water is piped to hotels. In Barbados, golf courses are consuming as much water as 7,000 people.

Summary

In this unit you have learned that:

- As incomes rise, demand for **leisure** increases.

- Leisure activities are supplied by the private, public and voluntary sectors.

- Demand for a particular leisure activity is influenced by price, price of substitutes and complements, income, tastes, gender, age structure and advertising.

- Sport can be divided into participatory and spectator sports.

- Playing sport provides both a consumption and an investment benefit.

- Football has become big business.

- Tourism is the world's fastest-growing industry.

- Expanding leisure industries include gaming, film, TV, radio and music industries.

- A large home market gives the USA a competitive advantage in TV and film.

- Market failure in leisure industries arise from price not being set at the equilibrium level, lack of information, existence of externalities, inequity and abuse of market power.

- The government intervenes in the leisure industry by making the sale of tickets by ticket touts illegal, financing fully or partially some leisure activities and regulating the behaviour of firms.

- When the economy is doing well, leisure industries do well.

- Leisure industries generate income, employment and export revenue.

- Hosting a major sports event has a number of advantages, including revenue, more facilities and increased tourism.

Multiple choice questions

1 Which of the following would reduce the opportunity cost of an extra hour of leisure time?

A a reduction in the wage rate

B an increase in the price of leisure activities

C a reduction in the satisfaction gained from leisure

D a rise in the time taken to complete household chores

2 Leisure has:

A negative YED

B zero YED

C positive YED

D perfectly elastic YED

3 Participating in which sport is likely to provide the lowest investment benefit?

A athletics

B cricket

C darts

D swimming

4 Which of the following is a possible external cost of an increase in the number of tourists visiting the country?

A a reduction in pollution

B a decrease in water consumption

C an increase in congestion

D an increase in export revenue

5 Figure 3 shows the demand and supply of tickets for an international rugby match. What would be a possible disadvantage for society of price moving to the equilibrium level?

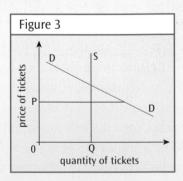

Figure 3

A the market would clear

B supply would contract

C some poor people would be unable to attend

D the black market in tickets would increase

6 Which leisure activity is likely to have the highest degree of income elasticity of demand?

A cycling

B running

C tenpin bowling

D yachting

The annual FA Premier League fans' survey paints a picture of a game that has a distinct north–south divide, but which is attracting more wealthy fans, spending on average £1,039 per season on following their team. More than one-third of all fans watching Premier League football earns more than £30,000 a year with the average season ticket costing £408.

Women make up 15% of fans attending Premier League games but they tend to be more attracted to the smaller clubs. More established teams, such as Liverpool, Arsenal and Newcastle United, attract relatively few women.

Clubs in London attract the wealthiest fans with 30% of Tottenham supporters and 32% of Chelsea supporters earning more than £50,000 per year. Clubs based in the north of England, such as Sunderland, Middlesbrough and Everton, attract a greater number of low-income fans.

The average cost of a ticket for a Premier League match is £26. Arsenal is the costliest club in the country with an

average season ticket of £747, followed by Chelsea at £614 and Tottenham at £546. ('Football's profile is white and wealthy', Vivek Chaudhary, Guardian, 27 February 2002)

a What type of income elasticity of demand does the extract suggest attending football matches has? [3]

b Why would you expect a ticket for matches at Sunderland's ground to be cheaper than a ticket for Chelsea? [3]

c What would you expect the cross elasticity of demand between tickets for Arsenal and Tottenham to be? [4]

d Explain two ways a football club could attract more female fans. [4]

e Discuss one advantage and one disadvantage to a city of having a Premier League football club. [6]

3 The environment

In this unit you will examine the nature of environmental problems. You will look at the causes of and approaches to environmental problems, and consider the need for a worldwide approach.

Environmental problems

The environment is a key economic resource. It includes natural resources such as the climate, oceans and rivers, forests and wildlife. Economists increasingly take the environment into account in their analysis and are becoming more involved in searching for solutions to environmental problems.

The three principal environmental problems facing the world today are pollution, global warming and loss of wildlife and wildlife habitats.

■ **Pollution** occurs when waste products are discharged into the environment – into the

atmosphere, rivers and the sea and on to land. When the rate of discharge is greater than the capacity of the environment to absorb the pollution problems arise, including damage to people's health, wildlife, fisheries, crops, farm animals and buildings.

■ **Global warming** involves the trapping of heat between the earth's surface and the atmosphere. This is caused by air pollution in the form of the emissions of greenhouse gases, most noticeably CO_2, methane and chlorofluorocarbons (CFCs). CO_2 emissions arise from the burning of fossil fuels, the use of vehicles and deforestation. Methane gas occurs naturally and when coal is burned, and CFCs are created in the production of refrigerators and air-conditioning.

- **Wildlife** is lost largely because of the destruction of its habitats. More intensive farming, the construction of more roads and buildings, the felling of trees in rainforests and the reclamation of land are all reducing wildlife habitats.

These problems are interlinked and threaten sustainable development.

- Pollution is making some land unusable, some water undrinkable and is destroying some wildlife.
- Global warming has already resulted in holes in the ozone layer in the Antarctic and the Arctic. This damage means that harmful ultra-violet radiation is not filtered out. This leads to climate change and environmental problems, such as melting ice caps, rising sea levels, droughts, floods and hurricanes. As a result, there is a loss of human life, wildlife, farm stock, buildings and wetlands.
- The destruction of wildlife and its habitats is reducing biodiversity. This is limiting advances in medicines and agriculture, reducing the range of raw materials available and further harming the environment.

Causes of environmental problems

Economic activity can cause environmental problems when there is market failure. Among the causes of market failure are short termism, the public good nature of some environmental goods, lack of knowledge and the existence of externalities.

- Some firms are more concerned with current profits than with sustainability. They may therefore use up non-renewable resources, turn some renewable resources into non-renewable resources and discharge pollution at rates which threaten sustainable development.
- In the case of some environmental goods, such as the sea and air, no one owns them and no one has the ability to prevent free riders using them. They may therefore be overexploited.
- Lack of knowledge means that consumers and producers create high levels of pollution and overuse the environment, for instance through overfishing.

Consumption and production can impose external costs not only at the time they take place but also in the future. Transport is a major cause of pollution. When people are deciding whether to drive or walk to a particular destination, they do not take into account the pollution, congestion, damage to buildings and other negative externalities they will cause by using their cars. The building of houses can cause negative externalities by destroying wildlife habitats such as flood plains. Industry, particularly manufacturing industry, also contributes to environmental problems by, for example, discharging waste into rivers.

Approaches to environmental problems

In seeking to reduce pollution, the UK and most other countries follow the **polluter pays principle**. This aims to correct market failure by making the polluters pay the costs of use or damage to environmental resources. Pollution taxes, fines, tradable permits and the creation of property rights are all based on this principle.

The UK and other governments are also pursuing long-term polices to improve the environment. These include encouraging the use of clean renewable energy – such as solar, tidal, wind and wave power – changing farming practices, planting new forests and managing existing ones, promoting recycling and setting up nature reserves.

Activity 3

The government requires energy suppliers to take 3% of their power from green sources. This will rise by 10% by 2010 and is likely to go up to 20% by 2020.

The government has a carrot and stick approach to promoting green fuel. Grants are available to help with the building of renewable energy installations, and fines are imposed if production quotas are not met.

a Explain what is meant by a carrot and stick approach.

b Give two examples of green energy sources.

Current issue: the global dimension of pollution

The effect of pollution and other environmental damage created in one country will not be restricted to that country. Environmental problems have a global dimension, and there is increasing awareness that these problems have to be tackled on a global level. If only one or a few countries introduce pollution taxes, for instance, firms may just relocate.

Of course, achieving a global approach is not easy because it is difficult to get international agreement. Some countries, most noticeably the USA, cause more pollution than others, and the effects of environmental damage are not evenly spread.

Poor countries want to increase their production, and their citizens want to enjoy the same standard of living experienced in richer countries. Any restrictions on pollution and resource use based on current levels would penalise the poor countries more. There is also the free rider problem, with the possibility that some countries will benefit from any environmental improvement without contributing to it.

In 2001, 186 countries signed the Kyoto protocol. This included an agreement by 38 industrialised countries to binding targets to reduce their greenhouse gases and the start of an international trade in carbon. However, the effectiveness of the protocol has been reduced by the USA's failure, so far, to sign up to it.

Summary

In this unit you have learned that:

■ The three main environmental problems facing the world are pollution, global warming and loss of wildlife and its habitats.

■ Environmental damage is being caused by more intensive farming, construction of new roads and buildings, destruction of rainforests and emissions of greenhouse gases.

■ Environmental damage is making some land unusable and some water undrinkable, reducing air quality, causing flooding and reducing biodiversity.

■ Environmental problems arise from market failure caused by short-termism, the public good nature of the environment, lack of information and externalities.

■ Most solutions to pollution are based on the **polluter pays principle**.

■ Among the measures being taken to improve the environment are the planting of forests, managing existing ones, changing farming practices, introducing cleaner technologies, recycling waste and setting up nature reserves.

Multiple choice questions

1 Some firms act as free riders in connection with the environment. They can do this because of:

A the fact that all natural resources are renewable

B the public good nature of the environment

C the demerit good nature of the environment

D the inferior good nature of the environment

2 Figure 1 shows the marginal external cost caused by pollution. Why is the marginal external cost at Z zero?

A the environment can absorb some pollution

B marginal social cost exceeds marginal private cost

C marginal external cost is less than marginal private cost

D marginal social cost is greater than marginal social benefit

Figure 1

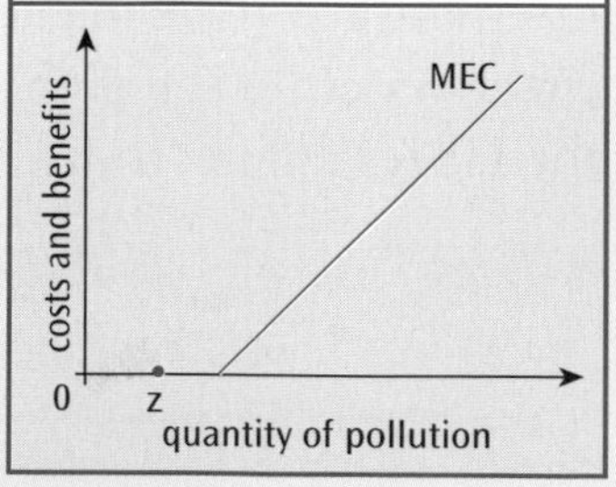

3 The theory behind property rights is that by clearly defining and policing property rights:

A private costs are reduced

B externalities are eliminated

C house prices will rise

D output increases beyond the socially optimum level

4 Which of the following is a possible disadvantage of a pollution tax?

A it may be equal to marginal external cost

B it may increase firms' private costs

C it may be regressive in its impact

D it may be imposed worldwide

5 Which of the following measures to reduce pollution is not in keeping with the polluter pays principle?

A a pollution tax

B tradable permits

C regulation backed up by fines

D subsidies given to polluters to introduce cheaper production methods

6 Which of the following could reduce global warming?

A an increase in the use of cars

B the ending of tradable permits

C the planting of more rainforests

D more intensive farming practices

Data response question: a new way of dealing with externalities

America's largest power generator has found a unique way to avoid legal challenges from a town it has polluted – buy it, lock, stock and barrel, for $20 million (£13.7 million).

American Electric Power, which also runs the UK's coal-fired Ferrybridge power station, is buying Cheshire, Ohio, which found itself under the brown and blue clouds from AEP's coal-burning General James M. Gavin plant that looms over the town.

All 221 residents will leave after accepting a deal that gives 90 homeowners cheques for three times the assessed value of their homes, about $150,000 each, totalling $13.5 million. Those renting homes in the town will each get $25,000.

AEP gets signed pledges that townsfolk will never sue the power company for property damage or health problems. No one yet has sued AEP for the asthma attacks, grime, headaches, burning eyes, sore throats and lips, mouth blisters or white coloured burns on lips, tongues and insides of mouth caused by sulphur dioxide and sulphuric acid emissions.

These emissions worsened last year [2001] after installation of a new $195 million emissions control system meant to cut nitrogen oxide emissions.

That is when the blue plumes arrived – because the new gear did not work well with the emissions-control technology installed earlier, a blue acid haze fell on Cheshire, usually on hot, humid days when exhaust from the 830ft smokestacks fell down into the town rather than going up into the sky.

The Environment Protection Agency had accused AEP two years ago of violating the Clean Air Act and threatened to force the plant to stop burning cheaper high-sulphuric coal. ('Power giant buys town to avoid pollution lawsuits', Brian Hale, The Times, 14 May 2002)

a What motivated AEP to buy the town of Cheshire? [2]

b What evidence is there in the extract of the existence of property rights influencing policy? [4]

c Identify four external costs caused by AEP's emissions of gases. [4]

d Explain whether the purchase of the town by AEP will eliminate the external costs caused by its gas emissions. [4]

e Discuss two measures the American Environmental Protection Agency could take to make firms use cleaner fuels. [6]

In considering the performance of a country's economy, economists examine a number of macroeconomic indicators both over time and among countries. In this unit you will examine these indicators. You will see how an economy's performance can be assessed by examining changes in its output, number of workers without jobs, price level and international trade position. You will consider how these indicators are measured, the problems involved in measurement and how to interpret the figures calculated.

Indicators of economic performance

Economists use four main indicators in assessing a country's economic performance.

- **Output.** Higher output (economic growth) is likely to raise people's living standards.
- **Unemployment.** Low unemployment means that most labour resources are being utilised and an economy should be producing close to its production possibility curve.
- **Inflation.** A low and stable inflation rate should encourage investment and promote international competitiveness.
- **Balance of payments.** A healthy international trade position should reflect a good economic performance and enable a country to continue to grow.

Activity 1

Which economy do you think performed best in 2001? Explain your answer.

Table 1: Economic indicators for three countries in 2001 (%)

	Increase in output	Increase in prices	Unemployment
Germany	0.8	2.4	7.9
Ireland	5.6	4.0	3.8
UK	2.4	1.2	5.1

Measuring output

A common measure of output is gross domestic product, often referred to by its initials **GDP**. Gross means total, domestic means produced by resources based in the country and product is output. So UK GDP is the total output produced by firms and other organisations located in the UK.

There are three methods of calculating the total output that has been produced: output, income and expenditure. They should all give the same figure as the output produced generates income which is then spent on the output. This relationship is known as the circular flow of income. Figure 1 shows a simplified version of the circular flow.

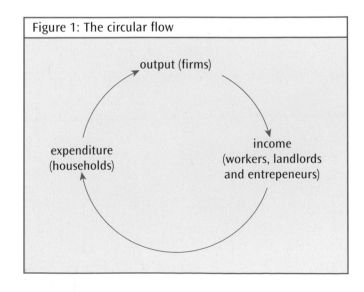

Figure 1: The circular flow

Activity 2

Figure 2 shows a slightly more sophisticated version of the circular flow. Fill in the missing flows.

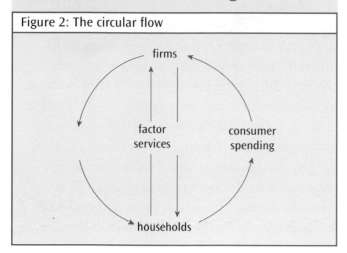

Figure 2: The circular flow

The output method

This measures the output produced by all the industries in the country. This sounds straightforward, but it is important to avoid double counting because the output of some firms can include the outputs of other firms. So, for example, if the output of a paper mill is £40,000 and the output of a book publisher is £720,000, it might be assumed that the combined output of the firms is £760,000. This would be incorrect since the value of the paper is included in the value of the books. To overcome this potential problem, economists use the concept of **value added**. They add only the value added (the difference between the sales revenue received and the cost of raw materials used) by each firm at each stage of production. In the example, the

Table 2: Value added in greetings card production (£m)			
	Value of output	Cost of intermediate products	Value added
Paper producers	25	0	25
Designers	52	25	27
Card producers	85	52	33
Retailers	140	85	55
			140

Activity 3

Using Figure 3:

a Decide which industry group had the highest value added.

b Decide which industry group had the lowest value added.

c Discuss whether you would have expected these results.

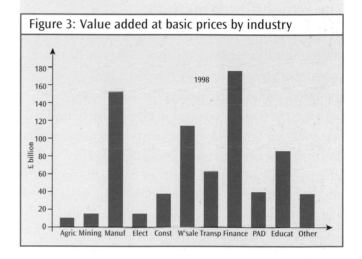

Figure 3: Value added at basic prices by industry

value added by the book publisher would have been £680,000. The total of the values added at each stage is the same as the total value of the final products, as illustrated in Table 2.

The income method

The value of output corresponds to the incomes created in its production. So to calculate output, incomes in the form of wages, rent, interest and profit are totalled. In this method it is important to include only incomes received in return for providing a good or service. **Transfer payments** – transfers of income from one group to another not in return for providing a good or service – must not be included. For example, social security payments, which represent a transfer of income from taxpayers to recipients of state benefits, including pensions, are not included because there is no corresponding output of goods and services.

Indicators of economic performance

Activity 4

Decide which of the following are transfer payments:

a job seeker's allowance

b housing benefit

c civil servants' pay

d birthday payments

The expenditure method

In this method, national output is calculated by adding up all spending on the country's finished products. So spending on raw materials is not included. Spending on exports is included because they are produced in the country and generate incomes for the country's population. In contrast, spending on imports is excluded because they are made in other countries and create incomes for foreign people. The main forms of spending are consumption (spending by households), investment (spending by firms on capital goods), government spending on goods and services, and exports minus imports.

Activity 5

Calculate the UK's GDP in 1999 using the information in Table 3:

Table 3	
	£ billion
Consumer spending	536.5
Investment	155.7
Government spending	149.1
Exports	258.9
Imports	297.2

Nominal and real GDP

The output, income and expenditure methods should produce the same figure for GDP. However, when they are first calculated there are often slight differences between them. Government economists and statisticians reconcile the figures and arrive at one figure for GDP. This figure is valued in terms of the prices operating in the year in which the output is produced and is referred to as **nominal GDP**, money GDP or GDP at current prices.

Nominal figures have not been adjusted for inflation, so nominal GDP may rise because products are selling for higher prices not because more are being made. Economists adjust nominal GDP by taking out the effects of inflation using a price index series. Multiplying nominal GDP by the price index in the base year divided by the price index in the current year gives GDP at constant prices. This is also known as **real GDP**. For example, in 2001 UK nominal GDP was £847.2 billion. If 1995 is used as the base year and the price index in 2001 is 112.6 then:

$$\frac{\text{Nominal GDP} \times \text{price index in base year}}{\text{price index in current year}} = \text{real GDP}$$

$$£847.2\text{bn} \times \frac{100}{112.6} = £752.4\text{bn}$$

Real GDP figures show clearly what is happening to output. If real GDP rises, the country is producing more.

Activity 6

A country's nominal GDP in 2000 is £500 billion. The price index is 100. By 2005 its nominal GDP has risen to £800 billion and its price index has increased to 125. Calculate:

a the percentage increase in nominal GDP from 2000 to 2005

b the real GDP for 2005

c the percentage increase in real GDP from 2000 to 2005

224

Problems of measuring GDP

Two main problems arise in seeking to gain an accurate measure of the output of a country. These are how to calculate the size of the hidden economy and the value of non-marketed goods and services.

The hidden economy is also known as the black or shadow economy. It consists of economic activity that is not declared to the government. There are two main reasons people may not be open about the goods and services they produce: they may be seeking to evade paying tax on their earnings; or the activity they are involved in may be illegal, such as selling non-prescribed drugs.

The existence of the hidden economy means that GDP figures understate the output produced. Non-marketed goods and services have the same effect. GDP figures include only goods and services which are bought and sold and thus have a price attached to them. They do not include items which are not bought and sold, such as DIY activities, child rearing by parents and voluntary work. This means that if more people do their own decorating or clean their own homes, GDP will fall although the output of services may not have changed.

Activity 7

Which of the following is likely to reduce the size of the hidden economy?

a a rise in marginal tax rates

b a rise in the penalties imposed for tax evasion

c a reduction in the number of activities which are declared illegal

d a reduction in social disapproval of tax evasion

e a reduction in illegal drug trading detection rates

Economic growth

Economic growth is usually associated with increases in output. The rate of economic growth is the percentage increase in output over a 12-month period. So a growth rate in real GDP of 2.5% means that output this year is 2.5% higher than in the previous year. It is important to recognise that a fall in the economic growth rate represents not a fall in output but a fall in the rate at which output is increasing. A negative economic growth rate indicates that output has fallen. For example, a growth rate of –2.0% would mean that output has fallen by 2% over the year.

Activity 8

Explain what happened to output from 1998 to 2001 in:

a Japan

b the USA

Table 4: Economic growth rates (% change in real GDP)		
	Japan	USA
1998	–1.0	4.3
1999	0.7	4.1
2000	2.2	4.1
2001	–0.3	1.1

Interpreting economic growth figures

An important economic objective is to raise people's living standards, and it is generally thought that increases in output will do this as they will be able to enjoy more goods and services. This is usually the case, but care must be taken in interpreting economic growth rate figures.

If real GDP increases but at a lower rate than the country's population, the average standard of living is likely to have fallen. This is why economists compare real GDP per head, which is found by dividing real GDP by population.

The composition of output is also important. If real GDP increases because of a rise in the output of capital goods, current living standards will not rise. However, future living standards will rise as the capital goods will produce more goods and services. An increase in the output of some goods and services, which are known as regrettables, may reflect a decline in the quality of people's lives. For instance, an increase in the value of police services may reflect a rise in crime, and people would probably prefer to have less crime.

Higher output may not raise people's living standards if it is accompanied by a fall in the quality of the products produced, an increase in working hours and/or deterioration in working conditions.

In calculating real GDP, externalities are not taken into account. If pollution were taken into account, real GDP would be lower. Undeclared economic activity is also not included, although changes in the size of the hidden economy over time can affect living standards. For example, real GDP may rise from one year to the next, but if all of the rise is accounted for by people declaring economic activity they had previously not declared, living standards may not have changed.

Furthermore, if any rise in real GDP is unevenly spread, only a small number of people may experience a rise in their incomes and spending power.

Activity 9

Decide whether the following would:

i   increase, decrease or leave unchanged real GDP

ii increase, decrease or leave unchanged living standards

a   a terrorist threat which leads to an increase in the size of the country's armed forces

b   an increase in leisure hours which has no effect on output

c   a reduction in infant mortality resulting from an increase in government expenditure on the NHS

d   an increase in traffic congestion caused by a rise in the number of cars produced and driven in the country

e   the closure of some textile factories leading to a rise in unemployment

International comparisons of real GDP

Real GDP per head is the indicator most commonly used to compare living standards in different countries because it is not distorted by differences in inflation rates and population sizes. However, the inhabitants of a country with a high real GDP per head may experience lower living standards than those experienced in a country with a lower real GDP per head for other reasons.

For example, the accuracy of real GDP per head figures may vary because of differences in the number of non-marketed goods and services and the sizes of countries' hidden economies. In some developing countries much agriculture is still at a subsistence level and it is difficult to estimate a value for this output. Some transitional economies have a large hidden economy because adequate systems to collect tax and detect tax evasion are still being developed.

Income distribution also varies among countries. Two countries may have a similar real GDP per head, but if they have different distributions of income, the living standards of their inhabitants may be very different. Living standards are also affected by differences in working hours and conditions, pollution levels and the composition of output.

Another problem when making international comparisons is that this has to be done in a common unit of measurement. If a currency is used the comparison may be distorted, as exchange rate values may not reflect the purchasing power of the currencies. For example, £1 may buy the same in the UK as $2 does in the USA, but speculation, say, may raise the value of the pound to £1 = $3. This, however, would not mean that someone in the UK with an income of £30,000 would have the same purchasing power as someone in the USA with an income of $90,000.

To overcome this problem, economists use **purchasing power parity exchange rates**. These seek to measure the cost of a typical basket of goods and services in different countries. If a typical basket of goods and services costs

£10,000 in the UK and $17,000 in the USA, the ratio is 1:1.7, and the effective exchange rate used to convert real GDP figures would be £1 = $1.7.

Activity 10

Discuss, from the data given, whether countries with high real GDP per head have higher living standards than those with low real GDP per head.

Table 5

	Real GDP per head (PPP US$)	Life expectancy at birth (years)	Adult literacy rate
Norway	28,433	78.4	99.0
UK	22,093	77.5	99.0
Portugal	16,064	75.5	91.9
Brazil	7,037	67.5	84.9
Angola	3,179	45.0	42.0
Pakistan	1,834	59.6	45.0
Sierra Leone	448	38.3	32.0

Note: 1999 figures.

Source: Table 1, *Human Development Report* 2001.

Unemployment

The level of **unemployment** is the number of people who are seeking work but are not in employment. The **rate of unemployment** is the number of people unemployed as a percentage of the number of people in the labour force. The labour force includes all economically active people, that is people who are willing and able to work. So it includes both employed and unemployed people. For instance, if there are 1 million people unemployed and 19 million in employment, the labour force is 20 million and the unemployment rate is:

$$\frac{\text{unemployed}}{\text{labour force}} \times 100 = \text{unemployment rate}$$

$$\frac{1m}{20m} \times 100 = 5\%$$

Measuring unemployment

There are two main measures of unemployment.

1. The claimant count. This is sometimes known as headline unemployment. It counts as unemployed people who are

Activity 11

A country has 2 million unemployed workers and 28 million people in employment. Calculate:

a the country's labour force

b the country's unemployment rate

Activity 12

The rate of unemployment fell unexpectedly for the third month in a row, tumbling to its lowest for more than 26 years in March [2002].

The unemployment data showed the headline claimant count fell by 6,000 to 939,600 last month [March], the lowest since October 1975. On the government's preferred, survey-based measure, unemployment in the three months to February was 1.52 million, down 14,000 from the previous three-month period. ('Further fall in jobless rate strengthens recovery hope', Gary Duncan, The Times, 18 April 2002)

a Define the rate of unemployment.

b Give two reasons why the survey-based measure may be preferred.

claiming unemployment-related benefits and have declared themselves as willing and able to work.

The advantages of the claimant count are that it is inexpensive and quick to collect the information as the details are gathered when benefits are paid out.

The disadvantages are that it provides only limited analysis of the characteristics of unemployed people, and the numbers recorded as unemployed will be affected by changes in entitlement rules. In this measure, who is entitled to receive job seeker's allowance affects who is counted as unemployed. This leads to criticism on the grounds that it excludes some people who are out of work and are actively seeking employment, such as people aged over 60 and under 18, people on government training schemes and married women seeking to return to work. A few people who are claiming benefit may not be actively seeking employment, but these are thought to be outweighed by people who are actively seeking employment but are not entitled to benefits. Thus the claimant count understates unemployment.

2. The labour force survey. This has a wider coverage and is given more prominence by the government. It is based on the International Labour Office's definition and is sometimes called the ILO method. The ILO's definition includes as unemployed all people who are actively seeking and available to start work, whether or not they are claiming benefits. As its name suggests, this measure is based on a survey of the labour force, which is carried out four times a year.

The advantages are that it is thought by many to give a more accurate measure of unemployment. As it is based on an internationally standardised definition, it is the measure most commonly used when making international comparisons. It also collects information about the labour market, such as the qualifications of potential workers and how many people are seeking part-time employment.

The disadvantages are that the information is costly to compile and is subject to sampling and response error. It also takes time to complete and analyse, so there is some delay before the figures become available.

Measurement problems

If the labour force survey measure is used, it is important to ensure that the sample used is representative and that care is taken in interpreting people's responses. If the claimant count is used, it is difficult to compare unemployment figures internationally because most countries' unemployment figures are based on the ILO definition. It is also difficult to compare unemployment figures over time, as changes in the eligibility criteria for unemployment benefit has altered the coverage of the measure.

Activity 13

Decide whether the following are characteristics of the claimant count measure or of the labour force survey measure.

a It is usable for inter-country comparisons.

b It provides considerable potential for analysis of other labour market characteristics.

c It is available quickly on a monthly basis.

d Its coverage depends upon administrative rules.

Interpreting unemployment data

When analysing unemployment data it is important to consider not just the level and the rate but also the time that people have been out of work. An unemployment rate of 10% with people, on average, being out of work for four months may be regarded as less of a problem than a rate of 4% with an average duration of two years.

It is also important to realise that a fall in unemployment may not be matched by a rise in employment. Finding a job is only one reason someone stops being unemployed. Other reasons include reaching retirement age, entering further or higher education, joining a government training scheme, becoming sick, emigrating or even giving up the search for employment.

When a fall in unemployment does result in a rise in employment, it is necessary to consider the nature of the jobs gained. Low-quality, temporary and part-time jobs may not have a significant impact on the country's output and are not likely to be very beneficial for those who take them up.

Activity 14

a Compare the unemployment performance of the UK and Japan between 1999 and 2003.

b Comment on what additional information it would be useful to have in making your assessment.

Table 6		
	Unemployment rates (%)	
	UK	Japan
1999	6.0	4.7
2000	5.5	4.7
2001	5.1	5.0
2002	5.4	5.9
2003	5.6	6.3

Inflation

Inflation is defined as a sustained rise in the general price level. This means that it is a situation where the general price level is rising over a period of time. It also means that although some prices may be falling, these are more than offset by rises in the prices of other products so that, on average, prices are increasing.

The inflation rate is the percentage by which the general price level is increasing. An annual inflation rate of 6% in June 2004 would mean that on average prices were 6% higher than in June 2003.

If the inflation rate falls, for example, from 6% to 3%, it means that prices are still rising but they are rising more slowly. If, on average, prices are falling, the inflation rate will be

negative. So an inflation rate of –2% would mean that the general price level is falling by 2%. A fall in the general price level is sometimes referred to as **deflation**.

When inflation occurs, the cost of living rises. What happens to the standard of living depends on whether incomes rise at a higher, a lower or the same rate as the cost of living. For instance, if incomes rise by more than the price level, people's real purchasing power will increase and so the standard of living is likely to be higher.

Activity 15

Explain what happened to the general price level in Germany between 1999 and 2002.

Table 7	
	Annual inflation rate in Germany (%)
1999	0.6
2000	1.8
2001	1.8
2002	1.6

Measuring inflation

One of the best-known measures of inflation in the UK is the **retail price index (RPI)**. It receives widespread coverage in the press and the media and is often referred to as the headline rate of inflation. It is a measure of changes in consumer prices and is a weighted price index. The weights take into account the proportion spent on different items.

Calculating the RPI

A Family Expenditure Survey is carried out to find out what people spend their money on. Households are asked to keep a record of their spending in diaries. From the information obtained, different weights are attached to various categories of goods and services. Products which people spend a large amount on receive a greater weighting than products they spend less on. This is because the degree to which people are affected by price changes is influenced by their expenditure patterns. Each year the weights are revised to reflect changes in spending patterns.

Changes in the prices of about 6,000 selected items are collected from retail outlets around the country. These price changes are then multiplied by the weights to give a weighted price index.

For example, in a country people spend £100bn on fuel and light, £250bn on food, £50bn on motoring, £200bn on leisure goods and services, £100bn on clothing and footwear and £300bn on housing. In the year in question, it is found that the price of fuel and light rises by 20%, the price of food falls by 10%, the price of motoring remains unchanged, the price of leisure goods and services rises by 5%, the price of clothing and footwear rises by 6% and there is a 5% rise in the price of housing.

To find the weights, total spending is calculated – in this case it is £1,000bn. Then spending is expressed as a fraction of total spending. The weights are then multiplied by the price changes and the individual weighted price changes are totalled to give the inflation rate.

Table 8: Calculating the RPI					
Category of product	weight		price change		weighted price change
Fuel and light	1/10	x	20%	=	2%
Food	1/4	x	−10%	=	−2.5%
Motoring	1/20	x	0%	=	0%
Leisure goods & services1%	2/10	x	5%	=	1%
Clothing & footwear	1/10	x	6%	=	0.6%
Housing	3/10	x	5%	=	1.5%
Inflation rate					2.6%

Other measures of inflation

RPI is adapted to provide two other measures of inflation.

RPIX is RPI minus mortgage interest payments. This measure is sometimes known as underlying inflation. This is because it measures price changes without taking

into account changes in the rate of interest, which may have been increased specifically to reduce inflation.

RPIY removes not only mortgage interest payments but also local authority taxes and indirect taxes. This measure is also called core inflation as it measures inflationary pressures in the economy undistorted by changes in the government policy measures of interest rates and indirect taxes.

Problems of measuring inflation

There are problems involved in measuring inflation. Surprisingly, higher prices may not mean that inflation is occurring because the products themselves may be changing. For example, a car produced now is relatively more expensive than one produced ten years ago, but it contains many more features and is of a higher quality. Consumers will be getting better value if quality has risen by more than price.

As well as not taking into account changes in quality, RPI, RPIX and RPIY may overestimate inflation because they do not consider special price offers, prices charged at car boot sales and prices in charity shops.

There is also the question of how representative the spending patterns revealed in the Family Expenditure Survey are of the whole population and so how accurate the weights are. The accuracy of the weights is also affected by the introduction of new products. The weights are reviewed each year, but new products are coming on to the market with increasing speed.

Activity 18

Which of the following may reduce the accuracy of the RPI as a measure of inflation?

a a decrease in the proportion of products bought at car boot sales

b a decrease in the frequency with which the weights are reviewed

c an increase in the accuracy of the Family Expenditure Survey

d an increase in the number of items sold at discounted prices

Interpreting inflation figures

Factors taken into account when interpreting inflation figures include the following.

■ What the inflation rate is. For example, a rate of 10% is likely to have more of an impact on the economy than one of 2%.

■ Whether the rate is rising or stable. It is more difficult for firms and households to plan if inflation is fluctuating than if it is stable. A rising inflation rate may generate further inflation. For example, if workers expect prices to be significantly higher in the future, they are likely to press for wage rises. If granted, such rises may result in higher costs of production and then higher prices.

■ Whether the rate has been correctly anticipated. If the rate is correctly anticipated its effects may have been offset by appropriate measures.

■ How the rate compares with that in other countries. Inflation is less likely to have a harmful effect on a country if it is below that of competitor countries. It might be thought that very low and negative inflation would be beneficial, but this is unlikely to be the case. Low price rises may discourage increases in output and investment. A fall in the price level may lead to a recession with people postponing buying products now in the expectation that products will be cheaper in the future.

■ The causes of inflation. Inflation caused by increases in costs of production is likely to have a more harmful effect on the economy than inflation caused by increases in demand.

Activity 19

a Comment on what happened to the general price level in Ireland between 1999 and 2002.

b Discuss why inflation may have caused more problems to the Irish economy in 2000 than in 2002.

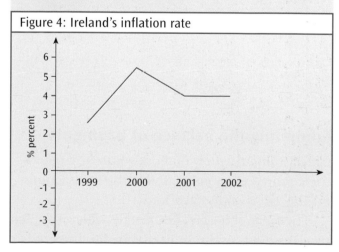
Figure 4: Ireland's inflation rate

The balance of payments

The **balance of payments** is a record of all economic transactions between the residents of a country and the rest of the world over a period of a year. It records all money entering and leaving the country. On the balance of payments account, money coming into the country is a credit item and money leaving the country is a debit item.

Money comes into the country as a result of transactions, including:

- selling goods and services abroad (exports);
- money being placed in the country's financial institutions by people and firms abroad;
- foreigners lending money to the country's citizens and firms;
- foreigners buying the country's shares and government bonds;
- foreign firms setting up in the country.

Money leaves the country when imports of goods and services are purchased from abroad and when the country's citizens and firms buy foreign financial assets (portfolio investment) and foreign factories, businesses, houses and land (direct investment).

Activity 20

Decide whether the following would be credit or debit items on the UK's balance of payments:

a imports of car components

b the purchase of a Portuguese theme park by a UK firm

c exports of organic beef

d a loan by an Italian bank to a UK firm

Compiling the balance of payments

In recording the flow of money into and out of the country, economists divide the transactions into sections and subsections.

The first section is the current account, which receives most attention in the media. It records exports and imports of goods and services, incomes flowing into and out of the economy and transfers of money into and out of the country. These details appear in four subsections.

1. Trade in goods. This covers exports and imports of goods such as cars, TV sets and food. The balance of exports and imports of goods is known as the balance on trade in goods, or sometimes by its old name, the visible balance. If the value of exports exceeds the value of imports, there is a trade surplus. A deficit occurs when the value of imports is greater than the value of exports.

2. Trade in services. This covers the export and import of services such as banking, insurance, transport, tourism and financial services. A surplus on the trade in services balance would mean that the value of exports of services exceeds the value of imports of services. The services balance is occasionally referred to by its old name, invisible balance.

The trade in goods and the trade in services combined gives the balance on trade in goods and services.

3. Income. This includes incomes flowing into and out of the country, including wages. However, the main item is investment income, which covers profit, dividends and interest receipts from abroad minus profit, dividends and interest paid abroad. Investment income is earned on loans, and portfolio and direct investment.

4. Current transfers. These include central government transfers and international transfers of money by private individuals and firms. Central government transfers include the UK's net contribution to the EU and aid given to developing countries. International transfers by private individuals and firms include money sent to and received from relatives abroad.

The balances of the four subsections are totalled to give the **current account balance**. A current account deficit occurs when the value of debit items exceeds the value of credit items. A current account surplus is where the value of credit items is greater than the value of debit items.

The second section is the capital account. A new capital account came into existence in 1998. It includes government investment grants and the purchase and sale of patents, trademarks and land for foreign embassies. The balance on the capital account usually contributes a small net figure to the balance of payments.

In contrast, the third section, the financial account, is an important part of the balance of payments as it involves substantial flows of money. Confusingly, before 1998 this section was known as the capital account. It covers direct and portfolio investment leaving and entering the country. A surplus on this account means that more investment is entering the country than leaving it.

The current, capital and financial accounts form the central part of the balance of payments. An associated section, which is published alongside the balance of payments, is the international investment position. This shows the country's holding of external assets and other countries' holdings of its assets (that is, its liabilities).

Activity 21

Decide:

i in which section of the balance of payments each item appears

ii whether the item is a debit or a credit

a the payment of interest to a UK bank on a loan taken out by a French citizen

b the purchase of seats on a UK airline by US citizens

c the purchase of shares in a Japanese firm by UK citizens

d the purchase of Italian leather goods by UK retailers

Measurement problems

In theory, the total outflow of money, debit items, should equal the total inflow of money,

Table 9: UK balance of payments, 2001 (£m)	
Trade in goods	−33,048
Trade in services	11,703
Trade in goods & services	−21,345
Income	11,151
Current transfers	−7,246
Current balance	−17,440
Capital balance	1,439
Net financial transactions	19,885
Net errors and omissions	−3,854

Source: ONS, Table 16.1, *Monthly Digest of Statistics*, April 2002.

credit items. So the net total of the current, capital and financial accounts should equal zero. However, drawing up the balance of payments involves processing vast amounts of information drawn from numerous sources. Some items are left out, some are put in the wrong sections or subsections and some are miscalculated, and there is a delay in recording some items.

To reflect these mistakes and to make the balance of payments balance, with credit items equalling debit items, a net errors and omissions figure is included. A positive net errors and omissions figure means that more money has flowed into the country than recorded figures suggest. Table 9 shows the UK's balance of payments in 2001.

Activity 22

Using the information in Table 10:

a calculate the net errors and omissions figure

b briefly comment on what this figure means

Table 10: UK balance of payments, 2000 (£m)	
Trade in goods & services	−16,244
Income	8,556
Current transfers	−9,337
Current balance	−17,025
Capital balance	1,676
Net financial transactions	18,010

Source: ONS, Table 16.1, *Monthly Digest of Statistics*, April 2002.

Interpreting balance of payment figures

Care must be taken in interpreting balance of payments figures. For instance, in considering the significance of a deficit on the trade in goods and services balance, economists take into account its size, duration and cause. A large deficit that has lasted a long time is likely to be more serious than a small, short-term deficit. If the country is importing more than it is exporting because its products are not price competitive and/or of poor quality, the deficit is unlikely to be self-correcting. If the deficit has arisen because the country is importing a large quantity of raw materials to be converted into finished products, some of which will be exported, the deficit will probably be short-lived.

A deficit on the financial account may not be a bad thing. In the short term money will be flowing out of the economy. However, in the longer term it will generate an inflow of funds as profit, interest and dividends come into the country.

Current issue: harmonised index of consumer prices

In November 2003, the UK inflation target was changed from 2.5% as measured by RPIX to 2% as measured by the harmonised index of consumer prices (HICP). This is a measure used in all EU countries. From January 1999 it has been used by the European Central Bank as the measure for its definition of price stability across the euro area.

It has two advantages over the RPI. One is technical: it uses more sophisticated weights. The other is that it has a wider coverage, including nearly 100% of consumer spending, and takes more account of high-tech items than the RPI. It does not include council tax.

The HICP is usually lower than the RPI, largely because of the greater weighting it gives to high-tech items, the prices of which are often falling.

Summary

In this unit you have learned that:

■ The main indicators of a country's economic performance are its economic growth, its level and rate of unemployment, its inflation rate and its balance of payments position.

■ A country's output can be measured by the output, income and expenditure methods. In the output measure, care must be taken to avoid double counting; in the income method, **transfer payments** should not be included; and in the expenditure method, exports should be added and imports deducted.

■ Economic growth is measured by changes in **real GDP**.

■ **Nominal GDP** is total output measured in current prices; real GDP is nominal GDP adjusted for inflation.

■ The two main problems in calculating a country's output are estimating the size of the hidden economy and non-marketed goods and services.

■ In deciding whether incomes in real GDP per head are raising living standards, it is important to consider the composition of output, the quality of products produced, changes in the size of the hidden economy and the distribution of income.

■ In making international comparisons of real GDP per head, economists usually use **purchasing power parity exchange rates**.

■ The level of **unemployment** is the number of people actually seeking employment, whereas the **rate of unemployment** is the number of people unemployed as a percentage of the labour force.

Summary continued

■ The two main measures of unemployment are the claimant count, which includes those receiving unemployment-related benefits, and the labour force survey measure, which is based on the ILO definition of unemployment.

■ The claimant count has the advantages of being quick, but the labour force survey is thought to provide a more accurate measure and is more useful for international comparisons.

■ In analysing unemployment data, attention must be paid not just to the numbers out of work but also to how long they have been out of work and the quality of the jobs some may eventually gain.

■ The best-known measure of inflation is the **RPI**, a weighted index of consumer prices. Other measures include the **RPIX**, RPIY and the HICP.

■ Problems involved in measuring changes in the general price level include changes in the quality of products, what to do about price discounts and the accuracy of weights used.

■ High, unstable and unanticipated **inflation** may cause problems to a country, especially if it is above that of other countries.

■ The **balance of payments** records money flowing into and out of the country. It has three main sections: the current account, the capital account and the financial account.

■ The accounting complexity involved in compiling the balance of payments means that mistakes are made and items are left out. So to bring the balance of payments into balance, a net errors and omissions figure is used.

■ Whether a deficit on any of the sections of the balance of payments is a problem or not is influenced by its size, duration and cause.

Multiple choice questions

1 What is real GDP?
A nominal GDP divided by the population
B nominal GDP divided by the labour force
C nominal GDP divided by the price index in the current year
D nominal GDP multiplied by the price index in the base year divided by the price index in the current year

2 Why may GDP per head measured at constant prices underestimate the changes in a country's living standards?
A the rate of inflation has increased
B the size of the hidden economy has decreased
C the average number of hours worked has decreased
D the level of air pollution has increased

3 Which of the following is an advantage of the claimant count as a measure of unemployment?
A it is quick to calculate
B it is based on an internationally standardised measure
C it provides a significant amount of information about the labour market
D it includes all those willing and able to take up employment

4 What do the weights in the retail price index indicate?
A seasonal fluctuations in prices
B the number of people buying each product
C the relative amount spent on each product
D the rise in the prices of all the products included in the index

5 RPIX is:
A RPI plus direct taxes
B RPI minus mortgage interest payments
C RPI minus mortgage interest payments and indirect taxes
D RPI plus the prices of capital goods

6 Which of the following would appear as a credit item in the UK's balance of payments on current account?
A spending by Dutch tourists in Scotland
B the sale of a US television series to the BBC
C the purchase of a UK factory by a German firm
D the transfer of profit from a US firm based in the UK back to its parent firm

Data response question: calculating the rate of inflation

Every year the nation's bean counters – the government's official statisticians – must decide what items should be counted when it comes to calculating the rate of inflation on the high street. In its annual review of the 'basket' of goods and services used to calculate the monthly rate at which prices are rising, the Office for National Statistics (ONS) has chucked out a range of cooking ingredients that no shopping basket was once complete without. So chilled reduced-calorie and frozen vegetarian meals, processed sliced cheese, a range of ethnic takeaway meals and frozen prawns are what the British consumer now favours over canned salmon, loose tea, stock cubes and red potatoes.

The whole exercise is part of the task of calculating how fast high street prices are rising to help the Bank of England set interest rates. Unless the statisticians are looking at goods and services that people are buying, the final number will probably be wrong.

[The latest] revisions to the basket showed that households are spending even more of their hard-earned spare cash on leisure and entertainment. It now includes DVD players, disposable cameras and cable telephone charges. They will replace personal stereos and the cassettes to play in them as well as blank video tapes and, perhaps oddly given the continuing popularity of the sport, sets of darts.

No clothing items have been thrown out, which may be fortunate as the ONS has a mixed record when it comes to calling fashion. It ejected men's cardigans in 1997 just as craze for buttoned knitwear, inspired by the Pulp singer, Jarvis Cocker, was sweeping the high street. They were brought back in 1999.

When the annual review does get it right it is sometimes a rather belated mark of changing trends and fashions. ('Goodbye, Oxo Mum. Hello Ally McBeal. UK's price index catches up with the times', Philip Thornton, Independent, *10 March 2002)*

a Define what is meant by the rate of inflation. [2]

b Drawing on information from the passage, comment on how spending patterns have changed in recent years. [3]

c Explain how the information about people's spending patterns is:
   i   obtained [3]
   ii used to calculate the rate of inflation. [4]

d What problem of calculating the rate of inflation is discussed in the passage? [3]

e Explain why 'unless the statisticians are looking at goods and services that people are buying, the final number will probably be wrong'. [5]

2 Aggregate demand

In this unit you will examine the meaning of **aggregate demand** and discover what influences the components of aggregate demand. You will distinguish between movements along and shifts in the aggregate demand curve.

The meaning of aggregate demand

Aggregate demand is total spending on domestic output at a given price level. There are four components of aggregate demand (AD): consumption (C), investment (I), government spending (G) and net exports (exports minus imports (X – M)). So:

$$AD = C + I + G + (X - M)$$

Activity 1

From the information in Table 1 calculate what proportion of UK aggregate demand in 2001 was accounted for by its components of consumption, investment, government spending and net exports.

Table 10: UK aggregate demand 2001	
	£ million
Consumption	580,225
Investment	158,074
Government spending	158,056
Net exports	–50,369

Consumption

Consumption is the amount households spend on goods and services to satisfy their current needs and wants. It is the largest component of aggregate demand.

The main influence on household spending is income, more specifically disposable income. The more disposable income a household has the more it is able to spend. In general, as income rises people usually spend more, but they spend a smaller proportion of their income because they can afford to save some of it.

For example, a family with a disposable income of £10,000 a year is likely to have to spend all (100%) of its income to meet its needs and wants. A family with a disposable income of £80,000 will almost certainly spend more in total but even if it spends £60,000 a year this is only 75% of its disposable income compared with the poorer family's 100%.

Various other factors influence people's willingness and ability to spend.

- Wealth. If there is an increase in the value of assets, people are likely to feel more confident and will be able to borrow more based on the value of their assets. Most people's main asset is their house, so when house prices rise, consumption usually increases.
- Optimism about economic prospects. If the economy is expected to grow, people are likely to anticipate greater job security, higher incomes and more promotion opportunities.
- A fall in the rate of interest. This makes it cheaper to borrow and reduces the incentive to save.
- Advances in technology. New consumer products are created and households are encouraged to update existing products.

Investment

Investment consists of spending by firms on capital goods including machinery, factories and offices. It fluctuates more than the other components of aggregate demand.

Various factors influence firms' willingness to increase investment.

■ An increase in income. Firms are likely to expect a rise in demand for their products, so they may want to expand their capacity and buy more capital goods.

■ A fall in the rate of interest. Firms will be encouraged to expand because they will anticipate that demand for their products will rise. If they finance their investment spending by borrowing, it will be cheaper. If they use retained profits to buy capital goods, they will find the opportunity cost of investment has fallen – the decision to invest rather than place profits in financial institutions will result in less interest being forgone.

■ Changes in expectations. If entrepreneurs become more optimistic about the future, they will invest more.

■ Advances in technology. New and more productive equipment and transport vehicles are created.

■ A fall in the cost of capital goods.

■ A rise in profit levels.

■ Cuts in corporation tax.

■ An increase in government investment subsidies.

Government spending

Government spending includes spending on defence, education, health care and transport. A government's political views will determine its approach. An interventionist government is likely to spend more than one that believes market forces work well.

Among the factors that influence the level of government spending are:

■ National income (real GDP). A fall in real GDP may lead to a government increasing its spending to stimulate economic activity.

■ Tax revenue. Higher tax revenue will enable a government to spend more to achieve its objectives.

■ Demographic changes. An ageing population will put pressure on a government to increase spending.

■ Demand for merit and public goods. Increased demand for higher education and better health care will pressurise a government to increase spending.

■ Technology advances. These lead to increased government spending on e.g. medical equipment and school computers.

Activity 2

Decide whether the following are likely to increase or decrease consumption:

a a more even distribution of income

b a rise in the availability of credit

c an increase in the range of goods and services available

d an increase in state benefits

e a rise in direct taxes

Activity 3

In the late 1990s investment in the UK increased significantly, rising by more than 12% in 1998. However, in 2001 the growth in investment slowed. The slowdown occurred largely because of the world recession.

a Identify two causes of an increase in investment.

b Explain why a world recession may cause a slowdown in investment.

Activity 4

Explain what effect the following are likely to have on government spending:

a the approach of a general election

b a fall in tax revenue

c a rise in crime levels

d a fall in population

e an increase in air pollution

Net exports

Net exports make a negative contribution to the UK's aggregate demand.

Various factors influence the level of net exports.

■ Income levels at home and abroad. If income levels at home rise, consumers may buy more imports and some products may be diverted from the export to the home market. In contrast, a rise in incomes abroad should increase UK exports.

■ Price and quality competitiveness of domestic and foreign products. UK exports should increase and imports fall if UK products become more competitive relative to foreign products.

■ The exchange rate. This can have a significant effect on net exports. A fall in the value of a currency relative to other currencies will make its exports cheaper and imports more expensive. If demand for exports and imports is elastic, there will be a rise in export revenue and a fall in import expenditure.

Activity 5

In 2001 spending in Spain grew at a faster rate than spending in Spain's main exports markets. Net exports were expected to have increased in 2002 with the fall in the value of the euro.

a Distinguish between spending in Spain and spending on Spanish products.

b Discuss how Spain's net exports are likely to have been affected by spending in Spain growing at a faster rate than spending in its export markets.

c Explain why Spanish net exports would be expected to increase as a result of a fall in the value of the euro.

The aggregate demand curve

An aggregate demand curve plots aggregate demand at different price levels. The curve slopes down from left to right showing that as the price level falls, aggregate demand extends (see Figure 1).

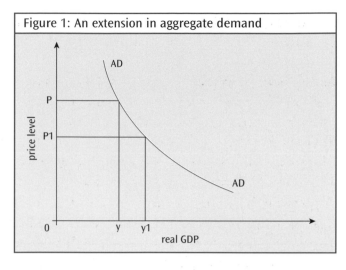

Figure 1: An extension in aggregate demand

There are three principal reasons for this inverse relationship.

■ A lower price level will make UK products more price competitive, which should cause exports to rise and imports to fall. This is known as the international trade effect.

■ Lower prices increase the purchasing power of wealth held in the form of bank and building society accounts (the wealth or real balances effect).

■ A fall in the general price level is usually accompanied by a fall in interest rates (the interest rate effect). Lower interest rates are likely to result in a rise in investment and consumption.

Activity 6

Explain three reasons why a rise in the price level will cause a contraction in aggregate demand.

Shifts in aggregate demand curves

A change in the price level will cause a movement along an aggregate demand curve, but other influences on the components of aggregate demand will shift the curve (see Figure 2).

An increase in aggregate demand can be caused by, for example, a fall in interest rates, a cut in direct taxes, a fall in the exchange rate, a rise in expectations and advances in technology.

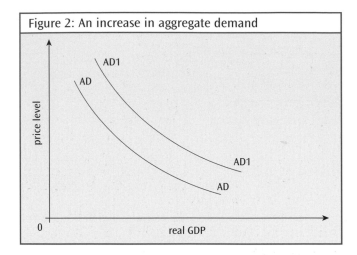

Figure 2: An increase in aggregate demand

Current issue: expectations affect aggregate demand

Expectations play an important role in determining consumption and investment and so aggregate demand. This is illustrated by events in Japan at the start of the 2000s, when Japanese households and firms became pessimistic about the future of the economy. Households increased their saving and reduced their consumption. Firms reduced their investment. The government tried to stimulate consumption and investment by cutting direct taxes, slashing interest rates, raising government spending and urging banks to lend more. So great were people's worries about future job prospects, however, that aggregate demand continued to fall in the first three years of the 2000s.

Summary

In this unit you have learned that:

■ **Aggregate demand** consists of consumption, investment, government spending and net exports.

■ In the UK, the largest component of aggregate demand is consumption, the most volatile is investment and net exports usually make a negative contribution.

■ The main influence on consumption is income. As incomes rise, people usually spend more in total but a smaller proportion of their income. Other influences include wealth, expectations, the rate of interest and advances in technology.

■ Investment is influenced by income, the rate of interest, expectations, advances in technology, cost of capital, profit levels, corporation tax and government subsidies.

■ The amount a government spends is influenced by its political views on government intervention.

■ Net exports are affected by income levels at home and abroad, price and quality competitiveness of domestic products and exchange rates. A fall in the exchange rate will be likely to increase exports and reduce imports and so increase aggregate demand.

■ A movement along an aggregate demand curve is caused by a change in the price level.

■ The aggregate demand curve slopes down from left to right because a fall in the price level makes domestic products more price competitive, increases wealth and reduces the rate of interest.

■ The aggregate demand curve will shift if anything, apart from a change in the price level, influences aggregate demand.

Multiple choice questions

1 Which of the following is the largest component of aggregate demand?

A consumption

B government spending

C investment

D net exports

2 What does an aggregate demand curve show?

A total spending on goods and services in a country at different price levels

B total spending on domestic output at different price levels

C the total of consumption, government spending and investment at different price levels

D the total of consumption, government spending and imports at different price levels

3 Which of the following explains why the aggregate demand curve slopes down from left to right?

A a rise in the general price level makes the country's products less price competitive

B a rise in the general price level encourages firms to undertake more investment

C a fall in the general price level leads to a reduction in wealth

D a fall in the general price level discourages investment

4 Which of the following may have caused the movement in aggregate demand from Y to Y1 as shown in Figure 3.

A a rise in direct taxes

B a rise in the price level

C a decrease in optimism

D a decrease in foreign incomes

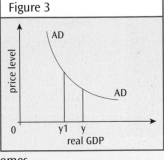
Figure 3

5 Which of the following would cause a decrease in aggregate demand?

A a reduction in the rate of interest

B a decrease in imports

C an increase in corporation tax

D an increase in consumer optimism

6 Which of the following could have caused the shift in the aggregate demand curve shown in Figure 4?

A a decrease in government spending

B a reduction in the exchange rate

C an increase in income tax

D an increase in the cost of capital goods

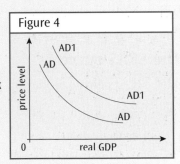
Figure 4

Data response question: US aggregate demand

In 2001 US aggregate demand rose by 1.2%, largely because of an increase in consumption. Americans were spending more partly as a result of cuts in direct taxation and interest rates.

US investment actually declined. Profit levels were 12.5% lower in 2001 than in 2000, and many firms had spare capacity with a backlog of unemployed capital goods.

Net exports made a negative contribution to US aggregate demand in the year. The value of the dollar rose throughout most of 2001 and incomes fell in some of the US's export markets.

a Which component of aggregate demand is not mentioned in the passage? [2]

b Explain why cuts in direct taxes and interest rates would be expected to increase aggregate demand. [8]

c Using the information in the passage, explain why US investment fell in 2001. [4]

d Discuss two other influences on investment. [4]

e Explain what is meant by net exports making a negative contribution to aggregate demand. [2]

3 Aggregate supply

In this unit you will examine what factors influence a country's output in the short and long run. You will consider the relationship between the price level and total output and distinguish between the views of two groups of economists on the shape of the **long run aggregate supply curve**.

Meaning of aggregate supply

Aggregate supply is the total output that all the producers of in economy are willing and able to supply at each price level.

Economists distinguish between **short run aggregate supply (SRAS)** and **long run aggregate supply (LRAS)**. Short run aggregate supply is the output supplied in a time period when the prices of inputs, including labour and raw materials, remain unchanged. Long run aggregate supply is the output supplied after the price level and factor prices have fully adjusted after any shifts in aggregate demand.

The SRAS curve

The SRAS curve slopes up from left to right as shown in Figure 1.

A rise in the price level results in an extension in output from Y to Y1.

There are two main reasons for this direct relationship between the price level and SRAS. A higher price level will:

- enable firms to cover any increase in average costs that may occur as output rises – for example, although in the short run it is assumed that the wage rate does not change, firms may have to pay overtime to persuade workers to work longer hours.
- increase firms' willingness to supply more because profit margins usually rise as the price level increases.

There are also two main causes of a shift in the SRAS curve: changes in the payments to factors of production and changes in productivity.

The SRAS curve will shift to the left if productivity decreases, wage rates rise or the prices of raw materials increase. Figure 2 illustrates a decrease in short run

Activity 1

In 2001, while the world's 500 biggest companies increased their capital expenditure by 17%, the UK's top 500 companies increased their spending by only 12%.

a What effect will an increase in investment have on a country's:
  i aggregate demand
  ii potential output

b Identify two reasons why the world's 500 biggest companies might have invested more in percentage terms than the UK's top 500 biggest companies.

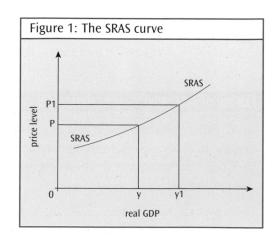

Figure 1: The SRAS curve

aggregate supply from SRAS to SRAS1. At each price level less is supplied.

Shifts in the SRAS curve caused by unexpected events, such as a sudden rise in the price of oil or a hurricane, are sometimes referred to as supply-side shocks. Unexpected shifts in the demand curve can be called demand-side shocks.

LRAS curve

There are two main views on the shape of the LRAS curve.

■ **Keynesians** are economists whose ideas are based on the work of John Maynard Keynes. They believe that market failure is a common occurrence and a serious problem. They think that government intervention is needed to improve the workings of markets and that it can be effective.
■ **New classical economists** believe that markets usually work efficiently. They think that government intervention can make the situation worse so it should be kept to a minimum. The government's main role should be to ensure that laws, regulations and institutions operate in such a way as to enable market forces to provide economic agents with sufficient information and incentives.

Keynesians believe that the LRAS curve is perfectly elastic at low levels of output, elastic as output rises, inelastic as output approaches full capacity and then perfectly inelastic as full employment of resources is reached. When output is low, firms can purchase more factors of production without raising their prices, so more can be produced without increasing average cost. As output rises, firms start to compete for resources, their prices rise and the cost of production increases. As shortages of resources increase, the LRAS curve becomes increasingly inelastic until the economy is producing its maximum output with all existing resources employed and given technological knowledge. Figure 3 shows the Keynesian view of the shape of the LRAS curve.

New classical economists believe that the economy will operate at full capacity in the long run, so they think the LRAS curve is a vertical line (see Figure 4).

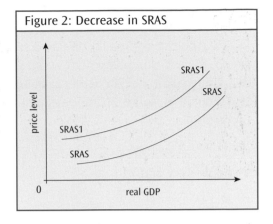
Figure 2: Decrease in SRAS

Activity 2

Explain what effect the following are likely to have on the SRAS curve:

a an increase in the price of oil

b a rise in wages matched by an increase in productivity

c a fall in corporation tax

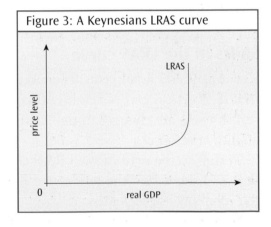
Figure 3: A Keynesians LRAS curve

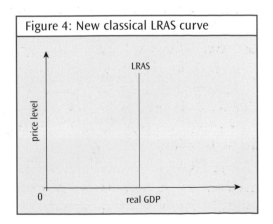
Figure 4: New classical LRAS curve

Aggregate supply

Activity 3

In 2001 output in Greece rose by 3.8%, inflation was 3.7% and unemployment was 11.2%. Using this information, decide at which point on the LRAS curve in Figure 5 Greece appeared to be producing in 2001:

a between 0 and Y

b between Y and Y1

c at Y1

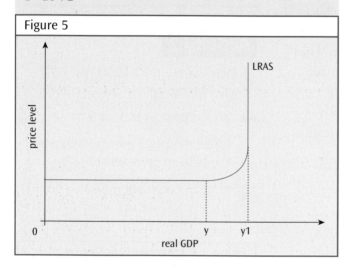

Figure 5

Shifts in the LRAS curve

Keynesians and new classical economists agree that the vertical part of the LRAS curve will shift if there are changes in the quantity or quality of resources.

A shift to the right of the LRAS curve (see Figure 6) shows that the productive capacity of the economy has increased.

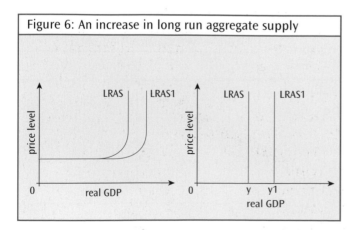

Figure 6: An increase in long run aggregate supply

Activity 4

Decide whether the following would cause the LRAS curve to shift to the right or the left:

a net emigration

b advances in technology

c worn out machines not being replaced

d improvements in the quality of education

e an outbreak of foot-and-mouth disease among the country's sheep and cows

Factors which can influence the quantity and quality of resources and thus the maximum output that the country can produce include changes in the size of the labour force, investment, training, education, health care and technology.

Current issue: raising educational standards

When it was elected in May 1997, the Labour government stated that education was its top priority. The UK has a good record in higher education, but its performance in secondary education and adult literacy is not so strong. People who go to university are more likely to graduate and to undergo further training after university than is the case in most EU countries. However, one in three young people fails to achieve five good GCSE passes, and a report published in 2001 found that a staggering 7 million adults in the UK were functionally illiterate.

The government is keen to raise educational standards and achievements in order to improve the quality of people's lives and to increase productivity. Better educated people are able to exercise more choice and to make better informed decisions. A better educated labour force would also be more productive, which would increase the country's productive potential, shifting its LRAS curve to the right.

244

Summary

In this unit you have learned that:

■ The **short run aggregate supply (SRAS)** curve slopes up from left to right because a higher price enables firms to cover higher average costs and to enjoy higher profit margins.

■ The two main causes of shifts in the SRAS curve are changes in the payments to factors of production and changes in productivity.

■ **Keynesians** think that the **long run aggregate supply (LRAS)** curve is perfectly elastic at low levels of output, elastic as factor prices start to rise, inelastic as shortages become more acute and perfectly inelastic when the economy's resources are fully employed.

■ **New classical economists** believe that the economy works at full capacity in the long run and that the LRAS curve is vertical.

■ The LRAS curve will shift if the quantity or quality of resources changes.

Multiple choice questions

1 What is aggregate supply?
A the average output of domestic firms and government concerns
B the average increase in output of an economy
C the quantity of goods and services that firms and government concerns choose to produce and sell at any price level
D the total of all planned output at any level of income

2 Which of the following could cause a shift to the left of the SRAS curve?
A a reduction in consumption
B a decrease in net exports
C an increase in labour productivity
D an increase in raw material costs

3 Which of the following would cause a decrease in long run aggregate supply?
A an increase in unemployment
B an increase in the general price level
C a decrease in investment
D a decrease in demand for exports

4 Which of the following could have caused the shift in the LRAS curve in Figure 7?
A an increase in consumption
B an increase in the quality of training
C a decrease in the stock of capital goods
D a decrease in the productivity of labour

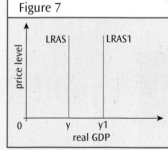
Figure 7

5 What does it mean if an economy is operating on the vertical part of its LRAS curve?
A aggregate demand is decreasing
B aggregate supply is perfectly elastic
C it is producing at its full capacity level of output
D it is producing where its export revenue matches its import expenditure

6 What effect would net emigration (the numbers of emigrants exceeding the number of immigrants) have on aggregate demand and aggregate supply?

	Aggregate demand	Aggregate supply
A	increase	increase
B	increase	decrease
C	decrease	decrease
D	decrease	increase

Data response question: the skills gap

The industry minister Kim Howells conceded yesterday that Britain has a skills and recruitment crisis, partly due to a collective failure to train a modern workforce.

He also challenged the relevance to industry of much sixth form and university education. 'I am worried by the skills gap,' he said. 'It is a real constraint on growth.' He urged companies to become 'much more involved in what is taught in education'.

Mr Howells [was] preparing for a tour to promote greater corporate social responsibility, including a bigger commitment from companies to train and retrain their workforce.

The Cabinet Office [was] publishing a paper on the scale of the skills gap and the role immigrants could play in meeting the shortages.

The report follows a call by the immigration minister, Barbara Roche, for a debate on whether immigration laws need to be relaxed in specific areas to plug the skills gap.

Claiming that Britain was close to becoming a full employment society, as defined by the economist, John

Maynard Keynes, he said there needed to be much more private sector involvement in formulating the best way to get young people to go into IT, and later on retraining people. ('Britain "in crisis" on skills and filling jobs', Patrick Wintour, Guardian, *22 January 2001)*

a Does the passage suggest that education always increases labour productivity? [3]

b Discuss the effect on the LRAS curve of:
   i an increase in training
   ii immigration [6]

c Explain why a lack of skilled workers could act as a real constraint on growth. [4]

d Explain at what point on its LRAS curve an economy will be operating if it is close to becoming a full employment society. [3]

e Discuss two causes, other than training and immigration, of a shift in the LRAS curve. [4]

---

4 Equilibrium output and price level

In this unit you will examine how the interaction of aggregate demand and supply determine a country's output and price level at any particular time. You will consider how changes in aggregate demand and aggregate supply can alter output and the price level.

Macroeconomic equilibrium output and price level

Macroeconomic equilibrium output and price level occur where aggregate demand and aggregate supply are equal, as shown in Figure 1.

At an output of Y, there are no pressures causing the price level or output to change. If the price level and output were higher, for example at P1 and Y1, there would be

disequilibrium, and aggregate demand and aggregate supply would be unequal. A surplus of unsold products would cause the price level to fall. Aggregate supply would contract and aggregate demand would expand until equilibrium was restored. However, if the price was at P2 and output at Y2, there would be a shortage of products. In this case the price level would rise, leading to a contraction in aggregate demand and an expansion in aggregate supply.

When the economy is in equilibrium, **injections** are equal to **withdrawals** (also known as leakages). Injections, consisting of investment, government spending and exports, are forms of spending that are additional to the circular flow of income. Withdrawals are leakages from the circular flow in the form of savings, taxation and imports. Figure 2 illustrates the circular flow with injections and withdrawals.

If injections exceed withdrawals, the extra spending in the system will cause output to rise. In contrast, if withdrawals are greater than injections, output will fall.

Activity 1

Decide which of the following are injections into and which are withdrawals from the circular flow:

a   corporation tax paid by UK firms

b   the purchase of UK banking services by German firms

c   spending on capital goods by UK firms

d   spending on Japanese products by UK citizens

Short run and long run equilibrium

It is possible for an economy to be in short run but not long run equilibrium. For example, an economy can produce an output above the full employment level if workers work overtime and equipment is fully used. This, however, cannot be sustained. The resulting higher average costs will shift the SRAS curve to the left, causing the economy to return to the full employment output but at a higher price level (see Figure 3). In the short run the economy is in equilibrium at Y, above the full employment level of real GDP at Yfe.

As firms compete for scarce labour, raw materials and machines, average costs will rise. The SRAS curve shifts to SRAS1 and output returns to Yfe but at a price level of P1.

New classical economists think that if the economy is in short run equilibrium below the full employment level of output, it will return to the full employment level in the long run. Figure 4 shows that the economy is initially in equilibrium at Y. The existence of unemployment, they argue, will mean that workers will be prepared to accept lower wages. The fall in costs of production shifts the SRAS curve to the right and output returns to the full employment level of Yfe.

In contrast, Keynesians argue that in the long run, equilibrium output can occur at any level of employment.

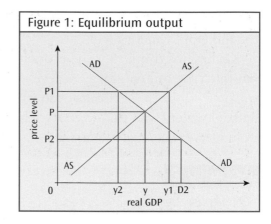

Figure 1: Equilibrium output

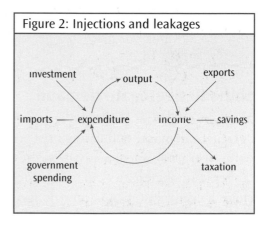

Figure 2: Injections and leakages

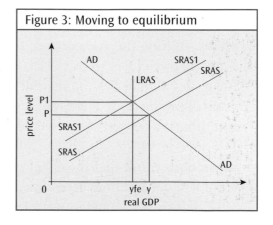

Figure 3: Moving to equilibrium

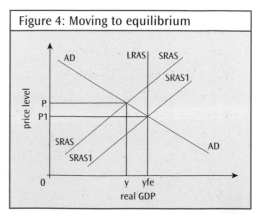

Figure 4: Moving to equilibrium

Figure 5 shows aggregate demand equalling LRAS well below the full employment level.

Keynesians think that the economy will not automatically return to the full employment level. They believe that workers will resist wage cuts even when there is high unemployment and that even if such a cut occurred, they would lower aggregate demand.

Activity 2

Distinguish between:

a market equilibrium and macroeconomic equilibrium

b macroeconomic equilibrium and macroeconomic disequilibrium

Shifts in aggregate demand

New classical economists believe that an increase in aggregate demand will cause a rise in the price level and an extension in aggregate supply in the short run, and that a decrease in aggregate demand will lower the price level and cause a contraction in short run aggregate supply. However, they think that in the long run changes in aggregate demand affect only the price level and leave output at the full employment level (see Figure 6). Aggregate demand increases, shifting the AD curve to the right (AD1) and causing the price level to rise to P1.

Increasing output beyond the full employment level pushes up costs of production. The SRAS curve shifts to the left. This returns output to the full employment level but at a higher price level.

Keynesians think that the effect of an increase in aggregate demand will depend on where the economy is initially operating. If the economy is operating with considerable spare capacity and unemployment, a rise in aggregate demand may increase output but have no effect on the price level (see Figure 7).

When the economy is close to or starting to experience shortages of resources, an increase in aggregate demand will raise both output and the price level (see Figure 8).

If the economy is experiencing full employment of resources, an increase in aggregate demand will raise the price level but have no effect on output. Figure 9 shows the aggregate demand curve shifting to the right, causing the price level to rise to P1, but leaving output at Y.

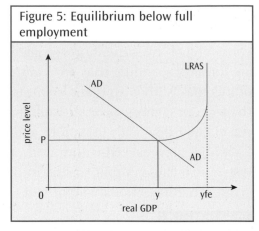

Figure 5: Equilibrium below full employment

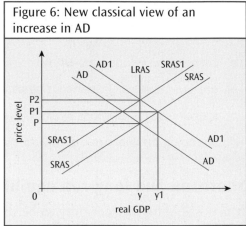

Figure 6: New classical view of an increase in AD

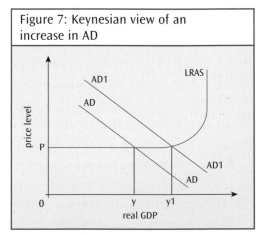

Figure 7: Keynesian view of an increase in AD

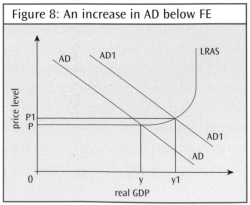

Figure 8: An increase in AD below FE

Shifts in the SRAS and LRAS curves

New classical economists and Keynesian economists agree that increases in the costs of production or a fall in productivity will shift the SRAS curve to the left, raise the price level and reduce output (see Figure 10).

An increase in SRAS will lower the price level and increase output (see Figure 11).

The two groups disagree about the effects of a shift in the LRAS curve. New classical economists believe that an increase in LRAS will cause a rise in output and a fall in the price level (see Figure 12).

Keynesians think that the effect of a shift in the LRAS curve will depend on the initial equilibrium position. If the economy is operating at a high level of unemployment, an increase in LRAS will raise potential but not actual output. The LRAS curve moves to the right, showing an increase in the productive capacity of the economy (see Figure 13). However, output will remain at Y owing to a lack of aggregate demand.

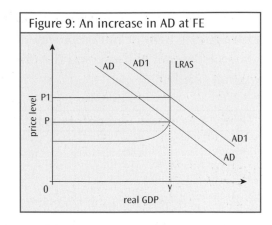

Figure 9: An increase in AD at FE

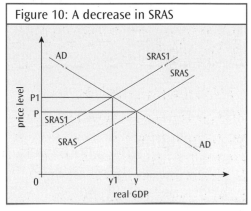

Figure 10: A decrease in SRAS

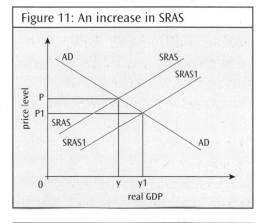

Figure 11: An increase in SRAS

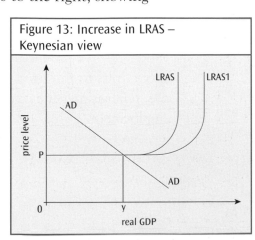

Figure 13: Increase in LRAS – Keynesian view

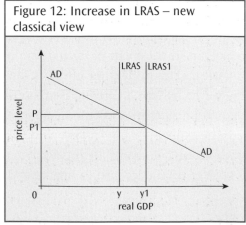

Figure 12: Increase in LRAS – new classical view

If LRAS increases when the economy is experiencing high or full employment of resources, output will rise and the price level will fall (see Figure 14).

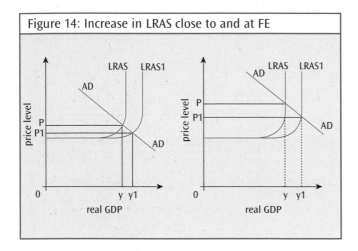

Figure 14: Increase in LRAS close to and at FE

The multiplier

An increase in aggregate demand will cause additional increases in aggregate demand because of the knock-on effect on spending. Economists call this the **multiplier** effect. For example, if the government raised its spending on medical equipment by £10 billion, the aggregate demand curve would initially move to the right by £10 billion. The firms supplying the medical equipment are likely to experience higher profits, raise wages and take on extra workers. The firms' owners and workers, earning higher incomes, are likely to spend more. This causes the AD curve to move to the right again. Higher demand will again lead to higher income, so the AD curve will move again. The increases in aggregate demand get smaller as more of the extra income leaks out in the form of saving, imports and taxation. The multiplier effect is illustrated in Figure 15, where an initial increase in aggregate demand results in additional spending.

The multiplier effect also works in reverse, with an initial fall in aggregate demand causing a greater final decrease in aggregate demand.

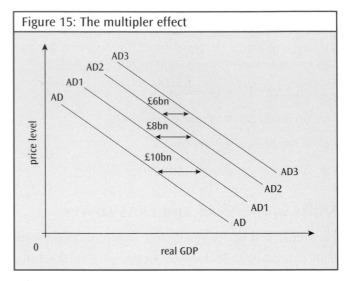

Figure 15: The multipler effect

Current issue: effects of changes in oil prices

In the last three decades, changes in the price of oil have had dramatic effects on the price level in Japan, the USA and EU countries. In the mid-1970s the price of oil quadrupled, and at the start of the 1980s it doubled. Crude oil is an important component in the production of many products, including petrol. So in these years production and transport costs rose. The countries' SRAS curves shifted to the left and they experienced rises in their price levels, falls in output and higher unemployment.

When oil prices fall, as they did in the mid-1980s, costs of production fall and so the SRAS curve shifts to the right. This causes output to rise, reduces pressure on price rises and increases employment.

Summary

In this unit you have learned that:

- The economy is in **macroeconomic equilibrium** when aggregate demand equals aggregate supply and **injections** equal **withdrawals**.

- New classical economists believe that in the short run an economy can be producing at any level of output, but in the long run it will return to equilibrium at the full employment level of output. In contrast, Keynesians think that the economy can be in equilibrium at any level of employment.

- New classical economists think that shifts in the AD curve will affect the price level and output in the short run, but in the long run will affect only the price level. Keynesians, however, think that the effect of an increase in aggregate

demand will be determined by the initial equilibrium position.

- A shift of the SRAS curve to the left will raise the price level and reduce output, whereas a shift to the right will lower the price level and raise output.

- New classical economists believe that an increase in LRAS will lower the price level and increase output. Keynesians think that the effect will depend on the initial equilibrium position. If there is a low level of economic activity, an increase in LRAS may raise potential but not actual output.

- An increase or decrease in aggregate demand has a knock-on effect (the **multiplier** effect), causing the final change in spending to be greater than the initial change.

Multiple choice questions

1 When does macroeconomic equilibrium occur?

A when aggregate demand is equal to aggregate supply

B when government spending is equal to tax revenue

C when exports are equal to imports

D when investment is equal to saving

2 At which point on the Keynesian LRAS curve will an increase in aggregate demand cause the largest rise in employment?

A where it is perfectly elastic

B where it is elastic

C where it is inelastic

D where it is perfectly inelastic

3 Figure 16 shows a change in a country's price level and output. Which of the following could have caused this change?

A a decrease in demand for exports

B a decrease in corporation tax

C an increase in investment

D an increase in wage rates

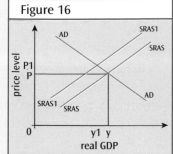

Figure 16

4 An economy's LRAS curve is perfectly inelastic. What effect will an increase in aggregate demand have on the economy's price level, output and employment?

	Price level	Output	Employment
A	increase	increase	increase
B	increase	leave unchanged	leave unchanged
C	leave unchanged	leave unchanged	leave unchanged
D	leave unchanged	increase	increase

5 Which of the following would cause both a fall in the price level and a rise in output?

A an increase in aggregate demand

B a decrease in aggregate demand

C a decrease in short run aggregate supply

D an increase in short run aggregate supply

6 An economy is operating below full employment. Which of the following would increase output?

A an increase in imports

B an increase in government spending

C a decrease in investment

D a decrease in the labour force

Data response question: low output growth in the UK

At the end of 2001 UK output was increasing only slowly. In the last three months of 2001, real GDP increased by only 0.2% compared with the previous quarter, despite continuing growth in consumption and government spending. Indeed, the government was spending more than it was raising in taxation.

Economists expressed concern that even the low rise in output might not be sustainable. These worries arose from the poor performance of aggregate supply. The terrorist attack in the USA on 11 September 2001 had reduced business confidence, which had lowered investment. Unemployment was at a low level and firms were finding it difficult to recruit skilled workers.

To ensure that output would continue to rise, some economists argued that the government should increase spending on education, permit more immigration and encourage more investment by reducing interest rates.

a i Which three components of aggregate demand are referred to in the passage? [3]

ii Identify the other component of aggregate demand. [1]

b Using an aggregate demand and supply diagram, explain why a rise in output may not be sustainable. [5]

c Using an aggregate demand and supply diagram, analyse the effects of an increase in government spending. [7]

d Explain why reducing interest rates may raise investment. [4]

5 Objectives of government policy

In this unit you will consider the four main macroeconomic objectives of governments. You will discover what most governments seek to achieve in their management of the economy and what influences their priorities.

Macroeconomic policy objectives

There are four main macroeconomic policy objectives. These are:

- steady and sustainable economic growth;
- low and stable inflation;
- full employment;
- a satisfactory balance of payments position.

The emphasis on these objectives varies as economic circumstances alter, government administrations change and different economic theories are followed. In recent years economic growth has been seen as a priority. Full employment is again seen as achievable, inflation is less of a threat and the balance of payments position is considered to be less significant than was once thought.

A government may also be pursuing other macroeconomic objectives, including a reduction in poverty and a cleaner environment.

Activity 1

At the start of 2002 some economists expressed concern that the slowdown in the rate at which UK real GDP was increasing might lead to increases in job losses.

Which two government macroeconomic objectives are referred to above?

Economic growth

The principal objective of the Labour governments elected in 1997 and 2001 was economic growth. The argument was that economic growth would raise living standards and reduce poverty by increasing job opportunities and by increasing the amount of tax revenue the government has to spend on helping people who are unable to work.

What constitutes a desirable rate of economic growth? It used to be thought that the UK economy was capable of increasing output by approximately 2.5% a year, largely through advances in technology and improved educational standards. In 1999 Gordon Brown, the chancellor of the exchequer, stated that he thought the UK's ability to grow had increased to around 2.75% because advances in technology were occurring at a more rapid rate.

It is also generally thought to be growth that is both steady and sustainable. Fluctuations in output, with periods of rapid economic growth (boom) and negative economic growth (bust), create uncertainty and make it difficult for governments, firms and households to plan. Governments want aggregate supply to rise steadily in line with increases in aggregate demand. They are also placing increasing emphasis on **sustainable economic growth**, ensuring that output is increased in a way that does not damage the environment and permits economic growth to continue in the future.

Low and stable inflation

Governments do not want a high inflation rate because it can cause problems, such as a reduction in a country's international price competitiveness, a decline in saving and a fall in the real income of people whose incomes do not rise in line with inflation. Very high levels of inflation, known as **hyperinflation**, may result in political instability and people resorting to barter.

Nor do they want zero inflation, for two main reasons. First, measures of inflation often overestimate price rises so that a zero inflation rate may be masking a fall in the general price level. Second, a small rise in the general price level may bring benefits, such as encouraging firms to raise their output and enabling them to cut their real costs of production by raising wage rates by less than the inflation rate rather than by cutting jobs.

So governments seek to achieve a low inflation rate. They also want a stable inflation rate, because fluctuations create uncertainty, making it difficult for governments, firms and households to plan, and discourage investment.

The Labour government elected in May 1997 set the Bank of England the target of achieving an inflation rate, as measured by RPIX, of 2.5% with a margin of 1 percentage point either way. The target was changed in November 2003 to an inflation rate of 2% or below as measured by the HICP.

Activity 2

Britain's longest ever period of economic expansion officially came to a shuddering halt as new figures showed the economy failed to grow in the final months of last year [2001].

This marked the end of the record 37 quarters of unbroken peacetime expansion which began at the end of the last recession in the third quarter of 1992. The revision, however, left in tact the estimate of 2.4% growth for 2001. ('UK's decade of economic growth grinds to a halt as services falter', Philip Thornton, Independent, 28 February 2002)

a Explain what is meant by an economy failing to grow.

b Explain two advantages of a long period of economic expansion.

Activity 3

Cut-price mortgages dragged the headline inflation rate down to 0.7% in December [2001] from 0.9% in November, the Office for National Statistics said. That represents the lowest rate since April 1960.

The underlying inflation rate rose slightly last month [December 2001] to 1.9%, boosted by higher food prices and phone bills.

Measured on an internationally comparable basis, Britain's inflation rate is even lower: 0.8% in November [2001], making it the lowest in Europe. ('Inflation hits 42-year low', Heather Stewart, Independent, *16 January 2002)*

a Distinguish between the headline rate of inflation and the underlying rate.

b Discuss whether the information in the extract suggests the government should have been concerned about inflation at the start of 2002

Full employment

In 1944 the wartime coalition government published a White Paper which committed the Labour and Conservative parties to the idea that a government should aim for full employment. The paper did not define full employment, but it was generally understood to be a situation where around 3% of the labour force was unemployed and there were as many unfilled vacancies as unemployed people. It was not zero unemployment, as there will always be people leaving one job and spending time seeking a new job.

Between 1944 and 1980, all administrations were committed to the objective of achieving full employment as defined above. However, in the 1980s and 1990s politicians dropped this objective because they thought changing economic conditions meant that 3% unemployment was no longer attainable. They adopted a more imprecise objective: to achieve as high employment and as low unemployment as possible.

In the 1980s new classical economists developed the concept of the **natural rate of unemployment** (also known as the non-accelerating inflation rate of unemployment – NAIRU). This is the level of unemployment existing when the labour market is in equilibrium and people willing and able to work at the going wage rate can find employment. They argue that the natural rate can change over time as a result of, for instance, cuts in jobseeker's allowance, which make people reduce the time they spend searching for a new job.

At the start of the 2000s, with falling unemployment, the idea that full employment was achievable was back as a credible political and economic concept. The Labour and Conservative parties again said their aim was to achieve full employment.

Activity 4

The number of people out of work and claiming benefit fell by 6,000 in August [2001] to 945,000, the lowest level since October 1975.

This means that the claimant count rate was unchanged at 3.1%, the same as in July.

The government's preferred measure of unemployment showed a rise of 13,000, its second successive monthly increase.

Meanwhile, the number of unemployed people rose 13,000 to 28.2 million, the smallest rise for several quarters. ('Unemployment falls by 6,000 to fresh 26-year low', Philip Thornton, Independent, *13 September 2001)*

a Explain how the number of people claiming benefit could fall while the claimant count remains the same.

b What is the government's preferred measure of unemployment?

c Explain why the claimant count and the government's preferred measure may give different figures for unemployment.

Balance of payments position

A government will be concerned about a deficit on its balance of payments if it thinks that this reflects a structural weakness in the economy and that it will affect its exchange rate. A deficit on the trade in goods balance as a result of low productivity will be a cause for concern. It may also put downward pressure on the country's exchange rate, and a government may be worried about the effects this may have on its inflation rate.

In recent years UK governments have been less concerned about balance of payments deficits in the belief that they are not caused by structural problems and can be covered by an inflow of investment income.

Current issue: risks of deflation

Some economists have expressed concern that the Bank of England is more worried when the inflation rate is just above the 2.5% target than when it is below it. They argue that the UK is more at risk from deflation than from inflation. They point to the reduction in inflationary pressure in both the domestic and global markets and to the serious consequences that can arise when there is deflation in an economy. Falling prices can transform an economy – Japan is a good example.

In the 1980s Japan enjoyed rapid economic growth, low inflation, very low unemployment and a large balance of payments surplus. In 2002 it was experiencing deflation, negative economic growth and rising unemployment. It still had a balance of payments surplus, but this was a result not of its international competitiveness but of low consumer demand in Japan.

Activity 5

Britain suffered its worst ever balance of payments deficit in the final quarter of 2001 as the downturn in the global economy took its toll on companies operating in recession-hit countries abroad.

British firms saw returns on investment abroad (investment income) completely wiped out as economic slowdown tightened its grip in the last three months of the year, increasing the current account deficit to a record £7.6 billion, according to the Office for National Statistics.

Ross Walker, of Royal Bank of Scotland, said that the sharp crunch in investment returns reflected the difficult trading conditions abroad in the final months of 2001.

'In some ways the surprise is that this has taken so long,' he said. Mr Walker was optimistic that a recovery in the global economy would help to reverse some of the deficit in the coming months. 'Most of the evidence shows the fourth quarter of last year was the low point for the global economy.' ('Record deficit for UK as global slump takes toll', Heather Stewart, Guardian, *28 March 2002)*

a Identify two components of the current account other than investment income.

b Does the article suggest that the UK government should have been worried about the record current account deficit? Explain your answer.

Summary

In this unit you have learned that:

■ The four main macroeconomic objectives are steady and **sustainable economic growth**, low and stable inflation, full employment and a satisfactory balance of payments position.

■ A desirable rate of economic growth is considered to be one that is steady and sustainable.

■ Fluctuations in economic growth cause uncertainty and discourage investment.

■ Governments want to avoid high and fluctuating inflation rates and deflation.

■ The UK's government inflation target is 2% as measured by HICP.

■ Full employment is generally taken to be 3% unemployment.

■ New classical economists developed the concept of the **natural rate of unemployment** in the 1980s.

■ Whether a deficit on the balance of payments is a cause for concern is influenced by whether it reflects structural problems in the economy and the effect it has on the exchange rate.

Multiple choice questions

1 Which of the following is not a government macroeconomic policy objective?
A   low inflation
B   high unemployment
C   steady economic growth
D   balance of payments equilibrium

2 Why would a government be likely to prefer a pattern of annual economic growth of 2%, 3%, 2% and 3% than one of 5%, 0%, 1% and 4%?
A   it will give a higher average annual growth rate
B   it will make it easier for firms and households to plan
C   it does not include a period of recession
D   it is growing more rapidly at the end of the period

3 Which of the following would mean that the Bank of England had failed to achieve the inflation target set for it by the UK government?
A   inflation as measured by RPI is 4%
B   inflation as measured by RPIX is 1.4%
C   inflation as measured by RPIY is 5.5%
D   inflation as measured by HICP is 0.8%

4 Which of the following combinations of economic performance would give the UK government the greatest cause for concern?

	Economic growth rate (%)	Inflation rate (%)	Unemployment rate (%)
A	1	2	4
B	2	2	2
C	3	3	3
D	5	−2	5

5 What is generally understood by the term 'full employment'?
A   no one being unemployed
B   only 3% of the labour force being unemployed
C   all those people of working age being in employment
D   an unemployment rate being below the average of other industrialised countries

6 Why might an outflow of portfolio and direct investment not be a cause for concern?
A   it will reduce potential employment in the country
B   it may be offset by a deficit on the current account
C   it may be into projects that are not viable in the long run
D   it will generate profits, interest and dividends in the long run

Data response question: interpreting unemployment figures

Times change. The last time the unemployment claimant count went through 1 million in 1975 it was seen as an economic disaster. When it edged below 1 million [in the second week of March 2001] it was a cause for celebration, occasioning a press conference featuring Tony Blair and half his Cabinet.

Figures change too. There have been some 30 changes in the way the count is made and in the 1980s there was a deliberate policy of encouraging people off the dole and on to long term sickness and disability benefits and early retirement. Today's numbers bear as much relation to those of 1975 as a Morris Marina of that year does to a modern car.

What caught my eye was the fact that for the first time in nearly 30 years, there are more job vacancies than there are unemployed people to fill them. There are 390,000 officially recorded job-centre positions. These, according to government statisticians, account for only a third of all vacant jobs in the economy.

Multiplying the number of vacancies by three gives us a grand total of 1.17 million vacancies, which is nearly 200,000 more than the claimant count. The government's dream of a return to full employment is, it seems, merely a matter of slotting the unemployed into available jobs.

It is not, of course, as straightforward as that. The unemployment claimant count may have dropped below

1 million, but the International Labour Organisation measure, the government's preferred one (or it used to be) stands at 1.54 million. As well as these, people there are 2.25 million others who, according to the Labour Force Survey, would like to work but are not actively seeking it.

The question is whether we now have a situation in which the mismatch between vacancies and those able to fill them has got worse. The answer is that we probably have.

One of the oddities about Britain's job market is that high levels of unemployment persist in areas close to places of full employment. There are also certain types of job for which the supply of suitable people will always lag a long way behind demand. ('Jobs go begging but not for long', David Smith, Sunday Times, 18 March 2001)

a Explain one reason why a fall in unemployment may be a 'cause for celebration'. [4]

b Why, when using the claimant count measure, is it difficult to compare unemployment figures over time? [4]

c Explain one reason why people may want to work but do not actively seek it. [3]

d Define full employment. [3]

e Explain two reasons why unemployment may persist despite there being no shortage of jobs available. [6]

6 Economic growth

In this unit you will distinguish between **actual** and **potential economic growth**. You will examine the causes of economic growth and explore some of its benefits and costs. You will also consider recent trends in economic growth.

Actual and potential economic growth

Economists sometimes distinguish between actual and potential economic growth. **Actual economic growth** refers to increases in output, as measured by rises in real GDP. In the short run, an economy can increase its output by using either previously unemployed resources or new and/or higher-quality resources.

    Potential economic growth occurs when the productive potential of the economy rises. An economy can increase its maximum potential output through increases in the quantity and/or quality of resources.

    In the long run, for output to continue to rise potential economic growth must occur. If the productive potential of the economy does not increase, it will experience a supply constraint. Figure 1 shows output increasing from Y to Y1, Y1 to Y2 and Y2 to Y3. However, when an output of Y4 is reached output cannot rise unless the aggregate supply curve shifts to the right.

Trend growth

Trend growth, which is also sometimes called the natural rate, is the expected rate of potential growth. In the short run, if an economy is operating below its productive potential, actual economic growth can exceed potential economic growth. However, in the long run an economy can only grow at the rate determined by the growth of its productive capacity, as illustrated by the movement to the right of the LRAS and production possibility curves. This is why some economists argue that economic growth is best interpreted as increases in productive capacity.

    An economy's trend growth rate indicates how rapidly it can increase its output without generating higher inflation.

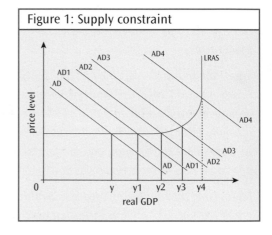

Figure 1: Supply constraint

Activity 1

Using Figure 2, decide which movement represents an increase in:

a actual but not potential output

b actual and potential output

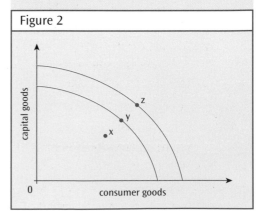

Figure 2

It used to be thought that the UK's trend growth rate was 2.25%, but the government has revised its estimate upwards to between 2.5% and 2.75%, largely because of the faster rate of advances in technology.

Activity 2

In recent years, both the British and US economies have grown at a rate far exceeding what was regarded as their rate of growth of productive potential, but with minimal inflation.

The growth of productive potential is often referred to by economists as the natural rate of growth.

What both the British and US economies have demonstrated is the simple Keynesian point that sustained demand expansion can lead to sustained higher output growth without inflation as long as supply responds and costs do not rise. ('Unnatural rate of growth', Tony Thirlwall, The Guardian, 6 November 2000)

a Explain what is meant by the 'rate of growth of productive potential' of an economy.

b Illustrate how demand expansion can lead to higher output 'as long as supply responds and costs do not rise'.

Causes of economic growth

In the short run, if an economy has unused resources, output can rise because of an increase in aggregate demand. Figure 3 uses an aggregate demand and aggregate supply diagram with a production possibility curve to illustrate output rising as an economy moves towards its productive capacity.

Increases in aggregate demand may themselves stimulate increases in long run aggregate supply. This is important, because for output to continue to increase, the productive potential of the economy must grow. A rise in investment will first increase aggregate demand and then, as the capital is put to use, long run aggregate supply. An increase in consumption,

especially if it is steady and sustained, may stimulate firms to undertake more investment. Higher government spending on education, training and research and development can also increase both aggregate demand and LRAS – in the latter case by raising productivity.

Increases in investment, technological progress and education and training are thought to be particularly important in raising a country's productive potential and so its ability to experience economic growth.

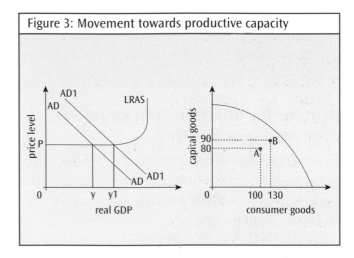

Figure 3: Movement towards productive capacity

For example, if firms buy more capital equipment than is wearing out, there will be additions to the country's capital stock (**net investment**). Even if firms just replace worn-out capital equipment, maximum potential output will increase if the new capital equipment embodies advanced technology.

As well as improving the productivity of machinery, technological progress can result in the development of new capital equipment, new methods of production, better organisation of resources, new consumer products and more efficient systems of transport and communications.

Having better capital equipment will not increase output unless workers have the skills to make the best use of it. So investment in **human capital**, by increasing the quantity and quality of education and training, is an important factor in improving labour productivity and generating economic growth. A better skilled labour force is also more likely to be more productive, because it will be more innovative, flexible and occupationally mobile.

Activity 3

Italy's real GDP grew by 1.8% in 2001. This was above the average for the EU as a whole for the first time since 1995. It was, however, lower than the country's growth rate in 2000, when it grew by an impressive 2.9% largely because of a 7.5% increase in investment.

a Explain what is meant by an increase in real GDP.

b Using an aggregate demand and supply diagram, explain why the Italian economy grew in 2000.

Reasons for differences in countries' economic growth rates

Economies grow at different rates. Some developing countries have low economic growth rates, but so do some industrialised countries. If the exact combination of factors needed for a good, steady and sustainable growth rate were known, far more countries would be likely to achieve what they regard as a satisfactory growth rate. As already indicated, capital, investment, technological progress and investment in human capital are thought to be important factors. Poor countries find it difficult to achieve high levels of investment because most of their resources have to be devoted to producing basic necessities.

Other influential factors include the following.

- **Stability.** Stable growth of aggregate demand and the avoidance of frequent changes in government policies make it easier for firms to plan and are likely to encourage investment.
- **A good export performance.** If a country is internationally competitive it will have access to larger markets at home and abroad. This will enable it to take advantage of economies of scale and provide it with the finance to buy capital goods to increase its productive capacity.

- **Low international debt.** Many developing countries have a high level of international debt. Paying interest on loans reduces their ability to spend money on, for example, education and health care.
- **Willingness to change.** Many developing countries are willing to accept change and are able to copy technology developed in other countries. When a country achieves a high level of output there may be more resistance to changing legal, educational and working practices. Countries such as the USA and UK, which are at the forefront of technological advances, are often unable to take advantage of research and development carried out in other countries.

Activity 4

Investment in human capital is increasing in Egypt, but it is still significantly below that in industrialised countries. For example, 81% of boys and 80% of girls attend primary school; 80% of boys but only 68% of girls go to secondary school. There are 4 million children aged between 9 and 13 who are illiterate and out of school.

a Explain what is meant by investment in human capital.

b Explain the effect an increase in Egyptian government spending would be likely to have on Egyptian output.

Benefits of economic growth

Many poor countries are desperate to increase their output in order to provide their populations with basic necessities. Economic growth can transform people's lives. In many industrialised countries, most people have a long life expectancy, reasonable leisure time and are able to consume a wide range of good-quality products.

The main benefits of economic growth are as follows.

- Increased material standards of living. People in the UK now enjoy better quality housing, more leisure goods and services and more advanced health care than ever before.
- More choices. If output per worker rises, a country can produce the same or a higher output with fewer workers. This enables workers to enjoy more leisure time, people to retire earlier and/or more people to enter higher education.
- The ability to reduce poverty. A higher output allows households to enjoy more goods and services. It will also generate higher incomes and so, without increasing tax rates, government tax revenue will rise. Some of this increased revenue can be spent on benefits for poor people and on measures, including education and training, to take them out of poverty.
- Increased economic status and power. The USA, with the world's highest real GDP, has vast economic power. In contrast, Bangladesh, with a real GDP less than Wal-Mart, a US supermarket chain, has very little economic power.

Activity 5

In 2001 more than 40 million people in Mexico were living on an income of 26 pesos ($3) or less a day. Around 14 million were living in houses with dirt floors and more than 6 million in shacks with cardboard roofs. The country had, however, made progress. In 1991–2001, the economy grew by an average of 5%, infant mortality rates dropped by nearly a half and basic health care was extended to 99.5% of Mexicans. Families living in extreme poverty also fell from approximately 35% to 26%.

a Discuss two benefits Mexico achieved as a result of economic growth in the 1990s.

b Explain two reasons why Mexico wanted its economy to grow in the 2000s.

Costs of economic growth

Economic growth also has costs for both developing and industrialised countries. If a country is producing at or close to its productive capacity, economic growth may involve an opportunity cost. To increase its productive capacity, a country may have to divert some resources from producing consumer goods to producing capital goods. This is, however, a short-term opportunity cost, since in the longer term more capital goods will enable the country to produce more consumer and capital goods.

What causes more concern is the effect that economic growth can have on the environment and the quality of people's lives.

- Rapidly increasing output may generate more pollution, destroy areas of outstanding natural beauty and deplete non-renewable resources. This why economists and increasingly politicians are anxious to achieve sustainable economic growth. Higher output may, indeed, improve rather than reduce environmental conditions if it permits more resources to be devoted to cleaning up the environment.
- People may have to work longer hours or under more stress. In a dynamic economy, some industries will be expanding and some will be contracting, so some people will have to learn new skills and some will have to change the jobs they do and where they live. This can be unsettling and some people may find it difficult to cope.
- Having more goods and services may not make people feel happier. For example, more people now own and drive cars, giving them more flexibility in terms of when and where they travel. However, it is also resulting in more traffic congestion and road accidents and makes it more difficult for children to play in the streets. People also have more clothes, televisions and music equipment than ever before but most are still not satisfied and want more.

Activity 6

Increased car use in the USA has led to significant increases in CO_2 emissions and in cases of asthma. Cars have killed more Americans than every war in US history.

a Explain the link between economic growth and car use.

b Identify a cost, other than those mentioned above, of increased car use in the USA.

Recent trends in economic growth

Since the early 1980s the UK economy has grown at a reasonably impressive average of 2.7% a year. Unfortunately, the growth has not been steady. For example, there was rapid economic growth in 1982–88 and a recession in 1990–91, and although the growth rate was 3% in 2000, it fell to 2.2.% in 2001.

Activity 7

a Explain what is meant by a recession.

b Explain one disadvantage of a fluctuating economic growth rate.

Current issue: changing economic relationships

In the 1990s the USA enjoyed high economic growth, low unemployment and low inflation. This led some economists to suggest that it is becoming easier for economies to increase their output without hitting a supply constraint and causing inflationary pressure. They attribute this change largely to advances in computer technology and communications. These have increased the quality of capital goods and made labour more productive, and so have shifted the LRAS curve to the right. Advances in technology have also reduced price rises by increasing competition both domestically and globally. New technology is reducing barriers to entry into a number of industries and making it easier for firms to sell their products throughout the world.

However, the slowdown in world economic activity that started in late 2001 demonstrated the need to increase not only productive potential but also aggregate demand. If both LRAS and AD increase, the extra capacity created will be put to use and output will continue to rise.

Summary

In this unit you have learned that:

- **Actual economic growth** can occur as a result of using unemployed resources or new and/or higher-quality resources.

- **Potential economic growth** occurs as a result of more or better quality resources. For economic growth to be sustained, potential economic growth has to occur.

- A country's **trend growth** rate shows the expected rate of potential growth.

- Output can rise in the short term as a result of increases in aggregate demand. However, for output to continue to rise, long run aggregate supply has to shift to the right.

- Among the factors that are thought to be significant in promoting economic growth are investment, technological advances, education and training.

- Among the factors that are thought to explain differences in countries' economic growth rates are capital investment, technological progress, investment in **human capital**, stability, export performance, level of international debt and the extent to which the countries are willing to accept change.

- The potential benefits of economic growth include higher material standards of living, greater ability to reduce poverty and increased economic status.

- The possible costs of economic growth include a short-term opportunity cost in terms of forgone consumer goods, environmental damage, pollution and increased stress.

- Since the early 1980s the average UK economic growth rate has been relatively high but it has not been stable.

Multiple choice questions

1 What is meant by potential economic growth?

A an increase in the willingness of foreign consumers to buy the country's products

B an increase in the productive potential of the economy

C an increase in the population size the country can support

D an increase in an economy's real GDP

2 Figure 4 shows the growth of a country's actual output and trend growth. At point X what must be the relationship between the country's aggregate demand and LRAS?

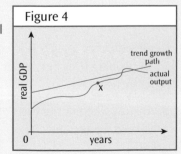

Figure 4

A AD and LRAS are equal

B AD exceeds LRAS

C LRAS exceeds AD

D AD is growing at the same rate as LRAS

3 Which of the following would be likely to result in an increase in a country's output?

A a decrease in aggregate demand

B net emigration

C net investment

D soil erosion

4 What is meant by a demand constraint on economic growth?

A investment rises more rapidly than consumption

B not all the components of aggregate demand are increasing

C productive potential increases but demand does not rise to encourage producers to make use of the extra capacity

D actual output matches potential output and potential output does not increase

Multiple choice questions continued

5 When does economic growth occur?

A when nominal GDP per head of the country increases

B when the country's population increases

C when the range of products produced in the economy increases

D when the productive capacity of the economy increases

6 Which of the following would reduce the average standard of living in a country?

A a rise in real GDP and a greater percentage rise in population

B no change in real GDP and a fall in population

C a rise in real GDP and no change in population

D a fall in real GDP and a greater percentage fall in population

Data response question: statistics and the quality of life

Why is it that despite growth in economic output, 'the quality of life for all but the wealthiest declines?'

This is the question the People-Centred Development Forum, an international alliance of economic and public policy researchers, is posing government statisticians. They are engaged in a battle for governments and official institutions to provide statistics that will illustrate more than mere economic trends.

'The world's brightest economists maintain our national accounting systems with a calculator that has a plus key but no minus key,' jokes a report from the Foundation for the Economics of Sustainability, the Dublin-based pressure group for 'sustainable economic systems'. The joke is employed to make the point that there is 'no way of knowing whether the costs of economic growth have exceeded the benefits'.

Gross domestic product, the most visible economic statistic, is the sum of an economy's money transactions, but it has no regard for broader economic health or welfare.

Critics identify a number of problems with mainstream data:

- *Resource depletion is ignored. GDP rises when an environmental asset is consumed and turned into an income flow but no negative adjustment is made for depletion of a non-renewable resource.*

- *The environmental impact of activity is ignored. Pollution often boosts 'growth' – an oil tanker journey will contribute more to GDP if there is an oil spill and additional resources are brought in to clean up.*

- *There is no allowance for welfare. Productivity gains could be reflected in either increased output or more leisure time. Only the former would boost 'growth' as increased leisure, less stress or improved health have no value in GDP.*

('Statistics may not add up in quality of life test', Simon Briscoe, Financial Times, *16 August 2001)*

a Explain two benefits of economic growth. [4]

b Explain what effect an increase in pollution may have on:
  i real GDP [3]
  ii the quality of people's lives [2]

c Describe two factors that could improve the quality of people's lives but would not cause real GDP to increase. [4]

d Discuss whether the costs of economic growth always exceed the benefits. [7]

7 Inflation

In this unit you will examine the main causes and consequences of inflation. You will consider recent trends in UK inflation.

Cost-push inflation

The causes of inflation can be divided into two main categories: cost-push and demand-pull. **Cost-push inflation** occurs when the price level is pushed up by sustained increases in the costs of production which are independent of changes in aggregate demand. Higher costs of production cause the aggregate supply curve to shift to the left and the price level to rise (see Figure 1).

Inflation will occur if the rise in the costs of production causes a series of rises in the price level. For example, if wages rise at a faster rate than productivity, firms' costs of production will increase. To cover these higher costs, firms are likely to raise the prices they charge. The price level will then rise and set off a period of inflation, with workers seeking to gain further increases in wages to cover the increased cost of living.

Other causes of cost-push inflation include the following.

- Increases in raw materials costs. A fall in the exchange rate would push up the price of imported raw materials. A decrease in the supply of raw materials, as a result, for example, of a poor crop or the action of producers to restrict supply, would raise the costs of production. Several times in recent decades cost-push inflation has been initiated by the actions of the international cartel OPEC (Organisation of Petroleum Exporting Countries) in restricting the supply of oil.
- Increases in profit margins. One way firms with market power may seek to increase their profit margins is to raise the prices they charge, independent of changes in consumer demand. This may provoke a series of further rises as workers seek to maintain their real wages.
- Increases in indirect taxes. Rises in VAT, for example, can force up firms' costs of production and so push up the general price level.

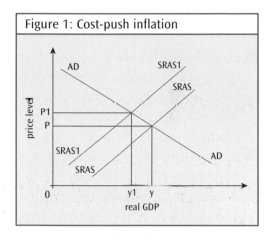

Figure 1: Cost-push inflation

Activity 1

In April 2000 Eddie George, governor of the Bank of England, warned of the threat to inflation that could be caused by a fall in the value of the pound. Speaking to the British Chambers of Commerce annual conference in London, he said that if the pound fell it might be difficult to slow the economy to a sustainable rate.

Explain how a fall in the value of the pound could:

a cause inflation

b lead the economy to grow at an unsustainable rate

Demand-pull inflation

Demand-pull inflation occurs when the price level is pulled up by increases in aggregate demand taking place when the economy is at or close to its maximum capacity. Figure 2 shows the price level rising from P to P1 when aggregate demand rises from AD to AD1.

When an economy is at its maximum capacity with all its resources employed, any increases in aggregate demand will be purely inflationary, as illustrated in Figure 3.

Demand-pull inflation can be initiated in various ways.

- A consumer boom. When confidence is high about future economic prospects, households tend to increase their spending. In an attempt to meet the higher aggregate demand, firms compete for resources, driving up costs of production and the price level.
- An increase in government spending and net exports. A government, in an attempt to raise economic output, may increase its spending. This will be inflationary if the extra spending is based on an overestimate of the gap between actual and potential output, or if it does not generate a rise in LRAS.
- An increase in net exports. This may cause inflation if the economy is using all or nearly all its resources. More exports will result in the country having more money to spend but fewer products to spend it on.
- The money supply growing faster than output. One group of economists, known as **monetarists**, argue that this is the only cause of inflation. They believe that an excessive growth of the money supply will increase aggregate demand. In the short run output may increase, but in the long run the rise in the money supply will lead to demand-pull inflation.

The costs of inflation

The costs of inflation depend on its rate, whether it is stable or not and how it compares with other countries' inflation rates.

Rate

As inflation increases so do what are known as menu costs, shoe leather costs and administrative costs.

- **Menu costs** are the costs involved in changing price lists, labels and catalogues.

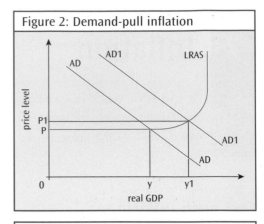

Figure 2: Demand-pull inflation

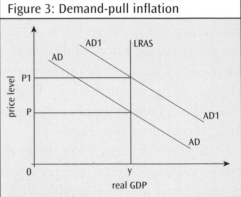

Figure 3: Demand-pull inflation

Activity 2

Inflation in the first half of 2002 was low, but some economists suggested that high consumer spending might push up the rate. In the second half of the 1990s consumer spending rose, on average, by 7% a year, but in 2001 it rose by 13%. Much of this extra spending was on so-called white goods, including fridges and washing machines, and brown goods, including televisions and DVDs. Two factors were thought to be significant causes of the rise in consumer spending: a buoyant housing market and low interest rates.

a Explain how consumer spending could continue to increase without causing inflation.

b Explain why a buoyant housing market and low interest rates would be likely to encourage high consumer spending.

- **Shoe leather costs** are the costs firms incur in moving money in and out of financial institutions in search of the highest rate of interest. During a period of high inflation, firms will not be able to afford to leave money lying idle and losing its value before they use it, for example, to pay wages and buy raw materials.
- Administrative costs are the costs of staff time and effort used in adjusting accounts, estimating the prices to charge and negotiating wage rises.

Inflation creates what is known as **inflationary noise**. People find it difficult to make decisions about which prices offer value for money. They cannot be sure whether a rise in the price of a product reflects an increase in its relative price or is just a rise in line with inflation. Consumer decisions can become distorted, so markets may not allocate resources to their best use.

During periods of inflation, workers with weak bargaining power are likely to find it difficult to keep gaining wage rises to cover the increased cost of living.

Stability

If inflation is unstable it will be unpredictable and its costs will be even higher. Menu, shoe leather and administrative costs will be greater and there will be more inflationary noise. There will also be what is known as an arbitrary redistribution of income, in which income is redistributed from one group to another in a way that has nothing to do with need or merit. For example, income will be redistributed from savers to borrowers if the rate of interest is not adjusted in line with inflation. People will pay more in tax in real terms if tax bands are not raised in line with inflation. **Fiscal drag** occurs when tax bands are not changed and income is transferred from taxpayers to the government.

Unstable inflation creates uncertainty. In particular, firms may be discouraged from

investing if they are uncertain about future costs and revenue. This will reduce the growth in the country's productive potential.

If inflation is stable, households, firms and the government will find it easier to judge changes in relative prices and to offset the effects of inflation. Households can check that their savings will give them a reasonable return in real terms; workers will know how much their wages need to rise; and the government can adjust tax rates and estimate how much it will have to raise state benefits to maintain their real value.

Comparison with other countries

Whether inflation is stable or unstable, it can pose a threat to a country's international competitiveness. If it has a higher inflation rate than other competing countries, its exports will become less price competitive at home and abroad. This will lead to a deterioration in the country's balance of payments position and possibly a fall in its exchange rate. If the exchange rate falls, inflation is likely to rise further.

Activity 3

Inflation in May 2002 was unchanged on the previous month at 2.3%. The main cause of the rise in the price level in May was an increase of 4p a litre in the price of unleaded petrol.

a Explain what would be happening to the price level if the rate of inflation remained unchanged.

b Would a rise in the price of unleaded petrol lead to cost-push or demand-pull inflation?

c Identify two possible costs of inflation.

Benefits of inflation

A low and stable level of demand-pull inflation may provide some benefits to the economy. Some firms, seeing the rising demand and increased prices for their products, may be encouraged to expand their output.

Firms may benefit from low real interest rates and the opportunity to cut the real wages they pay. When inflation is low, nominal and real rates of interest are usually low. For example, in May 2002 the UK nominal interest rate was 4% and the headline rate of inflation was 1.3%, giving a real interest rate of 2.7%. A fall in real interest rates will reduce firms' current costs, make future investment cheaper and increase consumer demand for their products.

Inflation makes it easier for firms in financial difficulties to cut their real wage bill by not raising money wages in line with inflation. In the absence of inflation, firms could cut their wage costs only by reducing workers' money wages, which workers are likely to resist, or reducing employment, which would have adverse effects.

Activity 4

Which of the following would reduce any possible adverse effects of inflation?

a its rate is stable

b it is possible to predict its rate

c its rate is above that of its international competitors

d its rate is above 10%

Recent trends in inflation

In recent years inflation has fallen to a low and stable level. As measured by the RPI, it averaged 11.4% in the 1980s and 4.1% in the 1990s, but it was 2.9% in 2000 and 1.8% in 2001.

Inflationary pressures have fallen for several reasons.

- Technological advances. These are reducing costs of production and removing barriers to entry into a number of industries.
- **Globalisation.** Improved communication and the reduction in trade barriers is increasing world competitive pressures.
- The experience of low inflation. Households and firms no longer expect high inflation so they are not acting in ways which would cause inflation. People are not seeking to bring purchases forward or pressing for high wage rises just to maintain real wages. Firms are not

raising prices purely in the expectation that their costs will rise.

- The high value of the pound at the start of the 2000s. This kept down the cost of imported raw materials and finished products and increased competitive pressure on UK producers to keep their prices low.

Current issue: the dangers of deflation

In the 1970s, 1980s and the first half of the 1990s economists focused their attention on the risks posed by inflation. With falling inflation in the second half of the 1990s and the experience of Japan, attention shifted to the dangers of deflation.

Deflation is a sustained fall in the general price level. Falling prices can result in various economic problems.

- A decline in output. Consumers may postpone some of their purchases, believing they will be cheaper in the future. Firms experiencing declines in their orders are likely to reduce output, investment and employment. This may lead to a downward spiral of economic activity, with lower employment reducing aggregate demand further.
- A decline in firms' ability to invest. During deflation people often switch from holding shares, which may fall in value because of declining demand for products, to holding cash and bank deposits, which will be rising in real value. Firms that find it difficult to raise the finance to invest by selling shares may have to forgo some profitable investment opportunities.
- Deflationary noise. Consumers and producers may misread price signals, resulting in wrong decisions being made and inefficiency.
- Deflationary expectations. If these are firmly held, it can be difficult for a government to stimulate economic activity. For instance, it may reduce the rate of interest in a bid to increase consumption and investment. However, this may have little effect if households and firms are pessimistic about the future.

Summary

In this unit you have learned that:

- The two main causes of inflation are cost-push and demand-pull.

- **Cost-push inflation** can occur because of increases in wage rates above productivity increases, higher raw material costs caused by reductions in supply or a fall in the exchange rate, firms raising profit margins and increases in indirect taxes.

- **Demand-pull inflation** can be initiated by a consumer boom, increases in government spending, net exports or, according to **monetarists**, an excessive growth of the money supply.

- The significance of the costs of inflation depends on the rate of inflation, whether it can be predicted with some certainty and how it compares with other countries' inflation rates.

- The costs of inflation include **menu costs**, **shoe leather costs**, administrative costs, **inflationary noise**, an arbitrary redistribution of income, uncertainty and a reduction in international price competitiveness.

- Possible benefits of low and stable inflation include increased producer optimism, low real interest rates and the ability to lower wage costs without reducing employment.

- In recent years UK inflation has been low because of advances in technology, **globalisation**, reduced expectations of inflation and the high value of the pound.

Multiple choice questions

1 Which of the following could cause inflation?
A an increase in the exchange rate
B an increase in raw material costs
C a decrease in net exports
D a decrease in consumption

2 Which of the following is a possible cause of cost-push inflation?
A an increase in the money supply
B an increase in bank lending
C a fall in labour productivity
D a decrease in corporation tax

3 Which of the following is a likely consequence of inflation?
A a reduction in the nominal rate of interest
B a redistribution of income from the government to taxpayers
C a redistribution of income from borrowers to lenders
D an increase in administrative costs

4 A country has a nominal interest rate of 8% and an inflation rate of 2%. What is its real rate of interest?
A 2%
B 4%
C 6%
D 10%

5 Which of the following must occur if a country's price level rises?
A a fall in the value of money
B a decline in the volume of exports sold
C an increase in real wages
D an increase in the real burden of taxation

6 Which of the following is a possible benefit of a low rate of demand-pull inflation?
A an arbitrary redistribution of income
B a rise in the value of money
C an absence of menu costs
D a stimulus to production

Data response question: the death of inflation?

Government figures show there are reasons to be cautious about declaring inflation dead and buried. There is a striking disparity between the inflation rate for internationally traded goods, where prices are down by 0.3% over the past year, and that for services, now rising at 4.1%.

Audiovisual equipment is 11% cheaper than a year ago, but foreign holidays are up 7%. Booming retail sales, the seemingly insatiable appetite of consumers for credit and the strength of house prices support the thesis that higher inflation is an accident waiting to happen. All the recent evidence, however, is that the Britain of 2002 is operating in a very different climate from that of 1973 or 1988.

Globalisation has added an extra dimension, with prices of manufactured goods in the west now strongly affected by goods provided from newly industrialised countries in Asia.

Slow growth in the west means commodity prices are under serious downward pressure, reflected in the 13% fall in the cost of petrol and oil in Britain over the past year.

Finally, there have been some factors specific to the UK. The Bank of England has cut interest rates aggressively to ensure the economy does not slide into recession, and these reductions feed through into the headline inflation rate.

The Bank's action means that Britain is expected to be the fastest growing economy in the group of industrialised nations, the G7, in 2001 and 2002 – which has attracted capital into London, keeping the value of the pound up and the cost of imports down.

Will inflation stay low? If the world economy recovers strongly, if the pound falls and if consumers keep spending at breakneck speed, it may not. But these are big ifs in a world awash with spare capacity. Low inflation is here to stay. ('Analysis', Larry Elliott, The Guardian, *16 January 2002)*

a Explain one advantage that would arise from inflation being 'dead'. [3]

b Discuss one cause of demand-pull inflation referred to in the passage. [4]

c Discuss one cause of the recent low level of inflation mentioned in the passage. [3]

d Explain why a fall in the rate of interest may stimulate economic growth. [5]

e Using an aggregate demand and aggregate supply diagram, explain why the existence of spare capacity is likely to reduce inflationary pressure. [5]

8 Unemployment

In this unit you will consider why some people may be out of work while there are job vacancies. You will examine the causes and consequences of unemployment and look at recent trends in unemployment.

Causes of unemployment

New classical economists believe that the economy operates in the long run at full employment, with the total demand for labour equalling the total supply of labour. Full employment does not mean that no one is unemployed. It means that everyone who is willing and able to work at the going wage rate has a job.

People who are out of work, new classical economists argue, are those unwilling to work, between jobs or unable to work. They also argue that there is likely to be some voluntary unemployment; for example, some people are prepared to live on jobseeker's allowance and do not actively seek employment.

New classical economists think that there can be frictional unemployment and structural unemployment.

Frictional unemployment arises when people are between jobs or seeking their first job. It is caused by imperfect information in the labour market, which means that it takes time to match job applicants to vacancies. It can be subdivided into three main types: search, casual and seasonal.

- Search unemployment occurs when people who are out of work do not accept the first job on offer but look for one with better pay or prospects. Sometimes the term is applied to frictional unemployment as a whole.
- Casual unemployment occurs when people are regularly out of work between periods of employment, for example actors, builders and supply teachers.
- Seasonal unemployment occurs when people are out of work because demand for what they produce falls at certain times of the year. For example, some people working in tourism may be unemployed in the winter months.

Structural unemployment is a more long-term problem and arises when changes in the pattern of demand and supply alter the structure of the economy. People are out of work because there is a mismatch between their skills and the skills required in the job vacancies. The unemployment continues because of the geographical and occupational immobility of labour.

Structural unemployment can also be divided into three main types: technological, regional and international.

- Technological unemployment arises from the introduction of new technology. For example, advances in telephone and internet banking have reduced the number of jobs in banking.
- Regional unemployment occurs when declining industries are concentrated in particular areas of the country. For example,

the decline in shipbuilding reduced employment in Belfast and the Upper Clyde.
- International unemployment arises when workers lose their jobs as demand for domestically produced products is replaced by demand for foreign workers. For example, workers in the South Wales steel industry have been losing their jobs as more steel is bought from countries such as Malaysia and Brazil.

Keynesians agree that there is always likely to be some frictional unemployment and some structural unemployment. However, they think there is also a risk that **cyclical unemployment** may occur. This is caused by a lack of aggregate demand. When there is a downturn in economic activity, unemployment can rise to high levels, particularly if the economy experiences a recession.

Figure 1 shows an economy operating with a low level of aggregate demand. Output is well below the full employment level of Yfe.

If aggregate demand grows more slowly than the increase in the productive potential of the economy, some resources will be unemployed.

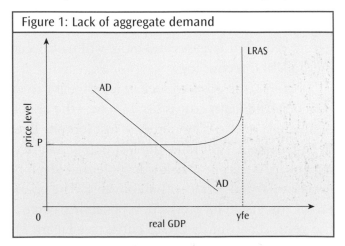

Figure 1: Lack of aggregate demand

The effects of unemployment

The effects of unemployment can be considered in terms of its impact on both unemployed people themselves and society as a whole.

Unemployed people

A few people may benefit from being out of work because it may give them time to explore job opportunities and to benefit from government training and education schemes. If they make the most of these, they may gain more rewarding jobs.

For most people, however, the costs of being unemployed far exceed any benefits. They experience a fall in income, sometimes a significant fall, as a result of being out of work. They and their families often suffer from loss of self-esteem and stress. These experiences may lead to physical and mental health problems, marriage breakdown, alcoholism and even suicide.

Unemployment can also itself cause unemployment – a situation economists refer to as **hysteresis**. The longer people are out of work, the more difficult it may be for them to find another job. This is because their skills can become rusty, they lose the work habit and they do not benefit from training in new methods, technology and skills.

The people most likely to experience unemployment lack skills, live in regions of high unemployment and come from ethnic minorities.

Society

Society may benefit from unemployment. It can create greater flexibility and put downward pressure on inflation. Firms are able to expand if there are appropriately qualified unemployed workers, and the existence of unemployed workers may make those in work more reluctant to press for excessive wage increases and more willing to accept new methods and technology.

However, the costs to society are thought to exceed the benefits. The main cost is lost output – the opportunity cost of unemployment. The output is lost forever. Even if unemployment later falls, the lost output can never be regained. As output is below its potential level, people enjoy fewer goods and services than possible. The country will be producing inside its production possibility curve and not on the vertical part of its LRAS curve (see Figure 2).

Society will experience other costs.

■ The government will receive less revenue from direct and indirect taxes as unemployment causes incomes and expenditure to fall.

■ At the same time, the government will have to spend more on unemployment-related benefits.

Activity 1

If the number of jobs being created is broadly the same as the number being lost, why worry? Simply because the types of jobs being created are unlikely to be filled by those who have recently found themselves without work. The job losses are in the main high tech, the job creations mainly retail, with a little bit of construction and public sector employment thrown in for good measure.

Someone who has earned his living making mobile phones, installing fibre optic cables or fixing computers is unlikely to have either the skills or the inclination to fill the numerous retail jobs being created round the country. Neither will he or she be qualified to nurse, to teach or to take up many of the other public sector vacancies on offer. ('Plenty of jobs, not for the jobless', Lea Paterson, The Times, *20 August 2001)*

a Is the unemployment discussed in the extract frictional, structural or cyclical? Explain your answer.

b Explain what would cause an increase in public sector employment.

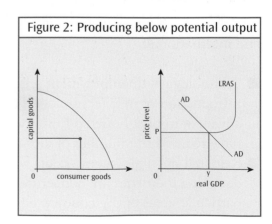

Figure 2: Producing below potential output

There is likely to be an increased burden on the NHS and social services caused by the adverse effects of unemployment on health and relationships.

There is evidence of a link between unemployment and crime, particularly in the case of young men. When people are out of work, some may become alienated from society and resort to crime to increase their income and self-esteem.

Recent trends

Unemployment in the UK was high in the 1980s. It fell at the end of the 1980s and then rose as the country entered a period of recession at the start of the 1990s.

From 1993 to the early 2000s unemployment fell steadily, reaching full employment levels, as measured by the claimant count. A large part of the remaining unemployment was thought to be frictional and structural.

Current issue: economic inactivity

Although UK unemployment has been falling in recent years, economists are concerned about the relatively high numbers of people, particularly men, who are economically inactive. These are people of working age who are not working and not seeking employment. They include those with a long-term illness, full-time students, family carers, those who have retired early and those who regard themselves as discouraged workers.

Between 1975 and 1998 the proportion of men of working age neither working nor unemployed increased from 2.6% to 13.2%. This rise in inactivity has been greatest among unqualified and unskilled men. In 2000, nearly one-third of unskilled men with no qualifications were inactive. Many of these were claiming disability benefit, which pays more than jobseeker's allowance.

If some of the economically inactive people would like a job, even though they are not actively seeking it, the claimant count and ILO measures may give a misleading picture of the extent of unemployment.

Activity 2

Paul Hughes (not his real name) is still trying to pluck up the courage to tell his children the bad news. On Good Friday, Hughes was made redundant and the timing, with his family moving home, was far from ideal. 'The hardest bit was telling my wife. And we haven't told the kids yet because they would get too upset.' Hughes, 39, was earning £100,000 a year as manager of European operations for a London-based broker but, for some time, had been nervous about his future. He says: 'I have enough money for six months and then I will start to panic.' ('How safe is your job', Kirstie Hamilton and John O'Donnell, Sunday Times, 22 April 2001)

a Discuss two disadvantages Paul Hughes is likely to experience as a result of losing his job.

b What evidence is there that Paul Hughes might have been experiencing search unemployment?

Activity 3

In July 2000 unemployment in the UK, using the claimant count measure, fell to 3.7%, its lowest level since November 1975. The ILO measure fell by 91,000 to 1.62 million in the three months to June, taking it down to 5.5%. Employment rose by 106,000 over the same period to a record level of 27.93 million.

a Explain how the number of people in employment can rise by more than the fall in unemployment.

b Explain two benefits of a fall in unemployment.

Summary

In this unit you have learned that:

- Economists agree that unemployment can be frictional or structural. Keynesians think that an economy may also experience cyclical unemployment.

- **Frictional unemployment** arises when workers are between jobs. Some people may spend time searching for a good job, some may be out of work during particular seasons and some may regularly experience periods of unemployment.

- **Structural unemployment** usually lasts longer than frictional unemployment. It occurs when there are changes in the structure of the economy caused by changes in demand and supply conditions, including technological advances, the decline of industries and an increase in competitiveness of foreign products.

- **Cyclical unemployment** is caused by a lack of aggregate demand and can be on a large scale.

- The costs people experience as a result of being unemployed include loss of income and self-esteem, stress, and physical and mental ill health. The longer they are out of work, the more difficulty they are likely to experience in finding another job.

- The main cost to society of unemployment is lost output. Other costs include loss of government tax revenue, the need for increased government expenditure and increased crime.

- Unemployment fell from 1993 to the early 2000s, when it reached the full employment level.

Multiple choice questions

1 Steelworkers are made redundant as a result of the closure of steelworks. This is an example of:
A cyclical unemployment
B frictional unemployment
C structural unemployment
D voluntary unemployment

2 What is the main cause of frictional unemployment?
A lack of information
B lack of aggregate demand
C structural change
D technological change

3 What is the main cost to society of unemployment?
A lost output
B lower tax rates
C lower productivity
D reduced burden on the NHS

4 Shop assistants are made redundant as a result of the country entering a recession. This is an example of:
A cyclical unemployment
B frictional unemployment
C search unemployment
D structural unemployment

5 The chances of gaining another job fall the longer people are out of work. Which of the following is not a reason for this?
A the minimum wage they are prepared to accept rises
B they start to lose the work habit
C their skills become out of date
D their confidence falls

6 Which of the following is a benefit of a fall in unemployment?
A a fall in aggregate demand
B a move to the left inside the production possibility curve
C an increase in crime detection rates
D an increase in government tax revenue

Data response question: falling unemployment

After climbing above 3 million in the mid-80s and almost reaching the 3 million mark again in the early 90s, the claimant count has fallen steadily. It is now 1,051,000. Unemployment is 3.6%. An alternative measure, the labour force survey, which uses availability and searching for work to calculate those who are jobless, has dropped slightly less spectacularly to 1.58 million – 5.3% of the workforce.

Another way of assessing the state of the labour market is by looking at the number of people with jobs. Here, the recent improvement has also been impressive, with a record 28 million in work. The employment rate (the proportion of all those of working age, including students, who are in jobs) is close to 75% – close to its all-time high in the early 70s.

But if some parts of the country already enjoy full-employment, there are pockets left untouched by growth. Tower Hamlets, for example, Liverpool and Sefton and Glasgow. The inner cities remain employment black spots along with remote rural areas such as the Scottish highlands and islands and resorts such as Thanet and Brighton. Full employment in such areas will depend on action being taken to counteract the forces making work harder to find, including age and racial discrimination. White applicants for jobs are three times more likely to get an interview than people from Asian backgrounds with equivalent qualifications and five times more likely than black people.' ('It's working', Larry Elliott, The Guardian, 17 October 2000)

a Describe what happened to unemployment between 1985 and 2000. [3]

b Define what is meant by the employment rate. [2]

c Explain how unemployment can exist when a country is described as having full employment. [5]

d Explain why unemployment may exist in one region while there are vacancies in other regions. [5]

e Discuss whether the passage suggests that the costs of unemployment are evenly spread. [3]

9 Balance of payments

In this unit you will examine the causes and consequences of a current account deficit and a financial account disequilibrium. You will consider what can cause a current account surplus and a financial account surplus, and look at recent trends in the UK's balance of payments position. You will also consider the significance of deficits.

Balance of payments disequilibrium

An imbalance can occur on any part of the balance of payments. For example, there will be a surplus on the financial account if the value of investment into the country exceeds the value of the country's investment abroad. Most attention, however, focuses on the causes and consequences of an imbalance on the current account, particularly a current account deficit.

The causes of a current account deficit

A country's current account might move into a deficit or a larger deficit for various reasons.

■ A rise in the exchange rate. This will cause the price of the country's exports to rise (in terms of foreign currencies) and the price of imports to fall (in terms of the domestic currency). If demand for its exports is elastic, the country will experience a fall in its export revenue, and if demand for its imports is elastic, it will spend more abroad.

- A rise in the inflation rate and a decline in labour productivity. Both will adversely affect the country's international price competitiveness. Demand for its exports is likely to fall and its demand for imports is likely to increase.
- A fall in the quality of products produced. This is also likely to cause exports to fall and imports to increase, especially if there are declines in the after-sales service the country's firms provide and the effectiveness of their marketing.
- A fall in incomes abroad. This would reduce foreigners' ability to buy the country's exports. It may also mean that foreign firms, experiencing difficulties selling products in their own countries, may try to increase their exports.
- A rise in domestic incomes. This is likely to lead to an increase in demand for goods and services, which may cause an increase in imports and possibly a fall in exports if products are diverted from the export to the buoyant home market.

Activity 1

In July 2000 the USA exported goods worth $89.67 billion and imported goods worth $121.56 billion.

Estimate whether the USA experienced a trade in goods equilibrium, deficit or surplus in July 2000.

The causes of a financial account deficit

A financial account deficit arises when direct, portfolio and other investment abroad exceeds inward investment. Direct investment abroad may be thought to be good because of the strength of foreign currencies, lower tax rates, low costs of production, a ready supply of good factors of production and limited government regulations. Portfolio and other investment would be attracted abroad by high interest rates, high profit levels and high demand for loans.

Activity 2

A country has a current account surplus. Which of the following would be likely to increase the surplus?

a a fall in the country's exchange rate

b a rise in the productivity of the country's labour force

c a fall in incomes abroad

d an improvement in foreign firms' marketing techniques

e a rise in the design standards of the country's products

Activity 3

A country has a balance on its financial account. Which of the following would be likely to cause it to move into a surplus?

a a rise in its economic growth rate

b a reduction in corporation tax in the country

c an increase in the productivity of the country's labour force

d a decrease in income tax in the country

e a fall in its interest rate

The consequences of a current account deficit

A current account deficit means that a country is consuming more goods and services than it is producing. This is sometimes referred to as the country living beyond its means.

A deficit often reduces inflationary pressure as it involves a net leakage of demand and income. However, if a country could increase the quantity of goods and services it sells at home and abroad, its economic growth and employment would be greater.

The consequences of a financial account deficit

Net investment abroad involves money leaving the country in the short run. In the long run, however, it will cause more money to enter the country in the form of profits, interest and dividends (recorded in investment income).

The net outflow of investment funds may reduce potential output and employment in the domestic economy. If a firm does not invest abroad, though, it does not necessarily mean that it will invest at home.

Activity 4

In March 2002 Japan's trade in goods surplus increased by nearly 40% compared with a year earlier. This caused some commentators to suggest that an export-led recovery might pull Japan out of its long period of recession. However, some leading government officials, including the economy minister, warned that the larger trade surplus was the result of an increase in global demand and a weaker yen rather than a fundamental improvement in the Japanese economy.

a Explain how an increase in global demand and a weaker yen could increase Japan's trade in goods surplus.

b Discuss two reasons why the improvement may not have lasted.

Activity 5

Explain:

a what is meant by a financial account surplus

b the short and long run effects of a financial account surplus

Recent trends in the UK balance of payments

The UK economy has always had a surplus on its trade in services. Its investment income fluctuates: at the start of the 1990s it was in deficit, but from 1994 to 2001 it was in surplus. Trade in goods is usually in deficit, and this often outweighs the surplus on trade in services, resulting in a current account deficit.

The UK's current account deficit increased to high levels in 1999, 2000 and 2001. This worsening of the current account position was largely attributed to the high value of the pound and, in 2001, to the slowdown in world economic growth.

Although the high value of the pound had an adverse effect on the current account balance, it attracted an inflow of portfolio investment. The UK also attracted this and other investment (bank deposits and loans) because its interest rate was above that prevailing in the USA and the euro area. Foreign direct investment in the UK was encouraged by the strength of the economy. There was a surplus on net financial transactions from 1987 to 2001, with the exception of 1997.

Activity 6

In 2001 the USA, UK and Germany were the top three locations for foreign direct investment. The UK was seen as an attractive destination because of the English language, low business taxes and a good skills base, particularly in financial services.

a Explain why the English language encourages foreign direct investment into the UK.

b Identify one other reason why the UK may have attracted foreign direct investment.

The significance of a current account deficit

The significance of a current account deficit depends on its size, duration, cause and the position on the financial account. A small deficit moving to equilibrium or a surplus would not be a problem.

A longer-term deficit may be financed by a surplus on the financial account. A net inflow of investment funds may increase output and employment in the country. However, such an inflow will mean that foreigners have a greater claim on the country's assets and will cause an outflow of profits, interest and dividends in the long run.

A deficit caused by changes in income and the exchange rate may be corrected without government intervention. As incomes start to rise abroad, the country's exports should rise and its imports may fall. The existence of a deficit will put downward pressure on the exchange rate. If it falls, exports will become cheaper and imports more expensive, so a current account equilibrium may be restored.

If, however, the deficit has arisen because of problems in the economy – such as low labour productivity, poor-quality products, production of products with low world income elasticity of demand and poor marketing – it will not be self-correcting.

In recent decades, UK governments and politicians have been less concerned about current account deficits. This is largely because they believe that they are sustainable, as they can be financed by a net inflow of funds, and that they do not indicate serious problems in the economy.

Activity 7

In July 2001 the UK experienced a record deficit on its trade in goods. The deterioration was attributed to the contrasting states of the world and UK economies. Although there was a global economic downturn, UK domestic demand was still strong enough to keep import demand relatively strong. Economists were not too concerned about the deficit, believing it would fall with an improvement in the global economy and a decrease in the value of the pound.

Give two reasons, other than those mentioned, why the UK's trade in goods deficit may have fallen after 2001.

The significance of a financial account disequilibrium

A government may not be concerned about a financial account deficit because in the long run it will generate profit, interest and dividends.

However, it may become concerned if the deficit occurs at a time of low investment in the domestic economy and reflects a lack of profitable investment opportunities at home.

In the short run, a government may be happy to see a financial account surplus because it can finance a current account deficit. It may also bring in new technology and production methods and increase output and employment. A government is likely to welcome this, but it knows that in the long run inward investment will involve net outflow in the form of investment income. It may also be concerned that **hot money flows** – flows of short-term finance that move around the world to take advantage of differences in interest rates and possible exchange rate changes – may have a destabilising effect on the economy as they can be pulled out of the country at short notice.

Current issue: a high exchange rate

At the end of the 1990s and start of the 2000s, UK firms expressed concern that their ability to compete in their home and overseas markets was being hampered by the high value of the pound.

Manufacturing firms were particularly affected, especially those that had high price elasticity of demand for their products. Manufacturers were affected more than firms in the tertiary sector because a higher proportion of manufactured goods than services are traded internationally.

If export revenue falls and import expenditure rises as a result of a high exchange rate, this would put downward pressure on the exchange rate. However, this may be offset by a net inflow of investment funds. Indeed, in the early 2000s the UK was experiencing both a relatively high value of the pound and a current account deficit.

Summary

In this unit you have learned that:

■ A balance of payments disequilibrium will arise on a section of the balance of payments when money leaving the country is not equal to money entering the country.

■ The possible causes of a current account deficit include a rise in the exchange rate, a rise in inflation, a fall in productivity, a fall in the quality of products produced, a fall in incomes abroad and a rise in incomes at home.

■ A financial account deficit may arise because of higher interest rates, higher profit levels and more attractive investment opportunities abroad.

■ A current account deficit enables a country to consume more goods and services than it is producing and reduces inflationary pressure, but it means that income and employment opportunities go abroad.

■ A deficit on the financial account involves money leaving the country in the short run and may reduce potential output and employment in the domestic economy. In the long run it will generate an inflow of money into the investment income section of the current account.

■ The UK usually has a deficit on its current account because the deficit on its trade in goods is greater than its trade in services surplus and surplus in investment income.

■ The significance of a current account deficit is influenced by whether it can be financed and whether it is a symptom of economic problems.

■ A financial account surplus can finance a current account deficit, but in the long run it will involve a net outflow of investment income.

Multiple choice questions

1 What is meant by a surplus on the current account of the balance of payments?

A there is net inward investment

B revenue earned abroad exceeds expenditure abroad

C the trade in goods section is in surplus

D the trade in goods deficit is larger than the trade in services and investment income surpluses

2 Which of the following would be likely to cause imports into the UK to decrease?

A a fall in UK GDP

B a rise in the value of the pound

C the UK inflation rate rising above that of competitor countries

D the quality of foreign products improving more quickly than the quality of UK products

3 What would be meant by a deficit on the UK's financial account of the balance of payments?

A a net inflow of investment funds

B UK citizens' purchase of foreign shares exceeding foreigners' purchase of UK shares

C UK citizens investing more money abroad than is invested in the UK by foreigners

D profits, interest and dividends paid abroad exceeding profit, interest and dividends received by UK citizens from abroad

Multiple choice questions continued

4 Which of the following would be most likely to improve the UK's current account balance?

A the holding of a major sports event in the UK

B an improvement in the after-sales service provided by foreign firms

C a recession experienced by other EU countries

D an inflow of foreign direct investment

5 A country moves from having a current account deficit to having a current account surplus. What effect is this likely to have on the economy?

A an increase in its unemployment rate

B an increase in its aggregate demand

C a fall in its economic growth rate

D a fall in its exchange rate

6 In which of the following circumstances would a government be most concerned about a current account deficit?

A imports of raw materials exceed exports of raw materials

B income levels abroad are falling

C domestic productivity levels are decreasing

D the country's exchange rate is artificially high

Data response question: Britain's trade gap

Britain's trade gap with the rest of the world widened to a new record in June [2001], as buoyant consumer demand sucked in imports, while manufacturers struggled to sell their goods on world markets.

Britain's trade gap with the rest of the world stood at £2.3bn in June, as a record £3.2bn deficit on its trade in goods swallowed up a £900m surplus for the service sector. The deficit in the three months to June set another record, hitting £8.5bn.

Exports to the recession-hit Japanese economy fell by 15% in the three months to June, and exports to the US by 6%, as a global slowdown weakened demand, and the strength of sterling made British goods costly on world markets. Imports from the US increased by 10% over the same period.

The rise in imports was boosted by so-called erratic items such as aircraft and precious stones, with a £600m increase over the month in imports of aircraft from the US.

One chink of light for the hard-pressed export manufacturing sector came from the motor industry. The

number of cars made for export last month [May 2001] rose to 73,456 – just over 10% up on July last year – helped by rising output of new models.

The overall export total for the year to date is still almost 22% down on the same period in 2000 however.

Analysts expect things to get worse before they get better. 'The near-term outlook for the trade deficit looks pretty nasty, with net trade set to make a significant negative contribution to GDP growth later this year,' said David Kaye, UK economist at Capital Economics. ('Trade gap hits £2.3bn', Heather Stewart and Mark Milner, Guardian, *21 August 2001)*

a Explain what is meant by a deficit on trade in goods. [2]

b Discuss the causes of the increase in the UK's deficit in June 2001. [10]

c Discuss two reasons why UK car exports may rise. [4]

d Explain what effect the worsening of the trade deficit would have on employment and economic growth. [4]

7 The international economy

1 The nature of international trade

In Section 1, Unit 9, you saw how international (external) trade differs from internal trade and considered the advantages of international trade. In this unit you will examine the general pattern of UK international trade and how membership of the EU has affected it. You will also examine the nature of globalisation.

The general pattern of UK international trade

The UK trades with most other countries in the world, but the bulk of its trade is now with other developed economies. Its four main trading partners are the USA, Germany, France and the Netherlands.

European Union (EU) countries figure prominently in the UK's international trade. In 2001 eight of the top ten destinations for UK exports were members of the EU, as were seven of the top ten sources of UK imports.

The UK trades heavily with other developed countries because it has social and economic links with them and because they provide products that the UK wants to buy at competitive prices and demand the types of products it produces.

Over the last 50 years the UK's trade with developing countries, as a proportion of its total trade, has declined. However, this trend may change as the income and international competitiveness of developing countries, most noticeably China, increases.

The products the UK trades in are also changing. Trade is still mainly in goods, but trade in services is becoming increasingly important, and the trade in services surplus continues to grow. Manufactured goods remain the most important part of trade in goods. However, the decline in the competitiveness of UK manufacturing has meant that the country has not had a surplus in manufactures since 1982. It is, however, competitive in some goods, particularly civil aviation, computer software, formula one racing cars and pharmaceuticals, as well as business and financial services.

The impact of EU membership

As well as being an important source of imports and destination for exports, the EU accounts for a growing percentage of the UK's total trade, while the percentage of trade with Commonwealth countries, including Australia, Canada and New Zealand, continues to decline.

The EU is the world's most important **trade bloc**. It started as a **customs union**, with member countries operating a common external tariff on imports from non-member countries. In 1986 the signing of the Single Market Act moved the area towards a single market with the free movement of both goods and services and labour and capital among member countries. It is now moving towards economic and monetary union. By early 2003, 12 members had adopted a single currency.

The UK joined the European trade bloc on 1 January 1973. It can trade with other members without restrictions on its products, but it has to impose taxes on products imported from non-members. This, of course, encourages the UK to trade with other EU member countries.

Activity 1

a Calculate the proportion accounted for by EU countries in 2001 of:
  i total UK exports
  ii total UK imports

b Which part of the world was the second most important trading partner for the UK in 2001?

c With which part or parts of the world did the UK have a trade surplus in 2001?

d With which products did the UK have a trade surplus in 2001?

Table 1: Destination and sources of exports and imports 2001

Area	Exports (£ billion)	Imports (£ billion)
EU	110,832	115,538
Other western Europe	7,182	12,548
North America	33,867	35,156
Other OECD* countries	10,925	17,417
Oil exporting countries	6,483	4,003
Rest of the world	21,922	39,597
Total	191,211	224,259

* Organisation for Economic Co-operation and Development (OECD), a group of developed countries that meets to discuss policies to promote economic growth, international trade and assistance to developing countries. Here it includes Australia, Czech Republic, Hungary, Japan, New Zealand, Poland, South Korea.
Sources: Tables 15.8 and 15.9, *Monthly Digest of Statistics*, ONS, April 2002

Table 2: Categories of products exported and imported in 2001

Product categories	Exports (£ billion)	Imports (£ billion)
Food & live animals	5,537	14,304
Beverages & tobacco	4,209	4,620
Crude materials	2,470	5,928
Fuels	16,496	10,763
Animal & vegetable oils & fats	144	526
Chemicals	28,034	22,994
Manufactured goods	133,283	163,841
Other commodities	1,038	1,283

Sources: Tables 15.6 and 15.7, *Monthly Digest of Statistics*, ONS, April 2002

Activity 2

a Which EU country is:
  i most dependent on trade with other EU countries
  ii least dependent on trade with other EU countries

b How does the UK's proportion of intra-EU trade in goods compare with that of other EU countries?

Table 3: Trade integration in the EU. Intra-EU trade in goods as a percentage of total trade

Country	%
Belgium/Luxembourg	73.06
Denmark	63.15
Germany	56.73
Greece	68.55
Spain	68.52
France	62.81
Ireland	62.77
Italy	56.91
Netherlands	66.82
Austria	76.87
Portugal	77.68
Finland	55.03
Sweden	61.03
UK	55.18
EU 15	61.19

('Is it time to jump off the European Express?', Sarah Hogg, *Independent*, 28 February 2000)

Globalisation

The world is fast becoming one global market. Improved communications, reduced transport costs and removal of some of the barriers to the free movement of products and capital are encouraging international trade and the movement of firms. National differences in tastes, skill levels and infrastructure are disappearing. Consumers can, for example, buy a McDonald's hamburger and watch satellite television almost anywhere in the world, and through the internet order products such as cars and books from an increasing number of countries. Firms are locating factories, offices and shops, and also parts of their production process, throughout the world. For instance, British Airways has its call centre in India and parts of US computers are produced in Taiwan. Firms are thinking globally, using the same brand name and brand image, and are constantly checking potential production sites and their costs around the world.

Globalisation is increasing competitive pressure on firms. This has benefits for consumers in the form of lower prices and high quality, but it also puts downward pressure on workers' wage rises. Firms will switch production from a plant in one country to a plant in another if costs rise. The increased integration of economies also means that countries are even more vulnerable to other countries' economic problems.

When more countries join the EU, there will be a change in the pattern of the UK's trade. The removal of trade restrictions will mean these countries will feature more prominently as the source of UK imports and the destination of UK exports. The EU as a whole is likely to account for an even higher proportion of the UK's international trade.

Activity 3

The globalisation of production has been praised for ensuring more efficient allocation of resources and greater employment opportunities throughout the world. However, it also means that most countries are now much more dependent on the performance of the US economy. Explain how globalisation:

a   improves the efficient allocation of resources

b   makes the world more dependent on the performance of the US economy

Current issue: EU enlargement and UK trade

The EU is preparing for an enlargement, with up to ten more countries joining by as early as 2004. The countries are Cyprus, Czech Republic, Estonia, Hungary, Latvia, Lithuania, Malta, Poland, Slovakia and Slovenia.

The enlargement would be the biggest expansion since the EU was established in 1952 (as the European Coal and Steel Community) and would mean that its new borders would stretch to Russia. It is, however, dependent on the unanimous backing of the 15 member states.

Summary

In this unit you have learned that:

- The UK's four main trading partners are the USA, Germany, France and the Netherlands.

- The main area of the world with which the UK trades is the EU.

- The UK trades mainly in goods but its trade in services is growing.

- The EU is the world's most important **trade bloc**.

- Improvements in communications, the removal of restrictions on the movement of products and capital and reductions in transport costs are breaking down national barriers and creating a global market.

Multiple choice questions

1 With which area of the world does the UK trade most?

A European Union

B North America

C other western Europe

D oil exporting countries

2 What can be concluded from the Table 4?

A there was a trade surplus on beverages and petroleum and petroleum products

B there was an overall trade surplus on the four products

C there was a larger trade deficit on clothing than on road vehicles

D road vehicles accounted for a higher proportion of UK exports than petroleum and petroleum products

Table 4: International trade in a selection of commodities, 2001		
Commodity	Exports (£ million)	Imports (£ million)
Beverages	3,270	2,863
Petroleum & petrol products	14,944	9,509
Road vehicles	13,996	26,533
Clothing	2,581	9,192

3 Which of the following combinations of countries are all members of the EU?

A Austria, Finland and Sweden

B Denmark, Greece and Norway

C Portugal, Spain and Switzerland

D Iceland, Irish Republic and Luxembourg

4 Which of the following countries accounts for the largest percentage of the UK's international trade?

A Australia

B France

C Japan

D Switzerland

5 EU membership has reduced the importance of which country in the UK's international trade?

A Belgium

B Italy

C New Zealand

D Portugal

6 What does globalisation involve?

A an increase in world economic growth

B the creation of trade blocs

C the creation of world markets in goods, services and capital

D a reduction in the mobility of capital throughout the world

Data response question: the textile industry

The young women who make Littlewoods clothes at the Dressmen factory – something of a showcase in the mushrooming Bangladeshi garment industry – get less than a fiftieth of the hourly rate earned by their relatively low-paid British counterparts. Unskilled workers start on the industry minimum of 930 takas a month for a six-day week – £12 at the going exchange rate. The more experienced are on 1,295 takas (£16.80) basic. Ten-hour days are the norm.

The British textile industry is losing 2,000 jobs a week, and it is mostly to factories such as Dressmen that those jobs are going. Clothing imports have tripled in the past 15 years, overwhelmingly from the developing world, and now account for over half the clothes sold in Britain, as the big retailers and brand-name multinationals have switched production to cheap labour contractors in countries such as China, Indonesia, Morocco and Bangladesh.

The same process is happening throughout western Europe, and while consumers have benefited from falling prices in real terms, the corporations and buyers – who dictate terms to producers in the developing world – have benefited far more from burgeoning mark-ups and arms-length control. ('Textile workers build solidarity in Bangladesh', Seumas Milne, *The Guardian, 9 May 2001*)

a Explain why it is difficult for UK textile firms to compete with those of Bangladesh. [4]

b What may enable a western textile firm to compete with those of Bangladesh? [6]

c Discuss one way that the UK could benefit from a growth of the Bangladeshi textile industry. [4]

d Discuss two effects of globalisation touched on in the extract.[6]

2 Free trade and protectionism

Despite the advantages of free international trade, all countries impose some restrictions on imports. In this unit you will consider the benefits of international trade presented in Section 1, Unit 9, exploring comparative advantage with some numerical examples. You will also consider the main methods of protecting domestic industries from foreign competition and explore the arguments for and against their imposition.

The benefits of free trade

Free trade is the exchange of products across national frontiers without restrictions or special taxes. Engaging in international trade enables consumers to obtain a greater variety of products at lower prices and producers to have access to more sources of raw materials and services in a larger market.

The main benefits of international trade are higher output and higher consumption. As explained in Section 1, Unit 9, if countries specialise in products in which they have a comparative advantage and then trade, they can enjoy higher material living standards.

The concept of comparative advantage can be illustrated by using numerical examples. Two countries, such as the USA and Poland, may have the resources to produce cars and grow wheat. One country, in this case the USA, may be capable of producing both products using fewer resources than the other country. However, it will still be beneficial for the USA to engage in trade with Poland provided there is a difference in the countries' opportunity cost ratios. This will enable the USA to concentrate on the product it is even better at producing and to obtain the other product through trade at a lower cost.

Table 1 gives hypothetical output figures for the two countries.

The USA has the absolute advantage in producing both products but has the comparative advantage in producing cars. It can make five times as many cars as Poland but only twice as much wheat. Its opportunity cost for producing cars is lower than Poland's. In the USA, 10 units of wheat have to be given up to obtain an extra car, whereas in Poland the opportunity cost is 25 units of wheat. Poland has the lower opportunity cost in wheat – $1/25$ a car in comparison to the USA's $1/10$ a car. So, on the basis of comparative advantage, the USA should concentrate on producing cars and Poland on growing wheat and the countries should trade.

Methods of protection

Countries use various methods to protect their industries from the competition of other

Activity 1

a What is the opportunity cost of one television in:
  i France
  ii Germany

b Which country has the comparative advantage in:
  i televisions
  ii CDs

Table 1: Output per worker per week		
	Cars	Wheat (units)
USA	5	50
Poland	1	25

Table 2: Output per worker per week		
	Televisions	CDs
France	4	200
Germany	6	600

Free trade and protectionism

countries' industries. The most common method is a tariff, sometimes called customs or import duty. Tariffs are taxes imposed on imported products. They are sometimes used to raise revenue, but their main function is to encourage domestic consumers to switch from foreign to domestic products. Figure 1 illustrates how a tariff is intended to work.

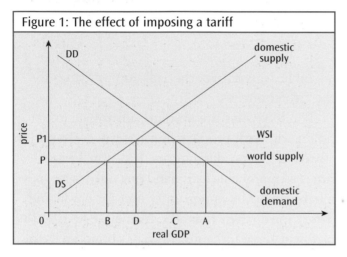

Figure 1: The effect of imposing a tariff

When the country engages in free international trade the price (P) is set where domestic demand equals world supply. Domestic consumers buy A amount at this price. Of this quantity, 0–B amount is bought from domestic suppliers and B–A is imported. The imposition of a tariff causes a decrease in foreign products sold in the home market, shifting world supply to WS1. Domestic consumption falls to C, of which 0–D comes from domestic suppliers and D–C is imported. Domestic consumers experience a rise in price from P to P1 and reduce their consumption from A to C. Imports, though, are reduced from B–A to D–C and domestic output increases from 0–B to 0–D.

Governments also use non-tariff methods, including the following.

- **Quota.** Limits the quantity of a good that may be imported in a given time period. A country may use quotas to control imports from specific countries or from all countries.

- Embargo. A legal ban on trade in a particular product or with a particular country and the harshest form of restriction. For example, during the BSE outbreak in the UK in 2001–02, some countries banned imports of UK beef.
- Exchange control. Seeks to limit imports by restricting the availability of foreign currency with which to buy them. It was ended in the UK in 1979 and no longer exists in any EU member countries. However, it is still used in some developing countries.
- Voluntary export restraint or restriction (VER). An agreement between two countries where the government of a country agrees to restrict the value of its exports. It may do this in exchange for the other country agreeing to do the same or to avoid tariffs or quotas being imposed on its protects.
- Quality standards. Some governments discourage imports by setting high and complex standards on, for instance, electrical goods, making it more expensive for foreign producers to sell their products in the country.
- Bureaucratic red tape. Having to complete bureaucratic forms and facing delays makes it more difficult and expensive for firms to import products.
- Subsidies. Government subsidies are an indirect way of protecting domestic industries. They may enable domestic industries to sell their products at a lower price than imports.

Arguments for and against protection

The restriction of free trade prevents countries taking full advantage of comparative advantage and so prevents an efficient allocation of resources. Consumers' welfare is reduced. Potential output is lower, choice of products is restricted, quality is lower and prices are higher.

However, some workers and producers in import-competing firms may be threatened by foreign competition. The following arguments support the restriction of free trade.

286

Brazil is the largest agricultural exporter among developing countries.

Increases in productivity and cultivated land, based largely on new technologies and investment over the past two decades, have won Brazil considerable comparative advantage over farm production in most industrialised nations. Production costs are lower than in the US by roughly 20% for soybeans, 50% for cotton, and between 10% and 60% for sugar.

Brazilian exports face tariffs in the US of 56% on orange juice, between 180% and 350% on tobacco, in addition to an 80,200 tonne quota, and 170% on sugar above a 162,000 tonne quota, according to the trade ministry. The EU taxes beef imports from Brazil over 5,000 tonnes at 114% and imposes non-tariff barriers on chicken, soy, tobacco, orange juice and other products, the government says. 'Wherever we increase our exports we face barriers,' says Sergio Amaral, the trade minister. ('Brazil looks to Doha for progress on fairer farm trade', Raymond Colitt, Financial Times, 6 November 2001)

a Explain how Brazil has gained a comparative advantage in many farm products.

b What barriers does Brazil face in trying to export its farm products?

To protect infant (sunrise) industries

This is perhaps the best known argument. If a country is developing a new industry in which it has a potential comparative advantage, it may find it difficult to compete with established firms. For example, the industry may have high start-up costs and may not be large enough to enjoy economies of scale. If it is protected, it may be able to grow and take advantage of economies of scale, and so become internationally competitive.

An argument against protecting infant industries is that it is difficult to determine which new industries have the potential to become internationally competitive. Another is that protecting the industry from competition during its growing stage may reduce the pressure and incentive for it to reduce its average costs and increase its responsiveness to consumer demand. The risk is that the industry may become dependent on protection.

To protect declining (sunset) industries

Comparative advantages are constantly changing. This means that there are always some declining industries. If resources were perfectly mobile, they would move smoothly from the contracting to the expanding industries. However, not all capital and especially not all labour is mobile. If an industry is allowed to go out of business quickly, there may be a sudden and possibly significant rise in unemployment. So there is often political pressure to protect the industry, allowing it to decline gradually and giving the resources time to move to other industries. The risk is that those within the industry will resist the removal of the protection.

To protect strategic industries

To ensure the country's national security, many governments protect defence-related industries that do not enjoy a comparative advantage. Most governments want to avoid being dependent on imports in case military conflicts develop with the foreign suppliers. The risk is that many industries, from telecommunications to petrochemicals, could claim to be defence-related.

To improve the country's balance of payments position

Some governments have imposed trade restrictions to reduce or eliminate a deficit on their current account. This may succeed in reducing imports in the short run. However, it may also provoke a trade war, with other countries retaliating. The fall in imports may then be matched by a fall in exports, leaving the current account no better off.

If the deficit has been caused by a lack of price competitiveness, poor quality and/or poor marketing, then imposing trade restrictions will not prove to be a long-term solution. If other measures are not taken, the deficit will reappear.

To protect domestic employment

The purchase of imported products reduces demand for domestically produced products and so reduces employment in the country. Placing tariffs on certain products, encouraging consumers to switch from imports to domestically produced products, may raise domestic employment. However, the net effect may be the opposite. Reducing foreign competition may mean that domestic firms charge higher prices to consumers, thereby reducing consumer welfare, and to other firms, making them less internationally competitive.

For example, if tariffs are imposed on steel imports, domestic steel producers may feel they can raise the prices they charge domestic car producers. Higher costs of imported and domestic steel would make it more difficult for domestic car producers to compete in world markets. If their sales fall, employment in the industry may decline, so jobs in the steel industry may have been 'bought' at the cost of jobs in the car industry. Overall unemployment may rise if other countries retaliate. There is also a risk of a trade war developing, with tariffs being pushed higher and higher in a tit-for-tat spiral, causing world employment to fall.

To protect industries from low wage competition

Some industries ask for protection against competition from developing countries that pay much lower wages. However, low wages do not necessarily mean low costs of production. The USA pays high wages but has high productivity and low production costs, because it has high levels of education and training and a high quality and quantity of capital goods. In many

developing countries, a lack of capital goods and low levels of training and education mean that productivity is low and production costs are high.

In some cases, particularly labour-intensive, low-tech manufacturing and agricultural industries, low-wage developing countries may have a comparative advantage. Imposing trade restrictions would reduce allocative efficiency and lower employment in such countries, which would push wages even lower.

To protect industries from unfair foreign competition

There is a stronger case for imposing trade restrictions where foreign countries engage in unfair labour market and trade practices. In some countries, powerful employers keep wages below equilibrium rates and working conditions are poor and unsafe. Child labour and slave labour may also be used to keep costs low.

Dumping is a common unfair trading practice. It occurs when producers sell their products at below cost, perhaps because they are receiving government subsidies or because they are willing

Activity 3

The United States was looking totally isolated over its global trade policy after the world's other rich nations accused it of jeopardising free trade with a return to protectionist policies.

A host of industrialised countries attacked the US for imposing tariffs on steel and pumping billions of dollars into subsidising its farming industry. ('US condemned over return to protectionist policy', Philip Thornton, Independent, *17 May 2002*)

a Draw a diagram to illustrate the effect of the US government subsidising its agricultural industry.

b Explain how government subsidies can be regarded as a protectionist measure.

c Identify another protectionist measure mentioned in the extract.

to make a loss in the short term in the belief that selling at low prices will drive out the domestic producers. In the latter case, domestic consumers may benefit from low prices in the short term, but if the foreign firms gain a strong market position, they may face higher prices and less choice.

It can be difficult to determine whether firms are engaging in dumping. Governments that suspect dumping is occurring may refer cases to the **World Trade Organisation (WTO)**, which operates a trade dispute settlement system.

Current issue: trade restrictions and health and safety

Health and safety standards are becoming an important form of trade restriction, particularly between the EU and the USA. The EU bans all hormone-treated beef and has a temporary ban on approving new genetically modified (GM) crops. It claims that such measures are increasing world welfare, rather than reducing it, because of concerns about potential health and environmental risks.

The USA claims these restrictions are illegal and are costing it hundreds of millions of dollars a year in lost exports. US farmers commonly use hormones in beef production and there is significant use of GM crops in the USA.

Summary

In this unit you have learned that:

- Two countries will still benefit from specialisation and trade even if one country has the absolute advantage in producing both products, provided there is a difference in comparative advantage.

- If countries specialise in products in which they have a comparative advantage, world output and welfare should be higher.

- The most common method of protection is **tariffs**. A tariff increases the price of imported products and is designed to encourage consumers to switch from imports to domestically produced products.

- Other methods of protection include **quotas**, embargoes, exchange control, voluntary export restraints, quality standards and complex customs procedures. Government subsidies may be used as an indirect method of protection.

- **Protectionism** reduces international specialisation and is likely to reduce the potential level of world output. Consumers may have to pay higher prices and buy lower-quality products, and they may have less choice.

- Despite the advantage of free trade, there are arguments in favour of imposing trade restrictions: to protect infant, declining and strategic industries; to improve the country's balance of payments position; to protect domestic employment; to protect industries from low wage competition and from unfair foreign competition.

- There are risks in imposing trade restrictions. Industries may become reliant on the protection, inefficiency may increase and other countries may retaliate.

Multiple choice questions

1 According to the theory of comparative advantage, a country should:

A   seek to diversify as much as possible

B   trade on the basis of absolute advantage

C   impose import restrictions to protect its industries

D   trade if its opportunity costs of production differ from those of its trade partners

2 Which of the following measures would increase competition from abroad?

A   the imposition of more import quotas

B   an increase in tariffs

C   the removal of subsidies to domestic producers

D   a raising of health and safety standards on imports

3 What effect is the imposition of a tariff likely to have on the domestic price level and domestic output?

	Domestic price level	domestic output
A	reduce	reduce
B	increase	increase
C	increase	reduce
D	reduce	increase

4 What is meant by dumping?

A   the removal of tariff barriers

B   the sale of products below cost price

C   the closure of non-competitive industries

D   the imposition of tariffs and quotas on developing countries

5 The time required to take advantage of economies of scale is a reason given for protecting which types of industries?

A   infant industries

B   labour-intensive industries

C   strategic industries

D   sunset industries

6 In which circumstance is the imposition of tariffs on imported products likely to raise employment in the country imposing the tariffs the least?

A   other countries do not retaliate

B   domestic firms have spare capacity

C   price elasticity of demand for imports is significantly less than 1

D   the price of imports is initially just below that of domestically produced products

Data response question: the steel industry

The fact is that Third World economies make steel cheaper than Britain does. Compared with making computer parts or designing motor cars, it is not a difficult art to master and for countries at the start of their industrial development, it offers better jobs and pay than are available elsewhere.

The West, nevertheless, insists on making steel in competition with low-cost producers and the result is more steel than the world can consume. Much more. For every three tonnes used, there is capacity to produce at least four.

The cost to the taxpayer of keeping people in unnecessary jobs has been enormous. Before it was privatised in 1988, £7.5 billion of public money had been poured into British Steel's furnaces.

A better-educated workforce demanding higher standards of living has already realised that old-fashioned industry does not provide all the answers. So has business: manufacturing now constitutes less than 20% of the UK economy and in other developed countries, such as the US, the proportion is lower still.

If government is still so addicted to throwing cash at problems, then spend taxpayers' money developing new industries – such

as the electronics and banking of South Wales – rather than prolonging the death of the old economy.

The Far East already produces many of the world's computers: now countries such as India are taking on much of the programming, data and other back-office functions from the West. The danger of hanging on to the dinosaur businesses, such as steel, is that Britain will be overtaken in the race to embrace the industries of the future. ('Better to shut down than prolong steel's dying agony', Richard Northedge, Sunday Business, *4 February 2001*)

a   What evidence is there in the passage of:

   i   comparative advantage changing between industries [4]

   ii   a misallocation of resources [4]

b   Discuss a possible economic argument for the government subsidising the electronics and banking industries of South Wales. [6]

c   Discuss the arguments for and against the government protecting the UK's steel industry. [6]

1 The nature of government policy

In this unit you will examine the main types of policies that a government uses to achieve its macroeconomic objectives, which you explored in Section 6, Unit 5. You will consider some of the possible policy conflicts and the factors that influence the effectiveness of policy measures.

Types of government policies

A government uses policies to achieve its macroeconomic objectives. It decides what its objective is, considers what it needs to do to achieve that objective and then chooses a policy instrument. For example, in 2002 the UK government wanted to boost aggregate demand and to raise the standard of public services. In his spending review, Gordon Brown, the chancellor of the exchequer, announced an overall rise in government spending of £93 billion, of which one-third was allocated to health and one-quarter to education. There was, however, concern that the extra spending would not guarantee higher-quality services. To reduce this risk, the chancellor announced public-sector reforms and new monitoring and inspection arrangements.

A government can use two types of policies.

- Demand-side policies are concerned with achieving the government's economic objectives by influencing aggregate demand. There are two main demand-side policies:
  – **Fiscal policy** involves changes in government spending and taxation; so fiscal policy measures include changes in income tax, VAT and government spending on education and health care.
  – **Monetary policy** covers changes in the money supply, the rate of interest and the exchange rate.
- **Supply-side policies** seek to shift the LRAS curve to the right and so increase the economy's productive potential.

Activity 1

In May 2002 Sir Edward George, governor of the Bank of England, said that the Bank had been successful in keeping inflation low. He also said that low inflation had helped to achieve stable economic growth and low unemployment.

a Explain two advantages of low inflation.

b Discuss two reasons why low inflation may contribute to stable economic growth and low unemployment.

Conflicts of policy objectives

In the long run all the government's macroeconomic policy objectives are likely to benefit from appropriate supply-side policies. However, in the short run a conflict may arise when demand-side policies are used. Economic growth and employment generally benefit from policy measures that increase domestic spending. In contrast, inflation and the balance of payments may be helped by measures to reduce domestic spending. For example, a government may cut taxes and increase its own spending in order to reduce unemployment. The resulting rise in aggregate demand is likely to stimulate firms to expand their output and take on more staff. However, the higher aggregate demand may raise the price level. As unemployment falls, inflationary pressure may increase further. The newly employed workers will spend more, and wages are likely to increase as competition for workers increases and unions feel more confident in pressing for wage rises. So a government may have to accept higher inflation if it wants to reduce unemployment and a higher rate of unemployment if it wants to reduce inflation.

Some measures a government may take to reduce a deficit on the current account of the balance of payments may harm economic growth. In particular, expenditure-reducing measures, such as increasing taxes and cutting government spending, are likely to reduce output growth. Other measures, such as a reduction in the exchange rate, may stimulate economic growth.

Some economists believe that the risk of policy conflicts is decreasing. Advances in technology are making it easier to increase productive potential in line with increases in aggregate demand. Also greater international competition and lower inflationary expectations are reducing the risk of inflation.

Activity 2

In early 2002 the Bank of England was criticised for keeping interest rates too high. Some economists argued that the Bank had overestimated the risk of inflation and that had the interest rate been lower, output would have been higher.

a Explain two factors that the Bank of England may take into account when estimating future inflation rates.

b Explain why a lower interest rate might have led to a higher rate of economic growth.

The effectiveness of government policies

Factors affecting the effectiveness of government policies are listed below.

- Quality of information. If the government lacks accurate information about, for example, consumers' spending plans and firms' investment plans, it may inject too much extra spending into the economy in order to reduce unemployment. It may also underestimate the

Figure 1: The risk of underestimating the multiplier effect

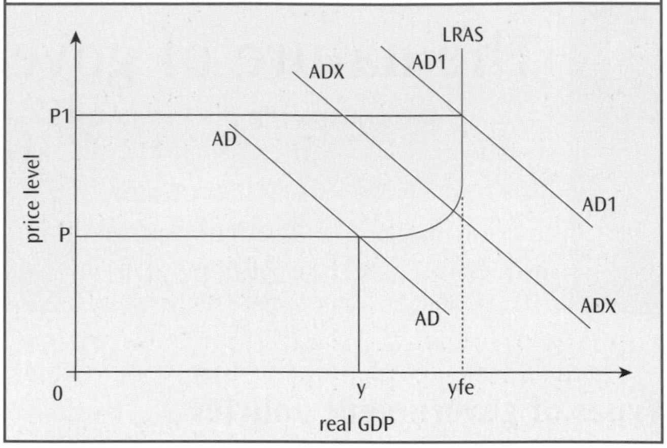

multiplier effect of extra spending. Figure 1 shows aggregate demand being initially below the full employment level of Yfe.

An increase in government spending based on inaccurate forecasting causes aggregate demand to increase from AD to AD1. There is a significant rise in the price level to P1. A rise in AD to ADX would have had a more beneficial effect on the economy.

- The time taken to influence the economy. It takes time for a government to recognise that there is a problem and to introduce a policy measure, and for that measure to influence economic behaviour. During this period, economic conditions may change, making the policy measures inappropriate. For instance, the Bank of England may decide to raise the rate of interest to reduce inflationary pressure. However, by the time mortgage and loan interest rates are changed and households and firms have responded, the economy may be moving into a recession. Supply-side policies in particular, such as improvements in education, take a long time to influence the economy.

- Unexpected responses. An unexpected response from households and firms can have an adverse effect. For instance, the government may increase income tax in order to reduce the growth in consumer spending. However, if people are optimistic about the future they may spend more, despite a fall in disposable income, by reducing their savings.

- Offsetting factors. The impact of the introduction of a government policy measure may be offset by, for example, the economic performance of other countries. A government may introduce measures to increase aggregate demand, but if a world recession occurs, the fall in demand for the country's exports and reduction in confidence may mean that aggregate demand will fall.

- Restrictions. The policies of major economies and membership of international organisations may restrict the measures a government can take. For example, the UK cannot have an interest rate markedly out of line with the Federal Reserve of the USA and the European Central Bank without generating unstable hot money flows. Nor can the government impose significantly higher direct and indirect taxes without risking losing workers, firms and sales abroad.

Membership of the EU means that the UK cannot impose tariffs on other members and that it follows similar policies in other areas, such as agreeing to keep its standard rate of VAT above 15%. The UK's use of trade restrictions is also limited by its membership of the World Trade Organisation.

Current issue: forecasting future economic activity

The success of policy measures depends crucially on the government's ability to forecast future economic activity. It employs its own economists, who make use of the Treasury economic model to make predictions. It also draws on the work of commercial and academic economists and their increasingly sophisticated economic models. These include, for example, the National Institute of Economic and Social Research (NIESR), the Confederation of British Industry (CBI) and Oxford Economic Forecasting.

Economists use indicators to make forecasts. The main forecasting tool is leading indicators. These are variables that change before real GDP changes. They include, for example, changes in consumer borrowing, changes in retail sales, and surveys of business and consumer confidence.

Coincident and lagging indicators are used to confirm forecasts. Coincident indicators are variables that change at the same time as real GDP changes. They include changes in the price level, household income and industrial production. Lagging indicators occur after the change in real GDP has taken place. The best-known are the unemployment rate and investment.

Summary

In this unit you have learned that:

- A government decides what its objectives are, what it needs do to achieve them and then what policy instruments to use.

- A government can use demand-side policies (**fiscal** and **monetary policies**) and **supply-side policies** to achieve its objectives.

- Economic growth and employment generally benefit from increases in aggregate demand, but such increases may cause inflation to rise and lead to a larger deficit on the current account.

- The development of the new economy may be making it easier for a government to achieve all its economic objectives simultaneously.

- The effectiveness of government policy measures is influenced by, for example, the quality of the information it has, how long it takes for its policy measures to have an effect, how households and firms respond, changes in economic activity in other countries and membership of international organisations.

Multiple choice questions

1 Changes in the rate of interest are an instrument of:
A fiscal policy
B monetary policy
C regional policy
D supply-side policy

2 A country is experiencing high unemployment, an inflation rate of 4%, a deficit on the current account of its balance of payments and low economic growth. Which of the following two policy objectives are most likely to benefit from an increase in domestic spending?
A balance of payments equilibrium and economic growth
B economic growth and full employment
C full employment and low inflation
D low inflation and balance of payments equilibrium

3 Which of the following factors could reduce the effectiveness of an increase in government spending in moving output to the full employment level?
A accurate forecasts
B a lack of a time lag
C an increase in foreign incomes
D a miscalculation of the size of the multiplier effect

4 Which of the following is an instrument of monetary policy?
A tariffs
B the money supply
C value added tax
D government expenditure on the NHS

5 Why may a cut in income tax by the government not result in a significant rise in UK aggregate demand?
A households spend less on imports
B households save most of the rise in disposable income
C households increase the amount they are borrowing
D government spending rises despite the cut in income tax

6 In which situation is a rise in interest rates most likely to have no effect on consumption?
Expectations of:

	wage rates	how long interest rates will remain high
A	rise	short time
B	rise	long time
C	fall	long time
D	fall	short time

Data response question: calculating current and future real GDP

In June 2002 there was a dispute over the accuracy of the GDP figures produced by the Office for National Statistics (ONS). The figures suggested that in the first quarter of 2002 the UK economy stagnated. Productivity growth had been poor, investment had not been increasing and profits had suffered.

However, economists and newspaper commentators argued that the official figures understated UK economic growth. They pointed out that rising employment, a buoyant housing market and increasing retail sales suggested a reasonably healthy economic growth rate.

Calculating real GDP involves collecting information from many sources and then processing and interpreting it. For example, the ONS has to ensure that transfer payments are not included in the income method, and it has to convert nominal into real GDP.

Calculations of current and estimates of future real GDP assist the government with its economic planning. For instance, if the rate of economic growth is slowing and it is predicted that output will fall in the future, the government may decide to stimulate aggregate demand.

a Discuss two influences on investment. [6]

b Explain one reason why official GDP figures may underestimate the country's output. [4]

c Identify the two methods of measuring GDP not mentioned in the passage. [2]

d Using an AD and AS diagram, explain the possible effect of an increase in AD on two government macroeconomic policy objectives. [8]

2 Fiscal policy

In this unit you will examine how the government can use changes in government spending and taxation in order to achieve its economic objectives. You will consider what influences the effectiveness of these policy measures.

The nature of fiscal policy

Fiscal policy involves changes in government spending and taxation. It can be used to influence the level of economic activity and to improve the performance of particular markets. The government's spending (also called public expenditure) and taxation plans are outlined by the chancellor of the exchequer in the annual **budget**. There may be a **budget deficit**, when government expenditure exceeds government revenue, a balanced budget, when the two are equal, or a **budget surplus**, when tax revenue is greater than government expenditure.

Four important areas of government spending are social security (benefit payments), health, education and defence. The government imposes direct and indirect taxes.

- Direct taxes are imposed on the income and wealth of individuals and the profits of firms. They include income tax, corporation tax and inheritance tax.
- Indirect taxes, sometimes called expenditure or outlay taxes, are imposed on spending on goods and services. They include VAT (value added tax) and excise duties.

Changes in government spending and tax revenue can result from a deliberate government decision to alter its spending levels and tax rates, referred to as **discretionary fiscal policy**, or from changes in real GDP. The revenues from some taxes and some forms of government spending – referred to as

automatic stabilisers – change automatically to dampen down fluctuations in real GDP. For example, when real GDP rises, government revenue from income tax and VAT rises without any changes in tax rates, and government spending on jobseeker's allowance falls without any change in the benefit rate. This is because higher real GDP is likely to reduce unemployment, raise incomes and increase spending.

The government can alter aggregate demand by allowing automatic stabilisers to work or by deliberately changing its spending levels and/or lowering tax rates. **Reflationary** (or expansionary) **fiscal policy** seeks to raise aggregate demand whereas **deflationary** (or contractionary) **fiscal policy** aims to reduce it.

Activity 1

In April 2002 the chancellor of the exchequer estimated that in the financial year 2002/03 the government would raise £407 billion from taxes, including £118 billion from income tax, and would spend £418 billion, of which £115 billion would go on social security.

Calculate:

a what proportion of total tax revenue in 2002/03 was expected to come from income tax

b what proportion of total public expenditure in 2002/03 was expected to go on social security benefits

c whether there was expected to be a balanced budget, a budget deficit or a budget surplus in 2002/03

Fiscal policy and employment

If there is cyclical unemployment, with the economy operating below its maximum capacity, the government may seek to increase employment opportunities by implementing reflationary fiscal policy – cutting taxes and increasing government spending.

A cut in indirect tax rates would probably increase consumption. So would a cut in income tax, as this would raise people's disposable income and so their ability to spend. Higher consumption and a fall in corporation tax would probably stimulate investment. The higher spending arising from tax cuts would have a knock-on effect and cause aggregate demand to rise by a multiple amount.

An equivalent increase in government spending would have an even greater effect on aggregate demand. This is because some of the extra spending arising from tax cuts is likely to leak out of the system in the form of saving and spending on imports. In addition, if households and firms are pessimistic about the future, cutting tax rates may not stimulate much of a rise in consumption and investment.

A government is also likely to allow automatic stabilisers to work. A rise in unemployment will automatically increase government spending on jobseeker's allowance if benefit levels are not changed, and tax revenue will fall if tax rates are not changed.

An increase in aggregate demand, occurring below the full employment level, will increase output (see Figure 1).

As output increases, firms are likely to take on more workers. There may be an initial time lag, with firms waiting to see if the higher demand will last. In the short run, firms can produce more by paying existing workers to work overtime, but in the longer run they will have to take on more workers. Employment may not rise proportionately with output, since there may be advances in technology which cause productivity levels to rise.

Activity 2

In his 2001 budget, the chancellor of the exchequer raised government spending by £6 billion and cut both direct and indirect taxes.

a Distinguish between direct and indirect taxes.

b Was the 2001 budget a reflationary or a deflationary budget? Explain your answer.

c Discuss the likely effect the changes in government spending and taxation would have had on unemployment.

Fiscal policy and economic growth

As Figure 1 shows, a government can, if the economy is operating below full employment, achieve an increase in output by raising aggregate demand. However, for output to continue to rise and sustained economic growth to be achieved, aggregate supply also has to increase. Figure 2 shows output increasing from Y to Y1 as aggregate demand rises and then from Y1 to Y2 as the productive capacity of the economy increases.

The fiscal policy measures a government can use to increase long run aggregate supply are:

- to increase spending on education and training in order to raise the quality of the labour force (although this may take some time to have an effect);

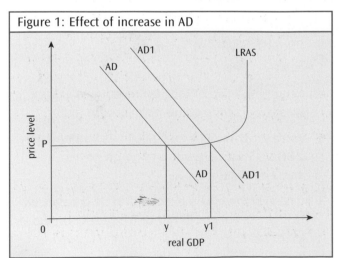

Figure 1: Effect of increase in AD

- to cut corporation tax, which, if it stimulates investment, will increase both aggregate demand and aggregate supply in the long run;
- to cut income tax rates, if it believes this will encourage existing workers to work more hours and persuade economically inactive people to enter the workforce.

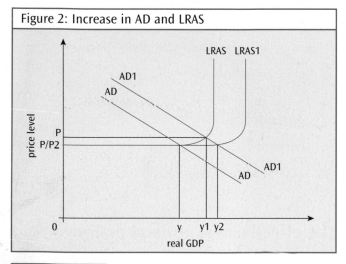

Figure 2: Increase in AD and LRAS

Activity 3

In 1963 the US economic growth rate fell, so the US government made large cuts in income tax. Two years later tax revenue increased by 2.5% and the economic growth rate rose to an impressive 5.8%.

Explain how tax cuts could increase:

a tax revenue

b the economic growth rate

Fiscal policy and inflation

To reduce demand-pull inflation, a government has two options: to reduce aggregate demand or to increase long run aggregate supply.

To reduce aggregate demand, it may employ deflationary fiscal policy, reducing government spending and raising taxes. Cutting government spending directly reduces one of the components of aggregate demand and will have knock-on effects on consumption and investment. Raising income tax rates will reduce disposable income and so people's ability to spend.

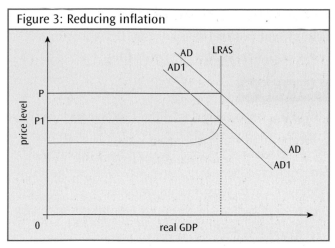

Figure 3: Reducing inflation

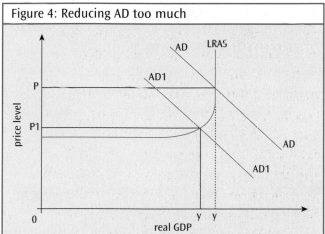

Figure 4: Reducing AD too much

Reducing aggregate demand when the level is high relative to the productive capacity of the country may only reduce inflation and have no effect on output and employment (see Figure 3).

However, if aggregate demand is reduced by too much the government will succeed in reducing inflation but at the cost of some unemployment and lower output (see Figure 4).

Tackling the problem of inflation by increasing aggregate supply is likely to be a long-term policy approach. If the government can encourage the growth of the productive potential of the economy, for example through investment subsidies, the economy will be able to sustain a higher level of aggregate demand.

Fiscal policy and the balance of payments

If a country is experiencing a deficit on the current account of its balance of payments, its government may decide to try to reduce it by using fiscal policy measures. In the short run, these could take one of two forms.

Activity 4

In 1993 Tanzania had a budget deficit and was experiencing great difficulty in paying interest on its international loans. It sought help from the International Monetary Fund, which, in return for help with loan repayments, required it to reduce its budget deficit by cutting government spending on education and health care.

a Explain the effect that cuts in government spending on education and health care would have on aggregate demand.

b Discuss the likely effects that such cuts in government spending might have on the country's inflation rate in:
   i the short run
   ii the long run

■ Expenditure reducing measures aim to reduce expenditure on imports by reducing consumers' demand for all products. Increasing income tax and cutting government spending will reduce spending on all products, including imports. Lower spending in the country may also increase exports, as domestic firms, facing a smaller home market, may seek to export more of their products.

■ Expenditure switching measures aim to encourage domestic consumers and/or foreigners to switch their purchases from foreign to domestic products. For example, the imposition of a tariff on an imported product may encourage some consumers to switch to a domestic product. Government spending on subsidies to home producers may be used to persuade both domestic consumers and foreigners to buy more of the country's products. The government may seek to raise foreigners' demand for its products by setting up or exhibiting at trade fairs in other countries.

In the long run, to correct a deficit on the current account arising from problems in the economy, a government is likely to introduce policies to increase long run aggregate supply and the performance of the economy, in particular to increase productivity.

Activity 5

Decide whether the following are expenditure reducing or expenditure switching methods:

a an increase in VAT

b the granting of a subsidy to domestic car producers

c the imposition of a quota

d a cut in state pensions

The effectiveness of fiscal policy

Fiscal policy can have a significant impact on the economy, especially when there is a large multiplier effect. It can be targeted at particular products, areas of the country and groups of the population. For instance, higher taxes can be imposed on demerit goods, the government can give subsidies to firms to set up in areas of high unemployment, and it can help vulnerable groups by providing state benefits.

Fiscal policy can influence every component of aggregate demand and can affect the quantity and quality of resources and hence long run aggregate supply.

As already noted, some fiscal policy measures adjust automatically to dampen down fluctuations in economic activity. There are, however, some limitations on the effectiveness of fiscal policy.

■ It can be difficult to estimate by how much aggregate demand will alter as a result of automatic stabilisers or deliberate changes in government spending and tax rates (discretionary fiscal policy).

■ It is somewhat inflexible. It takes time to change tax rates and introduce new or abolish old taxes. Changes in taxes are announced in the annual budget, and there is often a delay before they are implemented to give civil servants, employers and retailers time to make the necessary changes. It is also difficult to reduce some forms of government spending. For example, it is difficult to reduce the pay of teachers, nurses and doctors without cutting their numbers (an unpopular move), or to stop a large-scale investment project, such as a hospital or motorway, once it is under way.

■ There is usually a time lag before the measure takes effect. So policies may affect the economy when economic conditions have changed. For instance, during a recession a government may seek to increase aggregate demand by cutting taxes. By the time lower taxes encourage households to consume more and firms to buy more capital goods, aggregate demand may have picked up anyway.

It may take time to feel the full effect of measures to improve the quality and quantity of resources, such as government spending on education and health care. There is also no guarantee that such spending will improve the quality of the services provided.

■ It is not always easy to obtain sufficient and accurate information for the government to implement successful policies. It may, for instance, cut income tax because it believes that real GDP is lower than it actually is.

■ A measure or measures designed to achieve one objective may have unintended, adverse effects on other objectives. For example, reflationary fiscal policy measures intended to increase employment may also increase inflation and a current account deficit.

■ Some measures may have a disincentive effect. For example, a rise in corporation tax may reduce the profit incentive, and increases in income tax and/or a rise in state benefits may discourage some people from working.

■ A country's fiscal policy is increasingly influenced by that of other countries. For example, if the UK had much higher direct and indirect tax rates than other countries, it might experience an outflow of workers and firms and a fall in demand for its products.

Activity 6

In the second half of the 1990s the Japanese government switched from having budget surpluses to having budget deficits. However, the net injection of extra government spending was offset by a rise in household saving. This meant that the multiplier effect of the higher government spending and lower taxes was very small.

a Explain what is meant by a budget surplus.

b Explain why a reflationary fiscal policy may not have much impact on the economy.

Recent fiscal policy

In recent years the government has used fiscal policy largely to increase the long-term growth potential of the economy, to improve the performance of particular markets and to increase the provision and quality of state education and health care. It has tried to take a more long-term approach to fiscal policy, avoiding altering government spending and tax rates in response to short-term economic difficulties. It has introduced three-year spending reviews for government departments so they can plan ahead, and it has stated that in the long run it will borrow only to finance investment projects, not current government spending.

It has largely left the short-term management of economic activity to monetary policy, in the form of interest rates, although when it has considered it necessary it has been prepared to use fiscal policy to influence aggregate demand.

Current issue: jobseeker's allowance and employment levels

Economists debate what effect an increase in jobseeker's allowance would have on employment levels.

Keynesians argue that at times of high unemployment, raising benefits should increase aggregate demand, output and employment opportunities. Unemployed people are poor and are likely to spend a high proportion of any extra disposable income. So a rise in benefits is likely to have a large knock-on effect on aggregate demand.

New classical economists argue that reducing the gap between paid employment and benefits will reduce the incentive to work and increase voluntary unemployment.

Summary

In this unit you have learned that:

- Fiscal policy measures include changes in government spending on, for example, social security, health, education and defence, as well as direct and indirect taxes.

- Government spending and tax revenue can alter as a result of changes in real GDP and of government decisions to alter its spending levels and tax rates.

- To increase employment, a government could cut direct and indirect taxes and increase government spending.

- In the short run, a government could seek to increase output by increasing aggregate demand, but to achieve sustained economic growth, aggregate supply must also increase.

- To reduce inflation, a government may, in the short run, seek to reduce aggregate demand by increasing taxes and reducing government spending. In the long run, it is likely to seek to reduce inflationary pressures by increasing long run aggregate supply.

- To reduce a current account deficit, a government may, in the short run, use expenditure reducing or expenditure switching measures. For example, it may increase income tax, cut government spending or impose tariffs. In the longer run, it is likely to try to increase the performance of the economy, in particular to increase productivity.

- Fiscal policy can have a significant impact on aggregate demand and can be used to influence aggregate supply. Its effectiveness, though, can be limited by difficulties in estimating its effects on the economy, its inflexibility, time lags, lack of information, possible adverse effects on other objectives, disincentive effects and the influence of other countries' fiscal policies.

- The government has been using fiscal policy mainly to improve the long-run performance of the economy.

Multiple choice questions

1 Which of the following is an example of a fiscal policy measure?

A   minimum wage legislation

B   a reduction in the exchange rate

C   an increase in jobseeker's allowance

D   a cut in interest rates

2 Which of the following is an example of an expansionary fiscal policy measure?

A   a reduction in interest rates

B   a reduction in excise duties

C   an increase in the money supply

D   an increase in the budget surplus

3 A country is experiencing high demand-pull inflation. Which of the following is a fiscal policy measure designed to tackle the problem?

A   the imposition of tariffs

B   an increase in government spending

C   a rise in income tax

D   the imposition of price controls

4 Which of the following may limit the effectiveness of fiscal policy?

A   time lags

B   a large multiplier effect

C   the absence of a disincentive effect

D   beneficial side effects on other objectives

5 Figure 5 shows the effect of a fiscal policy measure. Which of the following measures could have caused this outcome?

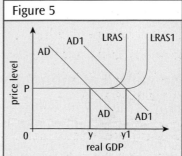

Figure 5

A   an increase in direct taxes

B   an increase in government spending on training

C   a cut in government spending on health care

D   a reduction in tariffs

6 Which of the following is an automatic stabiliser?

A   TV licence fees

B   government spending on defence

C   government spending on state pensions

D   corporation tax

Data response question: problems with fiscal policy

Fiscal policy can be used to influence aggregate demand and the long run performance of the economy. If there are concerns that economic growth may slow below its potential, a government can adopt a reflationary fiscal policy. In contrast, if there is a risk of inflation, a government may implement deflationary fiscal measures. A government may also use fiscal policy to increase the productive potential of the economy.

However, using fiscal policy may present problems. David Smith, an economist, has written:

There are long-term economic questions about public spending, which reach deeply into such matters as the optimal balance between state and private sector, and when the tax burden reaches the point where it becomes a serious disincentive.

Better transport improves the supply-side of the economy, while a health service that got people back to work more quickly would also have an effect. The effect of better education, however, takes decades to affect economic performance, while most other government spending does nothing for such performance, while requiring taxation to pay for it. ('Dangers of turning on the tap', David Smith, Sunday Times, *14 January 2001*)

a Explain two fiscal policy measures which could be used to increase aggregate demand. [4]

b Distinguish between reflationary and deflationary fiscal policy. [2]

c Using an aggregate demand and supply diagram, analyse the effect on the economy of:

i   an increase in government spending on transport [5]

ii an increase in income tax [5]

d Discuss one limitation of fiscal policy not mentioned in the passage. [4]

Monetary policy

In this unit you will examine the nature of monetary policy and how it affects the government's macroeconomic objectives. You will consider recent monetary policy and the factors that influence its effectiveness. The emphasis is on interest rate changes, because the government now uses these as the principal monetary policy tool.

The nature of monetary policy

Monetary policy includes measures that influence aggregate demand by changing the price or quality of money, such as changes in the exchange rate, the money supply and the rate of interest – although some economists treat the exchange rate as a separate measure.

In the 1980s, the main government policy objective was to reduce inflation. The main policy tool used was control of the growth of the money supply, but this did not prove successful. At the start of the 1990s, the emphasis of monetary policy switched to control of the exchange rate. The government sought to maintain a high exchange rate, but this was not found to be sustainable. It then decided to use interest rates to influence aggregate demand and control inflation. This remains the main policy tool for short-term management of the economy.

Activity 1

Decide which of the following measures are monetary policy measures and which are fiscal policy measures:

a a cut in corporation tax

b a restriction on bank lending

c a reduction in the country's budget deficit

d an increase in government spending on investment subsidies

e an increase in the country's exchange rate resulting from a rise in its interest rate

The exchange rate

A government can seek to influence its economic objectives by changing the value of its currency. To raise output and employment and to reduce a current account deficit in the short run, a government may try to reduce the value of its currency. A fall in the value of the pound, for example, would make UK exports cheaper and imports more expensive. This should increase demand for UK products, shifting the aggregate demand curve to the right. If the economy is operating below its productive capacity, output and employment should rise.

In contrast, if a government wants to reduce inflation it may raise or encourage a rise in its exchange rate. This would increase the price of exports and lower the price of imports. Cheaper imports should put downward pressure on inflation. Costs of production should fall, imported finished products should become cheaper and there will be more pressure on domestic firms to keep their costs and prices low. The upward pressure on export prices may also result in domestic firms taking measures to raise productivity and cut costs.

However, if a high exchange rate does not encourage domestic firms to become more price competitive, it can lead to a fall in output and employment. Changes in the exchange rate are also discriminatory, affecting the manufacturing sector (because it engages more in international trade) more than the services sector. It is also difficult for a government to keep an exchange rate at, or move it towards, a rate which is not equal to its long run equilibrium level.

Activity 2

In April 2000 UK export orders fell, largely because of the high value of the pound. Firms blamed the strong pound not just for the loss of overseas orders but also for the slow growth of their domestic sales. The Bank of England was reluctant to take measures to cut the value of the pound for fear that it would put the whole economy at risk of accelerating inflation.

a What effect will a high value of the pound have on UK export and import prices?

b Explain why a high value of the pound may reduce the growth of sales on the home market.

c Why might a fall in the value of the pound accelerate inflation?

The money supply

A government, through its central bank, can try to influence the money supply. For example, if the Bank of England wants to reduce inflation by restricting the growth of the money supply, it could restrict the number of notes it prints or try to reduce the ability of commercial banks to lend. To achieve the latter, it could raise the rate of interest, which is likely to reduce demand for loans.

Reducing the growth of the money supply may reduce inflationary pressure and limit a current account deficit. In contrast, if the government wants to increase output and employment it may instruct the Bank of England to increase the money supply. This is likely to increase aggregate demand and, Keynesians would argue, may increase output and employment. However, monetarists, a group of new classical economists, claim this is more likely to cause inflation in the long run and leave output and employment unchanged.

There are three main problems involved in using the money supply to influence economic activity.

■ Defining what is meant by money and deciding what to target. The two main measures of the money supply are M0, which includes notes, coins and commercial banks' accounts at the Bank of England, and M4, which includes the M0 items plus bank and building society accounts. It is difficult, though, to decide what to include. For instance, should savings accounts count as money?

■ Controlling the items included.

■ The tendency for the money supply to act erratically. In the 1980s, when the government sought to limit the growth of the money supply, it grew at a faster rate than expected and changes in the money supply were not found to have the expected relationship with the price level.

So the UK, the USA and the euro area now concentrate on using the rate of interest.

Activity 3

In the 1980s the usefulness of money growth as a guide to policy became questionable. The changes in the money supply at the start of the 1980s gave little warning of the recessions suffered in the USA and UK. In the 1990s there was a closer link between changes in the money supply and aggregate demand, but it was not consistent. Throughout the 1980s, 1990s and early 2000s there were problems in measuring the money supply and in the stability of its relationship with aggregate demand.

a Explain what relationship you would expect to find between changes in the money supply and aggregate demand.

b Why are measurement problems likely to reduce the effectiveness of the money supply as a policy tool?

Activity 4

In June 2002, after considering a range of information, the MPC decided to leave the interest rate unchanged. Some of the data studied suggested that an interest rate rise might be appropriate. House sales and prices were rising rapidly, surveys suggested business confidence was rising and unemployment was still falling. Consumer borrowing was also very high and concern was being expressed that the consumer debt burden would build up to unsustainable levels.

However, the MPC considered that this information was more than outweighed by economic growth figures for the last quarter of 2001 and the first quarter of 2002. These showed that the UK only just managed to escape recession as the economy absorbed the double shock of 11 September 2001 and the US recession.

Explain why:

a falling unemployment might lead to inflation

b low interest rates might lead to unsustainable levels of consumer debt

c the MPC was reluctant to raise the rate of interest in June 2002

The rate of interest as a policy tool

In May 1997 the government gave the Bank of England operational independence to set the rate of interest. The current inflation target is 2% or below as measured by HICP.

The **Monetary Policy Committee (MPC)**, which includes the governor and four employees of the Bank of England and four independent economists appointed by the chancellor of the exchequer, meets each month to decide whether to change the rate of interest. It first considers whether inflation is likely to stay within the target range and then whether the rate of interest is having an adverse effect on economic growth and employment.

The information the committee uses in making its decision includes current and forecast levels of employment, increases in wages, the exchange rate, house prices, retail sales, world economic growth, and surveys of consumer and business confidence.

If the inflation target is not achieved, the governor has to write to the chancellor explaining why this has happened and what action the Bank is taking to correct the situation.

The rate of interest and inflation

If the Bank of England thinks there is a risk that inflation will rise above its target level, it will raise the rate of interest. This is likely to reduce inflationary pressure by lowering aggregate demand and putting pressure on firms to keep their costs down.

An increase in the rate of interest is likely to reduce the consumption and investment components of aggregate demand. A higher rate of interest will encourage saving at the expense of spending and discourage borrowing and so spending on, for example, houses, cars and white goods. It will also reduce the amount available to spend after people have paid more on loans that have variable interest rates. Investment is likely to fall as the direct and opportunity cost of investing will rise, firms that have borrowed in the past will face higher costs and firms will expect demand for their products to fall.

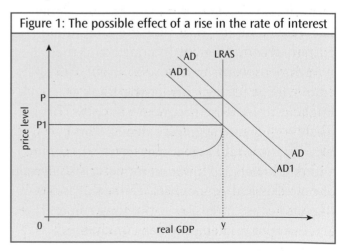

Figure 1: The possible effect of a rise in the rate of interest

A higher rate of interest may also reduce net exports, another component of aggregate demand, by attracting hot money flows into the country. Foreigners demand more pounds to put into British financial institutions, which causes the value of the pound to rise. A higher exchange rate raises the price of exports and lowers the price of imports, and the resulting loss of price competitiveness may cause net exports to fall.

Figure 1 shows the possible effect of a rise in interest rates.

Activity 5

In 2000 Poland experienced a rise in its inflation rate from 10.2% to 11.6%. This resulted from the exploitation of market power in sectors such as telecommunications, rising oil prices, a poor harvest and the imposition of tariffs on a number of farm products. In response, the Polish monetary authority raised interest rates above 20%.

a Was Poland in 2000 experiencing demand-pull or cost-push inflation? Explain your answer.

b Discuss how a rise in interest rates above 20% could affect two of the components of aggregate demand.

The rate of interest and employment and growth

If there is, or is a risk of, high unemployment and low or even negative economic growth, the Bank of England is likely to cut interest rates. This should increase aggregate demand and so raise output and employment.

A lower rate of interest should stimulate consumption by reducing the return from saving and the cost of borrowing and increasing the discretionary income of borrowers. Investment is likely to increase because the cost of borrowing will be lower, firms that have borrowed in the past will face lower costs and firms will expect consumption to rise. Net exports may also rise as a fall in interest rates may lead to a fall in the exchange rate.

The effect of the lower interest rate on output and employment will depend on the initial level of economic activity, the extent of the fall in the rate of interest, and the response of households and firms.

Figure 2 shows a fall in the rate of interest increasing aggregate demand and output.

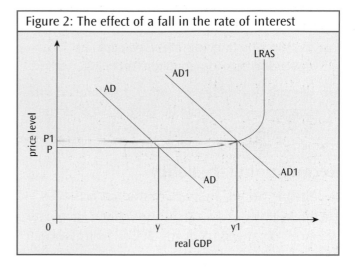

Figure 2: The effect of a fall in the rate of interest

Activity 6

In September 2001 the Bank of England cut the rate of interest from 5% to 4.75%. The move was criticised for being too little and too late to help to stimulate economic activity. Some economists were concerned that monetary policy might not work if there was widespread pessimism. In such circumstances, a cut in interest rates might not persuade firms to invest or consumers to spend.

a Explain how a cut in interest rates could stimulate economic activity.

b Why might a cut in interest rates not cause an increase in aggregate demand?

The rate of interest and the balance of payments

The rate of interest is not often used as a policy tool to correct a current account deficit because it has different effects in the short and the long run. In the short run, it may worsen a current account deficit because it often leads to an increase in the value of the currency. However, in the long run it is likely to reduce spending, including spending on imports. Even in the long run, though, it will not tackle problems caused by, for example, low productivity and poor marketing.

Activity 7

Interest rate rises could be described as an expenditure reducing method.

a Explain why interest rate rises could be described as an expenditure reducing method.

b Identify two measures, other than interest rate changes, which could be used in an attempt to improve the balance of payments.

Recent monetary policy

As already noted, the rate of interest has been the main policy tool used to influence aggregate demand. At the start of the 2000s, as inflationary pressure eased and there was some concern about the reduction in economic growth, the Bank of England reduced the rate of interest.

Activity 8

The strongish pound has helped hold down inflation. Were the pound to fall by very much and were imports to become more expensive, we would lose an important advantage. Curiously much of industry and the manufacturing unions still want a weaker pound, not realising that were that to happen there would have to be even faster rises in interest rates to choke off imported inflation.

Doubtless our exporters could live with a rise in rates provided they also had a slightly weaker currency, but what would be the effect of rising interest rates on domestic demand? ('We don't know which figures to believe but there's no hiding from a rate rise when it hits', Hamish McRae, Independent, 6 June 2002)

a Why might a fall in the exchange rate necessitate a rise in interest rates?

b Explain why a rise in interest rates may be harmful for firms.

The effectiveness of monetary policy

Problems in using the money supply and the exchange rate as policy tools mean that most governments now focus on the rate of interest.

In recent years, changes in the rate of interest have been effective in controlling inflation, keeping it within the government's target range. It is generally thought that the MPC has been successful in achieving a reduction in long-term inflation expectations. Changes in interest rates can have a significant impact on three of the components of aggregate demand. They also take less time to have an impact on the economy than some forms of fiscal policy, such as increased government spending on education or a motorway project. Nevertheless, there is an estimated time lag of approximately 18 months between a change in the rate of interest and the final change in aggregate demand.

There are other limitations to the effectiveness of interest rate policy.

- A change in the rate of interest can have adverse side effects. For instance, a rise in the rate of interest designed to reduce inflation may also cause a fall in output and employment.
- The use of interest rates depends on accurate, up-to-date information. In May 2002 the accuracy of the real GDP figures on which the MPC had been basing its interest rate decisions was questioned.
- The effects of interest rate changes do not fall on everyone equally. A rise in the rate of interest will benefit savers but harm borrowers and have a more harmful effect on manufacturers than on services firms.
- Changing interest rates may not be effective if firms and households hold strong views about future economic prospects. For instance, if consumers and firms are optimistic about the future, a rise in the rate of interest will not discourage them from spending and investing.

■ When the rate of interest is very low there is little room for the central bank to cut it further.

■ The central bank is restricted by the interest rate policies of other central banks. A central bank may, for example, be reluctant to lower its interest rate significantly below that operating in other countries, fearing that it may cause a large net outflow of hot money from the country, a fall in the exchange rate and a rise in inflationary pressures.

Summary

In this unit you have learned that:

■ The tools of monetary policy include the money supply, the rate of interest and the exchange rate. Most governments now use the rate of interest.

■ A fall in the exchange rate will generally increase output and employment and improve the current account position, but it will also increase inflation.

■ An increase in the money supply is likely to increase aggregate demand. It may be difficult to define and control the money supply.

■ The **Monetary Policy Committee** sets the rate of interest to achieve the government's objective of an inflation rate of 2%.

■ To reduce inflation, the Bank of England will raise the rate of interest. This is likely to reduce the consumption, investment and net export components of aggregate demand.

■ To increase employment and economic growth, the Bank of England will lower the rate of interest. A lower rate of interest is likely to encourage consumption and investment and may increase net exports via a fall in the exchange rate.

■ The effects of a change in the rate of interest on the current account of the balance of payments are likely to be different in the short and long run. In the short run the current account will be affected by the likely resulting change in the exchange rate and in the long run by the likely resulting change in aggregate demand.

■ Interest rate policy has been successful in controlling inflation, including reducing expectations of inflation. It can have a significant effect on aggregate demand and can act more quickly than some forms of fiscal policy. However, its effectiveness is limited by time lags, adverse side effects, lack of accurate information, its discriminatory nature, strong views held by consumers and firms about the future, little room to manoeuvre when the rate of interest is low and the interest rate policies pursued by other countries.

Multiple choice questions

1 Which of the following is a monetary policy measure?

A privatisation

B a rise in government spending

C a decrease in government spending

D a change in the growth of the money supply

2 What effect is an increase in the external value of the pound likely to have?

A increase the price of imports in the UK

B increase aggregate demand

C shift the aggregate supply curve to the right

D reduce the rate of inflation

3 A central bank may raise interest rates in a bid to reduce inflation. Which of the following is the most likely motive behind this move?

A to increase the money supply

B to stimulate investment

C to reduce consumer spending

D to lead to a fall in the exchange rate

4 An economy is operating at its full capacity level and is experiencing inflation. Which of the following policies is it most likely to adopt to tackle inflation in the short run?

A an increase in investment subsidies

B an increase in the rate of interest

C a reduction in income tax

D a decrease in the exchange rate

5 What effect would a fall in interest rates be likely to have?

A a reduction in bank lending

B a decrease in house prices

C an increase in investment

D an increase in the value of the currency

6 Which of the following would limit the effectiveness of monetary policy?

A the absence of time lags

B the absence of side effects

C the absence of accurate information

D the absence of a link between monetary policy measures and the exchange rate

Data response question: changing interest rates

Before the Bank of England was granted independence, interest rates were changed too slowly. For example, at the end of the 1980s, interest rates were doubled to 15% to control a consumer boom just as economic growth started to slow.

The risk of inflation is now much lower than in the past, partly because of lower inflationary expectations and globalisation. However, there is a risk of deflation. If consumer confidence falls as much as it did in Japan, cutting interest rates will not work.

Between February and November 2001, the Bank of England cut rates by 2 percentage points in seven stages to a 37-year low of 4%.

In mid-2002, there were signs that economic growth was recovering and that the need to keep rates low was passing. Some economists recommended a slightly higher interest rate. They argued that although this would be painful for house buyers and exporters, it would prevent the need for even higher interest rates in the future and would give the MPC more flexibility in its interest rate policy.

a Why would low inflationary expectations reduce the chances of inflation occurring? [4]

b Using an aggregate demand and supply diagram, analyse the effects of a cut in interest rates on the economy. [8]

c Why would a rise in the rate of interest be painful for home buyers and exporters? [4]

d Discuss two limitations of monetary policy mentioned in the passage. [4]

4 Supply-side policies

During the last 30 years supply-side policies have become increasingly important. Governments throughout the world now use them to improve their economic performance. In this unit you will consider the nature of supply-side policies. You will examine some of the main policies and consider their effectiveness.

The nature of supply-side policies

Supply-side policies seek to increase long run aggregate supply and so increase the productive potential of the economy. They aim to do this by increasing the quantity and quality of resources.

There are two main approaches to supply-side policies.

■ The free market approach. Favoured by new classical economists, this tries to raise productive potential by increasing work and investment incentives, removing restrictions on firms and increasing competitive pressures.
■ The interventionist approach. Favoured more by Keynesian economists, this seeks to shift the LRAS curve to the right through government intervention in markets to improve their performance by correcting market failure.

Activity 1

In 2001 the government increased its spending on training and teaching adults, especially those with poor basic skills needed by industry, by more than £2.5 billion.

a Decide whether the supply-side policy mentioned above is a free market or interventionist one.

b Explain whether spending on training will increase labour productivity.

Free market supply-side policies

The main policy measures that can be used to increase incentives, increase competitive pressures and reduce government intervention in markets are listed below.

■ **Reducing direct taxes.** Reducing income tax rates and corporation tax should raise productivity capacity by encouraging an increase in the quantity and quality of labour and capital available to the economy.

Lower income tax rates increase the disposable income that can be earned from working. This may motivate some existing workers to work longer hours and to undertake training to gain higher paid jobs. It may also persuade some of those not currently in work or seeking employment (economically inactive people) to look for work. For example, a lone parent may estimate that he or she can afford to pay for the childcare that would be needed if he or she worked.

Reducing corporation tax will increase the funds that firms have available to spend on research and development and new capital goods. It also provides more incentive for firms to purchase additions to their capital stock because they will be able to keep a greater proportion of any profits generated.

■ **Cutting unemployment benefits.** A reduction in jobseeker's allowance, especially if combined with a cut in income tax, will increase the gap between the income of those not in work and those in employment. This is particularly effective if the starting point for paying income tax is raised and the lower rates of income tax are reduced. The intention is to provide a greater incentive for those out of work to seek employment by making employment more attractive than living on unemployment benefit.

Some economists favour making the receipt of jobseeker's allowance dependent on unemployed people taking specific steps to gain employment, such as attending training sessions and participating in government work projects. Some also favour tightening the criteria for receiving disability benefit and checking more regularly that the recipients are unable to work.

■ **Reforming trade unions.** Some trade unions effectively operate as a monopoly or oligopoly. If one trade union bargains on behalf of all the workers in an industry, it becomes, in effect, a single seller of the workers' labour. It may use its labour market power to push the wage rate above the equilibrium level and to protect workers' jobs. In this case a reduction in trade union power may increase employment, labour market flexibility and efficiency.

■ **Privatisation.** New classical economists believe that firms work most efficiently in the private sector. If industries are transferred from the public to the private sector they will have more freedom to make decisions and encounter greater competition. State-run industries may experience delays in decision making, and the decisions that are made are not always based on commercial judgements. They also cannot go bankrupt, as the government guarantees their borrowings. In contrast, if private-sector firms do not produce what consumers want at low costs, they will go out of business if there are competing firms.

■ **Deregulation.** This involves removing laws, rules and regulations that restrict competition and the free workings of markets. Deregulation is designed to reduce barriers to entry and so make markets more economically efficient.

■ **Competition policy.** Promoting competitive pressures on firms is also designed to make markets more economically efficient.

Activity 2

Use an AD and AS diagram to explain the effect of a cut in corporation tax.

Interventionist supply-side policies

The main policies involving government intervention designed to shift the LRAS curve to the right are listed below.

■ **Education.** The Labour government elected in 1997 stated that its priorities would be 'education, education, education'. A greater quantity and higher quality of education should raise labour productivity and mobility and so increase the productive potential of the country. The argument for state intervention is that, if left to market forces, insufficient resources will be devoted to education and poor people will not have access to this crucial service. Education is a merit good, with some people undervaluing the private benefits to themselves and some not taking into account the benefits to third parties. If people had to pay for, or pay the full price of, their own and their children's education, some would not be able to afford it.

■ **Training.** As with education, training should raise labour productivity and mobility. It is also a merit good. Some firms may be reluctant to spend much on training for fear that other firms will gain the benefits by poaching staff. The government can provide training for its own workers and for unemployed people. It can also provide training for workers in private-sector firms or subsidise those firms to undertake their own training.

■ **Investment grants.** Short-termism, with firms seeking to earn money quickly, may mean that they underinvest. Lack of information may also mean that they invest in inappropriate areas. Government intervention grants are designed to increase the quantity and quality of investment. The government, for example, may give grants to infant industries if it believes that in the long run they will be efficient and have a comparative advantage.

■ **Regional policy.** If a country has some areas where there is a lack of workers and shortages of housing, schools and hospitals, and others where there is high unemployment and underused social capital, economic efficiency will not be achieved. Regional policy seeks to overcome this problem by regenerating depressed areas and influencing the distribution of firms and workers. Because firms are more geographically mobile than workers, the policy concentrates on providing incentives for firms to set up in depressed areas.

Activity 3

In 2000, a report by the National Skills Task Force found that 7 million adults in Britain were functionally illiterate. A year later, a report by the Organisation for Economic Co-operation and Development (OECD) found that Britain leads the world in higher education but performs badly in secondary education.

a Explain why illiteracy is likely to reduce labour productivity.

b Why may education be underprovided, even with state intervention?

Recent supply-side policies

UK, US and European governments are using a combination of free market and interventionist supply-side policies to increase their productive capacity. In the UK, recent supply-side policies have included cuts in income tax and corporation tax, a welfare to work programme

designed to move people off state benefits and into work, increased spending on education and projects to regenerate depressed inner city areas and regions.

Activity 4

The government intends to plug the skills gap with a series of training initiatives in some of Britain's most deprived areas. New schemes will pay employers who give their staff time off for training courses.

The moves are aimed primarily at the least skilled. The chancellor said, 'Thousands of employers are unable to recruit the skilled staff they need because training is so poor.'

But much of the problem is that training costs money – course fees, time off work, the need to hire temporary replacements, and employers fear that the expense will be wasted if a better skilled person moves to a job elsewhere.

A new government study, 'Developing Workplace Skills – Piloting a New Approach', says Britain has a significant skills gap compared with its main competitors 'at the lower to intermediate level. This limits productivity and hampers efforts to reduce social exclusion.' ('Employers given extra incentive to provide training', Tony Leverne, The Guardian, 18 April 2002)

a Identify two possible benefits that could arise from the government's training initiatives.

b Explain why some firms are reluctant to train their staff.

The effectiveness of supply-side policies

Supply-side policies recognise the need for a country to improve the efficiency of its product and labour markets and increase its productive capacity in order to achieve its macroeconomic objectives.

If a country becomes capable of producing more products at a lower cost, its balance of payments position should improve. A rise in the quality and quantity of labour and capital goods should raise its trend growth rate. Improved education, training and increased flexibility of labour should reduce unemployment.

Increasing productive capacity should also reduce the risk of inflation. Figure 1 shows a country's output rising without the price level increasing. This is because LRAS is rising in line with AD.

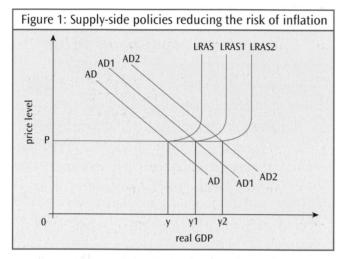

Figure 1: Supply-side policies reducing the risk of inflation

However, raising LRAS will not be effective if AD is below the full employment level. Figure 2 shows LRAS increasing but output remaining at Y.

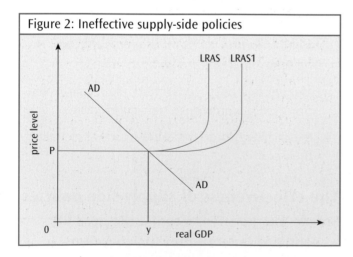

Figure 2: Ineffective supply-side policies

In this case a government would have to combine demand management and supply-side policies to achieve its macroeconomic objectives.

The effectiveness of supply-side policies can be influenced by other factors.

■ They can take time to have an effect. For example, it will be some years before improvements in primary and secondary education result in higher labour productivity.

■ They can be expensive to implement. Educational and training programmes, for example, can be very costly.

■ Workers and producers may respond to them in unintended ways. Reducing corporation tax, for instance, may result in firms paying higher dividends rather than undertaking more investment, and some workers may cut the hours they work when income tax is lowered.

■ There is no guarantee that they will work. Spending more on education does not always raise educational standards. Transferring industries from the public to the private sector does not always lead to increased competition and efficiency.

Current issue: the New Deal

In April 1988 the government introduced its **'New Deal'** or 'Welfare to Work' initiative. It has since added the Working Family Tax Credit (WFTC) and tightened up the eligibility criteria for disability allowance.

The New Deal aims to reduce unemployment by providing wage subsidies to employers to take on unemployed people, offering new training and education opportunities, helping with childcare costs and making work more attractive than unemployment.

Government policy has been driven by a desire to end the **unemployment trap**, where people are better off being out of work than working, and the **poverty trap**, where people's disposable income falls because benefits are withdrawn as earned income rises.

Increasing the financial incentives to work should encourage unemployed people to seek work more actively. Removing any difficulties they may be experiencing in finding work, including lack of skills and confidence and the cost of childcare, should make it easier for them to find work. However, if the economy experiences a fall in aggregate demand, even some motivated and skilled people may find it difficult to get a job.

Summary

In this unit you have learned that:

■ Supply-side policies seek to shift the LRAS curve to the right and so increase the productive potential of the economy.

■ Supply-side policies can be free market or interventionist.

■ Free market supply-side policies include reducing direct taxes, cutting unemployment benefit, reforming trade unions, privatisation, deregulation and competition policy.

■ Interventionist supply-side policies include state education, training, investment grants and regional policies.

■ To improve a country's balance of payments position, enable a country to grow, keep inflationary pressure low and achieve full employment, it is important that the quality and quantity of the country's resources continue to increase.

■ Supply-side policies can take a long time to have an effect, can be expensive to implement, and workers and firms may respond in unexpected ways.

■ Increasing LRAS will have no impact on the economy if AD remains low.

Multiple choice questions

1 What is the aim of supply-side policies?
A to shift the short run aggregate supply curve to the right
B to shift the short run aggregate supply curve to the left
C to shift the long run aggregate supply curve to the left
D to shift the long run aggregate supply curve to the right

2 Which of the following is a supply-side policy?
A a cut in interest rates
B an increase in income tax
C a reduction in the exchange rate
D an increase in government grants for retraining

3 An economy is experiencing high unemployment. Which of the following is a supply-side policy a government could use to tackle the problem?
A a cut in corporation tax
B a decrease in the money supply
C a rise in the minimum wage
D an increase in jobseeker's allowance

4 Which of the following is an objective of free market supply-side policies?
A to increase government intervention in the economy
B to increase economic incentives and the effectiveness of market forces
C to decrease the growth of the money supply
D to decrease aggregate demand

5 Which of the following policies would a supporter of free market supply-side policies advocate?
A deregulation
B regional policy
C reduced restrictions on the power of trade unions
D bringing privatised firms back into state ownership

6 In which circumstance would a supply-side measure which succeeds in increasing LRAS have no effect on output?
A if the economy is operating at full capacity
B if there is an equal increase in aggregate demand
C if the economy is operating well below full employment and there is no increase in aggregate demand
D if the economy is operating close to full employment and aggregate demand rises by less than LRAS

Data response question: improving productivity

The Labour government elected in May 1997 said that improving productivity was central to its efforts to raise the long run rate of economic growth. Increasing trend growth would create more jobs.

Among the measures it introduced were incentives for employee share ownership, cuts in corporation tax, capital allowances for small companies and the New Deal.

In its April 2002 budget, the government introduced further measures to make work pay for unemployed people and non-working parents. The New Deal was extended to those aged 25 and over and in pilot areas to jobseekers who had been unemployed for 18 months or more in the previous three years.

A mentoring service was introduced to provide support and advice to lone parents seeking to enter work through a personal adviser interview. All lone parents receiving income support with children under the age of five would have personal adviser interviews. Childcare co-ordinators would improve access to information about local childcare provision.

From April 2003, eligibility for the childcare tax credit element of the Working Family Tax Credit was extended to people using approved childcare in their own homes. This would benefit families needing home-based care, such as those with disabled children or parents working unconventional hours.

Further support was introduced to help jobseekers travel to work, including a £5 million fund to find solutions in deprived areas where transport is a barrier to work and an expansion of personal travel planning services in Jobcentres.

a Define:
   i productivity [3]
   ii economic growth [3]

b Explain why a rise in productivity would increase trend growth. [4]

c Explain why helping jobseekers travel to work should reduce unemployment. [4]

d Discuss why:
   i lone parents find it difficult to work [3]
   ii the effect of more lone parents entering the workforce. [3]

Glossary

absolute advantage the ability to produce a product with fewer resources than another country, region, firm or person

actual economic growth increases in real GDP

adverse selection where an insurance company does not know the extent to which different people are at risk and so charges them all the same premium

aggregate demand (AD) total spending on domestic output at a given price level

aggregate supply (AS) the total output all producers in the economy are willing and able to supply at a given price level

allocative efficiency where the appropriate quantity of resources is devoted to producing products, achieved when firms produce where MC = P

allocatively efficient output output where MSC equals MSB, also known as the socially optimum output

asymmetric information information not equally shared

automatic stabilisers forms of government spending and taxation that dampen down economic fluctuations without any deliberate changes in government policy

average cost total cost divided by output, sometimes called unit cost

average fixed cost fixed cost divided by output

average revenue total revenue divided by the quantity sold

average variable cost variable cost divided by output

balance of payments a record of a country's trade and investment with other countries

barriers to entry restrictions on the entry of firms into a market

barriers to exit restrictions on the exit of firms from a market

barter the direct exchange of products for other products

black market an unofficial market in which a product is sold for a price above its set price

budget a statement of government spending and tax revenues for the next financial year

budget deficit government spending exceeding tax revenue

budget surplus tax revenue exceeding government spending

buffer stock a stock of a commodity held to prevent price fluctuations by means of buying and selling the commodity

bundling the combining of two products for sale

business unit single workplaces such as factories, firms, offices and shops

capital goods man-made products used to make other products

capital-intensive using a high proportion of capital goods relative to other factors of production

cartel a group of countries or firms which collude to fix output and price in order to increase profits

ceteris paribus a Latin phrase often used in Economics meaning 'other things being equal'

change in demand a change in an influence on demand other than the price of the product

change in supply a change in an influence on supply other than the price of the product

Coase's theory the proposition that the extension of property rights can overcome the problem of externalities and result in the socially optimum level of output being achieved

cobweb theory the view that supply, particularly of agricultural products, can take time to adjust to market conditions

collusion a formal or informal agreement whereby competition is restricted

commodity a general term for a product or a term for a primary product or raw material

Common Agricultural Policy (CAP) an EU policy which seeks to assist farmers through intervention including setting minimum prices

comparative advantage the ability to produce a product at a lower opportunity cost than other countries, regions, firms or people

Competition Commission (CC) a government body which investigates firms which have or may gain dominant market power

complements products which are bought to be used together

concentration ratio a measure of the proportion of the total sales, output or employment of the largest firms

consumer goods goods which give immediate satisfaction

consumer sovereignty consumers' ability to determine what is produced by means of their purchases

consumer surplus the extra amount that consumers would be prepared to pay for a product above what they actually pay

consumers buyers and users of products

contraction in demand a movement along a demand curve caused by a rise in the price of the product

contraction in supply a movement along a supply curve caused by a fall in the price of the product

corporation tax a tax on firms' profits

cost-benefit analysis (CBA) a method of assessing investment projects which takes into account social costs and benefits

cost-push inflation increases in the price level resulting from increases in the costs of production

cross elasticity of demand a measure of the responsiveness of demand for one product to a change in the price of another product

current account balance a record of a country's trade in goods, trade in services, income and current transfers

customs union a trade bloc in which member countries remove trade restrictions among themselves and impose identical import restrictions on non-members

cyclical unemployment unemployment resulting from a lack of aggregate demand

decrease in demand a fall in demand caused by an influence other than a change in the price of the product

decrease in supply a fall in supply caused by an influence other than a change in the price of the product

deflation a sustained fall in the general price level

deflationary fiscal policy measures designed to decrease aggregate demand

demand the ability and willingness to buy a product

demand curve a curve showing the different quantities demanded at different prices

demand-pull inflation increases in the price level resulting from excessive increases in aggregate demand

demand schedule a table showing the different quantities demanded at a range of prices

demerit goods products which the government regards as harmful and which will be overconsumed if left to market forces

deregulation the removal of laws and regulations which restrict competition

developing countries countries with low incomes per head

diminishing returns output rising by less than resources, which causes marginal and average costs to rise

direct taxes taxes on income and wealth of people and firms

discounting technique a method of adjusting future costs and benefits to current values

discretionary fiscal policy deliberate changes in government spending and taxation

disequilibrium a situation of imbalance

disposable income income after the deduction of direct taxes and the addition of cash state benefits

dividends a share in the profits of a firm distributed to shareholders

division of labour the specialisation of workers on particular tasks in the production process

domestic trade the exchange of products within a country

dumping the sale of products at less than cost price

economic efficiency where an economy produces the products which reflect consumers' tastes at the lowest possible cost

economic goods products which are in limited supply and require resources to produce them and so have an opportunity cost

economic growth the growth of output of the economy and, in the long run, an outward shift of the production possibility curve

economic system the institutions, organisations and methods used to answer the fundamental economic questions

economies of scale lower average costs resulting from producing on a larger scale

effective demand the quantity of a product which people are willing and able to buy at a given price over some given period of time

elastic demand where demand responds by a greater percentage than the percentage change in price

elastic supply where a percentage change in price causes a greater percentage change in quantity supplied

elasticity the extent to which one variable responds to a change in another variable

elasticity of demand for labour the responsiveness of demand for labour to a change in the wage rate

elasticity of supply of labour the responsiveness of supply of labour to a change in the wage rate

enterprise the willingness to bear risks and organise the factors of production

entrepreneur a person who bears the risks of a business and organises the other economic resources

equilibrium a situation of balance

equilibrium output the output where demand equals supply

equilibrium price the price at which demand equals supply

equity fairness

exchange rate the price of a currency in terms of another currency or currencies

exports products sold abroad

extension in demand a movement along a demand curve caused by a fall in the price of the product

extension in supply a movement along a supply curve caused by a rise in the price of the product

external diseconomies of scale higher average costs resulting from the growth of an industry

external economies of scale lower average costs resulting from the growth of an industry

externalities the effects on third parties that arise from the production and consumption decisions of others

financial capital financial assets, such as savings accounts, shares and government bonds

firm an institution that hires factors of production and organises those factors to produce and sell goods and services

fiscal drag the reduction in disposable income that occurs if tax bands are not adjusted in line with inflation

fiscal policy changes in government spending and taxation

fixed costs costs which do not change when output changes

free goods products which are in unlimited supply and do not need resources to produce them and so have no opportunity cost

free trade trade across frontiers without restrictions or special taxes

frictional unemployment unemployment arising when people are between jobs

GDP total output produced in a country

geographical mobility the movement of an economic resource from one area to another

globalisation the creation of a world market

goods output which has a physical form (cars, televisions and clothes)

government failure government intervention reducing rather than increasing economic efficiency

Hicks-Kaldor criterion the view that the desirability of a project should be judged on the basis of whether those who benefit could compensate losers and still receive a net gain

hot money flows flows of short-term finance that move around the world to take advantage of differences in interest rates and possible exchange rate changes

housing associations organisations, some registered charities and some profit making, which provide social housing

human capital the knowledge and skills that workers acquire through education, training and experience

hyperinflation a very high rate of inflation which causes serious economic problems and political instability

hysteresis unemployment generating unemployment by reducing the confidence and relevance of the skills of unemployed people

imports products bought from abroad

income a flow of earnings

income distribution the extent to which different groups of households share in the total income of the country

income elastic where a percentage change in income causes a greater percentage change in demand

income elasticity of demand a measure of the responsiveness of demand to a change in income

income inelastic where a percentage change in income causes a smaller percentage change in demand

increase in demand a rise in demand caused by an influence other than a change in the price of the product

increase in supply a rise in supply caused by an influence other than a change in the price of the product

increasing returns output rising by more than resources, which causes marginal and average costs to fall

independent goods products which are unrelated and so have zero cross elasticity of demand

indirect taxes taxes on goods and services

industrial relations the relationships between employers and trade unions

industry a group of firms producing the same product

inelastic demand where demand responds by a smaller percentage than the percentage change in price

inelastic supply where a percentage change in price causes a smaller percentage change in quantity supplied

inferior goods products which fall in demand as income rises

inflation a sustained rise in the general price level

inflationary noise the distortionary effect inflation can have on price signals

injections spending on domestic output occurring outside the circular flow

internal diseconomies of scale higher average costs resulting from a firm growing in size

internal economies of scale lower average costs resulting from a firm growing in size

international trade the exchange of products across international boundaries

Keynesians economists who follow the ideas of John Maynard Keynes. They believe that market failure is a significant problem and that government intervention can improve the situation

kinked demand curve a diagram which suggests that oligopolists will be reluctant to change price because usually rivals will not follow price rises but will follow price cuts

labour mental and physical effort used to produce goods and services

labour-intensive industries industries which require a large labour force

labour market failure imperfections in labour markets resulting in a misallocation of labour resources and wage rates being above or below equilibrium

labour turnover people entering and leaving employment

land natural resources

legal tender money which, by law, has to be accepted in settlement of a debt

leisure time people have free to spend as they please

limit pricing setting price with the intention of discouraging the entry of new firms

liquidity preference the desire to hold wealth in a money form

long run aggregate supply (LRAS) the output supplied after the price level and factor prices have adjusted to any changes in aggregate demand

long run costs costs of production incurred when there is time to alter the quantity of all factors of production

loss where total cost exceeds total revenue

lump-sum tax a tax of a fixed amount which does not change even if the actions or circumstances of the taxpayer alter

macroeconomic equilibrium a situation where aggregate demand equals aggregate supply and so there are no forces to change the price level and output

marginal cost the change in total cost when output is changed by one unit

marginal revenue change in total revenue resulting from selling one more unit

market an arrangement which allows buyers and sellers to exchange products

market demand total demand for a product

market economy an economy where consumers determine what is produced, and resources are owned by individuals and groups of individuals and are allocated through the price mechanism

market failure the failure of market forces to achieve an efficient allocation of resources

market power the ability to influence price

market structure a classification of the principal characteristics of a market. The main structures are perfect competition, monopolistic competition, oligopoly and monopoly

market supply total supply

maximum price a price ceiling set by a government or other organisation

means-tested benefits benefits given to people assessed as needing assistance on the basis of their income

medium of exchange any item which is generally acceptable as a means of payment

menu costs costs involved in having to change prices as a result of inflation

merit goods products which the government regards as beneficial and which will be underconsumed if left to market forces

minimum price a price floor set by a government or other organisation

mixed economy an economy with a private and public sector, with some resources allocated through the price mechanism and some by government direction

mixed goods products which have some of the characteristics of both private and public goods

monetarists people who believe that the only cause of inflation is the money supply growing faster than output

monetary policy changes in the money supply, rate of interest and the exchange rate

Monetary Policy Committee (MPC) a committee of the Bank of England that determines the rate of interest with the objective of meeting the government's inflation target

money any item which is generally acceptable as a means of payment

monopolistic competition a market structure in which there are many firms producing a differentiated product and there is easy entry and exit

monopoly a market structure with a single supplier, high barriers to entry and exit, and a unique product

moral hazard the tendency for those insured to engage in more risky behaviour

mortgages loans for house purchase

multinational companies firms that produce products in a number of countries

multiplier the final effect on aggregate demand being greater than the initial effect

nationalised industries publicly owned industries

natural monopoly a market in which average costs will be lowest if the entire output is produced by just one firm

natural rate of unemployment the rate of unemployment that exists when the labour market is in equilibrium

negative cross elasticity of demand where a rise in the price of one product causes demand for another product to decrease

negative equity trap a situation where people are unable to move because the value of their properties is less than the mortgages they owe

negative externalities harmful effects on third parties for which they are not compensated, also called external costs

negative income elasticity of demand where a rise in income causes a decrease in demand

net investment additions to the capital stock

new classical economists economists who believe that markets usually work efficiently

New Deal a government initiative designed to encourage people to move from unemployment into employment

nominal GDP GDP measured at current prices

non-renewable resources natural resources which, with use, will run out

normal goods products which rise in demand as income rises

normal profit the minimum level of profit needed to keep a firm in the industry in the long run

normative statements statements based on opinions which cannot be tested

occupational mobility the movement of an economic resource from one use to another

Office of Fair Trading (OFT) a body set up in 1973 to run the UK's competition policy

oligopoly a market structure dominated by a few large firms and in which there are high barriers to entry and exit

opportunity cost the best alternative forgone when a choice is made

optimum output the output where average cost is minimised

Pareto efficiency where it is not possible to change the existing allocation of resources without making someone else worse off

perfect competition a market structure with no barriers to entry and exit, consisting of many firms producing an identical product

planned economy an economy where the government decides what to produce, how to produce it and who receives it

polluter pays principle an approach involving policy measures which make polluters pay for the pollution they cause

positive cross elasticity of demand where a rise in the price of one product causes demand for another product to increase

positive externalities beneficial effects on third parties for which they do not pay

positive income elasticity of demand where a rise in income causes an increase in demand

positive statements statements of fact which can be tested

postcode prescribing occurs when some health authorities offer treatments and others do not

potential economic growth increases in the ability of a country to produce goods and services

poverty trap a situation where poor people experience a fall in their disposable income as their gross income increases because they have to pay more tax and lose benefits

predatory pricing setting price low enough, often below cost price, to drive competitors out of the market

price competitive charging lower prices than rivals

price elasticity of demand (PED) a measure of the responsiveness of demand for a product to a change in the price of the product

price elasticity of supply the responsiveness of supply to a change in price

price leadership a situation where one firm sets the price and its rivals follow its price changes

private benefits benefits received by those who produce or consume a product

private costs costs incurred by those who produce or consume a product

private goods products which are rival and excludable

privatisation the transfer of assets from the public to the private sector

producer surplus the extra amount that producers are paid above what they were willing to accept to supply a product

product differentiation the process of creating real or apparent differences between products

production possibility curve a curve showing the maximum output of a combination of two types of products that can be produced efficiently with a country's existing resources and technology

productive efficiency where it is not possible to produce more of one product without producing less of another product and where firms produce at the lowest possible average cost

productivity output per worker hour

products goods and services

profit margin profit as a percentage of price

profit maximisation the objective of achieving the highest level of profits possible by producing where MC = MR

profit satisficing the objective of achieving a level of profit which will prove satisfactory for shareholders

progressive taxes taxes which take a greater percentage of the income of rich people than that of poor people

property rights the rights to use, change and transfer assets and products

protectionism restrictions of international trade

public goods products which are non-rival and non-excludable and have to be financed by taxation

purchasing power parity exchange rates exchange rates based on the cost of a basket of goods and services

QALY quality adjusted life year – a measure of both the quantity and quality of extra life gained by a medical treatment

quasi public goods products which come close to public goods but do not fully possess their defining characteristics

quota a limit on the supply of a product

rate of interest the price of money

rate of unemployment the number of people who are unemployed as a proportion of the total labour force

raw materials items which are processed into manufactured products

real disposable income disposable income adjusted for inflation

real GDP GDP adjusted for inflation

reflationary fiscal policy measures designed to increase aggregate demand

regional policy government measures designed to influence incomes, population and the number of firms in particular regions

regional unemployment people out of work in one area while there are job vacancies in another area

regressive taxes taxes which take a greater percentage of the income of poor people than that of rich people

regulatory capture a regulator acting in the interest of the industry rather than in the interest of the consumer

renewable resources natural resources which automatically replace themselves

resale price maintenance manufacturers insisting that their products are sold at recommended prices

resources human effort, man-made products and natural resources used to produce goods and services

retail price index (RPI) a weighted measure of changes in consumer prices

RPIX RPI minus mortgage interest payments

sales maximisation the objective of achieving the highest possible sales, usually subject to the constraint that AC = AR

sales revenue maximisation the objective of achieving the highest sales revenue by producing where marginal revenue is zero

scarcity not having enough resources to meet all wants

services output which does not have a physical form (banking, education and transport)

shoe leather costs costs involved in moving money around during a period of inflation in a bid to maintain its real value

short run the period of time when it is not possible to make a full adjustment to a change in market conditions

short run aggregate supply (SRAS) the output supplied in the time period when the price of inputs remains unchanged

short run costs costs of production incurred when the quantity at least one factor of production is fixed

sin taxes taxes designed to discourage unhealthy living

social benefits the total benefits to society of the production or consumption of a product, including private benefits and positive externalities

social capital capital used to produce goods and services for the community

social costs the total costs to society of the production or consumption of a product, including private costs and negative externalities

socially optimum output the output which maximises consumer welfare

specialisation concentration on a narrow range of products or tasks

stakeholders those with a direct interest in a firm's performance

standard for deferred payments any item used to enable people to borrow and lend

store of value an item used for saving

structural unemployment people out of work owing to a fall in demand for particular skills and occupations as some industries decline while demand for other skills and occupations increases as other industries expand

subsidies payments to encourage production or consumption

substitutes products which are seen as alternatives for each other

sunk costs costs which cannot be recovered should a firm leave the industry

superior goods products with positive and income elastic demand

supernormal profit profit above the normal profit level, earned when total revenue is greater than total cost (and so average revenue is greater than average cost)

suppliers sellers and providers of products

supply the ability and willingness to sell a product

supply curve a curve showing the different quantities supplied at a range of prices

supply schedule a table showing the different quantities supplied at a range of prices

supply-side policies policies designed to increase the economy's long-term growth potential

sustainable economic growth economic growth achieved in a way that does not endanger the country's ability to achieve economic growth in the future

tariff a tax on imports

total cost the total cost of production

total revenue the quantity sold multiplied by price per unit

tradable permits permits allowing firms to pollute which can be bought and sold

trade the exchange of products

trade bloc a group of countries with preferential trading agreements

transfer payments money transferred from one group to another not in return for providing a good or service

trend growth the expected annual increase in the ability of a country to produce goods and services

unemployment a situation where people who are willing and able to work are without jobs

unemployment trap a situation where some people are financially better off living on unemployment benefits than working

unit of account also known as a measure of value, an item used to measure the value of other items

universal benefits benefits available to everyone in a certain category, irrespective of income

value added value of output minus purchases of raw materials

value judgements assessment based on people's own views and priorities

variable an economic item which can change

variable costs costs which change as output changes

wage differentials differences in wages

wealth a stock of assets

wealth distribution the extent to which different groups of households share in the total wealth of the country

welfare loss a loss experienced by consumers when output occurs at a point where MSC is not equal to MSB

withdrawals parts of income which are not passed on in the circular flow of income (also known as leakages)

World Trade Organisation (WTO) a world trade organisation which aims to encourage the lowering of trade restrictions and to settle trade disputes

X-inefficiency a situation where firms are not forced to produce at the lowest average cost

zero cross elasticity of demand where a change in the price of one product has no effect on the demand for another product

zero income elasticity of demand where a change in income causes no change in demand

Index